P9-BJB-182

CHILTON'S
REPAIR & TUNE-UP GUIDE
CHEVROLET GMC PICK-UPS 1970-84

All U.S. and Canadian 2 and 4-wheel drive models including diesel engines and suburbans

Vice President and General Manager JOHN P. KUSHNERICK
Managing Editor KERRY A. FREEMAN, S.A.E.
Senior Editor RICHARD J. RIVELE, S.A.E.
Editor A. LINDSAY BROOKE

CHILTON BOOK COMPANY
Radnor, Pennsylvania
19089

SAFETY NOTICE

Proper service and repair procedures are vital to the safe, reliable operation of all motor vehicles, as well as the personal safety of those performing repairs. This book outlines procedures for servicing and repairing vehicles using safe, effective methods. The procedures contain many NOTES, CAUTIONS and WARNINGS which should be followed along with standard safety procedures to eliminate the possibility of personal injury or improper service which could damage the vehicle or compromise its safety.

It is important to note that repair procedures and techniques, tools and parts for servicing motor vehicles, as well as the skill and experience of the individual performing the work vary widely. It is not possible to anticipate all of the conceivable ways or conditions under which vehicles may be serviced, or to provide cautions as to all of the possible hazards that may result. Standard and accepted safety precautions and equipment should be used when handling toxic or flammable fluids, and safety goggles or other protection should be used during cutting, grinding, chiseling, prying, or any other process that can cause material removal or projectiles.

Some procedures require the use of tools specially designed for a specific purpose. Before substituting another tool or procedure, you must be completely satisfied that neither your personal safety, nor the performance of the vehicle will be endangered.

Although information in this guide is based on industry sources and is as complete as possible at the time of publication, the possibility exists that the manufacturer made later changes which could not be included here. While striving for total accuracy, Chilton Book Company cannot assume responsibility for any errors, changes, or omissions that may occur in the compilation of this data.

PART NUMBERS

Part numbers listed in this reference are not recommendations by Chilton for any product by brand name. They are references that can be used with interchange manuals and aftermarket supplier catalogs to locate each brand supplier's discrete part number.

ACKNOWLEDGMENTS

Chilton Book Company expresses appreciation to the Chevrolet Motor Division, General Motors Corporation, Detroit, Michigan 48202; and GMC Truck and Coach Division, General Motors Corporation, Pontiac, Michigan 48053 for their generous assistance.

Information has been selected from Chevrolet and GMC shop manuals, owner's manuals, data books, brochures, service bulletins, and technical manuals.

Copyright © 1984 by Chilton Book Company
All Rights Reserved
Published in Radnor, Pennsylvania 19089, by Chilton Book Company

Manufactured in the United States of America
  234567890   3210987654

Chilton's Repair & Tune-Up Guide: Chevrolet/GMC Pick-Ups and Suburban 1970–84
ISBN 0-8019-7464-X pbk.
Library of Congress Catalog Card No. 83-45306

CONTENTS

Quick Reference
Specifications For Your Vehicle

Fill in this chart with the most commonly used specifications for your vehicle. Specifications can be found in Chapters 1 through 3 or on the tune-up decal under the hood of the vehicle.

 # Tune-Up

Firing Order_____

Spark Plugs:

   Type_____

   Gap (in.)_____

Point Gap (in.)_____

Dwell Angle (°)_____

Ignition Timing (°)_____

   Vacuum (Connected/Disconnected)_____

Valve Clearance (in.)

   Intake_____   **Exhaust**_____

Capacities

Engine Oil (qts)

   With Filter Change_____

   Without Filter Change_____

Cooling System (qts)_____

Manual Transmission (pts)_____

   Type_____

Automatic Transmission (pts)_____

   Type_____

Front Differential (pts)_____

   Type_____

Rear Differential (pts)_____

   Type_____

Transfer Case (pts)_____

   Type_____

FREQUENTLY REPLACED PARTS
Use these spaces to record the part numbers of frequently replaced parts.

PCV VALVE

Manufacturer_____

Part No._____

OIL FILTER

Manufacturer_____

Part No._____

AIR FILTER

Manufacturer_____

Part No._____

General Information and Maintenance

HOW TO USE THIS BOOK

This book is intended to serve as a guide for the tune-up, repair and maintenance of ½, ¾ and 1 ton Chevrolet and GMC pick-ups and Suburbans from 1970 to 1984. All of the operations apply to both Chevrolet and GMC trucks unless specified otherwise.

To use this book properly, each operation should be approached logically and the recommended procedures read thoroughly before beginning the work. Before attempting any operation, be sure that you understand exactly what is involved. Naturally, it is considerably easier if you have the necessary tools on hand and a clean place to work.

When reference is made in this book to the "right side" or "left side" of the truck, it should be understood that these positions are to be viewed from the front seat. Thus, the left side of the truck is always the driver's side, even when one is facing the truck, as when working on the engine.

Information in this book is based on factory sources. Special factory tools have been eliminated from repair procedures wherever possible, in order to substitute more readily available tools.

TOOLS AND EQUIPMENT

It would be impossible to catalog each tool that you would need to perform each or any operation in this book. It would also not be wise for the amateur to rush out and buy an expensive set of tools on the theory that he may need one of them at some time. The best approach is to proceed slowly, gathering together a good quality set of those tools that are used most frequently. Don't be misled by the low cost of bargain tools. Forged wrenches, 12 point sockets and fine tooth ratchets are by far preferable to their less expensive counterparts. As any good mechanic can tell you, there are few worse experiences than trying to work on your truck with bad tools. Your monetary savings will be far outweighed by frustration and mangled knuckles.

Begin accumulating those tools that are used most frequently. In addition to a basic assortment of screwdrivers and a pair of pliers, you will need the following tools for routine maintenance and tune-up jobs:

1. One set each of both metric and S.A.E. sockets, including a ⅝ in. spark plug socket. Various length socket drive extensions and universals are also very helpful, but you'll probably acquire these as you need them. Ratchet handles are available in ¼, ⅜ and ½ in. drives, and will fit both metric and S.A.E. sockets (just make sure that your sockets are the proper drive size for the ratchet handle you buy).

2. One set each of metric and S.A.E. "combination" (one end open and one end box) wrenches.

3. Wire-type spark plug feeler gauge.

4. Blade-type feeler gauge for ignition and valve settings.

5. Slot and Phillips head screwdrivers in various sizes.

6. Oil filter strap wrench, necessary for removing oil filters (*never* used, though, for installing the filters).

7. Oil can filler spout, for pouring fresh oil from quart oil cans.

8. Pair of slip-lock pliers.

9. Pair of vise-type pliers.

10. Adjustable wrench.

11. A hydraulic floor jack of *at least* 1½ ton capacity. If you are serious about maintaining your own truck, then a floor jack is as necessary as a spark plug socket. The greatly increased utility, strength, and safety of a hydraulic floor jack makes it pay for itself many times over through the years.

12. At least two sturdy jackstands for working underneath the truck—any other type of support (bricks, wood and especially cinderblocks) is just plain dangerous.

13. Timing light, preferably a DC battery hookup type, and preferably an inductive type for use on trucks with electronic ignition.

This is an adequate set of tools, and the more work you do yourself on your truck, the larger you'll find the set growing—a pair of pliers here, a wrench or two there. It makes more sense to have a comprehensive set of basic tools as listed above, and then to acquire more along the line as you need them, than to go out and plunk down big money for a professional size set you may never use. In addition to these basic tools, they are several other tools and gauges you may find useful.

1. A compression gauge. The screw-in type is slower to use but it eliminates the possibility of a faulty reading due to escaping pressure.

2. A manifold vacuum gauge, very useful in troubleshooting ignition and emissions problems.

3. A drop light, to light up the work area (make sure yours is Underwriter's approved, and has a shielded bulb).

4. A volt/ohm meter, used for determining whether or not there is current in a wire. These are handy for use if a wire is broken somewhere and are especially necessary for working on today's electronics-laden vehicles.

As a final note, a torque wrench is necessary for all but the most basic work—it should even be used when installing spark plugs. The more common beam-type models are perfectly adequate and are usually much less expensive than the more precise "click" type (on which you pre-set the torque and the wrench "clicks" when that setting arrives on the fastener you are torquing).

Special Tools

Although a basic collection of hand tools is sufficient for the majority of service procedures in this guide, in a few cases special tools are necessary. Factory-approved tools are available from your dealer, or from:

Service Tool Division
Kent-Moore Corporation
1501 South Jackson Street
Jackson, Michigan 49203

In Canada, contact Kent-Moore of Canada, Ltd., 2395 Cawthra Mississauga, Ontario, Canada L5A 3P2.

SERVICING YOUR TRUCK SAFELY

It is virtually impossible to anticipate all of the hazards involved with automotive maintenance and service, but care and common sense will prevent most accidents.

The rules of safety for mechanics range from "don't smoke around gasoline," to "use the proper tool for the job." The trick to avoiding injuries is to develop safe work habits and take every possible precaution.

Dos

• Do keep a fire extinguisher and first aid kit within easy reach.

• Do wear safety glasses or goggles when cutting, drilling, grinding or prying. If you wear glasses for the sake of vision, they should be made of hardened glass that can serve also as safety glasses, or wear safety goggles over your regular glasses.

• Do shield your eyes whenever you work around the battery. Batteries contain sulphuric acid. In case of contact with the eyes or skin, flush the area with water or a mixture of water and baking soda and get medical attention immediately.

• Do use jack stands for any undercar service. Jacks are for raising vehicles; jack stands are for making sure the vehicle stays raised until you want it to come down. Whenever the truck is raised, block the wheels remaining on the ground and set the parking brake.

• Do use adequate ventilation when working with any chemicals or hazardous materials.

• Do disconnect the negative battery cable when working on the electrical system. The secondary ignition system can contain up to 40,000 volts.

• Do follow manufacturer's directions whenever working with potentially hazardous materials. Both brake fluid and antifreeze are poisonous if taken internally.

• Do properly maintain your tools. Loose hammerheads, mushroomed punches and chisels, frayed or poorly grounded electrical cords, excessively worn screwdrivers, spread wrenches, cracked sockets, slipping ratchets, or faulty droplight sockets can cause accidents.

• Do use the proper size and type of tool for the job being done.

• Do when possible, pull on a wrench handle rather than push on it, and adjust your stance to prevent a fall.

• Do be sure that adjustable wrenches are tightly closed on the nut or bolt and pulled so that the face is on the side of the fixed jaw.

• Do select a wrench or socket that fits the nut or bolt. The wrench or socket should sit straight, not cocked.

• Do strike squarely with a hammer; avoid glancing blows.

• Do set the parking brake and block the drive

wheels if the work requires the engine running.

Don'ts

• Don't run an engine in a garage or anywhere else without proper ventilation—EVER! Carbon monoxide is poisonous; it takes a long time to leave the human body and you can build up a deadly supply of it in your system by simply breathing in a little every day. You may not realize you are slowly poisoning yourself. Always use power vents, windows, fans, or open the garage doors.

• Don't work around moving parts while wearing a necktie or other loose clothing. Short sleeves are much safer than long, loose sleeves; hard-toed shoes with neoprene soles protect your toes and give a better grip on slippery surfaces. Jewelry such as watches, fancy belt buckles, beads or body adornment of any kind is not safe working around a truck. Long hair should be hidden under a hat or cap.

• Don't use pockets for toolboxes. A fall or bump can drive a screwdriver deep into your body. Even a wiping cloth hanging from the back pocket can wrap around a spinning shaft or fan.

• Don't smoke when working around gasoline, cleaning solvent or other flammable material.

• Don't smoke when working around the battery. When the battery is being charged, it gives off explosive hydrogen gas.

• Don't use gasoline to wash your hands; there are excellent soaps available. Gasoline may contain lead, and lead can enter the body through a cut, accumulating in the body until you are very ill. Gasoline also removes all the natural oils from the skin so that bone dry hands will suck up oil and grease.

• Don't service the air conditioning system unless you are equipped with the necessary tools and training. The refrigerant, R-12, is extremely cold when compressed, and when released into the air will instantly freeze any surface it contacts, including your eyes. Although the refrigerant is normally non-toxic, R-12 becomes a deadly poisonous gas in the presence of an open flame. One good whiff of the vapors from burning refrigerant can be fatal.

SERIAL NUMBER IDENTIFICATION

Vehicle

The Vehicle Identification Number (V.I.N.) is on a plate attached to the left hand door pillar, or on the left top of the dashboard (visible

| MFD. BY GENERAL MOTORS CORPORATION |
| GVWR |
| GAWR FRONT   GAWR REAR |
| VIN |
| CAMPER LOADING DATA |
| CWR   DIM A   DIM B |
| INFLATION DATA FOR TIRES FURNISHED WITH VEHICLE |
| FRONT   PRESSURE |
| REAR   PRESSURE |
| WARRANTY VOIDED IF LOADED IN EXCESS OF RATINGS |
| SEE OWNERS MANUAL FOR OTHER LOADING AND INFLATION DATA |

Typical vehicle identification (VIN) plate

through the windshield) on later models. The gross vehicle weight (GVW), or maximum safe total weight of the truck, cargo, and passengers, is also given on the plate.

1970

The first letter indicates the vehicle type, C for two wheel drive, K for four wheel drive. The second letter indicates the engine type, S for six cylinder, or E for V8. The first number is for the GVW range, either a 1, indicating ½ ton, or a 2, indicating ¾ ton. The second and third numbers are for the body type: 04 for fenderside, or Stepside; 34 for wideside, or Fleetside. The third letter indicates the assembly plant. The fourth letter is for the model year (Z is for 1970). The last five digits are the serial numbers.

1971

The plate is essentially the same as 1970, except that either a hyphen or a letter indicating the type of state certification appears between the body type numbers and the assembly plant letter. The model year number is 1.

1972–78

The plates for these years are the same, with the exception of the engine codes, and the model years, of course. The first letter indicates a Chevrolet (C) or GMC (T) vehicle. The second letter is the vehicle type, C or K. The third letter is the engine type. For 1972 this would be an S or an E. Later years are covered below. The first number is the GVW range, 1 (½ ton) or 2 (¾ ton). The second number is the model type, 4 for cab and pickup box. The third number is for the year, 2 for 1972, for example. The fourth letter indicates the assembly plant. The last six numbers are the serial numbers.

1973 Engine Codes:

Q	250 six
T	292 six
X	307 V8
Y	350 V8
Z	454 V8

1GCEC14D9BF123456

17-digit VIN, 1981 and later

1974 Engine Codes:
Same except:
V   350 V8 two barel
Y   350 V8 four barrel

1975 Engine Codes:
Same except: M 400 V8 Four barrel

1976 and 1977 Engine Codes:
D   250 six
T   292 six
V   350 V8 two barrel
L   350 V8 four barrel
V   400 V8 (R in 1977)
S   454 V8

1978 Engine Codes:
D   250 six
T   292 six
U   305 V8
L   350 V8
R   400 V8
S   454 V8
Z   350 V8 Diesel

1979–80

The VIN is on a plate attached to the upper left-hand side of the instrument panel. The interpretation for the VIN code is the same as outlined for 1972–78, except for the engine codes, which are:

D   250 six
T   292 six
U   305 V8
L   350 V8 four barrel
M   350 V8 two barrel
R   400 V8
S   454 V8
Z   350 V8 Diesel

1981 and Later

Beginning in 1981 a new 17 digit code is used. The interpretation is the same as previous years except that the engine code is the eighth digit. Additional engines/codes include the 305 V8 (F and H codes); a 350 V8 (P code); a "W"-code 454 V8 and a Chevrolet-built 379 cu. in. V8 diesel, in both C and J codes.

Engine

The engine number is located as follows:
• 6 Cylinder: On a pad on the right-hand side of the cylinder block, at the rear of the distributor.
• V8: On a pad at the front right-hand side of the cylinder block, except for 1979 and 1980 454 V8s, which have the code on a pad at the front top center of the engine block immediately forward of the intake manifold; and diesel

VIN location, inline sixes

Gasoline V8 engine VIN location

350 and 379 diesel engine VIN locations

Three and four-speed transmission serial number location—lower left side of the case adjacent to the rear cover

engines, which have the code on a label attached to the rear face of the left valve cover.

Example—F1210TFA:
- F—Manufacturing Plant. F-Flint and T-Tonawanda
- 12—Month of Manufacture (December)
- 10—Day of Manufacture (Tenth)
- T—Truck
- FA—Transmission and Engine Combination

Transmission

The Muncie or Saginaw three speed manual transmission serial number is located on the lower left side of the case adjacent to the rear of the cover. The three speed Tremec transmission has the number on the upper forward mounting flange. The four speed transmission is numbered on the rear of the case, above the output shaft. The Turbo Hydra-Matic 350 serial number is on the right rear vertical surface of the fluid pan. The Turbo Hydra-Matic 400 is identified by a light blue plate attached to the right side, which is stamped with the serial

H. THM 350C stamped I.D. location
I. THM 350C VIN location
J. THM 350C optional VIN locations

K. THM 400 I.D. tag location
L. THM 400 VIN location
M. THM 700-R4 stamped I.D. location
N. THM 700-R4 VIN location

Turbo Hydra-Matic 350, 400, and 700 series I.D. locations

number. The Powerglide transmission (through 1972 only) is stamped in the same location as the Turbo Hydra-Matic 350.

Transfer Case

The New Process 203, 205 and 208 transfer cases have a build date tag attached to the front of the case. Muncie Model 203 transfer cases have a build date on the front of the case above the output shaft.

Axles

From 1970 to 1973, the axle serial number for ½ ton Chevrolet and GMC trucks can be found on the bottom flange of the carrier housing. For ¾ and 1 ton, the number is stamped on the forward upper surface of the carrier. For all trucks, 1974 and later, the rear axle numbers are on the front of the right rear axle tube inboard of the upper control arm bracket, except for Dana-built axles, which are stamped on the rear surface of the right axle tube. Front axles on 4 x 4s are marked on the front of the left axle tube.

Rear axle serial number location

Powerglide serial number location

Service Parts Identification Plate

The service parts identification plate, commonly known as the option list, is usually located on the inside of the glove compartment door. On some trucks, you may have to look for it on an inner fender panel. The plate lists the vehicle serial number, wheelbase, all regular production options (RPOs) and all special equipment. Probably the most valuable piece of information on this plate is the paint code, a useful item when you have occasion to need paint.

Service parts identification plate

ROUTINE MAINTENANCE

The accompanying chart gives the recommended maintenance intervals for the components covered here. Refer to the text for the applicable procedures.

Air Cleaner
PAPER ELEMENT TYPE

Loosen the wing nut on top of the cover and remove the cover from the air cleaner housing. The element should be replaced when it has become oil saturated or filled with dirt. If the filter is equipped with a wetted wrapper, remove the wrapper and wash it in kerosene or similar solvent. Shake or blot dry. Saturate the wrapper in engine oil and squeeze it tightly in an absorbent towel to remove the excess oil. Leave the wrapper moist. Clean the dirt from the filter by lightly tapping it against a workbench to dislodge the dirt particles. Wash the top of the air cleaner housing and wipe it dry. If equipped, replace the crankcase ventilation filter, located in the air filter housing, if it appears excessively dirty. Replace the oiled wrapper on the air cleaner element and reinstall the element in the housing.

PCV Valve

The PCV valve is located on top of the valve cover. Its function is to purge the crankcase of

WING NUT
TORQUE AT 20 LBS IN.

POLYWRAP
AIR CLEANER ELEMENT
(BAND SHOWN)

NOTE: POLYURETHANE BAND MUST WRAP
OVER BOTH END SEALS OF PAPER ELEMENT AS
SHOWN.

AIR CLEANER
ELEMENT
(PAPER FILTER
PORTION)

NOTE: POLYURETHANE BAND MUST
COMPLETELY COVER THE OUTER SCREEN
SURFACE OF PAPER ELEMENT AS SHOWN.

POLYWRAP AIR
CLEANER ELEMENT
(BAND SHOWN)

PAPER FILTER PORTION
OF POLYWRAP AIR
CLEANER ELEMENT

Air cleaner with polyurethane wrap

harmful vapors through a system using engine vacuum to draw fresh air through the crankcase. The system reburns crankcase vapors, rather than exhausting them. Proper operation of the PCV valve depends on a sealed engine. If the oil begins to form sludge, which will be obvious as it is drained, and the PCV system is functioning properly, check the engine for possible causes.

Engine operating conditions that would indicate a malfunctioning PCV system are rough idle, oil present in the air cleaner, oil leaks or excessive oil sludging.

The simplest check for the PCV valve is to remove it from its rubber grommet on top of the valve cover and shake it. If it rattles, it is functioning; if not, replace it. In any event, it should be replaced at the recommended interval whether it rattles or not. Check the PCV hoses for breaks or restrictions. If necessary, the hoses should also be replaced. The plastic T-fittings used in this system break easily, so be careful.

To replace the PCV valve:

1. Pull the valve, with the hose still attached to the valve, from the rubber grommet in the rocker cover.

2. Use a pair of pliers to release the hose clamp; remove the PCV valve from the hose.

3. Install the new valve into the hose, slide the clamp into position, and install the valve into the rubber grommet.

Crankcase Depression Regulator and Flow Control Valve

Diesel Engines

The Crankcase Depression Regulator (CDR), found on 1981 and later diesels, and the flow control valve, used in 1980, are designed to scavenge crankcase vapors in basically the same manner as the PCV valve on gasoline engines. The valves are located either on the left rear corner of the intake manifold (CDR), or on the rear of the intake crossover pipe (flow control valve). On each system there are two ventilation filters, one per valve cover.

The filter assemblies should be cleaned every 15,000 miles by simply prying them carefully from the valve covers (be aware of the grommets underneath), and washing them out in solvent. The ventilation pipes and tubes should also be cleaned. Both the CDR and flow control valves should also be cleaned every 30,000 miles (the cover can be removed from the CDR; the flow control valve can simply be flushed with solvent). Dry each valve, filter, and hose with compressed air before installation.

NOTE: *Do not attempt to test the crankcase controls on these diesels. Instead, clean the valve cover filter assembly and vent pipes and check the vent pipes.*

Replace the breather cap assembly every 30,000 miles. Replace all rubber fittings as required every 15,000 miles.

Maintenance Intervals

See text for procedures concerning regular maintenance.

NOTE: *Heavy-duty operation (trailer towing, prolonged idling, severe stop-and-start driving) should be accompanied by a 50% increase in maintenance. Cut the interval in half for these conditions. Figures given are maintenance intervals when service should be performed.*

Maintenance	1970	1971–74	1975–84
Air Cleaner (Check and Clean)			
Paper element ①	24,000 mi (replace)	24,000 mi (replace)	30,000 mi (replace) ⑥
PCV Valve (Replace)	12 mo/12,000 mi	12 mo/12,000 mi	12 mo/15,000 mi ⑦ ⑧
Evaporative Canister			
Replace filter	—	12 mo/12,000 mi	24 mo/30,000 mi ⑧
Engine Oil			
Check	Each fuel stop	Each fuel stop	Each fuel stop
Replace	4 mo/6,000 mi	4 mo/6,000 mi	6 mo/7,500 mi ⑨ ⑬ ⑭
Engine Oil Filter (Replace)	At 1st oil change; then every 2nd	At 1st oil change; then every 2nd	At 1st oil change; then every 2nd ⑬
Fuel Filter			
Replace ⑮	12,000 mi	12,000 mi	12 mo/15,000 mi ⑥ ⑫
Powerglide Transmission Fluid			
Check	6,000 mi	6,000 mi	—
Replace	24,000 mi ⑤	24,000 mi	
Turbo Hydra-Matic Fluid & Filter			
Check fluid	6,000 mi	6,000 mi	Each oil change
Change fluid	24,000 mi	24,000 mi	30,000 mi
Replace filter	24,000 mi	24,000 mi	30,000 ⑧ ⑩
Manual transmission (All)			
Check lubricant	6,000 mi	4 mo/6,000 mi	6 mo/7,500 mi ⑨
Add lubricant	As necessary	As necessary	As necessary
Battery			
Lubricate terminal felt washer	6,000 mi ④	—	—
Clean terminals	6,000 mi	As necessary	As necessary
Check electrolyte level	Twice monthly	Twice monthly	Twice monthly
Coolant Level	Each fuel stop	Each fuel stop	Each fuel stop
Front Wheel Bearings			
Lubricate	30,000 mi	30,000 mi ③	30,000 mi ⑧ ⑪
Front and Rear Axle Lube			
Check	6,000 mi	6,000 mi	6 mo/7,500 mi ⑨
Replace	24,000 mi	24,000 mi	1st 15,000 mi w/Positraction
Brake Fluid (Master Cylinder)			
Check fluid level	6,000 mi	6,000 mi	6 mo/7,500 mi ⑨
Add fluid	As necessary	As necessary	As necessary
Manual Steering Gear Lubricant			
Check level	36,000 mi ②	36,000 mi ②	30,000 mi
Add lubricant	As necessary ②	②	②
Power Steering Reservoir			
Check fluid level	At each oil change	At each oil change	6 mo/7,500 mi
Add fluid	As necessary	As necessary	As necessary
Rotate Tires	6,000 mi	6,000 mi	Radial—1st 7,500 mi, then every 15,000 mi Bias Belted—every 7,500 mi
Chassis Lubrication	See Chassis Lubrication charts	See Chassis Lubrication charts	See Chassis Lubrication charts
Drive Belts			
Check and adjust (as necessary)	6,000 mi	6,000 mi	6 mo/7,500 mi

Maintenance Intervals (cont.)

Maintenance	1970	1971–74	1975–84
Transfer Case			
Check	4 mo/6,000 mi	4 mo/6,000 mi	4 mo/6,000 mi
Add	As necessary	As necessary	As necessary
Driveshaft Centering Ball			
Lubricate (4WD only)	6,000 mi	6,000 mi	7,500 mi ⑨

—Not applicable
mi—Miles
mo—Months
① Paper element air cleaners should be rotated 180° each time they are checked
② From 1970 on, no lubrication of the manual steering gear is recommended. The gear should be inspected for leaks at the seal (lubricant leaks, not filmy oil leaks). Seasonal change of the lubricant is not required and the housing should not be drained.
③ 24,000 miles in 1972–74
④ May be equipped with a felt terminal washer
⑤ 20 Series—every 12,000 miles
⑥ 12,000 mi in heavy duty emissions vehicles (C 10 or C-1500 over 6000 lbs. GVW; all K models)
⑦ 24 mo/30,000 mi 1976–84
⑧ 24,000 mi in heavy duty emission vehicles
⑨ 4 mo/6,000 mi in heavy duty emissions vehicles
⑩ 60,000 mi 1976–78, 100,000 mi 1979–84, light duty emissions vehicles
⑪ 12,000 mi in four wheel drive vehicles
⑫ 24 mo/24,000 mi in California 350 and 400 engines through 1977; 12,000 mi on 1979–84 heavy duty emissions vehicles
⑬ Change at 3,000 mile intervals for 350 Diesel; 6,000 miles for 1981 and later models
⑭ Change at 5,000 mile intervals for 379 (6.2L) Diesel; or every 2,500 miles when operating under extreme temperatures, extended high speed or idle conditions, or frequent trailer towing.
⑮ Figures include diesel fuel filters

DIESEL CRANKCASE VENTILATION SYSTEM   CRANKCASE DEPRESSION REGULATOR

Diesel crankcase ventilation flow and depression regulator

Evaporative Canister

The only regular maintenance that need be performed on the evaporative emission canister is to regularly change the filter and check the condition of the hoses. If any hoses need replacement, use only hoses which are marked "EVAP." No other types should be used. Whenever the vapor vent hose is replaced, the restrictor adjacent to the canister should also be replaced.

The evaporative emission canister is located on the left side of the engine compartment, with a filter located in its bottom. The filter should

Typical evaporative canister

be replaced according to the scheduled maintenance.

To service the canister filter:

1. Note the installed positions of the hoses, tagging them as necessary, in case any have to be removed.

2. Loosen the clamps and remove the bottom of the canister.

3. Pull the filter out and throw it away.

4. Install a new canister filter.

5. Install the bottom of the canister and tighten the clamps.

6. Check the hoses for cracks, restrictions or hose connection openings.

Heat Riser

The heat riser is a thermostatically or vacuum operated valve in the exhaust manifold. Not all engines have one. Heat riser-equipped V8s have only one valve, located in the right manifold. The valve opens when the engine is warming up, to direct hot exhaust gases to the intake manifold, in order to preheat the incoming fuel/air mixture. If it sticks shut, the result will be frequent stalling during warmup, especially in cold and damp weather. If it sticks open, the result will be a rough idle after the engine is warm. The heat riser should move freely. If it sticks, apply GM Manifold Heat Control Solvent or something similar (engine cool) to the ends of the shaft. Sometimes rapping the end of the shaft sharply with a hammer (engine hot) will break it loose. If this fails, components must be removed for further repairs.

Typical PCV valve locations. Inline six valve also in valve cover

Typical heater riser valve, six cylinder shown

Drive Belts

BELT TENSION

At the interval specified in the "Maintenance Intervals" chart, check the water pump, alternator, power steering pump (if equipped), air conditioning compressor (if equipped) and air pump (if equipped) drive belts for proper tension. Also look for signs of wear, fraying, separation, glazing, and so on, and replace the belts as required.

Belt tension should be checked with a gauge made for the purpose. If a tension gauge is not available, tension can be checked with moderate thumb pressure applied to the belt at its longest span midway between pulleys. If the belt has a free span less than twelve inches, it should deflect approximately ⅛–¼ inch. If the span is longer than twelve inches, deflection can range between ⅛ and ⅜ inches.

To adjust or replace belts:

1. Loosen the driven accessory's pivot and mounting bolts.

7" TO 10"
1/4" DEFLECTION

13" TO 16"
1/2" DEFLECTION

A gauge is recommended, but you can check belt tension with thumb pressure

To adjust belt tension or to replace belts, first loosen the component's mounting and adjusting bolts slightly

Push the component toward the engine and slip off the belt

Slip the new belt over the pulley

2. Move the accessory toward or away from the engine until the tension is correct. You can use a wooden hammer handle, or broomstick, as a lever, but do not use anything metallic, such as a prybar.

3. Tighten the bolts and recheck the ten-

HOW TO SPOT WORN V-BELTS

V-Belts are vital to efficient engine operation—they drive the fan, water pump and other accessories. They require little maintenance (occasional tightening) but they will not last forever. Slipping or failure of the V-belt will lead to overheating. If your V-belt looks like any of these, it should be replaced.

This belt has deep cracks, which cause it to flex. Too much flexing leads to heat build-up and premature failure. These cracks can be caused by using the belt on a pulley that is too small. Notched belts are available for small diameter pulleys.

Cracking or weathering

Oil and grease on a belt can cause the belt's rubber compounds to soften and separate from the reinforcing cords that hold the belt together. The belt will first slip, then finally fail altogether.

Softening (grease and oil)

Glazing is caused by a belt that is slipping. A slipping belt can cause a run-down battery, erratic power steering, overheating or poor accessory performance. The more the belt slips, the more glazing will be built up on the surface of the belt. The more the belt is glazed, the more it will slip. If the glazing is light, tighten the belt.

Glazing

The cover of this belt is worn off and is peeling away. The reinforcing cords will begin to wear and the belt will shortly break. When the belt cover wears in spots or has a rough jagged appearance, check the pulley grooves for roughness.

Worn cover

This belt is on the verge of breaking and leaving you stranded. The layers of the belt are separating and the reinforcing cords are exposed. It's just a matter of time before it breaks completely.

Separation

Pull outward on the component and tighten the mounting bolts

sion. If new belts have been installed, run the engine for a few minutes, then recheck and readjust as necessary.

It is better to have belts too loose than too tight, because overtight belts will lead to bearing failure, particularly in the water pump and alternator. However, loose belts place an extremely high impact load on the driven component due to the whipping action of the belt.

Air Conditioning

Regular maintenance for the air conditioning system includes periodic checks of the compressor drive belt tension, covered in the previous section. In addition, the system should be operated for at least five minutes every

GENERATOR

POWER STEERING

AIR CONDITIONING

379 diesel belt adjustments

The air conditioning sight glass on most models is located near the top of the VIR unit, mounted on the left side of the radiator

month. This ensures an adequate supply of lubricant to the bearings, and helps prevent the seals and hoses from drying out. To do this comfortably in winter, set the air conditioning lever to "Norm," the temperature lever to "Hot," and turn on the blower. This will engage the compressor, circulating lubricating oils within the system, but prevent the discharge of cold air.

The system can be checked for proper refrigerant charge using the appropriate procedure given below. Note that these procedures apply only to the factory-installed systems. If your truck has an aftermarket unit, you should consult the manufacturer of the unit for system checks.

If the system does not seem to be properly charged, take the truck to a trained professional for service. *Do not attempt to charge the air conditioning system yourself unless you are thoroughly familiar with its operation and the hazards involved.* Escaping refrigerant evaporates at subzero temperatures, and is cold enough to freeze any surface it contacts, including your skin and eyes.

SYSTEM CHECKS

1970–72

All Chevrolet and GMC pick-ups in these years have an air conditioning sight glass for checking the refrigerant charge.

1. Start the engine and set it on fast idle.
2. Set the controls for maximum cold with the blower on high.
3. If bubbles are present in the sight glass, the system is low on charge. If no bubbles are present in the sight glass, the system is either fully charged or empty.

4. Feel the high and low perssure lines at the compressor. The high pressure line should be warm and the low pressure line should be cool. If no appreciable temperature difference is felt, the system is empty or nearly empty.

NOTE: *Do not attempt to charge the refrigerant system unless thoroughly familiar with its operation and the procedures involved.*

Even though there is a noticeable temperature difference, there is a possibility of overcharge. If the refrigerant in the sight glass remains clear for more than 45 seconds before foaming and then settling away from the sight glass, an overcharge is indicated.

CAUTION: *No attempt should be made to discharge the system. Severe injury could result.*

If the refrigerant foams and then settles away from the sight glass in less than 45 seconds, it can be assumed that the system is properly charged.

High and low pressure lines on the 1970–72 factory-installed air conditioning compressor

1973–and Later

These air conditioning systems have no sight glass for checking.

1. Warm the engine to normal operating temperature.

2. Open the hood and doors.

3. Set the selector lever at A/C.

4. Set the temperature lever at the first detent to the right of COLD (outside air).

5. Set the blower on HI.

6. Idle the engine at 1,000 rpm.

7. Feel the temperature of the evaporator inlet and the accumulator outlet with the compressor engaged.

Both lines should be cold. If the inlet pipe is colder than the outlet pipe the system is low on charge.

Do not attempt to charge the system yourself.

Check engine crankcase oil level with the dipstick

The oil level should show between the "ADD" and "FULL" marks on the dipstick

Checking evaporator inlet and accumulator outlet line temperatures, 1973 and later

ACCUMULATOR OUTLET

EVAPORATOR INLET

Add oil through the capped opening in the valve cover

Fluid Level Checks

ENGINE OIL

The engine oil should be checked on a regular basis, ideally at each fuel stop. If the truck is used for trailer towing or for heavy-duty use, it would be safer to check it more often.

When checking the oil level it is best that the oil be at operating temperature, although checking the level immediately after stopping will give a false reading because all of the oil will not yet have drained back into the crankcase. Be sure that the truck is resting on a level surface, allowing time for the oil to drain back into the crankcase.

1. Open the hood and locate the dipstick. Remove it from the tube. The oil dipstick is located on the passenger's side of 6 cylinder engines and on the driver's side of V8s.

2. Wipe the dipstick with a clean rag.

3. Insert the dipstick fully into the tube, and remove it again. Hold the dipstick horizontally and read the oil level. The level should be between the FULL and ADD OIL marks. If the

oil level is at or below the ADD OIL mark, oil should be added as necessary. Oil is added through the capped opening on the valve cover(s) on gasoline engines. Diesel engines have a capped oil fill tube at the front of the engine. See "Oil and Fuel Recommendations" for the proper viscosity oil to use.

4. Replace the dipstick and check the level after adding oil. Be careful not to overfill the crankcase. Approximately one quart of oil will raise the level from ADD to FULL.

MANUAL TRANSMISSION

Check the lubricant level at the interval specified in the maintenance chart.

1. With the truck parked on a level surface, remove the filler plug from the side of the transmission case. Be careful not to take out the drain plug at the bottom.

2. If lubricant begins to trickle out of the hole, there is enough. If not, carefully insert a finger (watch out for sharp threads) and check that the level is up to the edge of the hole.

3. If not, add sufficient lubricant with a fun-

Capacities

Year	Engine Displace-ment (cu in.)	Engine Crankcase (qts)		Transmission (pts)			Drive Axle		Fuel Tank (gals)	Transfer Case (pts)	Cooling System (qts)		
		With Filter	Without Filter	Manual 3-spd	Manual 4-spd	Auto (Refill)	Front	Rear			w/o A/C	w/A/C	HD
1970	250	5	4	1.75 ①	8.0	②	5	③	21.5	5	12.5	—	—
	292	6	5	1.75 ①	8.0	②	5	③	21.5	5	12.5	13.0	13.5
	307	5	4	1.75 ①	8.0	②	5	③	21.5	5	17.5	18.5	18.0
	350	5	4	1.75 ①	8.0	②	5	③	21.5	5	17.0	18.5	18.5
	396	5	4	1.75 ①	8.0	②	5	③	21.5	5	24.0	—	24.5
1971–72	250	5	4	3.5	7.0	②	5	③	20.2 ④	5	12.2	12.9	12.9
	292	6	5	3.5	7.0	②	5	③	20.2 ④	5	12.6	13.3	13.3
	307	5	4	3.5	7.0	②	5	③	20.2 ④	5	16.0	16.0	16.0
	350	5	4	3.5	7.0	②	5	③	20.2 ④	5	16.2	17.7	17.7
	402	5	4	3.5	7.0	②	5	③	20.2 ④	5	23.2	24.7	24.7
1973–74	250	5	4	3.5	7.0	②	5	⑥	20 ⑩	5 ⑤	12.2	12.5	12.5
	292	6	5	3.5	7.0	②	5	⑥	20 ⑩	5 ⑤	12.6	13.3	13.3
	307	5	4	3.5	7.0	②	5	⑥	20 ⑩	5 ⑤	16.0	16.0	16.0
	350, 400	5	4	3.5	7.0	②	5	⑥	20 ⑩	5 ⑤	16.2	17.7	17.7
	454	5	4	3.5	7.0	②	5	⑥	20 ⑩	5 ⑤	18.5	21.0	21.0
1975	250	5	4	3.2 ⑦	8.3	②	5	⑥	20 ⑩	5 ⑤	14.8	15.4	14.8
	292	6	5	3.2 ⑦	8.3	②	5	⑥	20 ⑩	5 ⑤	14.8	15.6	14.8
	350	5	4	3.2 ⑦	8.3	②	5	⑥	20 ⑩	5 ⑤	17.6	18.0	18.0
	400	5	4	3.2 ⑦	8.3	②	5	⑥	20 ⑩	5 ⑤	19.6	20.4	20.4
	454	5	4	3.2 ⑦	8.3	②	5	⑥	20 ⑩	5 ⑤	24.8	24.8	24.8
1976–80	250	5	4	3.2 ⑦	8.0	②	5 ⑧	⑥	20 ⑩	5 ⑤	15.0	15.6	15.0
	292	6	5	3.2 ⑦	8.0	②	5 ⑧	⑥	20 ⑩	5 ⑤	14.8	15.4	14.8
	305	5	4	3.2 ⑦	8.0	②	5 ⑧	⑥	20 ⑩	5 ⑤	17.6	18.0	18.0
	350	5	4	3.2 ⑦	8.0	②	5 ⑧	⑥	20 ⑩	5 ⑤	17.6	18.0	18.0
	350 Diesel	7	6	—	—	5.0	—	⑥	20 ⑩	—	18.0	18.0	18.0
	400	5	4	3.2 ⑦	8.0	②	5 ⑧	⑥	20 ⑩	5 ⑤	20.4	20.4	20.4
	454	7	6	3.2 ⑦	8.0	②	5 ⑧	⑥	20 ⑩	5 ⑤	24.4 ⑨	24.7	24.7
1981	250	5	4	3	8	6	5	⑥	20 ⑩	5	15	15	15
	292	6	5	3	8	6	5	⑥	20 ⑩	5	15	15	15
	305	5	4	3	8	6	5	⑥	20 ⑩	5	17.5	17.5	17.5
	350	5	4	3	8	6	5	⑥	20 ⑩	5	17.5	17.5	17.5
	350 Diesel	7	—	3	8	6	5	⑥	20 ⑩	5	17.5	18	18
	400	5	4	3	8	6	5	⑥	20 ⑩	5	18	19	20
	454	7	6	3	8	6	5	⑥	20 ⑩	5	23	23	24
1982–84	250	5	4	3	8	⑭	5	⑥	⑬	5 ⑫	15.5	15.5	15.5
	292	6	5	3	8	⑭	5	⑥	⑬	5 ⑫	15.5	15.5	15.5
	305	5	4	3	8	⑭	5	⑥	⑬	5 ⑫	17.5	17.5	17.5

Capacities (cont.)

Year	Engine Displacement (cu in.)	Engine Crankcase (qts)		Transmission (pts)			Drive Axle		Fuel Tank (gals)	Transfer Case (pts)	Cooling System (qts)		
		With Filter	Without Filter	Manual		Auto (Refill)	Front	Rear			w/o A/C	w/A/C	HD
				3-spd	4-spd								
	350	5	4	3	8	⑭	5	⑥	⑬	5 ⑫	17.5	17.5	17.5
	379 Diesel	7	—	3	8	⑭	5	⑥	⑬	5 ⑫	24.5	24.5	24.5
	454	7	6	3	8	⑭	5	⑥	⑬	5 ⑫	23	23	24

① Heavy-duty 3-speed—3.5 pts
② Powerglide—4.0 pts
   Turbo Hydra-Matic 350—5.0 pts
   Turbo Hydra-Matic 400—7.5 pts
③ 3,300 and 3,500 lb. Chevrolet axles—4.5 pts
   5,200 and 7,200 lb. Chevrolet axles—6.5 pts
   5,500 lb. Dana axles—6.0 pts
   11,000 lb. Chevrolet axles—14.0 pts
④ 20 Series—21.0 gals
⑤ Full-time 4 wd—8 pts
⑥ 8½ in. ring gear—4.2 pts
   8⅞ in. ring gear (Chevrolet)—4.5 pts (3.5 pts 1977–82)
   9¾ in. ring gear (Dana) 6.0 pts.
   10½ in. ring gear (Chevrolet)—6½ pts
   10½ in. ring gear (Dana)—7.2 pts
   12½ in. ring gear (Chevrolet)—26.8 pts
⑦ Tremec 3-spd—4.0 pts
   Muncie 3-spd—3.0 pts
⑧ 8½ in. ring gear—4.25 pts (1977–80)
⑨ 22.8—1979–80
⑩ 16.0 gal—short wheelbase models
⑪ Not used
⑫ 10 pts on 30 Series vehicles
⑬ Short bed w/single tank: 16 gal., 32 gal. w/dual tanks
   Long bed w/single tank: 20 gal. Long bed w/dual tanks under 8600 GVWR 32 gal.
   Long bed w/dual tanks over 8600 GVWR 40 gal.
   All diesel w/dual tanks 40 gal.
⑭ Turbo Hydra-Matic 350—6 pts
   Turbo Hydra-Matic 400—7 pts
   Turbo Hyrda-Matic 700R4—10 pts

Filler Plug

Drain Plug

Manual transmission fill and drain plugs

nel and tube, or a squeeze bulb to bring it to the proper level. The correct lubricant to use is SAE 80W-90 GL-5 Gear Lubricant, or SAE 80W GL-5 for cold climates.

4. Replace the plug and check for leaks.

AUTOMATIC TRANSMISSION

Check the level of the fluid at the specified interval. The fluid level should be checked with the engine at normal operating temperature and running. If the truck has been running at high speed for a long period, in city traffic on a hot day, or pulling a trailer, let it cool down for about thirty minutes before checking the level.

1. Park on the level with the engine running and the shift lever in Park.
2. Remove the dipstick at the rear of the en-

Add automatic transmission fluid through the automatic transmission dipstick tube, using a funnel

Pry the retaining bail from the top of the master cylinder

gine compartment. Cautiously feel the end of the dipstick with your fingers. Wipe it off and replace it, then pull it again and check the level of the fluid on the dipstick.

3. If the fluid felt cool, the level should be between the two dimples below ADD. If it was too hot to hold, the level should be between the ADD and FULL marks.

4. If the fluid is at or below the ADD mark, add fluid through the dipstick tube. One pint raises the level from ADD to FULL when the fluid is hot. The correct fluid to use is DEXRON® II. Be certain that the transmission is not overfilled; this will cause foaming, fluid loss, and slippage.

(65° -85°F.)   (18° -29°C.)
COOL   HOT

ADD 1 PT.→ ←FULL HOT

WARM

NOTE: <u>DO NOT OVERFILL</u>. It takes only one pint to raise level from ADD to FULL with a hot transmission.

Automatic transmission dipstick markings

TRANSFER CASE

Check the four wheel drive transfer case lubricant level every 4 months or 6,000 miles.

1. With the truck parked on a level surface, remove the filler plug from the rear of the transfer case (behind the transmission). Be careful not to take out the drain plug at the bottom.

2. If lubricant trickles out, there is enough. If not, carefully insert a finger and check that the level is up to the edge of the hole, EXCEPT in full time four wheel drive systems. The lubricant level in full time four wheel drive cases should be ½ in. below the hole.

Lubricant may be added, if necessary, with a funnel and tube, or a squeeze bulb. Conventional transfer cases require SAE 80W or SAE 80W-90 GL-5 gear lubricant; full time systems use SAE 10W-30 or 10W-40 engine oil.

BRAKE MASTER CYLINDER

Chevrolet and GMC trucks are equipped with a dual braking system, allowing a vehicle to be brought to a safe stop in the event of failure in either the front or rear brakes. The dual master cylinder has two entirely separate reservoirs, one connected to the front brakes and the other connected to the rear brakes. In the event of failure in either portion, the remaining part is not affected.

1. Clean all of the dirt from around the cover of the master cylinder.

2. Be sure that the vehicle is resting on a level surface.

3. Carefully pry the clip from the top of the master cylinder to release the cover.

4. The fluid level should be approximately ⅛ in. from the top of the master cylinder. If not, add fluid until the level is correct. Only high quality brake fluids, such as General Motors Supreme No. 11 Hydraulic Brake Fluid, or fluids meeting DOT 3 specifications should be used.

NOTE: *It is normal for the fluid level to fall slightly as the disc brake pads wear, on 1971 and later trucks. However, if the level drops significantly between fluid level checks, or if the level is chronically low, the system should be examined for leakage.*

5. Install the cover of the master cylinder. On most models there is a rubber gasket under the cover, which fits into two slots on the cover. Be sure that this is seated properly.

6. Push the clip back into place and be sure that it seats in the groove on the top of the cover.

CAUTION: *Brake fluid damages paint. It also absorbs moisture from the air; never leave a container or the master cylinder uncovered any longer than necessary. All parts in contact with the brake fluid (i.e. master cylinder, and its lid, hoses, plunger assemblies, etc.) must be kept clean, since any contami-*

LEVEL CYLINDER   TILTED CYLINDER

Master cylinder fluid level

nation of the brake fluid will adversely affect braking performance.

COOLANT SERVICE

The coolant level should be checked at each fuel stop, ideally, to prevent the possibility of overheating and serious engine damage. If not, it should at least be checked once each month.

The cooling system was filled at the factory with a high quality coolant solution that is good for year around operation and protects the system from freezing down to −20°F. (−32°F in Canada). It is good for two full calendar years or 24,000 miles, whichever occurs first, provided that the proper concentration of coolant is maintained.

The 1973 and later cooling system differs slightly from those used on 1970–72 trucks. The 1973 and later system incorporates a plastic expansion tank connected to the radiator by a hose from the base of the radiator filler neck. The hot coolant level on 1973 and later trucks should be at the FULL HOT mark on the expansion tank and the cold coolant level should be at the FULL COLD mark on the tank. Do not remove the radiator cap to check the coolant level on 1973 and later trucks. On 1970–72 trucks, the cold coolant level should be approximately three inches below the bottom of the filler neck, and the hot level should be 1–1½ in. below the bottom of the filler neck.

To check the coolant level:

1. On 1973 and later models, check the level on the see-through expansion tank. On earlier models it will be necessary to CAREFULLY remove the radiator cap.

CAUTION: *The radiator coolant is under pressure when hot. To avoid the danger of physical harm, coolant level should be checked or replenished only when the engine is cold. To remove the radiator cap when the engine is hot, first cover the cap with a thick rag, or wear a heavy glove for protection. Press down on the cap slightly and slowly*

WARNING
ENGINE COOLANT ONLY

Coolant Recovery Tank

Typical coolant recovery tank

If you must remove the radiator cap when hot, cover the cap with a thick rag

Some radiator caps have levers to vent pressure before the cap is removed

Coolant protection can be checked with a simple float-type tester

The system should be pressure tested once a year

SEAL   GASKET

Check the radiator cap's rubber gasket and metal seal for deterioration at least once a year

Remove any debris from the radiator's cooling fins

turn it *counterclockwise until it reaches the first stop. Allow all the pressure to vent (indicated when the hissing sound stops). When the pressure is released, press down on the cap and continue to rotate it counterclock-*

wise. Some radiator caps have a lever for venting the pressure; lifting the lever will release the pressure, but you should still exercise extreme caution when removing the cap.

2. Check the level and, if necessary, add coolant to the proper level. Use a 50/50 mix of ethylene glycol antifreeze and water. Alcohol or methanol base coolants are not recommended. Anti-freeze solutions should be used, even in summer, to prevent rust and to take advantage of the solution's higher boiling point compared to plain water. This is imperative on air conditioned trucks; the heater core can freeze if it isn't protected. On 1974 and later models,

HOW TO SPOT BAD HOSES

Both the upper and lower radiator hoses are called upon to perform difficult jobs in an inhospitable environment. They are subject to nearly 18 psi at under hood temperatures often over 280°F., and must circulate nearly 7500 gallons of coolant an hour—3 good reasons to have good hoses.

A good test for any hose is to feel it for soft or spongy spots. Frequently these will appear as swollen areas of the hose. The most likely cause is oil soaking. This hose could burst at any time, when hot or under pressure.

Swollen hose

Cracked hoses can usually be seen but feel the hoses to be sure they have not hardened; a prime cause of cracking. This hose has cracked down to the reinforcing cords and could split at any of the cracks.

Cracked hose

Weakened clamps frequently are the cause of hose and cooling system failure. The connection between the pipe and hose has deteriorated enough to allow coolant to escape when the engine is hot.

Frayed hose end (due to weak clamp)

Debris, rust and scale in the cooling system can cause the inside of a hose to weaken. This can usually be felt on the outside of the hose as soft or thinner areas.

Debris in cooling system

coolant should be added through the coolant recovery tank, not the radiator filler neck.

CAUTION: *Never add large quantities of cold coolant to a hot engine. A cracked engine block may result.*

3. Replace the cap.

Each year the cooling system should be serviced as follows:

• Wash the radiator cap and filler neck with clean water.

• Check the coolant for proper level and freeze protection.

• Have the system pressure tested (15 psi). If a replacement cap is installed, be sure that it conforms to the original specifications.

• Tighten the hose clamps and inspect all hoses. Replace hoses that are swollen, cracked or otherwise deteriorated.

• Clean the frontal area of the radiator core and the air conditioning condenser, if so equipped.

DRAINING, FLUSHING AND TESTING THE COOLING SYSTEM AND COOLANT

The cooling system in your car accumulates some internal rust and corrosion in its normal operation. A simple method of keeping the system clean is known as "flushing" the system. It is performed by circulating a can of radiator flush through the system, and then draining and refilling the system with the normal coolant. Radiator flush is marketed by several different manufacturers, and is available in cans at auto departments, parts stores, and many hardware stores. This operation should be performed every 30,000 miles or once a year.

To flush the cooling system:

1. Drain the existing anti-freeze and coolant. Open the radiator and engine drain petcocks (located near the bottom of the radiator and engine block, respectively), or disconnect the bottom radiator hose at the radiator outlet.

NOTE: *Before opening the radiator petcock, spray it with some penetrating oil. Be aware that if the engine has been run up to operating temperature, the coolant emptied will be HOT.*

2. Close the petcock or re-connect the lower hose and fill the system with water—hot water if the system has just been run.

3. Add a can of quality radiator flush to the radiator or recovery tank, following any special instructions on the can.

4. Idle the entine as long as specified on the can of flush, or until the upper radiator hose gets hot.

5. Drain the system again. There should be quite a bit of scale and rust in the drained water.

6. Repeat this process until the drained water is mostly clear.

7. Close all petcocks and connect all hoses.

8. Flush the coolant recovery reservoir with water and leave empty.

9. Determine the capacity of your car's cooling system (see "Capacities" specifications in this guide). Add a 50/50 mix of ethylene glycol antifreeze and water to provide the desired protection.

10. Run the engine to operating temperature, then stop the engine and check for leaks. Check the coolant level and top up if necessary.

11. Check the protection level of your antifreeze mix with an antifreeze tester (a small, inexpensive syringe-type device available at any auto parts store). The tester has five or six small colored balls inside, each of which signify a certain temperature rating. Insert the tester in the recovery tank and suck just enough coolant into the syringe to float as many individual balls as you can (without sucking in too much coolant and floating all the balls at once). A table supplied with the tester will explain how many floating balls equal protection down to a certain temperature (three floating balls might mean the coolant will protect your engine down to 5°F, for example).

For problems with engine overheating, see Chapter 3.

AXLES

Locking front hubs should be run in the LOCK position for at least 10 miles each month to assure proper lubrication to the front axle.

Lubricant levels in both axles should be checked as specified in the "Maintenance" chart. To check the lubricant level in both front and rear axles:

1. Park on level ground.

2. Remove the filler plug from the differential housing cover.

3. If lubricant trickles out, there is enough. If not, carefully insert a finger and check that the level is up to the bottom of the hole. Front axles should be full up to the level of the hole when warm, and ½ in. below when cold.

4. Lubricant may be added with a funnel or a squeeze bulb. Front and rear axles use SAE 80W-90 GL-5 gear lubricant.

Positraction® limited slip axles must use a special lubricant available from dealers. If the special fluid is not used, noise, uneven operation, and damage will result. There is also a Positraction® additive to cure noise and slippage. Positraction® axles have an identifying tag, as well as a warning sticker near the jack or on the rear wheel well.

FILLER PLUG

Steering box lubrication points

The rear axle filler plug may be in either of the two locations shown here

Positraction® rear axle identification tag

STEERING GEAR

The steering gear is factory-filled with a lubricant which does not require seasonal change. The housing should not be drained; no lubrication is required for the life of the gear.

The gear should be inspected for seal leakage when specified in the "Maintenance" chart. Look for solid grease, not an oily film. If a seal is replaced or the gear overhauled, it should be filled with Part No. 1051052, which meets GM Specification GM 4673M, or its equivalent. Do not use EP Chassis Lube to lubricate the gear and do not overfill.

POWER STEERING RESERVOIR

The reservoir is part of the belt-driven power steering pump at the front of the engine.

1. Wipe off the cap and surrounding area, after stopping the engine with the wheels straight. On 1970–71 models, the wheels should be all the way to the left.

2. Remove the cap and attached dipstick.

3. Wipe the dipstick off with a clean, lint-free rag, replace the cap, and take a reading. If the fluid is hot, the level should be between HOT and COLD; if it is cold, it should be between COLD and ADD.

4. Either GM Power Steering Fluid or DEXRON® II Automatic Transmission Fluid may be used.

Power steering reservoir dipstick markings

Battery

Check the battery fluid level (except in Maintenance Free batteries) at least once a month, more often in hot weather or during extended periods of travel. The electrolyte level should be up to the bottom of the split ring in each cell. All batteries on Chevrolet and GMC trucks are equipped with an "eye" in the cap of one cell. If the "eye" glows or has an amber color to it, this means that the level is low and only distilled water should be added. Do not add anything else to the battery. If the "eye" has a

Fill each battery cell to the bottom of the split ring with distilled water

The specific gravity of the battery can be checked with a simple float-type hydrometer

Clean the battery posts with a wire brush, or the special tool shown

Special pullers are available to remove cable clamps

Clean the inside of the cable clamp with a wire brush

dark appearance the battery electrolyte level is high enough. It is wise to also check each cell individually.

At least once a year, check the specific gravity of the battery. It should be between 1.20–1.26. Clean and tighten the clamps and apply

Special tools are available for cleaning the terminals and cable clamps on side terminal batteries

a thin coat of petroleum jelly to the terminals. This will help to retard corrosion. The terminals can be cleaned with a stiff wire brush or with an inexpensive terminal cleaner designed for this purpose.

If water is added during freezing weather, the truck should be driven several miles to allow the electrolyte and water to mix. Otherwise the battery could freeze.

If the battery becomes corroded, a solution of baking soda and water will neutralize the corrosion. This should be washed off after making sure that the caps are securely in place. Rinse the solution off with cold water.

Some batteries were equipped with a felt terminal washer. This should be saturated with

Battery State of Charge at Room Temperature

Specific Gravity Reading	Charged Condition
1.260–1.280	Fully Charged
1.230–1.250	¾ Charged
1.200–1.220	½ Charged
1.170–1.190	¼ Charged
1.140–1.160	Almost no Charge
1.110–1.130	No Charge

engine oil approximately every 6,000 miles. This will also help to retard corrosion.

If a "fast" charger is used while the battery is in the truck, disconnect the battery before connecting the charger.

NOTE: *Keep flame or sparks away from the battery; it gives off explosive hydrogen gas.*

TESTING THE MAINTENANCE-FREE BATTERY

All later model trucks are equipped with maintenance-free batteries, which do not require normal attention as far as fluid level checks are concerned. However, the terminals require periodic cleaning, which should be performed at least once a year.

The sealed-top battery cannot be checked for charge in the normal manner, since there is no provision for access to the electrolyte. To check the condition of the battery:

1. If the indicator eye on top of the battery is dark, the battery has enough fluid. If the eye is light, the electrolyte fluid is too low and the battery must be replaced.

2. If a green dot appears in the middle of the eye, the battery is sufficiently charged. Proceed to Step 4. If no green dot is visible, charge the battery as in Step 3.

3. Charge the battery at this rate:

Charging Rate Amps	Time
75	40 min
50	1 hr
25	2 hr
10	5 hr

CAUTION: *Do not charge the battery for more than 50 amp/hours. If the green dot appears, or if electrolyte squirts out of the vent hole, stop the charge and proceed to Step 4.*

It may be necessary to tip the battery from side to side to get the green dot to appear after charging.

4. Connect a battery load tester and a voltmeter across the battery terminals (the battery cables should be disconnected from the battery). Apply a 300 amp load to the battery for 15 seconds to remove the surface charge. Remove the load.

5. Wait 15 seconds to allow the battery to recover. Apply the appropriate test load, as specified in the following chart:

Battery	Test Load
Y85-4	130 amps
R85-5	170 amps
R87-5	210 amps
R89-5	230 amps

Apply the load for 15 seconds while reading the voltage. Disconnect the load.

6. Check the results against the following chart. If the battery voltage is at or above the specified voltage for the temperature listed, the battery is good. If the voltage falls below what's listed, the battery should be replaced.

Temperature (°F)	Minimum Voltage
70 or above	9.6
60	9.5
50	9.4
40	9.3
30	9.1
20	8.9
10	8.7
0	8.5

Tires and Wheels

The tires should be rotated as specified in the "Maintenance Intervals" chart. Refer to the accompanying illustrations for the recommended rotation patterns.

The tires on your truck should have built-in tread wear indicators, which appear as ½ in. bands when the tread depth gets as low as ¹⁄₁₆ in. When the indicators appear in 2 or more adjacent grooves, it's time for new tires.

For optimum tire life, you should keep the tires properly inflated, rotate them often and have the wheel alignment checked periodically.

Some late models have the maximum load pressures listed on the V.I.N. plate on the left door frame. In general, pressure of 28–32 psi would be suitable for highway use with moderate loads and passenger car type tires (load range B, non-flotation) of original equipment size. Pressures should be checked before driving, since pressure can increase as much as 6 psi due to heat. It is a good idea to have an accurate gauge and to check pressures weekly.

Tire tread wear indicators appear as solid bands when the tire is worn out

Tread depth can be checked with a penny; when the top of Lincoln's head is visible, it's time for new tires

Tread depth can also be checked with an inexpensive gauge made for the purpose

Not all gauges on service station air pumps are to be trusted. In general, truck-type tires require higher pressures and flotation-type tires, lower pressures.

TIRE ROTATION

It is recommended that you have the tires rotated every 6,000 miles. There is no way to give a tire rotation diagram for every combination of tires and vehicles, but the accompanying diagrams are a general rule to follow. Radial tires should not be cross-switched; they last longer if their direction of rotation is not changed. Truck tires sometimes have directional tread, indicated by arrows on the sidewalls; the arrow shows the direction of rotation. They will wear very rapidly if reversed. Studded snow tires will lose their studs if their direction of rotation is reversed.

NOTE: *Mark the wheel position or direction of rotation on radial tires or studded snow tires before removing them.*

If your truck is equipped with tires having different load ratings on the front and the rear, the tires should not be rotated front to rear. Rotating these tires could affect tire life (the tires with the lower rating will wear faster, and could become overloaded), and upset the handling of the truck.

BIAS PLY TIRE   BIAS PLY TIRE
4 WHEEL ROTATION 5 WHEEL ROTATION

This rotation pattern is for bias or bias-belted tires only

5 WHEEL ROTATION   4 WHEEL ROTATION

This rotation pattern is for radical tires; it can also be used for bias or bias-belted tires if you wish. The radial spare can be used on the left side, too, but don't change its direction of rotation once used

TIRE USAGE

The tires on your truck were selected to provide the best all-around performance for normal operation when inflated as specified. Oversize tires (Load Range D) will not increase the maximum carrying capacity of the vehicle, although they will provide an extra margin of tread life. Be sure to check overall height before using larger size tires which may cause interference with suspension components or wheel wells. When replacing conventional tire sizes with other tire size designations, be sure to check the manufacturer's recommendations. Interchangeability is not always possible because of differences in load ratings, tire dimensions, wheel well clearances, and rim size. Also due to differences in handling characteristics, "70 Series" and "60 Series" tires should be used only in pairs on the same axle; radial tires should be used only in sets of four.

The wheels must be the correct width for the tire. Tire dealers have charts of tire and rim compatibility. A mismatch can cause sloppy handling and rapid tread wear. The old rule of thumb is that the tread width should match the rim width (inside bead to inside bead) within an inch. For radial tires, the rim width should be 80% or less of the tire (not tread) width.

The height (mounted diameter) of the new tires can greatly change speedometer accuracy, engine speed at a given road speed, fuel mileage, acceleration, and ground clearance. Tire manufacturers furnish full measurement specifications. Speedometer drive gears are available for correction.

NOTE: *Dimensions of tires marked the same size may vary significantly, even among tires from the same manufacturer.*

The spare tire should be usable, at least for low speed operation, with the new tires.

TIRE TYPES

For maximum satisfaction, tires should be used in sets of five. Mixing or different types (radial, bias-belted, fiberglass belted) should be avoided. Conventional bias tires are constructed so that the cords run bead-to-bead at an angle. Alternate plies run at an opposite angle. This type of construction gives rigidity to both tread and sidewall. Bias-belted tires are similar in construction to conventional bias ply tires. Belts run at an angle and also at a 90° angle to the bead, as in the radial tire. Tread life is improved considerably over the conventional bias tire. The radial tire differs in construction, but instead of the carcass plies running at an angle of 90° to each other, they run at an angle of 90° to the bead. This gives the tread a great deal of rigidity and the sidewall a great deal of flexibility and accounts for the characteristic bulge associated with radial tires.

Chevrolet and GMC trucks are capable of using radial tires and they are recommended in some years. If they are used, tire sizes and wheel diameters should be selected to maintain ground clearance and tire load capacity equivalent to the minimum specified tire. Radial tires should always be used in sets of five, but in an emergency radial tires can be used with caution on the rear axle only. If this is done, both tires on the rear should be of radial design.

NOTE: *Radial tires should never be used on only the front axle.*

CAUTION: *Radial tires must not be mounted on 16.5 in. rims unless the rims are stamped with the word "Radial". Ordinary rims are not strong enough to withstand the additional side loads.*

CARCASS PLIES   TREAD PLIES   TREAD

BIAS   BELTED RADIAL   BELTED BIAS

Types of tire construction

Snow tires should not be operated at sustained speeds over 70 mph.

On four wheel drive trucks, all tires must be of the same size, type, and tread pattern, to provide even traction on loose surfaces, to prevent driveline bind when conventional four wheel drive is used, and to prevent excessive wear on the center differential with full time four wheel drive.

Fuel Filter

GASOLINE ENGINES

The fuel filter should be serviced at the interval given on the "Maintenance Interval" chart. Two types of fuel filters are used, a bronze type and a paper element type. Inline fuel filters may be used on some engines which should be changed at the same time as the filter in the carburetor body. Filter replacement should be attempted only when the engine is cold. Additionally, it is a good idea to place some absorbent rags under the fuel fittings to catch the gasoline which will spill out when the lines are loosened. To replace the filter found in the carburetor body:

1. Disconnect the fuel line connecting at the intake fuel filter nut. Plug the opening to prevent loss of fuel.

2. Remove the intake fuel filter nut from the carburetor with a 1 in. wrench.

3. Remove the filter element and spring.

4. Check the element for restrictions by blowing on the cone end. Air should pass freely.

5. Clean or replace the element, as necessary.

6. Install the element spring, then the filter element in the carburetor. Bronze filters should have the small section of the cone facing out.

7. Install a new gasket on the intake fuel nut.

A bronze fuel filter is used on earlier types

Most carburetors use a paper element fuel filter

Install the nut in the carburetor body and tighten securely.

8. Install the fuel line and tighten the connector.

Some trucks may have an inline filter. This is a can-shaped device located in the fuel line between the pump and the carburetor. It may be made of either plastic or metal. To replace the filter:

1. Place some absorbent rags under the filter; remember, it will be full of gasoline when removed.

2. Use a pair of pliers to expand the clamp on one end of the filter, then slide the clamp down past the point to which the filter pipe extends in the rubber hose. Do the same with the other clamp.

3. Gently twist and pull the hoses free of the filter pipes. Remove and discard the old filter.

NOTE: *Most replacement filters come with new hoses that should be installed with the new filter.*

4. Install the new filter into the hoses, slide the clamps back into place, and check for leaks with the engine idling.

350 (5.7L) DIESEL ENGINES

The diesel fuel filter is mounted on a bracket at the top rear of the engine.

1. Unbolt the fuel pump line at the filter inlet (upper corner of the filter).

2. Unbolt the injector pump line at the lower corner of the fuel filter.

3. Loosen the center bolt holding the filter to the bracket, and remove the filter.

Installation is the reverse of removal. Tighten the two fuel line nuts to 20 ft. lbs., and check for leaks.

379 (6.2L) DIESEL ENGINES

These diesels utilize two fuel filters; a primary filter, located on the engine side of the firewall,

The 350 diesel engine fuel filter is located at the rear of the engine

379 (6.2L) diesel primary fuel filter is located on the firewall

and a secondary filter, which is bolted to the back of the intake manifold. Both filters are canister-type screw-on units, and should be replaced at the regular intervals specified in the "Maintenance" chart. See "Diesel Fuel System" in Chapter 4 for more information.

DRAINING WATER—PRIMARY FILTER

1. Open the petcock on the top of the filter housing.
2. Place a drain pan below the filter. Attach a length of hose to the petcock to direct the fluid down below the frame. Open the petcock on the bottom of the drain assembly.
3. After all the water has been drained, close the petcock lightly.
    NOTE: *If the filter is drained completely,*

remove the filter and refill it with clean diesel fuel before starting engine.
4. Close the upper petcock tightly.
5. Start the engine and let it run a bit. The engine may run roughly for a short time until the air is purged from the system.
    NOTE: *If the engine continues to run roughly, check that both petcocks at the primary filter are closed tightly.*

SECONDARY FUEL FILTER—REMOVAL AND INSTALLATION

1. Remove the air cleaner.
2. Disconnect and remove the fuel lines from the adaptor. Remove the fuel filter adaptor and remove the fuel filter.
3. To install, install the filter to the adaptor and tighten ⅔ turn after the filter contacts the gasket.
4. Install the adaptor to the intake manifold.
5. Install the filter inlet line only.
    NOTE: *Anytime the secondary filter is removed or replaced, air must be purged from the filter to prevent engine stalling or excessive cranking time to restart the engine.*
6. With the secondary fuel line disconnected, disconnect the pink electrical wire from the fuel injection pump to prevent the engine from starting.
7. Place a shop rag under the filter outlet. Crank the engine (10 seconds at the most) until fuel appears at the outlet port. If fuel is not observed after 10 seconds, wait 15 seconds and repeat the above procedure.
8. When fuel is seen at the outlet port, install the outlet line.
9. Reconnect the pink wire at the injection pump and reinstall the air cleaner.
10. Start the engine and let it idle for several minutes to purge any remaining air. Check all fittings for leakage.

Secondary fuel filter, 379 diesels

LUBRICATION

Oil and Fuel Recommendations

ENGINE OIL

The SAE grade number indicates the viscosity of the engine oil, or its ability to lubricate under a given temperature. The lower the SAE grade number, the lighter the oil; the lower the viscosity, the easier it is to crank the engine in cold weather.

The API (American Petroleum Institute) designation indicates the classification of engine oil for use under given operating conditions. Only oils designated for "Service SF" should be used. These oils provide maximum engine protection. Both the SAE grade number and the API designation can be found on the top of a can of oil.

NOTE: *Non-detergent should not be used.*

Oil viscosities should be chosen from those oils recommended for the lowest anticipated temperatures during the oil change interval.

The multi-viscosity oils offer the important advantage of being adaptable to temperature extremes. They allow easy starting at low temperatures, yet give good protection at high speeds and engine temperatures. This is a decided advantage in changeable climates or in long distance driving.

Diesel engines also require SF engine oil. In addition, the oil must qualify for a CC rating. The API has a number of different diesel engine ratings, including CB, CC, and CD.

NOTE: *1981 and later diesel engines can use either SF/CC, SF/CD.*

The diesel engine in the Chevrolet and GMC pick-ups requires SF/CC rated oil. DO NOT use an oil if the designation CD appears anywhere on the oil can. *Use SF/CC engine oil only. Do not use an oil labeled only SF or only CC. Both designations must appear.*

For recommended oil viscosities, refer to the chart. 10W-30 grade oils are not recommended for sustained high speed driving.

Single viscosity oil (SAE 30) is recommended for sustained high speed driving.

SYNTHETIC OIL

There are excellent synthetic and fuel-efficient oils available that, under the right circumstances, can help provide better fuel mileage and better engine protection. However, these advantages come at a price, which can be three or four times the price per quart of conventional motor oils.

Before pouring any synthetic oils into your car's engine, you should consider the condition of the engine and the type of driving you do. Also, check the truck's warranty conditions regarding the use of synthetics.

Generally, it is best to avoid the use of synthetic oil in both brand new and older, high mileage engines. New engines require a proper break-in, and the synthetics are so "slippery" that they can prevent this; most manufacturers recommend that you wait at least 5,000 miles before switching to a synthetic oil. Conversely, older engines are looser and tend to "use" more oil; synthetics will slip past worn parts more readily than regular oil, and will be used up fsater. If your car already leaks and/or "uses" oil (due to worn parts and bad seals or gaskets), it will leak and use more with a slippery synthetic inside.

Consider your type of driving. If most of your accumulated mileage is on the highway at higher, steadier speeds, a synthetic oil will reduce friction and probably help deliver better fuel mileage. Under such ideal highway conditions, the oil change interval can be extended, as long as the oil filter will operate effectively for the extended life of the oil. If the filter can't do its job for this extended period, dirt and sludge will build up in your engine's crankcase, sump, oil pump and lines, no matter what type of oil is used. If using synthetic oil in this manner, you should continue to change the oil filter at the recommended intervals.

Trucks used under harder, stop-and-go, short hop circumstances should always be serviced more frequently, and for these cars synthetic oil may not be a wise investment. Because of the necessary shorter change interval needed for this type of driving, you cannot take advantage of the long recommended change interval of most synthetic oils.

Gasoline Engine Oil Viscosity Chart

(© Chevrolet Motor Div.)

NOTES: 1. SAE 5W and 5W-20 are not recommended for sustained high speed driving.
2. SAE 5W-30 is recommended for all seasons in Canada

Diesel Engine Oil Viscosity Chart

(© **Chevrolet Motor Div.**)

Finally, most synthetic oils are not compatible with conventional oils and cannot be added to them. This means you should always carry a couple of quarts of synthetic oil with you while on a long trip, as not all service stations carry this oil.

FUELS

Gasoline Engines

1970–74 AND 1975–AND LATER MODELS WITHOUT CATALYTIC CONVERTER

Chevrolet and GMC trucks are designed to operate on regular grades of fuel (1970–71) commonly sold in the U.S. and Canada. In 1972–74 (and 1975–and later models without a catalytic converter), unleaded or low-lead fuels of approximately 91 octane (Research Octane) or higher are recommended. General Motors recommends the use of low-leaded or unleaded fuels (0–0.5 grams per gallon) to reduce particulate and hydrocarbon pollutants.

Use of a fuel which is too low in anti-knock quality will result in "spark knock." Since many factors affect operating efficiency, such as altitude, terrain and air temperature, knocking may result even though you are using the recommended fuel. If persistent knocking occurs, it may be necessary to switch to a slightly higher grade of gasoline to correct the problem. In the case of late model engines, switching to a premium fuel would be an unnecessary expense. In these engines, a slightly higher grade of gasoline (regular) should be used only when persistent knocking occurs. Continuous or excessive knocking may result in engine damage.

NOTE: *Your engine's fuel requirement can change with time, mainly due to carbon buildup, which changes the compression ratio. If your engine pings, knocks, or runs on, switch to a higher grade of fuel and check* the ignition timing as soon as possible. If you must use unleaded fuel, sometimes a change of brands will cure the problem. If it is necessary to retard the timing from specifications, don't change it more than about four degrees. Retarded timing will reduce power output and fuel mileage, and it will increase engine temperature.

1975–AND LATER MODELS WITH CATALYTIC CONVERTER

Chevrolet and GMC trucks with Gross Vehicle Weight Ratings (GVWR) which place them in the heavy-duty emissions class do not require a catalytic converter. However, almost all 1975 and later light-duty emissions trucks have a catalytic converter. The light-duty classification applies to all trucks with a GVWR under 6,000 lbs. through 1978, except for 1978 trucks sold in California. 1978 California models and all 1979 models with GVWR's under 8,500 lbs. fall into the light-duty category. In 1980 and later, the light-duty classification applies to all trucks with GVWR's under 8,600 lbs.

The catalytic converter is a muffler-shaped device installed in the exhaust system. It contains platinum and palladium coated pellets which, through catalytic action, oxidize hydrocarbon and carbon monoxide gases into hydrogen, oxygen, and carbon dioxide.

The design of the converter requires the exclusive use of unleaded fuel. Leaded fuel renders the converter inoperative, raising exhaust emissions to illegal levels. In addition, the lead in the gasoline coats the pellets in the converter, blocking the flow of exhaust gases. This raises exhaust back pressure and severly reduces engine performance. In extreme cases, the exhaust system becomes so blocked that the engine will not run.

Converter-equipped trucks are delivered with

the label "Unleaded Fuel Only" placed next to the fuel gauge on the instrument panel and next to the gas tank filler opening. In general, any unleaded fuel is suitable for use in these trucks as long as the gas has an octane rating of 87 or more. Octane ratings are posted on the gas pumps. However, in some cases, knocking may occur even though the recommended fuel is being used. The only practical solution for this is to switch to a slightly higher grade of unleaded fuel, or to switch brands of unleaded gasoline.

Diesel Engines

Diesel-engined pick-ups require the use of diesel fuel. Two grades of diesel fuel are manufactured, #1 and #2, although #2 grade is generally the only grade available. Better fuel economy results from the use of #2 grade fuel. In some northern parts of the U.S., and in most parts of Canada, #1 grade fuel is available in winter, or a winterized blend of #2 grade is supplied in winter months. If #1 grade is available, it should be used whenever temperatures fall below 20°F (−7°C). Winterized #2 grade may also be used at these temperatures. However, unwinterized #2 grade should *not* be used below 20°F (−7°C). Cold temperatures cause unwinterized #2 grade to thicken (it actually gels), blocking the fuel lines and preventing the engine from running.

Do not use home heating oil or gasoline in the diesel pick-up. Do not attempt to "thin" unwinterized #2 diesel fuel with gasoline. Gasoline or home heating oil will damage the engine and void the manufacturer's warranty.

Lubricant Changes
ENGINE OIL

Engine oil should be changed according to the schedule in the "Maintenance Interval Chart." Under conditions such as:

• Driving in dusty conditions,
• Continuous trailer pulling or RV use,
• Extensive or prolonged idling,
• Extensive short trip operation in freezing temperatures (when the engine is not throughly warmed-up),
• Frequent long runs at high speeds and high ambient temperatures, and
• Stop-and-go service such as delivery trucks, the oil change interval and filter replacement interval should be cut in half. Operation of the engine in severe conditions such as a dust storm may require an immediate oil and filter change.

Chevrolet and GMC recommended changing both the oil and filter during the first oil change and the filter every other oil change

thereafter. For the small price of an oil filter, it's cheap insurance to replace the filter at every oil change. One of the larger filter manufacturers points out in its advertisements that not changing the filter leaves one quart of dirty oil in the engine. This claim is true and should be kept in mind when changing your oil.

NOTE: *The oil filter on the diesel engines must be changed every oil change.*

To change the oil, the truck should be on a level surface, and the engine should be at operating temperature. This is to ensure that the foreign matter will be drained away along with the oil, and not left in the engine to form sludge. You should have available a container that will hold a minimum of 8 quarts of liquid, a wrench to fit the old drain plug, a spout for pouring in new oil, and a rag or two, which you will always need. If the filter is being replaced, you will also need a band wrench or filter wrench to fit the end of the filter.

NOTE: *If the engine is equipped with an oil cooler, this will also have to be drained, using the drain plug. Be sure to add enough oil to fill the cooler in addition to the engine.*

1. Position the truck on a level surface and set the parking brake or block the wheels. Slide a drain pan under the oil drain plug.

2. From under the truck, loosen, but do not remove the oil drain plug. Cover your hand with a rag or glove and slowly unscrew the drain plug.

CAUTION: *The engine oil will be HOT. Keep your arms, face and hands clear of the oil as it drains out.*

3. Remove the plug and let the oil drain into the pan.

NOTE: *Do not drop the plug into the drain pan.*

4. When all of the oil has drained, clean off the drain plug and put it back into the hole. Remember to tighten the plug 20 ft. lbs. (30 ft. lbs. for diesel engines).

5. Loosen the filter with a band wrench or special oil filter cap wrench. On most Chevrolet engines, especially the V8s, the oil filter is next to the exhaust pipes. Stay clear of these, since even a passing contact will result in a painful burn.

NOTE: *On trucks equipped with catalytic*

The oil drain plug is located at the lowest point of the engine oil pan

Use a strap wrench to loosen the oil filter; install the new filter by hand

Coat the gasket on the new oil filter with a film of oil

converters stay clear of the converter. The outside temperature of a hot catalytic converter can approach 1200°F.

6. Cover your hand with a rag, and spin the filter off by hand.

7. Coat the rubber gasket on a new filter with a light film of clean engine oil. Screw the filter onto the mounting stud and tighten according to the directions on the filter (usually hand-tight one turn past the point where the gasket contacts the mounting base). Don't overtighten the filter.

8. Refill the engine with the specified amount of clean engine oil.

9. Run the engine for several minutes, checking for leaks. Check the level of the oil and add oil if necessary.

When you have finished this job, you will notice that you now possess four or five quarts of dirty oil. The best thing to do with it is to pour it into plastic jugs, such as milk or antifreeze containers. Then, if you are on good terms with your gas station man, he might let you pour it into his used oil container for recycling. Otherwise, the only thing to do with it is to put the containers into the trash.

MANUAL TRANSMISSION

No intervals are specified for changing the transmission lubricant, but it is a good idea on a used vehicle, one that has been worked hard, or one driven in deep water. The vehicle should be on a level surface and the lubricant should be at operating temperature.

1. Position the truck on a level surface.

2. Place a pan of sufficient capacity under the transmission drain plug.

3. Remove the upper (fill) plug to provide a vent opening.

4. Remove the lower (drain) plug and let the lubricant drain out. The 1976–80 Tremec top-cover three speed is drained by removing the lower extension housing bolt.

5. Replace the drain plug.

6. Add lubricant with a suction gun or squeeze bulb. The correct lubricant is SAE 80W–90 GL-5 Gear Lubricant, or SAE 80W GL-5 for cold climates.

7. Reinstall the filler plug. Run the engine and check for leaks.

AUTOMATIC TRANSMISSION

The fluid should be drained with the transmission warm. It is easier to change the fluid if the truck is raised somewhat from the ground, but this is not always easy without a lift. The transmission must be level for it to drain properly.

1. Place a shallow pan underneath to catch the transmission fluid (about 5 pints). On earlier models, the transmission pan has a drain plug. Remove this and drain the fluid. For later models, loosen all the pan bolts, then pull one corner down to drain most of the fluid. If it sticks, VERY CAREFULLY pry the pan loose. You can buy aftermarket drain plug kits that makes this operation a bit less messy, once installed.

NOTE: *If the fluid removed smells burnt, serious transmission troubles, probably due to overheating, should be suspected.*

2. Remove the pan bolts and empty out the pan. On some models, there may not be much room to get at the screws at the front of the pan.

PUMP FILTER TO VALVE BODY   GASKET

The Turbo Hydra-Matic 350 filter mounts to the valve body

The Turbo Hydra-Matic 400 filter has an O-ring on the intake pipe; check the condition of this O-ring, and replace as necessary

Install the new gasket to the pan

Transmission fluid is added through the dipstick tube

3. Clean the pan with solvent and allow it to air dry. If you use a rag to wipe it out, you risk leaving bits of lint and threads in the transmission.

4. Remove the filter or strainer retaining bolts. On the Turbo Hydra-Matic 400, there are two screws securing the filter or screen to the valve body. A reusable strainer may be found on some models. The strainer may be cleaned in solvent and air dried thoroughly. The filter and gasket must be replaced.

5. Install a new gasket and filter.

6. Install a new gasket on the pan, and

tighten the bolts evenly to 12 foot pounds in a criss-cross pattern.

7. Add DEXRON® or DEXRON® II transmission fluid through the dipstick tube. The correct amount is in the Capacities Chart. Do not overfill.

8. With the gearshift lever in PARK, start the engine and let it idle. Do not race the engine.

9. Move the gearshift lever through each position, holding the brakes. Return the lever to PARK, and check the fluid level with the engine idling. The level should be between the two dimples on the dipstick, about ¼ in. below the ADD mark. Add fluid, if necessary.

10. Check the fluid level after the truck has been driven enough to thoroughly warm up the transmission. Details are given under Fluid Level Checks earlier in the Chapter. If the transmission is overfilled, the excess must be drained off. Overfilling causes aerated fluid, resulting in transmission slippage and probable damage.

TRANSFER CASE

Part Time Systems

No intervals are specified for changing transfer case lubricant, but it is a good idea for trucks that are worked hard or driven in deep water.

1. With the transfer case warmed up, park on a level surface.

2. Slide a pan of at least 6 pts. capacity under the case drain plug.

3. Remove the filler plug from the rear of the transfer case (behind the transmission). Remove the drain plug from the bottom.

4. Wipe the area clean and replace the drain plug.

5. Add lubricant with a suction gun or squeeze bulb. Conventional transfer cases require SAE 80W–90 GL-5 Gear Lubricant.

6. When the lubricant level is up to the bottom of the filler hole, replace the plug.

Full Time Four Wheel Drive

The full time system requires oil changes at regular intervals, according to the amount and type of work done by the unit. Trucks used for normal on-off road work should have the transfer case oil changed at 24,000 mile intervals. When used for heavy duty work, trailer towing, snowplowing, and the like, the interval should be halved to 12,000 miles. If the truck is exposed to extremely dusty or muddy conditions, the oil should be changed at 1,000 mile intervals.

The letters point out the draining locations on the full time four wheel drive transfer case. Letter A indicates the lowest bolt in the rear cover; B indicates the P.T.O. cover, and C shows the location of the speedometer driven gear. Use a suction gun at locations B and C.

The transfer case oil must be hot before changing. Drive the truck until the engine has reached normal operating temperature, and park on a level surface.

1. Slide a pan of at least 8 pts. capacity under the case drain plug.
2. Remove the filler plug.
3. Remove the lowest bolt from the front output shaft rear bearing retainer cover, and allow the lubricant to drain. Be careful—the oil will be hot. There may be a drain plug. If so, remove that instead.
4. Remove the six bolts on the left (driver's) side of the case which secure the P.T.O. (power take-off) cover. Remove this cover and allow the lubricant to drain out.
5. Remove the speedometer driven gear from the upper left rear corner of the case.
6. Use a suction gun to remove as much lubricant as possible from the case cover location and the speedometer gear location.
7. Install the speedometer driven gear, the P.T.O. cover, and the lowest bolt or drain plug.
8. Add approximately seven pints of oil through the filler plug opening. The proper oil to use is 10W–30 or 10W–40 engine oil.
9. Check the fluid level and add sufficient oil to raise the level to ½ in. below the filler plug opening. Replace the plug, and wipe the surfaces of the case and skid plate to remove any excess oil. Drive the truck and check for leaks.

AXLES

No intervals are specified for changing axle lubricant, but it is a good idea, especially if you have driven in water over the axle vents.

1. Park the vehicle on the level with the axles at normal operating temperature.
2. Place a pan of at least 6 pints capacity under the differential housing.
3. Remove the filler plug.
4. If you have a drain plug, remove it. If not, unbolt and remove the differential cover.
5. Replace the drain plug, or differential cover. Use a new gasket if the differential cover has been removed.
6. Lubricant may be added with a suction gun or squeeze bulb. Front axles use SAE 80W–90, GL-5 Gear Lubricant. Fill front axle to ½ in. below the filler plug opening. Rear axles use SAE 80W–90 gear oil. Positraction® axles must use special lubricant available from dealers. If the special fluid is not used, noise, uneven operation, and damage will result. There is also a Positraction® additive used to cure noise and slippage. Positraction axles have an identifying tag, as well as a warning sticker near the jack or on the rear wheel well. Rear axle lubricant level should be up to the bottom of the filler plug opening.

DRIVESHAFTS

The four wheel drive front driveshaft requires special attention for lubrication. The large constant velocity joint at the front of the transfer case has a special grease fitting in the centering ball; a special needle nose adapter for a flush type fitting is required, as well as a special lubricant, GM part no. 1050679. You can only get at this fitting when it is facing up toward the floorboards, so you need a flexible hose, too. To lubricate the sliding splines in the Dana type front driveshaft properly, first unscrew and slide back the spline seal collar. Pump chassis grease into the fitting until it oozes out the vent hole, then plug the vent hole with

LUBE FITTING

The front driveshaft constant velocity joint grease fitting must face up (toward the truck's underbody) so that a needle-nose adapter can be inserted.

your finger and pump in grease until it comes out past the seal. This isn't necessary on the GM style driveshaft, which has the grease fitting closer to the seal collar.

Water resistant EP chassis lubricant (grease) conforming to GM specification 6031-M should be used for all chassis grease points.

Chassis Greasing
FRONT SUSPENSION

Every year or 7,500 miles the front suspension ball joints, both upper and lower on each side of the truck, must be greased. Most trucks covered in this guide should be equipped with grease nipples on the ball joints, although some may have plugs which must be removed and nipples fitted.

Jack up the front end of the truck and safely support it with jackstands. Block the rear wheels and firmly apply the parking brake. If the truck has been parked in temperatures below 20°F for any length of time, park it in a heated garage for an hour or so until the ball joints loosen up enough to accept the grease.

Depending on which front wheel you work on first, turn the wheel and tire outward, either full-lock right or full-lock left. You now have the ends of the upper and lower suspension control arms in front of you; the grease nipples are visible pointing up (top ball joint) and down (lower ball joint) through the end of each control arm. If the nipples are not accessible enough, remove the wheel and tire. Wipe all dirt and crud from the nipples or from around the plugs (if installed). If plugs are on the truck, remove them and install grease nipples in the holes (nipples are available in various thread sizes at most auto parts stores). Using a hand-operated, low pressure grease gun loaded with a quality chassis grease, grease the ball joint only until the rubber joint boot begins to swell out.

NOTE: *Do not pump so much grease into the ball joint that excess grease squeezes out of the rubber boot. This destroys the water-tight seal.*

STEERING LINKAGE

The steering linkage should be greased at the same interval as the ball joints. Grease nipples are installed on the steering tie rod ends on most models. Wipe all dirt and crud from around the nipples at each tie rod end. Using a hand-operated, low pressure grease gun loaded with a suitable chassis grease, grease the linkage until the old grease begins to squeeze out around the tie rod ends. Wipe off the nipples and any excess grease. Also grease the nipples on the steering idler arms.

PARKING BRAKE LINKAGE

Use chassis grease on the parking brake cable where it contacts the cable guides, levers and linkage

AUTOMATIC TRANSMISSION LINKAGE

Apply a small amount of clean engine oil to the kickdown and shift linkage points at 7,500 mile intervals.

Body Lubrication
HOOD LATCH AND HINGES

Clean the latch surfaces and apply clean engine oil to the latch pilot bolts and the spring anchor. Also lubricate the hood hinges with engine oil. Use a chassis grease to lubricate all the pivot points in the latch release mechanism.

DOOR HINGES

The gas tank filler door and truck doors should be wiped clean and lubricated with clean engine oil once a year. The door lock cylinders and latch mechanisms should be lubricated periodically with a few drops of graphite lock lubricant or a few shots of silicone spray.

WHEEL BEARINGS

Refer to Chapter 7 (4 x 4s) for removal, installation, adjustment and repacking procedures. Refer to Chapter 9 for 2WD bearings.

PUSHING AND TOWING

Pushing

Chevrolet and GMC trucks with manual transmissions can be push started.

To push start, make sure that both bumpers are in reasonable alignment. Turn the ignition key to ON and engage High gear. Depress the clutch pedal. When a speed of about 10 mph is reached, slightly depress the gas pedal and slowly release the clutch. The engine should start.

Automatic transmission equipped trucks cannot be started by pushing.

Towing
TWO WHEEL DRIVE

Chevrolet and GMC trucks can be towed on all four wheels (flat towed) at speeds of less than 35 mph for distances less than 50 miles, providing that the axle, driveline and engine/transmission are operable. The transmission should be in Neutral, the engine should be off, the steering column unlocked, and the parking brake released.

TOWING FOUR WHEEL DRIVE

FRONT WHEELS OFF THE GROUND	
FULL TIME (4 X 4) AUTOMATIC TRANSMISSION	**PART TIME (4 X 4)** MANUAL TRANSMISSION
1. TRANSFER CASE IN NEUTRAL 2. TRANSMISSION IN PARK 3. MAXIMUM SPEED 35 MPH 4. MAXIMUM DISTANCE 50 MILES NOTE: For distances over 50 miles, disconnect rear propshaft at rear axle carrier and secure in safe position.	1. TRANSFER CASE IN 2 H 2. TRANSMISSION IN NEUTRAL 3. MAXIMUM SPEED 35 MPH 4. MAXIMUM DISTANCE 50 MILES NOTE: For distances over 50 miles, disconnect the rear propshaft at rear axle carrier and secure in safe position.
REAR WHEELS OFF THE GROUND	
CAUTION: When towing a vehicle in this position, the steering wheel should be secured to keep the front wheels in a straight ahead position.	
. FULL TIME (4 X 4)	**PART TIME (4 X 4)**
1. TRANSFER CASE IN NEUTRAL 2. TRANSMISSION IN PARK 3. MAXIMUM SPEED 35 MPH 4. MAXIMUM DISTANCE 50 MILES NOTE: For distances over 50 miles, disconnect front propshaft at front axle carrier and secure in safe position.	1. TRANSFER CASE IN 2 H 2. TRANSMISSION IN NEUTRAL 3. MAXIMUM SPEED 35 MPH 4. MAXIMUM DISTANCE 50 MILES NOTE: For distances over 50 miles, disconnect the front propshaft at front axle carrier and secure in safe position.
ALL FOUR WHEELS ON GROUND	
FULL TIME (4 X 4)	**PART TIME (4 X 4)**
1. TRANSFER CASE IN NEUTRAL 2. TRANSMISSION IN PARK NOTE: Do not exceed speed as per State laws for towing vehicles.	1. TRANSFER CASE IN 2 H 2. TRANSMISSION IN NEUTRAL 3. MAXIMUM SPEED 35 MPH 4. MAXIMUM DISTANCE 50 MILES NOTE: For speeds or distances greater than above, both propshafts must be disconnected at the axle carrier end and secured in a safe position. It is recommended that both propshafts be removed and stored in the vehicle. NOTE: Do not exceed speeds as per State laws for towing vehicles.

Four wheel drive towing chart

Do not attach chains to the bumpers or bracketing. All attachments must be made to the structural members. Safety chains should be used. It should also be remembered that power steering and brake assists will not be working with the engine off.

The rear wheels must be raised off the ground or the driveshaft disconnected when the transmission is not operating properly, or when speeds of over 35 mph will be used or when towing more than 50 miles.

CAUTION: *If a truck is towed on its front wheels only, the steering wheel must be secured with the wheels in a straight ahead position.*

FOUR WHEEL DRIVE

Details for towing procedures are given in the Towing Four Wheel Drive Chart.

Remember that the power steering and power brakes will not have their power assist with the engine off. The only safe way to tow is with a tow bar. The steering column must be unlocked and the parking brake released. Attachments should be made to the frame and to the bumper or its brackets. Safety chains are also required.

NOTE: *When towing a full time four wheel drive manual transmission truck with all four wheels on the ground, the transfer case must be in Neutral and the transmission in high gear. There is no speed restriction.*

JUMP STARTING

ALL EXCEPT DIESELS

The following procedure is recommended by the manufacturer. Be sure that the booster battery is 12 volt with negative ground.

CAUTION: *Do not attempt this procedure on a frozen battery; it will probably explode. Do not attempt it on a sealed Delco Freedom battery showing a light color in the charge indicator. Be certain to observe correct polarity connections. Failure to do so will result in almost immediate alternator and regulator destruction. Never allow the jumper cable ends to touch each other.*

1. Position the vehicles so that they are not touching. Set the parking brake and place automatic transmissions in Park and manual transmissions in Neutral. Turn off the lights, heater and other electrical loads.

2. Remove the vent caps from both the booster and discharged battery. Lay a cloth over the open vent cells of each battery. This isn't necessary on batteries equipped with sponge type flame arrestor caps, and it isn't possible on sealed batteries.

GREEN DOT   ALL DARK — CAN BE JUMP STARTED

ALL LIGHT — DO NOT JUMP START

No-maintenance battery charge indicators

DIESELS

Jump-Starting a Dual Battery Diesel

All GM V8 diesels are equipped with two 12 volt batteries. The batteries are connected in parallel circuit (positive terminal to positive terminal, negative terminal to negative terminal). Hooking the batteries up in parallel circuit increases battery cranking power without increasing total battery voltage output (12 volts). On the other hand, hooking two 12 volt batteries up in a series circuit (positive terminal to negative terminal, positive terminal to negative terminal) increases total battery output to 24 volts (12 volts + 12 volts).

CAUTION: *NEVER hook the batteries up in a series circuit or the entire electrical system will go up in smoke.*

In the event that a dual battery diesel must be jump started, use the following procedure.

1. Open the hood and locate the batteries. On GM diesels, the manufacturer usually suggests using the battery on the driver's side of the car to make the connection.

2. Position the donor car so that the jumper cables will reach from its battery (must be 12 volt, negative ground) to the appropriate battery in the diesel. *Do not allow the cars to touch.*

3. Shut off all electrical equipment on both vehicles. Turn off the engine of the donor car, set the parking brakes on both vehicles and block the wheels. Also, make sure both vehicles are in Neutral (manual transmission models) or Park (automatic transmission models).

4. Using the jumper cables, connect the positive (+) terminal of the donor car battery to the positive terminal of one (not both) of the diesel batteries.

5. Using the second jumper cable, connect the negative (−) terminal of the donor battery to a solid, stationary, metallic point on the diesel (alternator bracket, engine block, etc.). Be very careful to keep the jumper cables away from moving parts (cooling fan, alternator belt, etc.) on both vehicles.

6. Start the engine of the donor car and run it at moderate speed.

7. Start the engine of the diesel.

8. When the diesel starts, disconnect the battery cables in the reverse order of attachment.

Tune-Up and Performance Maintenance

2

TUNE-UP PROCEDURES

Neither tune-up nor troubleshooting can be considered independently since each has a direct relationship with the other.

It is advisable to follow a definite and thorough tune-up procedure. Tune-up consists of three separate steps: Analysis, the process of determining whether normal wear is responsible for performance loss, and whether parts require replacement or service; parts replacement or service; and adjustment, where engine adjustments are performed.

The manufacturer's recommended interval for tune-ups is every 12,000 miles or 12 months, whichever comes first for 1970–74, and 22,500 miles or 18 months for 1975–84, except for heavy duty emission models, which use the 12 mo/12,000 mi schedule in all years. These intervals should be shortened if the truck is subjected to severe operating conditions such as trailer pulling or off-road driving, or if starting and running problems are noticed. It is assumed that the routine maintenance described in Chapter 1 has been kept up, as this will have an effect on the results of the tune-up. All the applicable tune-up steps should be followed, as each adjustment complements the effects of the others. If the tune-up (emission control) sticker in the engine compartment disagrees with the information presented in the "Tune-up Specifications" chart in this chapter, the sticker figures must be followed. The sticker information reflects running changes made by the manufacturer during production. The light duty sticker is usually found on the underhood sheet metal above the grille. The heavy duty sticker is usually on top of the air cleaner.

Diesel engines do not require tune-ups *per se*, as there is no ignition system.

Troubleshooting is a logical sequence of procedures designed to locate a particular cause of trouble. The "Troubleshooting" chapter of this book is general in nature (applicable to most vehicles), yet specific enough to locate the problem.

It is advisable to read the entire chapter before beginning a tune-up, although those who are more familiar with tune-up procedures may wish to go directly to the instructions.

Spark Plugs

Rough idle, hard starting, frequent engine miss at high speeds and physical deterioration are all indications that the plugs should be replaced.

The electrode end of a spark plug is a good indicator of the internal condition of your engine. If a spark plug is fouled, causing the engine to misfire, the problem will have to be found and corrected. Often, "reading" the plugs will lead you to the cause of the problem. Spark plug conditions and probable causes are listed in the "Troubleshooting" chapter.

NOTE: *A small amount of light tan or rust red colored deposits at the electrode end of the plug is normal. These plugs need not be renewed unless they are severely worn.*

Heat range is a term used to describe the cooling characteristics of spark plugs. Plugs with longer nosed insulators take a longer time to dissipate heat than plugs with shorter nosed insulators. These are termed "hot" or "cold" plugs, respectively. It is generally advisable to use the factory recommended plugs. However, in conditions of extremely hard use (cross-country driving in summer) going to the next cooler heat range may be advisable. If most driving is done in the city or over short distances, go to the next hotter heat range plug to eliminate fouling. If in doubt concerning the substitution of spark plugs, consult your Chevrolet or GMC dealer.

Spark plugs should be gapped when they are

Spark plug heat range showing different electrode lengths. "Colder" plug (shorter electrode) is on left

Pull on the spark plug boot, not on the wire

checked or newly installed. Never assume that new plugs are correctly gapped.

1. Before removing the spark plugs, number the plug wires so that the correct wire goes on the plug when replaced. This can be done with pieces of adhesive tape.

2. Next, clean the area around the plugs by brushing or blowing with compressed air. You can also loosen the plugs a few turns and crank the engine to blow the dirt away.

3. Disconnect the plug wires by twisting and pulling on the rubber cap, not on the wire. On H.E.I. systems, twist the plug caps ½ turn in either direction to break the seal before removing the wire. Never remove the wires from H.E.I. systems when the engine is running. Severe shock could result.

4. Remove each plug with a rubber-insert spark plug socket, ⅝ in. for tapered seat plugs (designated with a letter T), ¹³⁄₁₆ in. for the rest. The tapered seat plugs are used in some engines in 1970 and all engines thereafter. Make sure that the socket is all the way down on the plug to prevent it from slipping and cracking the porcelain insulator. On some V8s the plugs are more accessible from under the truck.

5. After removing each plug, evaluate its condition. A spark plug's useful life is about 12,000 miles (optimistically 22,500 with H.E.I.). Thus, it would make sense to replace a plug if it has been in service that long. If the plug is to be replaced, refer to the "Tune-up Specifications" chart for the proper spark plug type.

The letter codes on the General Motors original equipment type plugs are read this way:
- R resistor
- S extended tip

PORCELAIN INSULATOR

INSULATOR CRACKS OFTEN OCCUR HERE

SHELL

(PROPER GAP)

CENTER ELECTRODE FILE FLAT WHEN ADJUSTING GAP— DO NOT BEND!

SIDE ELECTRODE (BEND TO ADJUST GAP)

Spark plug cutaway

¹³⁄₁₆ in. plug on right; ⅝ in. plug on left. ⅝ in. plug needs no gasket

Tune-Up Specifications

Year	Engine Displacement (cu in.)	Spark Plugs		Distributor		Ignition Timing (deg)		Fuel Pump Pressure (psi)	Compression Pressure (psi) ●	Idle Speed (rpm)*		Valve Clearance (in.)	
		Type	Gap (in.)	Point Dwell (deg)	Point Gap (in.) ▲	MT	AT			MT	AT	Ex	In
1970	250	R46T	0.035	31–34	0.019	TDC	4B	3.5–4.5	130	See Text	500	Hyd	Hyd
	292	R46T	0.035	31–34	0.019	TDC	4B	3.5–4.5	130	See Text	500	Hyd	Hyd
	307	R44	0.035	28–32	0.019	2B	8B	5.0–6.5	150	See Text	550	Hyd	Hyd
	350 (2 bbl)	R43	0.035	28–32	0.019	4B	—	7.0–8.5	150	See Text	500	Hyd	Hyd
	350 (4 bbl)	R43	0.035	28–32	0.019	TDC	4B	7.0–8.5	150	See Text	550	Hyd	Hyd
	396	R43T	0.035	28–32	0.019	4B	—	7.0–8.5	150	See Text	600	Hyd	Hyd
1971	250	R46TS	0.035	31–34	0.019	4B	4B	3.5–4.5	130	550	500	Hyd	Hyd
	292	R44T	0.035	31–34	0.019	4B	4B	3.5–4.5	130	550	500	Hyd	Hyd
	307 (200 HP)	R45TS	0.035	28–32	0.019	4B	8B	5.0–6.5	150	600	550	Hyd	Hyd
	307 (215 HP)	R45TS	0.035	28–32	0.019	4B	4B	7.0–8.5	150	550	500	Hyd	Hyd
	350	R44TS	0.035	28–32	0.019	4B	8B	7.0–8.5	150	600	550	Hyd	Hyd
	402	R44TS	0.035	28–32	0.019	8B	8B	7.0–8.5	150	600	600	Hyd	Hyd
1972	250	R46T	0.035	31–34	0.019	4B	4B	3.5–4.5	130	700	600	Hyd	Hyd
	292	R44T	0.035	31–34	0.019	4B	4B	3.5–4.5	130	700	700	Hyd	Hyd
	307	R44T	0.035	28–32	0.019	4B	8B①	5.0–6.5	150	900②	600	Hyd	Hyd
	350	R44T	0.035	28–32	0.019	4B	8B	7.0–8.5	150	800	600	Hyd	Hyd
	402	R44T	0.035	28–32	0.019	8B	8B	7.0–8.5	150	750	600	Hyd	Hyd
1973	250 (LD)	R46T	0.035	31–34	0.019	6B	6B	3.5–4.5	130	700	600	Hyd	Hyd
	250 (HD)	R46T	0.035	31–34	0.019	4B	4B	3.5–4.5	130	700	700	Hyd	Hyd
	292 (Fed)	R44T	0.035	31–34	0.019	4B	4B	3.5–4.5	130	700	700	Hyd	Hyd
	292 (Calif)	R44T	0.035	31–34	0.019	8B	8B	3.5–4.5	130	600	600	Hyd	Hyd
	307 (LD)	R44T	0.035	28–32	0.019	4B	8B	5.0–6.5	150	900	600	Hyd	Hyd

Tune-Up Specifications (cont.)

Year	Engine Displacement (cu in.)	Spark Plugs Type	Gap (in.)	Distributor Point Dwell (deg)	Point Gap (in.) ▲	Ignition Timing (deg) MT	AT	Fuel Pump Pressure (psi)	Compression Pressure (psi) ●	Idle Speed (rpm)* MT	AT	Valve Clearance (in.) Ex	In
1973	307 (HD)	R44T	0.035	28–32	0.019	TDC	TDC	5.0–6.5	150	600	600	Hyd	Hyd
	350 (LD)	R44T	0.035	28–32	0.019	8B	12B	7.0–8.5	150	900	600	Hyd	Hyd
	350 (HD)	R44T	0.035	28–32	0.019	4B	4B	7.0–8.5	150	600	600	Hyd	Hyd
	454 (LD)	R44T	0.035	28–32	0.019	10B	10B	7.0–8.5	150	900	600	Hyd	Hyd
	454 (HD)	R44T	0.035	28–32	0.019	③	④	7.0–8.5	150	700	700	Hyd	Hyd
1974	250 (LD, Fed)	R46T	0.035	31–34	0.019	8B	8B	3.5–4.5	130	850	600	Hyd	Hyd
	250 (LD, Calif)	R46T	0.035	31–34	0.019	8B	—	3.5–4.5	130	850	—	Hyd	Hyd
	250 (HD)	R44T	0.035	31–34	0.019	6B	6B	3.5–4.5	130	600	600	Hyd	Hyd
	292 (HD)	R44T	0.035	31–34	0.019	8B	8B	3.5–4.5	130	600	600	Hyd	Hyd
	350 (2 bbl)	R44T	0.035	29–31	0.019	4B	8B	7.0–8.5	150	900	600	Hyd	Hyd
	350 (4 bbl, Calif)	R44T	0.035	29–31	0.019	4B	8B	7.0–8.5	150	900	600	Hyd	Hyd
	350 (4 bbl, Fed)	R44T	0.035	29–31	0.019	6B	12B	7.0–8.5	150	900	600	Hyd	Hyd
	350 (4 bbl, HD)	R44T	0.035	29–31	0.019	8B	8B	7.0–8.5	150	700	700	Hyd	Hyd
	454 (LD)	R44T	0.035	29–31	0.019	10B	10B	7.0–8.5	150	800	600	Hyd	Hyd
	454 (HD)	R44T	0.035	29–31	0.019	8B	8B	7.0–8.5	150	700	700	Hyd	Hyd
1975	250	R46TX	0.060	—	—	10B	10B	3.5–4.5	130	900	550	Hyd	Hyd
	292 (HD)	R44TX	0.060	—	—	8B	8B	3.5–4.5	130	600	600	Hyd	Hyd
	350 (2 bbl)	R44TX	0.060	—	—	—	6B	7.0–8.5	150	—	600	Hyd	Hyd
	350 (4 bbl)	R44TX	0.060	—	—	6B	6B	7.0–8.5	150	800	600	Hyd	Hyd
	350 (HD, Fed)	R44TX	0.060	—	—	8B	8B	7.0–8.5	150	600	600	Hyd	Hyd
	350 (HD, Calif)	R44TX	0.060	—	—	2B	2B	7.0–8.5	150	700	700	Hyd	Hyd
	400 (HD, Fed)	R44TX	0.060	—	—	4B	4B	7.0–8.5	150	700	700	Hyd	Hyd
	400 (HD, Calif)	R44TX	0.060	—	—	2B	2B	7.0–8.5	150	700	700	Hyd	Hyd

Year	Model											
1976	454 (LD)	R44TX	0.060	—	—	16B	7.0–8.5	150	—	650	Hyd	Hyd
	454 (HD, Fed)	R44TX	0.060	—	8B	8B	7.0–8.5	150	700	700	Hyd	Hyd
	454 (HD, Calif)	R44TX	0.060	—	8B	8B	7.0–8.5	150	600	600	Hyd	Hyd
	250	R46TS	0.035	—	10B	10B	3.5–4.5	130	900	550	Hyd	Hyd
	250 (Calif)	R46TS	0.035	—	6B	10B	3.5–4.5	130	1000	600	Hyd	Hyd
	250 (HD)	R46T	0.035	—	6B	6B	3.5–4.5	130	600	600(N)	Hyd	Hyd
	292 (HD)	R44T	0.035	—	8B	8B	3.5–4.5	130	600	600(N)	Hyd	Hyd
	350	R45TS	0.045	—	2B	6B	7–8.5	150	800	600	Hyd	Hyd
	350 (4 bbl)	R45TS	0.045	—	8B	8B	7–8.5	150	800	600	Hyd	Hyd
	350 (4 bbl Calif)	R45TS	0.045	—	6B	6B	7–8.5	150	800	600	Hyd	Hyd
	350 (HD)	R44TX	0.060	—	8B	8B	7–8.5	150	600	600(N)	Hyd	Hyd
	350 (HD Calif)	R44TX	0.060	—	2B	2B	7–8.5	150	700	700(N)	Hyd	Hyd
	400 (HD)	R44TX	0.060	—	4B	4B	7–8.5	150	—	700(N)	Hyd	Hyd
	400 (HD Calif)	R44TX	0.060	—	2B	2B	7–8.5	150	—	700(N)	Hyd	Hyd
	454 (w/cat)	R45TS	0.045	—	12B	12B	7–8.5	150	—	600	Hyd	Hyd
	454 (w/o cat)	R45TS	0.045	—	8B	8B	7–8.5	150	—	600	Hyd	Hyd
	454 (HD)	R44T	0.045	—	8B	8B	7–8.5	150	700	700(N)	Hyd	Hyd
1977	250	R46TS	0.035	—	8B	12B	3.5–4.5	130	750	550	Hyd	Hyd
	250 (High Alt)	R46TS	0.035	—	8B	12B	3.5–4.5	130	750	600	Hyd	Hyd
	250 (Calif)	R46TS	0.035	—	6B	10B	3.5–4.5	130	850	600	Hyd	Hyd
	250 (HD)	R46T	0.035	—	6B	6B	3.5–4.5	130	600	600(N)	Hyd	Hyd
	292	R44T	0.035	—	8B	8B	3.5–4.5	130	600	600(N)	Hyd	Hyd
	305	R45TS	0.045	—	8B	8B	7–8.5	150	600	500	Hyd	Hyd
	305 (HD)	R44T	0.045	—	6B	6B	7–8.5	150	700	700(N)	Hyd	Hyd
	350	R45TS	0.045	—	8B	8B	7–8.5	150	700	500	Hyd	Hyd
	350 (High Alt)	R45TS	0.045	—	—	6B	7–8.5	150	—	600	Hyd	Hyd
	350 (Calif)	R45TS	0.045	—	6B	6B	7–8.5	150	700	500	Hyd	Hyd
	350 (HD)	R44T	0.045	—	8B	8B	7–8.5	150	700	700(N)	Hyd	Hyd

Tune-Up Specifications (cont.)

| Year | Engine Displacement (cu in.) | Spark Plugs | | Distributor | | Ignition Timing (deg) | | Fuel Pump Pressure (psi) | Compression Pressure (psi) ● | Idle Speed (rpm) * | | Valve Clearance (in.) | |
		Type	Gap (in.)	Point Dwell (deg)	Point Gap (in.) ▲	MT	AT			MT	AT	Ex	In
1977	350 (HD Calif)	R44TX	0.060	—	—	2B	2B	7–8.5	150	700	700(N)	Hyd	Hyd
	400 (HD)	R44T	0.045	—	—	—	4B	7–8.5	150	—	700(N)	Hyd	Hyd
	400 (HD Calif)	R44T	0.045	—	—	—	2B	7–8.5	150	—	700(N)	Hyd	Hyd
	454	R45TS	0.045	—	—	—	4B	7–8.5	150	—	600	Hyd	Hyd
	454 (HD)	R44T	0.045	—	—	8B	8B	7–8.5	150	700	700(N)	Hyd	Hyd
1978	250 (LD Fed)	R46TS	0.035	—	—	8B	8B	4.5–6.0	130	750	550	Hyd	Hyd
	250 (LD Calif)	R46TS	0.035	—	—	8B	8B	4.5–6.0	130	750	750	Hyd	Hyd
	250 (LD High Alt)	R46TS	0.035	—	—	8B	12B	4.5–6.0	130	750	600	Hyd	Hyd
	250 (HD)	R46T	0.035	—	—	6B	6B	4.5–6.0	130	600	600(N)	Hyd	Hyd
	292 (HD)	R44T	0.035	—	—	8B	8B	4.5–6.0	130	600	600(N)	Hyd	Hyd
	305 (LD)	R45TS	0.045	—	—	4B	4B	7.5–9.0	150	600	500	Hyd	Hyd
	305 (HD)	R44T	0.045	—	—	6B	6B	7.5–9.0	150	700	700(N)	Hyd	Hyd
	350 (LD)	R45TS	0.045	—	—	8B	8B	7.5–9.0	150	600 ⑤	500	Hyd	Hyd
	350 (HD Fed)	R44T	0.045	—	—	8B	8B	7.5–9.0	150	700	700(N)	Hyd	Hyd
	350 (HD Calif)	R44TX	0.060	—	—	2B	2B	7.5–9.0	150	700	700(N)	Hyd	Hyd
	400 (LD)	R45TS	0.045	—	—	—	4B	7.5–9.0	150	—	500	Hyd	Hyd
	400 (HD Fed)	R44T	0.045	—	—	—	4B	7.5–9.0	150	—	700(N)	Hyd	Hyd
	400 (HD Calif)	R44T	0.045	—	—	—	2B	7.5–9.0	150	—	700(N)	Hyd	Hyd
	454 (LD Fed)	R45TS	0.045	—	—	—	8B	7.5–9.0 ⑥	150	—	550	Hyd	Hyd
	454 (LD Calif)	R45TS	0.045	—	—	—	8B	7.5–9.0 ⑥	150	—	700(N)	Hyd	Hyd
	454 (HD)	R44T	0.045	—	—	8B	8B	7.5–9.0 ⑥	150	700	700(N)	Hyd	Hyd

Year	Engine											
1979	250 (LD Fed)	R46TS	0.035	—	10B	10B	4.5-6.0	130	750	600	Hyd	Hyd
	250 ⑦	R46TS	0.035	—	6B	8B	4.5-6.0	130	750	600	Hyd	Hyd
	292	R44T	0.035	—	8B	8B	4.5-6.0	130	700	700	Hyd	Hyd
	305	R45TS	0.045	—	6B	6B	7.5-9.0	150	600	500	Hyd	Hyd
	350 (LD)	R45TS	0.045	—	8B	8B	7.5-9.0	150	700	500	Hyd	Hyd
	350 (HD)	R44T	0.045	—	4B	4B	7.5-9.0	150	700	700(N)	Hyd	Hyd
	400	R45TS	0.045	—	—	4B	7.5-9.0	150	—	500	Hyd	Hyd
	454 (LD)	R45TS	0.045	—	8B	8B	7.5-9.0 ⑥	150	700	500	Hyd	Hyd
	454 (HD)	R44T	0.045	—	—	4B	7.5-9.0 ⑥	150	—	700(N)	Hyd	Hyd
1980	250 (LD Fed)	R46TS	0.035	—	10B	10B	4.5-6.0	130	750	650	Hyd	Hyd
	250 (LD Calif)	R46TS	0.035	—	10B	10B	4.5-6.0	130	750	600	Hyd	Hyd
	250 ⑦	R46TS	0.035	—	—	8B	4.5-6.0	130	—	600	Hyd	Hyd
	292	R44T	0.035	—	8B	8B	4.5-6.0	130	700	700(N)	Hyd	Hyd
	305	R45TS	0.045	—	8B	8B	7.5-9.0	150	600	500	Hyd	Hyd
	350 (LD)	R45TS	0.045	—	8B	8B	7.5-9.0	150	700	500	Hyd	Hyd
	350 (HD Fed)	R44T	0.045	—	4B	4B	7.5-9.0	150	700	700(N)	Hyd	Hyd
	350 (HD Calif)	R44T	0.045	—	6B	6B	7.5-9.0	150	700	700(N)	Hyd	Hyd
	400 (HD Fed)	R44T	0.045	—	—	4B	7.5-9.0	150	—	700(N)	Hyd	Hyd
	400 (HD Calif)	R44T	0.045	—	—	6B	7.5-9.0	150	—	700(N)	Hyd	Hyd
	454	R44T	0.045	—	4B	4B	7.5-9.0 ⑥	150	700	700(N)	Hyd	Hyd
1981	250 (Fed)	R45TS	0.035	—	10B	10B	4.5-6.0	130	750	650	Hyd	Hyd
	250 (Calif)	R46TS	0.035	—	10B	10B	4.5-6.0	130	750	650	Hyd	Hyd
	292	R44T	0.035	—	8B	84	4.5-6.0	130	700	700(N)	Hyd	Hyd
	305 2 bbl	R45TS	0.045	—	8B	8B	7.5-9.0	150	600	500	Hyd	Hyd
	305 4 bbl	R45TS	0.045	—	4B	4B ⑧	7.5-9.0	150	700	500	Hyd	Hyd

Tune-Up Specifications (cont.)

| Year | Engine Displacement (cu in.) | Spark Plugs | | Distributor | | Ignition Timing (deg) | | Fuel Pump Pressure (psi) | Compression Pressure (psi) ● | Idle Speed (rpm) * | | Valve Clearance (in.) | |
		Type	Gap (in.)	Point Dwell (deg)	Point Gap (in.) ▲	MT	AT			MT	AT	Ex	In
1981	350 (LD)	R45TS	0.045	—	—	8B	8B ⑨	7.5–9.0	150	700	500	Hyd	Hyd
	350 (HD-Fed)	R44T	0.045	—	—	4B	4B	7.5–9.0	150	700	700(N)	Hyd	Hyd
	350 (HD Calif)	R44T	0.045	—	—	6B	6B	7.5–9.0	150	700	700(N)	Hyd	Hyd
	454	R44T	0.045	—	—	4B	4B	7.5–9.0	150	700	700(N)	Hyd	Hyd
1982–84	All				See underhood specifications decal							Hyd	Hyd

▲ 0.016 in. for used points
● Maximum variation among cylinders—20 psi
B Before Top Dead Center
LD Light-duty
HD Heavy-duty
Fed Federal (49 states)
Calif California only
MT Manual transmission
AT Automatic transmission
N Neutral
NA Not available
— Not applicable
* Automatic transmission idle speed set in Drive unless otherwise indicated

Part numbers in this chart are not recommendations by Chilton for any product by brand name.
Cat catalytic converter
Hyd Hydraulic Lifters
① 4B—20 Series
② 950 rpm—California trucks
③ Federal—10B; California—5B
④ Federal—10B; California—8B
⑤ 700 rpm—California
⑥ 5.5–7.0 with vapor return line
⑦ California C-20, C-2500 only
⑧ Calif.: 8B, High Alt.: 2B
    Emission label code AAN: 6B
    Emission label code AAD: 8B
⑨ Calif.: 6B, Calif. w/emission label code AAD: 8B

Diesel Tune-Up Specifications

Year	Engine No. Cyl Displacement (cu in.)	Fuel Pump Pressure (psi)	Compression (lbs.)	Intake Valve Opens (deg)	Idle Speed (rpm) ●
1978–79	8-350	5.5–6.5	275 min.	16	650/675
1980	8-350	5.5–6.5	275 min.	16	750/600
1981	8-350	5.5–6.5	275 min.	16	575 ①
1982–84	8-379	5.5–6.5 ②	275 min.	NA	575/550 ③

NOTE: The underhood specifications sticker often reflects tune-up specifications changes made in production. Sticker figures must be used if they disagree with those in this chart.

● Where two idle speed figures appear separated by a slash, the first is for manual trans, the second is for auto trans.

① In drive: Calif. 600 rpm

② Transfer pump pressure given—injector opening pressure for used injector—1500 psi

③ '82 slow idle speed. '82 fast idle: 700 rpm. '83–'84 slow idle: 650 rpm; fast idle: 800 rpm

NA—Not available

- tapered seat
- X wide gap

The numbers indicate heat range; hotter running plugs have higher numbers.

6. If the plugs are to be reused, file the center and side electrodes flat with a fine, flat points file. Heavy or baked on deposits can be carefully scraped off with a small knife blade or the scraper tool on a combination spark plug tool. Check the gap between the electrodes with a round wire spark plug gapping gauge. Do not use a flat feeler gauge; it will give an inaccurate reading. If the gap is not as specified, use the bending tool on the spark plug gap gauge to bend the outside electrode. Be careful not to bend the electrode too far or too often, because excessive bending may cause the electrode to break off and fall into the combustion chamber. This would require removing the cylinder head to reach the broken piece, and could also result in cylinder wall, piston ring, or valve damage.

CAUTION: *Never bend the center electrode of the spark plug. This will break the insulator.*

7. Clean the plug threads with a wire brush. Lubricate the threads with a drop of oil.

Bend the side electrode to adjust the gap. Never bend the center electrode

8. Screw the plugs in finger tight, and then tighten them with the spark plug socket. Be very careful not to overtighten them. Just snug them in. If a torque wrench is available, torque them to 15 ft. lbs. for plug designations with a T, 25 ft. lbs. for all the rest.

9. Reinstall the wires. If, by chance, you have forgotten to number the plug wires, refer to the "Firing Order" illustrations in Chapter 3.

NOTE: *On 1975–77 six cylinder engines with HEI, the coil is not integral with the distributor cap. It is important that the coil wires be properly routed on these engines. On 250s, the coil wire goes in the wire loom clip above the plug wires. On 292s, the coil wire goes in the clip below the plug wires.*

Gap the plug with a wire gauge; a flat gauge will give an inaccurate reading

FIRING ORDERS

To avoid possible cross-wiring, replace spark plug wires one at a time.

Six-cylinder firing order. Distributor rotation—clockwise

V8 with electronic ignition firing order. Distributor rotation—clockwise

V8 with points-type ignition firing order. Distributor rotation—clockwise

Breaker Points and Condenser— Dwell Angle

1970–74

The usual procedure is to replace the condenser each time the point set is replaced. Although this is not always necessary, it is easy to do at this time and the cost is negligible. Every time you adjust or replace the breaker points, the ignition timing must be checked and, if necessary, adjusted. No special equipment

The six cylinder distributor cap is retained by two captive screws

The eight cylinder distributor cap has latches

Pull the six cylinder rotor straight up to remove

The eight cylinder rotor is held on by two screws

other than a feeler gauge is required for point replacement or adjustment, but a dwell meter is strongly advised. A magnetic screwdriver is handy to prevent the small points and condenser screws from falling down into the distributor.

Point sets using the push-in type wiring terminal should be used on those distributors equipped with an R.F.I. (Radio Frequency Interference) shield (1970–74). Points using a lockscrew-type terminal may short out due to contact between the shield and the screw.

1. Push down on the spring-loaded V8 distributor cap retaining screws and give them a half-turn to release. Unscrew the six-cylinder cap retaining screws. Remove the cap. You might have to unclip or detach some or all of the plug wires to remove the cap. If so, number the wires and the cap before removal.

2. Clean the cap inside and out with a clean rag. Check for cracks and carbon paths. A carbon path shows up as a dark line, usually from one of the cap sockets or inside terminals to a ground. Check the condition of the carbon button inside the center of the cap and the inside terminals. Replace the cap as necessary. Carbon paths usually cannot be successfully scraped off. It is better to replace the cap.

3. Pull the six-cylinder rotor up and off the shaft. Remove the two screws and lift the round V8 rotor off. There is less danger of losing the screws if you just back them out all the way and lift them off with the rotor. Clean off the metal outer tip if it is burned or corroded. Don't file it. Replace the rotor as necessary or if one came with your tune-up kit.

4. Remove the radio frequency interference shield if your distributor has one. Watch out for those little screws!

Typical V8 points-type distributor

5. Pull off the two wire terminals from the point assembly. One wire comes from the condenser and the other comes from within the distributor. The terminals are usually held in place by spring tension only. There might be a clamp screw securing the terminals on some older versions. There is also available a one-piece point/condenser assembly for V8s. The radio frequency interference shield isn't needed with this set. Loosen the point set hold-down

Areas to check on the distributor, rotor, cap and coil

The points are retained by screws; use a magnetic screwdriver to avoid losing them

LATERAL MISALIGNMENT

PROPER LATERAL ALIGNMENT

CORRECT LATERAL MISALIGNMENT BY BENDING FIXED CONTACT SUPPORT NEVER BEND BREAKER LEVER

Breaker point alignment

ADJUST DWELL ANGLE SETTING OR POINT OPENING

Adjusting the point gap (and therefore the dwell) on a six-cylinder distributor

WINDOW

"HEX" TYPE WRENCH

ADJUSTING SCREW

Setting the dwell on a 1970–74 V8 distributor

The condenser is also retained by a screw

screw(s). Be very careful not to drop any of these little screws inside the distributor. If this happens, the distributor will probably have to be removed to get at the screw. If the hold-down screw is lost elsewhere, it must be replaced with one that is no longer than the original to avoid interference with the distributor workings. Remove the point set, even if it is to be reused.

6. If the points are to be reused, clean them with a few strokes of a special point file. This is done with the points removed to prevent tiny metal filings from getting into the distributor.

Don't use sandpaper or emery cloth; they will cause rapid point burning.

7. Loosen the condenser hold-down screw and slide the condenser out of the clamp. This will save you a struggle with the clamp, condenser, and screw when you install the new one. If you have the type of clamp that is permanently fastened to the condenser, remove the screw and the condenser. Don't lose the screw.

8. Inspect the distributor cam lubricator. If you have the round kind, turn it around on its shaft at the first tune-up and replace it at the second. If you have the long kind, switch ends at the first tune-up and replace it at the second.

NOTE: *Don't oil or grease the lubricator. The foam is impregnated with a special lubricant.*

If you didn't get any lubricator at all, or if it looks like someone took it off, don't worry. You don't really need it. Just rub a match-head size dab of grease on the cam lobes.

9. Install the new condenser. If you left the

The points have a locating tab which fits into a hole in the breaker plate

Six cylinder point gap is adjusted with a screwdriver

clamp in place, just slide the new condenser into the clamp.

10. Replace the point set and tighten the screws on a V8. Leave the screw slightly loose on a six. Replace the two wire terminals, making sure that the wires don't interfere with anything. Some V8 distributors have a ground wire that must go under one of the screws.

11. Check that the contacts meet squarely. If they don't, bend the tab supporting the fixed contact.

NOTE: *If you are installing preset points on a V8, go ahead to step 16. If they are preset, it will say so on the package. It would be a good idea to make a quick check on point gap, anyway. Sometimes those preset points aren't.*

12. Turn the engine until a high point on the cam that opens the points contacts the rubbing block on the point arm. You can turn the engine by hand if you can get a wrench on the crankshaft pulley nut, or you can grasp the fan belt and turn the engine with the spark plugs removed.

CAUTION: *If you try turning the engine by hand, be very careful not to get your fingers pinched in the pulleys.*

On a stick-shift you can push it forward in High gear. Another alternative is to bump the starter switch or use a remote starter switch.

V8 point gap is adjusted with an Allen wrench

13. On a six, there is a screwdriver slot near the contacts. Insert a screwdriver and lever the points open or closed until they appear to be at about the gap specified in the "Tune-Up Specifications." On a V8, simply insert a ⅛ in. Allen wrench into the adjustment screw and turn. The wrench sometimes comes with a tune-up kit.

14. Insert the correct size feeler gauge and adjust the gap until you can push the gauge in and out between the contacts with a slight drag, but without disturbing the point arm. This operation takes a bit of experience to obtain the correct feel. Check by trying the gauges 0.001–0.002 larger and smaller than the setting size. The larger one should disturb the point arm, while the smaller one should not drag at all. Tighten the six-cylinder point set hold-down screw. Recheck the gap, because it often changes when the screw is tightened.

15. After all the point adjustments are complete, pull a white business card through (between) the contacts to remove any traces of oil. Oil will cause rapid contact burning.

NOTE: *You can adjust six-cylinder dwell at this point, if you wish. Refer to Step 18.*

16. Replace the radio frequency interference shield, if any. You don't need it if you are installing the one-piece point/condenser set. Push the rotor firmly down into place. It will only go on one way. Tighten the V8 rotor screws. If the rotor is not installed properly, it will break when the starter is operated.

17. Replace the distributor cap.

18. If a dwell meter is available, check the dwell. The dwell meter hookup is shown in the "Troubleshooting" Section.

NOTE: *This hookup may not apply to electronic, capacitive discharge, or other special ignition systems. Some dwell meters won't work at all with such systems.*

Dwell can be checked with the engine running or cranking. Decrease dwell by increasing the point gap; increase by decreasing the gap. Dwell angle is simply the number of degrees of distributor shaft rotation during which the points stay closed. Theoretically, if the point gap is correct, the dwell should also be correct. Adjustment with a dwell meter produces more exact, consistent results since it is a dynamic adjustment. If dwell varies more than 3 degrees from idle speed to 1,750 engine rpm, the distributor is worn.

19. To adjust dwell on a six, trial and error point adjustments are required. On a V8, simply open the metal window on the distributor and insert a ⅛ in. Allen wrench. Turn until the meter shows the correct reading. Be sure to snap the window closed.

20. An approximate dwell adjustment can be made without a meter on a V8. Turn the adjusting screw clockwise until the engine begins to misfire, then turn it out ½ turn.

21. If the engine won't start, check:
   a. That all the spark plug wires are in place.
   b. That the rotor has been installed.
   c. That the two (or three) wires inside the distributor are connected.
   d. That the points open and close when the engine turns.
   e. That the gap is correct and the hold-down screw (on a six) is tight.

22. After the first 200 miles or so on a new set of points, the point gap often closes up due to initial rubbing block wear. For best performance, recheck the dwell (or gap) at this time. This quick initial wear is the reason why the factory recommends 0.003 in. more gap on new points.

23. Since changing the gap affects the ignition timing, the timing should be checked and adjusted as necessary after each point replacement or adjustment.

1975 and Later

These engines use the breakerless HEI (High Energy Ignition) system. Since there is no mechanical contact, there is no wear or need for periodic service. There is an item in the distributor that resembles a condenser; it is a radio interference suppression capacitor which requires no service.

High Energy Ignition (HEI) System

The General Motors HEI system is a pulse-triggered, transistor-controlled, inductive discharge ignition system. Except on inline six-cylinder models 1975–77, the entire HEI system is contained within the distributor cap. Inline six-cylinder engines 1975–77 have an external coil. Otherwise, the systems are the same.

The distributor, in addition to housing the

Six-cylinder HEI distributor, 1975–77. 1978 and later models have the coil in the distributor cap

V8 HEI distributor

mechanical and vacuum advance mechanisms, contains the ignition coil (except on some inline six engines), the electronic control module, and the magnetic triggering device. The magnetic pick-up assembly contains a permanent magnet, a pole piece with internal "teeth," and a pick-up coil (not to be confused with the ignition coil).

In the HEI system, as in other electronic ignition systems, the breaker points have been replaced with an electronic switch—a transistor—which is located *within* the control module. This switching transistor performs the same function the points did in a conventional igni-

V8 HEI distributor components

tion system; it simply turns coil primary current on and off at the correct time. Essentially then, electronic and conventional ignition systems operate on the same principle.

The module which houses the switching transistor is controlled (turned on and off) by a magnetically generated impulse induced in the pick-up coil. When the teeth of the rotating timer align with the teeth of the pole piece, the induced voltage in the pick-up coil signals the electronic module to open the coil primary circuit. The primary current then decreases, and a high voltage is induced in the ignition coil secondary windings which is then directed through the rotor and spark plug wires to fire the spark plugs.

In essence then, the pick-up coil module system simply replaces the conventional breaker points and condenser. The condenser found within the distributor is for radio suppression purposes only and has nothing to do with the

ignition process. The module automatically controls the dwell period, increasing it with increasing engine speed. Since dwell is automatically controlled, it cannot be adjusted. The module itself is non-adjustable and non-repairable and must be replaced if found defective.

HEI SYSTEM PRECAUTIONS

Before going on to troubleshooting, it might be a good idea to take note of the following precautions:

Timing Light Use

Inductive pick-up timing lights are the best kind to use with HEI. Timing lights which connect between the spark plug and the spark plug wire occasionally (not always) give false readings.

Spark Plug Wires

The plug wires used with HEI systems are of a different construction than conventional wires. When replacing them, make sure you get the correct wires, since conventional wires won't carry the voltage. Also handle them carefully to avoid cracking or splitting them and *never* pierce them.

Tachometer Use

Not all tachometers will operate or indicate correctly when used on a HEI system. While some tachometers may give a reading, this does not necessarily mean the reading is correct. In addition, some tachometers hook up differently from others. If you can't figure out whether or not your tachometer will work on your truck, check with the tachometer manufacturer. Dwell readings, have no significance at all.

Internal components of the HEI distributor; later models have slightly different connectors at the module, but the wiring is the same

BATTERY TERMINAL
CONNECTED TO IGNITION SWITCH

TACHOMETER TERMINAL

GROUND TERMINAL

C-TERMINAL
CONNECT TACHOMETER FROM
THIS TERMINAL TO GROUND
(SOME TACHOMETERS
MUST CONNECT FROM
THIS TERMINAL TO
ENERGIZER POSITIVE +.
CONSULT TACHOMETER
MANUFACTURER.)

B + TERMINAL

CONNECTOR

LATCH (4)

HEI distributor connections

HEI System Testers

Instruments designed specifically for testing HEI systems are available from several tool manufacturers. Some of these will even test the module itself. However, the test given in the following section will require only an ohmmeter and a voltmeter.

TROUBLESHOOTING THE HEI SYSTEM

The symptoms of a defective component within the HEI system are exactly the same as those you would encounter in a conventional system. Some of these symptoms are:

• Hard or no Starting
• Rough Idle
• Fuel Poor Economy
• Engine misses under load or while accelerating

If you suspect a problem in the ignition system, there are certain preliminary checks which you should carry out before you begin to check the electronic portions of the system. First, it is extremely important to make sure the vehicle battery is in a good state of charge. A defective or poorly charged battery will cause the various components of the ignition system to read incorrectly when they are being tested. Second, make sure all wiring connections are clean and tight, not only at the battery, but also at the distributor cap, ignition coil, and at the electronic control module.

Since the only change between electronic and conventional ignition systems is in the distributor component area, it is imperative to check the secondary ignition circuit first. If the sec-

ondary circuit checks out properly, then the engine condition is probably not the fault of the ignition system. To check the secondary ignition system, perform a simple spark test. Remove one of the plug wires and insert some sort of extension in the plug socket. An old spark plug with the ground electrode removed makes a good extension. Hold the wire and extension about ¼ in. away from the block and crank the engine. If a normal spark occurs, then the problem is most likely *not* in the ignition system. Check for fuel system problems, or fouled spark plugs.

If, however, there is no spark or a weak spark, then further ignition system testing will have to be done. Troubleshooting techniques fall into two categories, depending on the nature of the problem. The categories are (1) Engine cranks, but won't start or (2) Engine runs, but runs rough or cuts out.

Engine Fails to Start

If the engine won't start, perform a spark test as described earlier. If no spark occurs, check for the presence of normal battery voltage at the battery (BAT) terminal in the distributor cap. The ignition switch must be in the "on" position for this test. Either a voltmeter or a test light may be used for this test. Connect the test light wire to ground and the probe end to the BAT terminal at the distributor. If the light comes on, you have voltage to the distributor. If the light fails to come on, this indicates an open circuit in the ignition primary wiring leading to the distributor. In this case, you will have to check wiring continuity back to the ignition switch using a test light. If there is battery voltage at the BAT terminal, but no spark at the plugs, then the problem lies within the distributor assembly. Go on to the distributor components test section.

Engine Runs, but Runs Rough or Cuts Out

1. Make sure the plug wires are in good shape first. There should be no obvious cracks or breaks. You can check the plug wires with an ohmmeter, but *do not* pierce the wires with a probe. Check the chart for the correct plug wire resistance.

2. If the plug wires are OK, remove the cap

HEI Plug Wire Resistance Chart

Wire Length	Minimum	Maximum
0–15 inches	3000 ohms	10,000 ohms
15–25 inches	4000 ohms	15,000 ohms
25–35 inches	6000 ohms	20,000 ohms
Over 35 inches		25,000 ohms

assembly, and check for moisture, cracks, chips, or carbon tracks, or any other high voltage leaks or failures. Replace the cap if you find any defects. Make sure the timer wheel rotates when the engine is cranked. If everything is all right so far, go on to the distributor components test section.

Distributor Components Testing

If the trouble has been narrowed down to the units within the distributor, the following tests can help pinpoint the defective component. An ohmmeter with both high and low ranges should be used. These tests are made with the cap assembly removed and the battery wire disconnected.

1. Connect an ohmmeter between the TACH and BAT terminals in the distributor cap. The primary coil resistance should be less than one ohm (zero or nearly zero).

2. To check the coil secondary resistance, connect an ohmmeter between the rotor button and the BAT terminal. Then connect the ohmmeter between the ground terminal and the rotor button. The resistance in both cases should be between 6,000 and 30,000 ohms.

3. Replace the coil *only* if the readings in step one and two are infinite.

NOTE: *These resistance checks will not disclose shorted coil windings. This condition*

Checking the pick-up coil

Distributor base and components

Checking coil resistance on the HEI system. Ohmmeter 1 shows the primary coil resistance connection. Ohmmeter 2 shows the secondary resistance connection. 1980 models shown, others similar

can be detected only with scope analysis or a suitably designed coil tester. If these instruments are unavailable, replace the coil with a known good coil as a final coil test.

4. To test the pick-up coil, first disconnect the white and green module leads. Set the ohmmeter on the high scale and connect it between a ground and either the white or green lead. Any resistance measurement *less* than infinity requires replacement of the pick-up coil.

5. Pick-up coil continuity is tested by connecting the ohmmeter (on low range) between the white and green leads. Normal resistance is between 650 and 850 ohms, or 500 and 1500 ohms on 1977 and later models. Move the vacuum advance arm while performing this test. This will detect any break in coil continuity. Such a condition can cause intermittent misfiring. Replace the pick-up coil if the reading is outside the specified limits.

6. If no defects have been found at this time, and you still have a problem, then the module will have to be checked. If you do not have

access to a module tester, the only possible alternative is a substitution test. If the module fails the substitution test, replace it.

COMPONENT REPLACEMENT

Integral Ignition Coil

1. Disconnect the feed and module wire terminal connectors from the distributor cap.
2. Remove the ignition set retainer.
3. Remove the 4 coil cover-to-distributor cap screws and coil cover.
4. Remove the 4 coil-to-distributor cap screws.
5. Using a blunt drift, press the coil wire spade terminals up out of distributor cap.
6. Lift the coil up out of the distributor cap.
7. Remove and clean the coil spring, rubber seal washer and coil cavity of the distributor cap.
8. Coat the rubber seal with a dielectric lubricant furnished in the replacement ignition coil package.
9. Reverse the above procedures to install.

Distributor Cap

1. Remove the feed and module wire terminal connectors from the distributor cap.
2. Remove the retainer and spark plug wires from the cap.
3. Depress and release the 4 distributor cap-to-housing retainers and lift off the cap assembly.
4. Remove the 4 coil cover screws and cover.
5. Using a finger or a blunt drift, push the spade terminals up out of the distributor cap.
6. Remove all 4 coil screws and lift the coil, coil spring and rubber seal washer out of the cap coil cavity.
7. Using a new distributor cap, reverse the above procedures to assemble, being sure to clean and lubricate the rubber seal washer with dielectric lubricant.

Rotor

1. Disconnect the feed and module wire connectors from the distributor.
2. Depress and release the 4 distributor cap to housing retainers and lift off the cap assembly.
3. Remove the two rotor attaching screws and rotor.
4. Reverse the above procedure to install.

Vacuum Advance

1. Remove the distributor cap and rotor as previously described.
2. Disconnect the vacuum hose from the vacuum advance unit.
3. Remove the two vacuum advance retain-

Pickup coil removed and disassembled

Be sure to coat the mating surfaces with silicone lubricant when replacing the HEI module

ing screws, pull the advance unit outward, rotate and disengage the operating rod from its tang.

4. Reverse the above procedure to install.

Module

1. Remove the distributor cap and rotor as previously described.
2. Disconnect the harness connector and pick-up coil spade connectors from the module. Be careful not to damage the wires when removing the connector.
3. Remove the two screws and module from the distributor housing.
4. Coat the bottom of the new module with dielectric lubricant supplied with the new module. Reverse the above procedure to install.

Ignition Timing

Timing should be checked at each tune-up and any time the points are adjusted or replaced. It isn't likely to change much with HEI. The timing marks consist of a notch on the rim of the crankshaft pulley or vibration damper and a graduated scale attached to the engine front (timing) cover. A stroboscopic flash (dynamic) timing light must be used, as a static light is too inaccurate for emission controlled engines.

There are three basic types of timing light available. The first is a simple neon bulb with two wire connections. One wire connects to the spark plug terminal and the other plugs into the end of the spark plug wire for the No. 1 cylinder, thus connecting the light in series with the spark plug. This type of light is pretty dim and must be held very closely to the timing marks to be seen. Sometimes a dark corner has to be sought out to see the flash at all. This type of light is very inexpensive. The second type operates from the vehicle battery—two alligator clips connect to the battery terminals, while an adapter enables a third clip to be connected to the No. 1 spark plug and wire. This type is a bit more expensive, but it provides a nice bright flash that you can see even in bright sunlight. It is the type most often seen in professional shops. The third type replaces the battery power source with 110 volt current.

Some timing lights have other features built into them, such as dwell meters or tachometers. These are convenient, in that they reduce the tangle of wires under the hood when you're working, but may duplicate the functions of tools you already have. One worthwhile feature, which is becoming more of a necessity with higher voltage ignition systems, is an inductive pickup. The inductive pickup clamps around the No. 1 spark plug wire, sensing the surges of high voltage electricity as they are sent to the plug. The advantage is that no mechanical connection is inserted between the wire and the plug, which eliminates false signals to the timing light. A timing light with an inductive pickup should be used on HEI systems.

To check and adjust the timing:

1. Warm up the engine to normal operating temperature. Stop the engine and connect the timing light to the No. 1 (left front on V8, front on six) spark plug wire. You can also use the No. 6 wire, if it is more convenient. Numbering is illustrated in Chapter 3. Under no circumstances should the spark plug wire be pierced to hook up a timing light. Clean off the timing marks and mark the pulley or damper notch and timing scale with white chalk. The timing notch on the pulley or damper can be elusive. The best way to get it to an accessible position for marking is to "bump" the engine around using either the ignition key or a remote starter.

2. Disconnect and plug the vacuum line at the distributor. This is done to prevent any distributor vacuum advance. A short screw, pencil, or a golf tee can be used to plug the line.

3. Start the engine and adjust the idle speed to that specified in the "Tune-Up Specifications" chart. With automatic transmission, set the specified idle speed in Park. It will be too high, since it is normally (in most cases) adjusted in Drive. However, it is safer to adjust the timing in Park and to reset the idle speed after all timing work is done. Some trucks require that the timing be set with the transmission in Neutral. Refer to the "Tune-up Specifications" chart or the under-hood sticker for details. You can disconnect the idle solenoid, if any, to get the speed down. Otherwise, adjust the idle speed screw. This is done to prevent any centrifugal (mechanical) advance.

The tachometer hookup for 1970–74 models is the same as the dwell meter hookup shown in the "Tune-Up and Trouble-shooting" sections. On 1975–77 HEI systems, the tachometer connects to the TACH terminal on the distributor (V8) or on the coil (six) and to a ground. For 1978 and later, all tachometer connections are to the TACH terminal. Some tachometers must connect to the TACH terminal and to the positive battery terminal. Some tachometers won't work with HEI.

CAUTION: *Never ground the HEI TACH terminal; serious system damage will result.*

4. Aim the timing light at the pointer marks. Be careful not to touch the fan, because it may appear to be standing still. Keep the timing light wires clear of the fan, belts, and pulleys. If the pulley or damper notch isn't aligned with the proper timing mark (see the "Tune-Up Speci-

Timing marks (on pulley) and timing indicator on 1975 and later gasoline V8s fications" chart), the timing will have to be adjusted.

NOTE: *TDC or Top Dead Center corresponds to 0 degrees. B, or BTDC, or Before Top Dead Center may be shown as BEFORE. A, or ATDC, or After Top Dead Center may be shown as AFTER.*

5. Loosen the distributor base clamp locknut. You can buy a special wrench which makes this task a lot easier on V8s. Turn the distributor slowly to adjust the timing, holding it by the body and not the cap. Turn the distributor in the direction of rotor rotation (found in the "Firing Order" illustration in Chapter 3) to retard, and against the direction of rotation to advance.

6. Tighten the locknut. Check the timing again, in case the distributor moved slightly as you tightened it.

7. Replace the distributor vacuum line. Correct the idle speed.

8. Stop the engine and disconnect the timing light.

Diesel Injection Timing

350 and 379 cu. in. Diesels

For the engine to be properly timed, the marks on the top of the engine front cover (379) or injection pump adapter (350) must be aligned with the marks on the injection pump flange. The engine must be "off" when the timing is reset.

NOTE: *On 49-state 379s, the marks are scribe lines. On California 379s, the marks are half-circles.*

1. Loosen the three pump retaining nuts. If the marks are not aligned, adjustment is necessary.

2. Loosen the three pump retaining nuts. Special tool #J-26987 is useful here on the 350.

3. Align the mark on the injection pump with

Diesel injection timing marks, 379 shown. Marks shown are in alignment

Injection pump timing marks location and alignment, 350 diesel shown

the mark on the front cover (379) or adapter (350). Tighten the nuts to 30 ft. lbs. on the 379, and 35 ft. lbs. on the 350.

NOTE: *Use a ¾ in. open-end wrench on the nut at the front of the injection pump to aid in rotating the pump to align the marks.*

3. Adjust the throttle linkage if necessary.

Carburetor

In most cases, the mixture screws have limiter caps, but in later years the mixture screws are concealed under staked-in plugs. Idle mixture is adjustable only during carburetor overhaul, and requires the addition of propane as an artificial mixture enrichener. For these reasons, mixture adjustments are not covered here for affected models.

See the emission control label in the engine compartment for procedures and specifications not supplied here.

NOTE: *See "Carburetor Identification in Chapter 4 for carburetor I.D. specifics.*

IDLE SPEED AND MIXTURE

1970

On all vehicles, disconnect the "FUEL TANK" line from the vapor canister. Remember to reconnect the line after setting the idle speed and mixture. The engine should be at operating temperature with the choke valve and air cleaner damper door fully open, air conditioning OFF and parking brake ON.

• 250–292 Engines, ½ ton models. Disconnect and plug the vacuum advance line. Turn the mixture screw in until it lightly contacts the seat, then back out 4 turns. Adjust the solenoid

Adjusting the idle solenoid

screw to obtain 800 rpm with manual transmission in Neutral or 630 rpm with automatic transmission in drive. Adjust the mixture screw to obtain 750 rpm with manual transmission in Neutral or automatic in Drive. Electrically, disconnect the solenoid and set the carburetor idle speed screw to obtain 400 rpm and connect the solenoid. Reconnect the vacuum line.

• 292 Engine, ¾ and 1 ton Series: Disconnect and plug the distributor vacuum line. Turn the mixture screws in until they lightly contact the seats and back the screw(s) out 4 turns. On manual transmission models, adjust the carburetor idle speed screw to obtain 600 rpm in Neutral. Then adjust the mixture screw to obtain 550 rpm in Neutral. On automatic transmission models, adjust the solenoid screw to obtain 550 rpm with transmission in Drive. Adjust the mixture screw to obtain 500 rpm with transmission in Drive. Disconnect the solenoid and set the carburetor idle speed screw to obtain 400 rpm and connect the solenoid. Reconnect the distributor vacuum line on all models.

• 307 V8, ½ ton Series: Disconnect and plug the distributor vacuum line. Turn the mixture screws in until they lightly contact the seats then back them out 4 turns. Adjust the carburetor idle speed screw to obtain 800 rpm with manual transmission in Drive. Adjust the mixture screw to obtain 630 rpm with automatic transmission in Drive. Adjust the mixture screws in equally to obtain 700 rpm with manual transmission in Neutral or 600 rpm with automatic transmission in Drive. Disconnect the solenoid and set the carburetor idle speed screw to obtain 450 rpm and reconnect the solenoid. Reconnect the vacuum line.

• 307 V8, ¾ and 1 ton Series: Disconnect and plug the distributor vacuum line. Set the mixture screws for maximum idle rpm and adjust the idle speed screw to obtain 700 rpm with manual transmission in Neutral or 600 rpm with automatic transmission in Drive. Adjust the mixture screws equally to obtain a 200 rpm drop, then back the screws out ¼ turn. As necessary,

adjust the idle screw on manual transmission models to obtain 700 rpm with the transmission in Neutral. On automatic transmission models, adjust the solenoid screw to obtain 600 rpm with the transmission in Drive. Disconnect the solenoid electrically and set the carburetor idle screw to obtain 450 rpm and reconnect the solenoid. Reconnect the vacuum line.

• 350 V8, ½ ton Series: Disconnect and plug the distributor vacuum line. Turn the mixture screws in until they lightly contact the seats. Back the screws out 4 turns. Adjust the idle speed screw to obtain 650 rpm with manual transmission in Neutral or 550 rpm with automatic transmission in Drive. Adjust the mixture screws equally to obtain 600 rpm with manual transmission in Neutral or automatic transmission in Drive. Reconnect the vacuum advance line.

• 350 and 396 V8, ¾ and 1 ton Series: Disconnect and plug the distributor vacuum line. Turn the mixture screws in until they lightly contact the seats and back them out 4 turns. Adjust the carburetor idle speed screw to obtain 775 rpm (manual transmission in Neutral) or 630 rpm (automatic transmission in Drive). Adjust the mixture screws equally to obtain 700 rpm (manual transmission in Neutral) or 600 rpm (automatic transmission in Drive). Reconnect the vacuum line.

1971

The engine should be running at operating temperature, choke valve fully open, parking brake ON and drive wheels blocked.

• 250–292 Engines, ½ tone Series: Disconnect the "FUEL TANK" line from the evaporative canister. Disconnect the vacuum advance line and plug the vacuum source. Adjust the carburetor speed screw to obtain 550 rpm with manual transmission in Neutral or 550 rpm with automatic transmission in Drive. Do not adjust the solenoid screw.

CAUTION: *Use the CEC solenoid screw to adjust the idle speed could result in a decrease in engine braking.*

Reconnect the "FUEL TANK" line and the vacuum advance line.

• 307 V8, ½ ton Series: Disconnect the "FUEL TANK" line from the evaporative canister. Disconnect the vacuum source opening. Adjust the carburetor speed screw to obtain 600 rpm with manual transmission in Neutral or 550 rpm with automatic transmission in Drive and air conditioner ON. Do not adjust the solenoid. See the previous "Caution." Reconnect the "FUEL TANK" line and the vacuum advance line.

• 350 and 402 V8, ½ ton Series: Disconnect

Idle speed and mixture screws, 1971

the "FUEL TANK" line from the evaporative canister. Disconnect the vacuum advance line and plug the vacuum source opening. Turn the air conditioner OFF and adjust the carburetor speed screw to obtain 600 rpm with manual transmission in Neutral or 550 rpm (600 rpm on 402 V8) with automatic transmission in Drive. Do not adjust the solenoid screw, or a decrease in engine braking could result. Place the fast idle cam follower on the second step of the fast idle cam and turn the air conditioner OFF. Adjust the fast idle to 1,350 rpm with manual transmission in Neutral or 1,500 rpm with automatic transmission in PARK. Reconnect the "FUEL TANK" and vacuum advance lines.

• 292 and 307 V8, ¾ and 1 ton Series: Disconnect the vacuum advance line and plug the vacuum source opening. Turn the air conditioner ON. Turn the mixture screws in until they lightly contact the seats and back them out 4 turns. Adjust the carburetor speed screw to obtain 600 rpm with manual transmission in Neutral and 500 rpm with automatic in Drive. Reconnect the vacuum advance hose.

• 350 and 402 V8, ¾ and 1 ton Series: Disconnect the distributor vacuum advance hose and plug the vacuum source opening. Turn the air conditioner off. Turn the mixture screws in until they contact the seats lightly. Back the screws out 4 turns. Adjust the carburetor speed screw to obtain 650 rpm with manual transmis-

sion in Neutral or 550 rpm with automatic transmission in Drive. Reconnect the vacuum advance hose.

1972

The engine should be at normal operating temperature on the choke valve fully open, parking brake ON and the drive wheels blocked. All carburetors are equipped with idle mixture limiter caps, which provide for only a small adjustment range. Normally, these should not be removed. However, if they are removed, the CO content of the exhaust should be checked to be sure that it meets Federal Emission Control limits.

• 250 and 292: Disconnect the "FUEL TANK" line from the vapor canister. Remember to reconnect it after making the adjustment. Disconnect and plug the vacuum line source. Adjust the idle stop solenoid to obtain 700 rpm with manual transmission in Neutral or 600 rpm with automatic transmission in Drive. Do not adjust the CEC solenoid screw.

CAUTION: *If the CEC solenoid screw is adjusted out of limits, a decrease in engine braking may result.*

Reconnect the vacuum line.

• 307 V8: Disconnect the "FUEL TANK" line from the vapor canister and remove and plug the vacuum line source. Adjust the idle stop solenoid screw to obtain 900 rpm (950 on Cali-

ROCHESTER CARBURETORS

Idle speed and mixture screws, 1972–75

fornia trucks) with manual transmission in Neutral or 600 rpm with automatic transmission in Drive. On trucks without TCS, adjust speed screw for 600 rpm with transmission in Neutral. With transmission in Park or Neutral, adjust the fast idle speed to obtain 1850 rpm. Reconnect the "FUEL TANK" line and the vacuum line.

• 350 V8: Disconnect the "FUEL TANK" line and disconnect and plug the vacuum line. On vehicles with TCS, turn the air conditioner OFF and adjust the idle solenoid screw to obtain 800 rpm with manual transmission in Neutral or 600 rpm with automatic transmission in Drive. On vehicles without TCS, adjust the carburetor speed screw to obtain 600 rpm with transmission in Neutral. Place the fast idle cam, turn the air conditioner OFF and adjust the fast idle to 1,350 rpm with manual transmission in Neutral or automatic transmission in Drive. Reconnect the "FUEL TANK" and vacuum lines.

• 402 V8: Disconnect the "FUEL TANK" line from the evaporative canister. Disconnect the vacuum advance hose and plug the vacuum source opening. On trucks with TCS, turn the air conditioning OFF and adjust the idle stop solenoid screw to obtain 750 rpm with manual transmission in Neutral or 600 rpm with automatic in Drive. On trucks without TCS, adjust the carburetor speed screw to obtain 600 rpm with transmission in Neutral. Place the fast idle cam follower on the second step of the fast idle cam, turn the air conditioner OFF and adjust the fast idle speed to 1,350 rpm with manual

transmission in Neutral or 1,500 rpm with automatic transmission in Drive. Reconnect the "FUEL TANK" line and the vacuum advance line.

1973–75

Emission system requirements necessitate the division of trucks as follows:
• Light-Duty: All ½ ton Series
• Heavy-Duty: ¾ and 1 ton
All adjustments should be made with the engine at operating temperature, choke fully open, air conditioner OFF, parking brake ON and drive wheels blocked.

• 250: Disconnect the "FUEL TANK" line and the vacuum source opening. Plug the vacuum line. Adjust the idle stop solenoid by turning the hex nut to obtain:

Rochester 2GC, 1975

700 rpm (1973) or 600 rpm (1974) on all heavy-duty vehicles with manual transmission in Neutral;

600 rpm (1973–74) on all light-duty vehicles with automatic transmission in Drive.

850 rpm (1974–75) on all light duty trucks with manual transmission.

Do not adjust the CEC solenoid on 1973 vehicles or a decrease in engine braking may result. Place automatic transmissions in Park and manual transmission in Neutral and adjust the fast idle to 1800 rpm, on the top step of the fast idle cam. Reconnect the "FUEL TANK" and vacuum lines.

• 292: Disconnect the vacuum advance line and plug the vacuum source opening. Adjust the idle stop solenoid screw to obtain 600 rpm on California (and all 1974–75) trucks or 700 rpm on all other trucks. Reconnect the vacuum advance line.

1973 307 V8: On light-duty vehicles, disconnect the "FUEL TANK" line from the vapor canister and plug the vacuum source opening. Adjust the idle stop solenoid to obtain 600 rpm with automatic transmission in Park or 900 rpm with manual transmission in Neutral. Disconnect the idle stop solenoid and adjust the low idle screw located inside the solenoid hex nut, to obtain 450 rpm in Neutral or Drive. Reconnect the idle stop solenoid, the "FUEL TANK" line, and the vacuum line.

• 350 V8: On light-duty vehicles, disconnect the "FUEL TANK" line from the vapor canister. Disconnect and plug the vacuum line. On heavy-duty vehicles, adjust the carburetor idle speed screw to obtain 600 rpm with automatic transmission in Park or manual transmission in Neutral. On light-duty vehicles, adjust the idle stop solenoid screw to obtain 600 rpm with automatic transmission in Drive or 900 rpm with manual transmission in Neutral. On light-duty vehicles with automatic transmission, reconnect the vacuum line and adjust the fast idle to 1600 rpm on the top step of the fast idle cam. On light-duty vehicles with manual transmission, adjust the fast idle screw to obtain 1300 rpm with the screw on the top step of the fast idle cam and the vacuum line disconnected. Reconnect the "FUEL TANK" line and the vacuum line.

• 454 V8: On light-duty trucks, disconnect the "FUEL TANK" line from the evaporative canister. Disconnect the vacuum advance line and plug the vacuum source opening. Adjust the idle speed with the idle stop solenoid screw to obtain:

700 rpm on all heavy-duty trucks with automatic transmission in Park and manual transmission in Neutral.

600 rpm on light-duty trucks with automatic transmission in Drive.

900 rpm (1973) or 800 rpm (1974–75) on light-duty trucks with manual transmission in Neutral.

On light-duty trucks with automatic transmission, reconnect the vacuum advance line. Adjust the fast idle screw to obtain 1,600 rpm with the screw on the top step of the fast idle cam.

On light-duty trucks with manual transmission, adjust the fast idle screw to obtain 1,600 rpm (1973) or 1,500 rpm (1974–75) with the screw on the top step of the fast idle cam and the vacuum hose disconnected.

Reconnect the "FUEL TANK" line and the vacuum advance line.

1976 IDLE SPEED ADJUSTMENT

All adjustments should be made with the engine at normal operating temperature, air cleaner on, choke open, and air conditioning off, unless otherwise noted. Set the parking brake and block the rear wheels.

• 250 and 292 Engines: Disconnect and plug the carburetor and PCV hoses at the vapor canister on the 250. On heavy duty emissions 250s and all 292s, disconnect the "FUEL TANK" hose at the vapor canister. If the engine has a solenoid located between the carburetor and the distributor on the vacuum hose line, disconnect and plug the vacuum line. Otherwise, leave the vacuum hose connected. On heavy duty 250s and all 292s turn the air conditioning on, if so equipped. With manual transmissions in Neutral, 250 automatics in Drive, and heavy duty 250 and 292 automatics in Neutral, turn the solenoid body in or out to set the idle speed to specified rpm. Disconnect the electrical wire from the carburetor solenoid, and turn the air conditioner off. Turn the $\frac{1}{8}$ in. hex (Allen head) screw located in the end of the solenoid body to set the low idle to 425 rpm for 250s and 450 rpm for heavy duty 250s and 292s. Reconnect the electrical wire and any hoses that were disconnected.

• 350, 400, and 454 Engines: On California emissions engines, disconnect and plug the "FUEL TANK" hose at the vapor canister. On heavy duty emissions 350s and 400s, turn the air conditioning on. Place the automatic transmission in Drive, manuals in Neutral, unless otherwise noted in the "Tune-Up Specifications" chart. Adjust the carburetor idle speed to the specified rpm by turning the idle speed screw. Reconnect the "FUEL TANK" hose on California engines. On engines equipped with four barrel carburetors, place the transmission in Park for automatics, and leave manual transmissions in Neutral. Disconnect and plug the vacuum hose at the EGR valve if so equipped. On 454 engines with electric chokes, disconnect and plug the vacuum hose to the front vacuum break unit located in front of the choke coil housing. Position the cam follower lever of the fast idle unit on the proper step on the cam, as specified on the underhood emissions sticker. Turn the fast idle screw to obtain the specified rpm on the sticker. Reconnect any hoses that were disconnected.

1977–78 IDLE SPEED ADJUSTMENT

All adjustments should be made with the engine at normal operating temperature, air cleaner on, choke open, and air conditioning off, unless otherwise noted. Set the parking brake and block the rear wheels. Automatics should be place in Drive, manuals in Neutral, except as noted in the "Tune-Up Specifications" chart.

• 250 and 292 Engines: Make certain that the fast idle follower is not on any of the steps marked "H", "2", or "L" on the cam. It should be resting against the first step below "L". Set the idle to specifications by turning the solenoid in or out. Do this with a wrench on the nut attached to the end of the solenoid body. Disconnect the electrical connector from the solenoid. The engine speed will drop. With a ⅛ in. hex (Allen head) wrench, turn the screw located inside the nut attached to the solenoid body, and set the idle speed to 425 rpm for light duty emissions trucks, 450 rpm for heavy duty 250s and 292s. Reconnect the solenoid wire and check idle speed.

• 305, 350, 400, and 454 Engines: Check the underhood emissions sticker to determine which hoses, if any, must be disconnected. On carburetors not equipped with a solenoid: For two barrel carburetors, make sure that the idle speed screw is on the low ("L") step of the fast idle cam. Then, for all engines except 1978 2bbl models with a solenoid but without air conditioning: Turn the idle speed screw to adjust idle speed to the specification found in the "Tune-Up Specifications" chart or on the underhood emissions sticker.

On 1978 trucks with a two barrel carburetor which have a solenoid, but without air conditioning, open the throttle slightly to allow the solenoid plunger to extend. Turn the solenoid screw to adjust the curb idle to specification, as given in the chart or on the emission control sticker in the engine compartment. Then disconnect the electrical connector from the solenoid. The idle speed will drop. Turn the idle speed screw to set the slow engine idle to the figure given on the emission control sticker. Reconnect the solenoid and shut off the engine.

On carburetors equipped with a solenoid and air conditioning: Turn the idle speed screw to set the idle to specifications. Then, disconnect the air conditioner compressor electrical lead at the compressor, and turn the air conditioner on. Open the throttle slightly to allow the solenoid plunger to fully extend. Turn the solenoid screw and adjust to 650 rpm, except light duty emissions trucks with manual transmissions, which should be set to 700 rpm. Reconnect the air conditioner compressor lead.

1979 AND LATER IDLE SPEED ADJUSTMENT

Idle mixture is not adjustable in these years, except for the heavy-duty emission 292 six-cylinder equipped with the 1ME carburetor, and

1 ENGINE MUST BE WARM-CHOKE WIDE OPEN-CAM FOLLOWER OFF STEPS OF CAM (SEE EMISSION LABEL)

3 TO ADJUST BASE IDLE, TURN 1/8" HEX SCREW (SOLENOID NOT ENERGIZED)

HEX WRENCH

2 SET CURB IDLE TO SPECIFICATIONS-TURN ASSEMBLY IN OR OUT TO ADJUST R.P.M. (SOLENOID ENERGIZED)

Idle speed adjustment for 250 and 292 sixes, 1979 and later

④ OPEN THROTTLE SLIGHTLY TO ALLOW SOLENOID PLUNGER TO FULLY EXTEND.

② TURN IDLE SPEED SCREW TO SET CURB IDLE SPEED TO SPECIFICATIONS – A/C OFF (SEE EMISSION LABEL)

THROTTLE LEVER

③ SOLENOID ENERGIZED – A/C COMPRESSOR LEAD DISCONNECTED AT A/C COMPRESSOR, A/C ON, A/T TRANSMISSION IN DRIVE.

ELECTRICAL CONNECTION

⑤ TURN SOLENOID SCREW TO ADJUST TO SPECIFIED RPM. (RECONNECT A/C COMPRESSOR LEAD AFTER ADJUSTMENT)

① PREPARE VEHICLE FOR ADJUSTMENTS – SEE EMISSION LABEL ON VEHICLE. NOTE: IGNITION TIMING SET PER LABEL.

Idle speed adjustment for V8 4-bbl. carburetors with solenoid, 1977

heavy-duty emission V8s equipped with the four barrel M4MC.

All adjustments should be made with the engine at normal operating temperature, air cleaner on, choke open, and air conditioning off, unless otherwise noted. Set the parking brake and block the rear wheels. Automatic transmissions should be set in Drive, manuals in Neutral, unless otherwise noted in the procedures or in the "Tune-Up Specifications" chart, or on the emission control label.

• 250 Engine: Check the emission control label for any special instructions. Open the throttle slightly to allow the solenoid plunger to extend. Turn the solenoid screw to adjust the curb idle to the figure given in the "Tune-Up Specifications" chart or on the emission control label. Disconnect the electrical connector from the solenoid. The idle speed will drop. Adjust the idle to the basic idle speed figure

given on the emission control label by means of the idle speed screw. Connect the solenoid lead and shut off the engine.

• 292 Engine: See the procedure given for 1977–78. Check the idle figures given against the emission control label in the engine compartment; the label figures must be used if different.

Idle mixture is adjustable on this carburetor (model 1ME):

1. Set the parking brake and block the rear wheels.

2. Remove the air cleaner but do not disconnect any of the hoses. Disconnect and plug the other hoses as directed on the emission control label.

3. The engine should be at normal operating temperature, choke open, and air conditioning off (if equipped). Connect an accurate tachometer to the engine.

③ TO ADJUST LOW IDLE TURN 1/8" HEX SCREW (SOLENOID NOT ENERGIZED)

HEX WRENCH

① NOTE: ENGINE MUST BE WARM – CHOKE WIDE OPEN – FAST IDLE CAM FOLLOWER OFF STEPS OF CAM (SEE EMISSION LABEL)

② SET CURB IDLE TO SPECIFICATIONS – TURN ASSEMBLY IN OR OUT TO ADJUST R.P.M. (SOLENOID ENERGIZED)

1977 and later inline six cylinder idle speed adjustment, MV and ME-type 1-bbls,

1979 and later 4 bbl adjustments without solenoid; 1978 4 bbl and 1979—81 V8 2 bbl (M2MC) models similar (© Chevrolet Motor Div.)

4. Disconnect and plug the vacuum advance hose at the distributor and check the ignition timing. Correct as necessary. Reconnect the vacuum advance hose.

5. Carefully remove the limiter cap from the idle mixture screw. Lightly seat the screw, then back it out just enough to allow the engine to run.

6. Place the transmission in Neutral.

7. Back the mixture screw out ⅛ turn at a time until the maximum idle speed is obtained. Adjust the idle speed to the figure given on the emission control label by means of the idle speed screw. Repeat this step until you are certain that the maximum speed has been obtained with the mixture screw.

8. Turn the mixture screw in ⅛ turn at a time until the idle speed drops to the figure given on the emission control label.

9. Reset the idle speed to the figure given on the emission control label by means of the idle speed screw. Check and adjust the fast idle as directed on the emission control label. Reconnect any vacuum hoses removed in Step 2, install the air cleaner, and recheck the idle speed. Correct, if necessary, by means of the idle speed screw.

• 305 Engine: Check the emission control label in the engine compartment to determine which hoses, if any, must be disconnected. Make sure the idle speed screw is on the low ("L") step of the fast idle cam. Turn the idle speed screw to adjust the idle speed to the figure given in the "Tune-Up Specifications" chart, or on the emission control label.

On carburetors equipped with a solenoid (air conditioned trucks): turn the idle speed screw to set the idle to specifications, as in the previous paragraph. Then, disconnect the air conditioner compressor electrical lead at the com-

1979 and later 4-bbl. adjustments with solenoid, 1978 4-bbl. and 1979 2-bbl. (M2MC) similar

① DISCONNECT ELECTRICAL LEAD FROM IDLE SPEED SOLENOID (IF SO EQUIPPED).

③ RECONNECT ELECTRICAL LEAD TO IDLE SPEED SOLENOID.

② ADJUST BASE IDLE SPEED SCREW TO R.P.M. SPECIFIED ON EMISSION LABEL (AUTOMATIC TRANSMISSION IN DRIVE OR MANUAL TRANSMISSION IN NEUTRAL).

1980–81 V8 2-bbl. (M2MC) idle speed adjustment with solenoid

pressor. Turn the air conditioning on. Open the throttle slightly to allow the solenoid plunger to fully extend. Turn the solenoid screw and adjust to 700 rpm with manual transmission (Neutral), or 600 rpm with automatic transmission (Drive). Reconnect the air conditioner electrical lead.

• 350, 400, and 454 Engines: The idle speed procedure is the same as given for 1977–78 models. Check the emission control label and the "Tune-Up Specifications" chart to determine the proper idle speeds.

Mixture is adjustable on heavy duty emissions V8s with the four barrel M4MC carburetor. This procedure will not work on light-duty emissions trucks.

1. The engine must be at normal operating temperature, choke open, parking brake applied, and the transmission in Park or Neutral. Block the rear wheels and do not stand in front of the truck when making adjustments.

2. Remove the air cleaner. Connect a tachometer and a vacuum gauge to the engine.

3. Turn the idle mixture screws in lightly until they seat, then back them out two turns. Be careful not to tighten the mixture screw against its seat, or damage may result.

4. Adjust the idle speed screw to obtain the engine rpm figure specified on the emission control label.

5. Adjust the idle mixture screws equally to obtain the highest engine speed.

④ OPEN THROTTLE SLIGHTLY TO ALLOW SOLENOID PLUNGER TO FULLY EXTEND

② TURN IDLE SPEED SCREW TO SET CURB IDLE SPEED TO SPECIFICATIONS – A/C OFF (SEE EMISSION LABEL)

③ SOLENOID ENERGIZED – A/C COMPRESSOR LEAD DISCONNECTED AT A/C COMPRESSOR, A/C ON, A/T TRANSMISSION IN DRIVE, M/T IN NEUTRAL

THROTTLE LEVER

ELECTRICAL CONNECTION

⑤ TURN SOLENOID SCREW TO ADJUST TO SPECIFIED RPM. (RECONNECT A/C COMPRESSOR LEAD AFTER ADJUSTMENT)

① PREPARE VEHICLE FOR ADJUSTMENTS – SEE EMISSION LABEL ON VEHICLE. NOTE: IGNITION TIMING SET PER LABEL.

2GC 2-bbl. slow idle adjustment, A/C-equipped

① PREPARE VEHICLE FOR ADJUST-
MENTS - SEE EMISSION LABEL
ON VEHICLE. NOTE: IGNITION
TIMING SET PER LABEL.

③ TURN FAST IDLE SCREW
iN OR OUT TO OBTAIN
SPECIFIED FAST IDLE
R.P.M. - (SEE LABEL)

②

PLACE FAST IDLE
SCREW ON HIGHEST
STEP OF FAST IDLE CAM

**FAST IDLE ADJUSTMENT
(ON VEHICLE)**

① PREPARE VEHICLE FOR ADJUSTMENTS -
SEE EMISSION LABEL ON VEHICLE.
NOTE: IGNITION TIMING SET PER LABEL.

② SOLENOID ENERGIZED - A/T IN DRIVE,
M/T IN NEUTRAL

⑥ RECONNECT
SOLENOID
ELECTRICAL
LEAD AFTER
ADJUSTMENT

④ TURN SOLENOID
SCREW TO ADJUST
CURB IDLE SPEED
TO SPECIFIED RPM
(SOLENOID ENERGIZED)

⑤ TURN IDLE SPEED SCREW
TO SET BASIC IDLE
SPEED TO SPECIFICATIONS
(SOLENOID DE-ENERGIZED)

③
OPEN THROTTLE
SLIGHTLY TO
ALLOW SOLENOID
PLUNGER TO
FULLY EXTEND

**IDLE SPEED ADJUSTMENT
WITH A/C (ON VEHICLE)**

**IDLE SPEED ADJUSTMENT
WITHOUT A/C (ON VEHICLE)**

① PREPARE VEHICLE FOR ADJUSTMENTS -
SEE EMISSION LABEL ON VEHICLE.
NOTE: IGNITION TIMING SET PER LABEL.

② TURN IDLE SPEED SCREW
TO SET CURB IDLE SPEED TO
SPECIFICATIONS -
(SEE EMISSION LABEL)

2SE 2-bbl. idle speed and fast idle adjustments

① **PREPARE VEHICLE FOR ADJUSTMENTS -
SEE EMISSION LABEL ON VEHICLE.
NOTE: IGNITION TIMING SET PER LABEL.**

③ **SOLENOID ENERGIZED - A/C
COMPRESSOR LEAD
DISCONNECTED AT A/C
COMPRESSOR, A/C ON,
A/T IN DRIVE, M/T IN NEUTRAL.**

⑤ **TURN SOLENOID
SCREW TO ADJUST
TO SPECIFIED RPM.
(RECONNECT A/C
COMPRESSOR LEAD
AFTER ADJUSTMENT).**

② **TURN IDLE SPEED SCREW
TO SET CURB IDLE SPEED TO
SPECIFICATIONS - A/C OFF
(SEE EMISSION LABEL)**

④ **OPEN THROTTLE
SLIGHTLY TO
ALLOW SOLENOID
PLUNGER TO
FULLY EXTEND.**

**ELECTRICAL
CONNECTION**

E2SE 2-bbl. idle speed adjustment with A/C, 1983

① PREPARE VEHICLE FOR ADJUSTMENTS - SEE EMISSION LABEL ON VEHICLE. NOTE: IGNITION TIMING SET PER LABEL

④ TURN SOLENOID SCREW TO ADJUST CURB IDLE SPEED TO SPECIFIED RPM (SOLENOID ENERGIZED)

② SOLENOID ENERGIZED - A/T IN DRIVE, M/T IN NEUTRAL

⑥ TURN IDLE SPEED SCREW TO SET BASIC IDLE SPEED TO SPECIFICATIONS. RECONNECT SOLENOID ELECTRICAL LEAD AFTER ADJUSTMENT

③ OPEN THROTTLE SLIGHTLY TO ALLOW SOLENOID PLUNGER TO FULLY EXTEND

⑤ DISCONNECT ELECTRICAL LEAD TO DE-ENERGIZE SOLENOID

E2SE 2-bbl. idle speed adjustment without A/C

① PREPARE VEHICLE FOR ADJUSTMENTS - SEE EMISSION LABLE ON VEHICLE. PLACE TRANSMISSION IN PARK/NEUTRAL.

② PLACE FAST IDLE SCREW ON HIGHEST STEP OF FAST IDLE CAM.

③ TURN FAST IDLE SCREW IN OR OUT TO OBTAIN SPECIFIED FAST IDLE R.P.M. - (SEE LABEL).

E2SE fast idle adjustment

FAST IDLE ADJUSTMENT

④ SUPPORT LEVER WITH PLIERS – BEND TANG IN OR OUT TO OBTAIN SPECIFIED FAST IDLE R.P.M. (SEE INSERT).

MANUAL CHOKE MODELS WITH SMOOTH CONTOUR CAM SURFACE – ROTATE FAST IDLE CAM CLOCK-WISE TO ITS FARTHEST UP POSITION.

③ PLACE CAM FOLLOWER TANG ON HIGH STEP OF CAM (SEE NOTE).

① PREPARE VEHICLE FOR ADJUSTMENTS – SEE EMISSION LABEL ON VEHICLE. IGNITION TIMING SET PER LABEL.

THIRD LOW
SECOND
HIGH

② ADJUST CURB IDLE SPEED WITH IDLE STOP SOLENOID.

FAST IDLE CAM STEPS

1ME 1-bbl. fast idle adjustment

6. Repeat Steps 4 and 5 until the best idle is obtained.

7. Shut off the engine, remove the tachometer and vacuum gauge, and install the air cleaner.

Diesel Fuel Injection

IDLE SPEED ADJUSTMENT

350 V8 Diesel

A special tachometer with an RPM counter suitable for the 350 V8 diesel is necessary for this adjustment; a standard tach suitable for gasoline engines will not work.

1. Place the transmission in Park, block the rear wheels and firmly set the parking brake.

2. If necessary, adjust the throttle linkage as described in Chapter 6.

3. Start the engine and allow it to warm up for 10–15 minutes.

4. Shut off the engine and remove the air cleaner.

5. Clean off any grime from the timing probe holder on the front cover; also clean off the crankshaft balancer rim.

FUEL SHUT- 90° ELBOW FUEL RETURN LINE
OFF SOLENOID CONNECTOR
PRE-SET—
DO NOT ADJUST

SLOW IDLE
ADJUSTMENT
SCREW

PRESSURE TAP
PLUG & SEAL

INLET

THROTTLE LEVER

350 diesel injection pump showing idle speed screws

6. Install the magnetic probe end of the tachometer fully into the timing probe holder. Complete the remaining tachometer connections according to the tach manufacturer's instructions.

7. Disconnect the two-lead connector from the generator.

8. Make sure all electrical accessories are OFF.

NOTE: *At no time should either the steering wheel or the brake pedal be touched.*

9. Start the engine and place the transmission in Drive (after first making sure the parking brake is firmly applied).

10. Check the slow idle speed reading against the one printed on the underhood emissions sticker. Reset if necessary.

11. Unplug the connector from the fast idle cold advance (engine temperature) switch, and install a jumper wire between the connector terminals.

NOTE: *DO NOT allow the jumper to ground.*

12. Check the fast idle speed and reset if necessary according to the specification printed on the underhood emissions sticker.

13. Remove the jumper wire and reconnect it to the temperature switch.

14. Recheck the slow idle speed and reset if necessary.

15. Shut off the engine.

16. Reconnect the leads at the generator and A/C compressor.

17. Disconnect and remove the tachometer.

18. If the car is equipped with cruise control, adjust the servo throttle rod to minimum slack, then put the clip in the first free hole closest to the bell rank or throttle lever.

19. Install the air cleaner.

379 V8 Diesel

NOTE: *A special tachometer suitable for diesel engines must be used. A gasoline engine-type tach will not work with the diesel engine.*

1. Set the parking brake and block the drive wheels.

2. Run the engine up to normal operating temperature. The air cleaner must be mounted and all accessories turned off.

3. Install the diesel tachometer as per the manufacturer's instructions.

4. Adjust the low idle speed screw on the fuel injection pump to 650 rpm in Neutral or Park for both manual and automatic transmissions.

379 (6.2L) diesel injection pump showing idle adjustments

NOTE: *All idle speeds are to be set within 25 rpm of the specified values.*

5. Adjust the fast idle speed as follows:

a. Remove the connector from the fast idle solenoid. Use an insulated jumper wire from the battery positive terminal to the solenoid terminal to energize the solenoid.

b. Open the throttle momentarily to ensure that the fast idle solenoid plunger is energized and fully extended.

c. Adjust the extended plunger by turning the hex-head screw to an engine speed of 800 rpm in neutral.

d. Remove the jumper wire and reinstall the connector to the fast idle solenoid.

6. Disconnect and remove the tachometer.

Valve Lash

All engines covered in this guide are equipped with hydraulic valve lifters. Engines so equipped operate with zero clearance in the valve train; because of this the rocker arms are non-adjustable. The hydraulic lifters themselves do not require any adjustment as part of the normal tune-up, although they occasionally become noisy (especially on high-mileage engines) and need to be replaced. In the event of cylinder head removal or any operation that requires disturbing or removing the rocker arms, the rocker arms have to be adjusted. Please refer to Chapter 3. Hydraulic lifter service is also covered in Chapter 3.

Engine and Engine Rebuilding

3

ENGINE ELECTRICAL

Distributor

REMOVAL AND INSTALLATION

1970–74

1. Remove the distributor cap and position it out of the way.
2. Disconnect the primary coil wire and the vacuum advance line.
3. Scribe a mark on the distributor body and the engine block showing their relationship. Mark the distributor housing to show the direction in which the rotor is pointing. Note the positioning of the vacuum advance unit.
4. Remove the hold-down bolt and clamp and remove the distributor.

To install the distributor with the engine undisturbed:

5. Reinsert the distributor into its opening, aligning the previously-made marks on the housing and the engine block.
6. The rotor may have to be turned either way a slight amount to align the rotor-to-housing marks.
7. Install the retaining clamp and bolt. Install the distributor cap, primary wire, and the vacuum hose.
8. Start the engine and check the ignition timing.

To install the distributor with the engine disturbed:

9. Turn the engine so the No. 1 piston is at the top of its compression stroke. This may be determined by covering the No. 1 spark plug hole with your thumb and slowly turning the engine over. When the timing mark on the crankshaft pulley aligns with the 0 on the timing scale and your thumb is pushed out by compression, No. 1 piston is at top-dead-center (TDC).
10. Install the distributor to the engine block so that the vacuum advance unit points in the correct direction.
11. Turn the rotor so that it will point to the No. 1 terminal in the cap.
12. Install the distributor into the engine block. It may be necessary to turn the rotor a little in either direction in order to engage the gears.
13. Tap the starter a few times to ensure that the oil pump shaft is mated to the distributor shaft.
14. Bring the engine to No. 1 TDC again and check to see that the rotor is indeed pointing toward the No. 1 terminal of the cap.
15. After correct positioning is assured, turn the distributor housing so that the points are just opening. Tighten the retaining clamp.
16. Install the cap and primary wire. Check the ignition timing. Install the vacuum hose.

1975 and Later

1. Disconnect the wiring harness connectors at the side of the distributor cap.
2. Remove the distributor cap and lay it aside.
3. Disconnect the vacuum advance line.
4. Scribe a mark on the engine in line with the rotor and note the approximate position of the vacuum advance unit in relation to the engine.
5. Remove the distributor hold-down clamp and nut.
6. Lift the distributor from the engine.
7. Installation is the same as for the standard (1970–74) distributor.

Alternator

Three basic alternators are used; the 5.5 in. Series 1D Delcotron, the 6.2 in. Series 150 Delcotron and the integral regulator 10 SI Delcotron.

Six cylinder point-type distributor

ALTERNATOR PRECAUTIONS

1. When installing a battery, ensure that the ground polarity of the battery, the alternator and the regulator are the same.

2. When connecting a jumper battery, be certain that the correct terminals are connected.

3. When charging, connect the correct charger leads to the battery terminals.

4. Never operate the alternator on an open circuit. Be sure that all connections in the charging circuit are tight.

5. Do not short across or ground any of the terminals on the alternator or regulator.

6. Never polarize an AC system.

REMOVAL AND INSTALLATION

1. Disconnect the battery ground cable.

2. Disconnect and tag all wiring to the alternator.

3. Remove the alternator brace bolt. If the truck is equipped with power steering, loosen the pump brace and mount nuts.

4. Remove the drive belt(s).

5. Support the alternator and remove the mounting bolts. Remove the alternator from the truck.

6. Installation is the reverse of removal. Adjust the belt(s) to have $\frac{1}{4}$–$\frac{1}{2}$ in. depression under thumb pressure on its longest run.

V8 point-type distributor

CAP

ROTOR

RADIO FREQUENCY
INTERFERENCE
SHIELD

WEIGHT SPRINGS

MAINSHAFT

ADVANCE WEIGHTS

CAM WEIGHT
BASE ASSEMBLY

CONDENSER

CONTACT POINT
ASSEMBLY

RETAINING RING

BREAKER PLATE

VACUUM ADVANCE UNIT

FELT WASHER

PLASTIC SEAL

HOUSING

TANGED WASHER

SHIM WASHER

DRIVE GEAR

DRIVE PIN

6

V 8

Typical alternator mounting, inline sixes and gasoline V8

Regulator

REMOVAL AND INSTALLATION

1970–72

1. Disconnect the ground cable from the battery.

2. Disconnect the wiring harness from the regulator.

3. Remove the mounting screws and remove the regulator.

4. Make sure that the regulator base gasket is in place before installation.

5. Clean the attaching area for proper grounding.

6. Install the regulator. Do not over-tighten the mounting screws, as this will cancel the cushioning effect of the rubber grommets.

AIR GAP
ADJUSTING NUT
ONLY

ADJUSTING SCREW
(Turn To Adjust
Voltage Setting)

Conventional regulator voltage adjustment

VOLTAGE ADJUSTMENT

The standard voltage regulator from 1970–72 is a conventional double contact unit, although an optional transistorized regulator was available. Voltage adjustment procedures are the same for both types except for the point of adjustment. The double contact adjusting screw is located under the cover and the transistorized regulator is adjusted externally after removing an allen screw from the adjustment hole. On 1973 and later models, the 10 SI Delcotron is used which is equipped with an integral regulator that cannot be adjusted.

1. Insert a ¼ ohm-25 watt fixed resistor into the charging circuit at the horn relay junction block, between both leads and the terminal. Use a ½ ohm-25 watt resistor for 1971–72.

2. Install a voltmeter as shown in the figure.

3. Warm the engine by running it for several minutes at 1,500 rpm or more.

4. Cycle the voltage regulator by disconnecting and reconnecting the regulator connector.

5. Read the voltage on the voltmeter. If it is between 13.5 and 15.2, the regulator does not need adjustment or replacement. If the voltage

Transistorized regulator voltage adjustments

Regulator voltage setting circuit

is not within these limits, leave the engine running at 1,500 rpm.

6. Disconnect the four-terminal connector and remove the regulator cover (except on transistorized regulators). Reconnect the four-terminal connector and adjust the voltage to between 14.2 and 14.6 volts by turning the adjusting screw while observing the volt-meter.

7. Disconnect the terminal, install the cover, and then reconnect the terminal.

8. Continue running the engine at 1,500 rpm to re-establish the regulator internal temperature.

9. Cycle the regulator by disconnecting/reconnecting the regulator connector. Check the voltage. If the voltage is between 13.5 and 15.2, the regulator is good.

CAUTION: *Always disconnect the regulator before removing or installing the cover in order to prevent damage by short-circuiting.*

Starter

No periodic lubrication of the starting motor or solenoid is required. Since the starting motor and brushes cannot be inspected without disassembling the unit, no service is required on these units.

REMOVAL AND INSTALLATION

The following is a general procedure for all trucks, and may vary slightly depending on model and series.

NOTE: *The starters on some engines re-*

6

V 8

Typical starter mountings

Exploded view of the 20MT starter motor used on the 350 diesel. Gasoline engine starters are almost identical; the only real difference is that they do not have the center bearing quire the addition of shims to provide proper clearance between the starter pinion gear and the flywheel. These shims are available in .015 in. sizes from Chevrolet dealers.

1. Disconnect the battery ground cable.

2. Raise and support the vehicle with jack stands.

3. Disconnect and tag all wires at the solenoid terminal.

NOTE: *1975 and later starters no longer have the "R" terminal. The High Energy Ignition System does not need a cable from solenoid to ignition coil.*

4. Reinstall all nuts as soon as they are removed, since the thread sizes are different.

5. Remove the front bracket from the starter and the two mounting bolts. On engines with a solenoid heat shield, remove the front bracket upper bolt and detach the bracket from the starter.

6. Remove the front bracket bolt or nut. Lower the starter front end first, and then remove the unit from the truck.

7. Reverse the removal procedures to install the starter. Torque the two mounting bolts to 25–35 ft. lbs.

SHIMMING THE STARTER

Starter noise during cranking and after the engine fires is often a result of too much or too little distance between the starter pinion gear and the flywheel. A high pitched whine during cranking (before the engine fires) can be caused by the pinion and flywheel being too far apart.

Likewise, a whine after the engine starts (as the key is released) is often a result of the pinion-flywheel relationship being too close. In both cases flywheel damage can occur. Shims are available in .015 in. sizes to properly adjust the starter on its mount. You will also need a flywheel turning tool, available at most auto parts stores or from any auto tool store or salesperson.

If your car's starter emits the above noises, follow the shimming procedure below:

1. Disconnect the negative battery cable.

2. Remove the flywheel inspection cover on the bottom of the bellhousing.

3. Using the flywheel turning tool, turn the flywheel and examine the flywheel teeth. If damage is evident, the flywheel should be replaced.

4. Insert a screwdriver into the small hole in the bottom of the starter and move the starter pinion and clutch assembly so the pinion and flywheel teeth mesh. If necessary, rotate the flywheel so that a pinion tooth is directly in the center of the two flywheel teeth and on the centerline of the two gears, as shown in the accompanying illustration.

5. Check the pinion-to-flywheel clearance by using a .020 in. wire gauge (a spark plug wire gauge may work here, or you can make your own). Make sure you center the pinion tooth between the flywheel teeth and the gauge—NOT in the corners, as you may get a false reading. If the clearance is *under* this minimum, shim the starter *away* from the flywheel

FRONT OF
ENGINE

1. Use shims as required
2. Shield

Starter Noise Diagnostic Procedure
1. Starter noise during cranking: remove 1–.015″ double shim or add single .015″ shim to *outer* bolt only.
2. High pitched whine after engine fires: add .015″ double shims until noise disappears.
See text for complete procedure.

Shimming the starter motor; diesel 350 shown at right

Flywheel-to-pinion clearance check

A .015" SHIM WILL INCREASE THE
CLEARANCE APPROXIMATELY
.005". MORE THAN ONE SHIM
MAY BE REQUIRED.

Meshing starter teeth

by adding shim(s) one at a time to the starter mount. Check clearance after adding each shim.

6. If the clearance is a good deal *over* .020 in. (in the vicinity of .050 plus), shim the starter *towards* the flywheel. Broken or severely mangled flywheel teeth are also a good indicator that the clearance here is too great. Shimming the starter towards the flywheel is done by adding shims to the outboard starter mounting pad only. Check the clearance after each shim is added. A shim of .015 in. at this location will decrease the clearance about .010 in.

STARTER OVERHAUL

Solenoid Replacement

1. Remove the screw and washer from the field strap terminal.

2. Remove the two solenoid-to-housing retaining screws and the motor terminal bolt.

3. Remove the solenoid by twisting the unit 90°.

4. To replace the solenoid, reverse the above procedure. Make sure the return spring is on the plunger, and rotate the solenoid unit into place on the starter.

Starter solenoid terminals through 1974

Drive Replacement

1. Disconnect the field coil straps from the solenoid.

2. Remove the through-bolts (usually 2), and separate the commutator end frame, field frame assembly, drive housing, and armature assembly from each other.

NOTE: *On the diesel starters, remove the insulator from the end frame. The armature on the diesel starter remains in the drive end frame.*

3. On diesel starters, remove the shift lever pivot bolt. On the diesel 25 MT starter only, remove the center bearing screws and remove the drive gear housing from the armature shaft. The shift lever and plunger assembly will now fall away from the starter clutch.

4. Slide the two-piece thrust collar off the end of the armature shaft.

5. Slide a ⅝ in. deep socket, piece of pipe or an old pinion onto the shaft so that the end of the pipe, socket, or pinion butts up against the edge of the pinion retainer.

Starter drive assembly removed

Use a piece of pipe or an old socket to drive the retainer toward the snap-ring

Snap-ring installation

6. Place the lower end of the armature securely on a soft surface, such as a wooden block or thick piece of foam rubber. Tap the end of the socket, pipe or pinion, driving the retainer towards the armature end of the snap ring.

7. Remove the snap ring from the groove in the armature shaft with a pair of pliers. If the snap ring is distorted, replace it with a new one during reassembly. Slide the retainer and starter drive from the shaft; on diesel starters, remove the fiber washer and the center bearing from the armature shaft. On gasoline engine starters, the shift lever and plunger may be disassembled at this time (if necessary) by removing the roll pin.

8. To reassemble, lubricate the drive end of the armature shaft with silicone lubricant. On diesel starters, install the center bearing with the bearing *toward the armature winding*, then

Removing shift lever and plunger from starter

install the fiber washer on the armature shaft.

9. Slide the starter drive onto the armature shaft *with the pinion facing outward* (away from the armature). Slide the retainer onto the shaft with the cupped surface facing outward.

10. Again support the armature on a soft surface, with the pinion on the upper end. Center the snap ring on the top of the shaft (use a new ring if the old one was misshapen or damaged). Gently place a block of wood on top of the snap ring so as not to move it from a centered position. Tap the wooden block with a hammer in order to force the snap ring around the shaft. Slide the ring down into the snap groove.

11. Lay the armature down flat on your work surface. Slide the retainer close up onto the shaft and position it and the thrust collar next to the snap ring. Using two pairs of pliers on opposite ends of the shaft, squeeze the thrust collar and the retainer together until the snap ring is forced into the retainer.

12. Lube the drive housing bushing with a silicone lubricant.

13. Engage the shift lever yoke with the clutch. Position the front of the armature shaft into the bushing, then slide the complete drive assembly into the drive gear housing.

NOTE: *On non-diesel starters the shift lever may be installed in the drive gear housing first.*

14. On the 25 MT diesel starter only, install the center bearing screws and the shift lever pivot bolt, and tighten securely.

15. Apply a sealing compound approved for this application onto the drive housing, to the solenoid flange where the field frame contacts it. Position the field frame around the armature shaft and against the drive housing. Work carefully and slowly to prevent damaging the starter brushes.

16. Lubricate the bushing in the commutator end frame with a silicone lubricant, place the leather washer onto the armature shaft, and

SWITCH TERMINAL — SOLENOID — PLUNGER — RETURN SPRING — SHIFT LEVER — GROMMET — COMMUTATOR — BUSHING — BUSHING — INSULATED BRUSH HOLDER — BRUSH — GROUNDED BRUSH HOLDER — RISER BARS — CONDUCTORS TO RISER BARS TO ARMATURE — ARMATURE — FIELD COIL — OVERRUNNING CLUTCH — PINION STOP

Cross-section of 10MT starter motor

then slide the commutator end frame over the shaft and into position against the field frame. On diesel starters, install the insulator and then the end frame onto the shaft. Line up the bolt holes, then install and tighten the through-bolts (make sure they pass through the bolt holes in the insulator).

17. Connect the field coil straps to the "motor" terminal of the solenoid.

NOTE: *If replacement of the starter drive fails to cure improper engagements of the starter pinion to the flywheel, there may be defective parts in the solenoid and/or shift lever. The best procedure is to take the assembly to a shop where a pinion clearance check can be made by energizing the solenoid on a test bench. If the pinion clearance is incorrect, disassemble the solenoid and shift lever, inspect, and replace the worn parts.*

Brush Replacement

1. Disassemble the starter by following steps 1 and 2 of the "Drive Replacement" procedure above.

2. Replace the brushes one at a time to avoid having to mark the wiring. For each brush: remove the brush holding screw; remove the old brush and position the new brush in the same direction (large end toward center of field frame), position the wire connector on top of the brush, line up the holes, and reinstall the screw. Make sure the screw is snug enough to ensure good contact.

3. Reassemble starter according to steps 8–17 above.

Battery

Refer to Chapter 1 for battery maintenance. Battery installation and removal varies with the truck model and series, making it impossible to detail all installations. However, observe the following precautions when dealing with batteries:

1. Always disconnect the grounded (negative) terminal first and install it last to avoid short circuits and sparks. Special pullers are available to remove clamp-type battery terminals.

2. Be sure that the battery tray is clean and free of debris, so that the battery will seat squarely.

3. When installing batteries, tighten the hold-down strap or clamp snugly, but not with such force that it cracks the cover or case.

4. Be sure that the cables are in good condition and that the terminal clamps are clean and tight. Wire brushes are available to clean these items. Make sure that the ground cable is clean and tight at the engine block or frame. When installing cables, never hammer them in place. The terminals should be coated lightly with grease after installation to reduce corrosion.

5. Always check the battery polarity before

installing cables. Reversed connections will destroy an alternator almost instantaneously.

ENGINE MECHANICAL

Design

All Chevrolet and GMC truck engines, whether six or V8, are water-cooled, overhead valve powerplants. All engines use cast iron cylinder blocks and heads.

The 250 and 292 cu in. inline six-cylinder engines are all very similar in design although some 250 cu in. sixes have an integral cylinder head and intake manifold beginning 1975. Crankshafts are supported in seven main bearings, with the thrust taken by No. 7. The camshaft is low in the block and driven by the crankshaft gear; no timing chain is used. Relatively long pushrods actuate the valves through ball-jointed rocker arms.

The small-block family of engines, which includes the 283, 305, 307, 327, 350, and 400 cu in. blocks, have all sprung from the basic de-

Electronic ignition troubleshooting chart, 1981 shown

INJECTION PUMP

INJECTION PUMP ADAPTOR

VACUUM PUMP

FUEL FILTER

FUEL RETURN SYSTEM

INJECTOR

INJECTION PUMP DRIVE GEARS

GLOW PLUG

PRECHAMBER

TIMING CHAIN

Cutaway view of the General Motors 350 diesel (Courtesy Oldsmobile Motor Div.)

sign of the 1955 265 cu in. engine. It was this engine that introduced the balljoint rocker arm design which is now used by many car makers. This line of engines features a great deal of interchangeability, and later parts may be utilized on earlier engines for increased reliability and/or performance.

The 396, 402, and 454 cu in. engines are known as the Mark IV engines or big-blocks. These engines feature unusual cylinder heads, in that the intake and exhaust valves are canted at the angle at which their respective port enters the cylinder. The big-block cylinder heads use balljoint rockers similar to those on the small block engines.

Two V8 diesel engines have been available in the Chevrolet pick-ups since 1978. The first was the Oldsmobile-built 350 cu. in. engine which was derived from a gasoline engine of the same displacement. Internal engine components such as the crankshaft, main bearings, connecting rods, pistons, wrist pins and piston rings all are heavier made to withstand the considerably higher pressures and stresses common to diesel engines.

Diesel ignition occurs because of heat developed in the combustion chamber during compression. This is the reason for the diesel's high compression ratio (22.5:1). Because the fuel ignites under compression, the need for spark plugs and high voltage ignition is eliminated.

A new V8 diesel of 379 cu. in. (6.2L) was introduced for the pick-ups in 1982, superceding the 350. This engine is built by Chevrolet;

GM's Detroit Diesel Division aided in much of the engine's design. The 379 is even stronger— component by component—than the 350. Designed "from the block up" as a diesel, it utilizes robust features such as four-bolt main bearing caps.

Engine Removal and Installation

The factory recommended procedure for engine removal is to remove the engine/transmission as a unit on two wheel drive models, except for the diesel. Only the engine should be removed on diesels and four wheel drive models.

1. Disconnect the negative battery terminal. On diesels, disconnect the negative cables at the batteries and ground wires at the inner fender panel.
2. Drain the cooling system.
3. Drain the engine oil.
4. Remove the air cleaner and ducts.
5. Scribe alignment marks around the hood hinges, and remove the hood.
6. Remove the radiator and hoses, and fan shroud if so equipped.
7. Disconnect and label the wires at:
   a. Starter solenoid.
   b. Alternator.
   c. Temperature switch.
   d. Oil pressure switch.
   e. Transmission controlled spark solenoid.

General Engine Specifications

Year	Engine No. Cyl Displacement Cu In.	Carburetor Type	Advertised Horsepower @ rpm ■	Advertised Torque @ rpm (ft. lbs.) ■	Bore and Stroke (in.)	Advertised Compression Ratio	Oil Pressure @ 2000 rpm
1970	6-250	1 bbl	155 @ 4200	235 @ 1600	3.875 x 3.530	8.5:1	40
	6-292	1 bbl	170 @ 4000	275 @ 1600	3.875 x 4.120	8.0:1	40
	8-307	2 bbl	200 @ 4600	300 @ 2400	3.875 x 3.250	9.0:1	40
	8-350	2 bbl	215 @ 4400	320 @ 2400	4.000 x 3.480	8.0:1	40
	8-350	4 bbl	225 @ 4600	355 @ 3000	4.000 x 3.480	9.0:1	40
	8-396	4 bbl	310 @ 4800	400 @ 3200	4.125 x 3.760	9.0:1	40
1971	6-250	1 bbl	145 @ 4200	235 @ 1600	3.875 x 3.530	8.5:1	40
	6-292	1 bbl	165 @ 4000	270 @ 1600	3.875 x 4.120	8.0:1	40
	8-307	2 bbl	200 @ 4600	300 @ 2400	3.875 x 3.250	9.0:1	40
	8-307	2 bbl	215 @ 4800	305 @ 2800	3.875 x 3.250	8.5:1	40
	8-350	4 bbl	250 @ 4600	350 @ 3000	4.000 x 3.480	8.5:1	40
	8-402	4 bbl	300 @ 4800	400 @ 3200	4.125 x 3.760	8.5:1	40
1972	6-250	1 bbl	110 @ 3800	185 @ 1600	3.875 x 3.530	8.5:1	40
	6-292	1 bbl	125 @ 3600	225 @ 2400	3.875 x 4.120	8.0:1	40
	8-307	2 bbl	135 @ 4000	230 @ 2400	3.875 x 3.250	8.5:1	40
	8-350	4 bbl	175 @ 4000	290 @ 2400	4.000 x 3.480	8.5:1	40
	8-402	4 bbl	210 @ 4000	320 @ 2800	4.125 x 3.760	8.5:1	40
1973	6-250	1 bbl	100 @ 3800	175 @ 2000	3.875 x 3.530	8.25:1	40
	6-292	1 bbl	120 @ 3600	225 @ 2000	3.875 x 4.120	8.0:1	40
	8-307	2 bbl	115 @ 3600	205 @ 2000	3.875 x 3.250	8.5:1	40
	8-307	2 bbl	130 @ 4000	220 @ 2200	3.875 x 3.250	8.5:1	40
	8-350	4 bbl	155 @ 4000	255 @ 2400	4.000 x 3.480	8.5:1	40
	8-454	4 bbl	240 @ 4000	355 @ 2800	4.125 x 4.000	8.25:1	40
	8-454	4 bbl	250 @ 4000	365 @ 2800	4.125 x 4.000	8.25:1	40
1974	6-250	1 bbl	100 @ 3600	175 @ 1800	3.875 x 3.530	8.25:1	40
	6-292	1 bbl	120 @ 3600	215 @ 2000	3.875 x 4.120	8.0:1	40
	8-350	2 bbl	145 @ 3800	250 @ 2200	4.000 x 3.480	8.5:1	40
	8-350	4 bbl	160 @ 3800	250 @ 2400	4.000 x 3.480	8.5:1	40
	8-454	4 bbl	230 @ 4000	350 @ 2800	4.125 x 4.000	8.25:1	40
	8-454	4 bbl	245 @ 4000	365 @ 2800	4.125 x 4.000	8.25:1	40
1975	6-250	1 bbl	105 @ 3800	185 @ 1200	3.875 x 3.530	8.25:1	40
	6-292	1 bbl	120 @ 3600	213 @ 2000	3.875 x 4.120	8.0:1	40
	8-350	4 bbl	160 @ 3800	250 @ 2400	4.000 x 3.480	8.5:1	40
	8-400	4 bbl	175 @ 3600	290 @ 2800	4.125 x 3.750	8.5:1	40
	8-454	4 bbl	245 @ 4000	355 @ 3000 ①	4.125 x 4.000	8.25:1	40
1976	6-250	1 bbl	105 @ 3800	185 @ 1200	3.875 x 3.530	8.25:1	40–60
	6-250 HD	1 bbl	100 @ 3600	175 @ 1800	3.875 x 3.530	8.25:1	40–60
	6-292	1 bbl	120 @ 3600	215 @ 2000	3.870 x 4.120	8.0:1	40–60
	8-350	2 bbl	145 @ 3800	250 @ 2200	4.000 x 3.480	8.5:1	40

General Engine Specifications (cont.)

Year	Engine No. Cyl Displacement Cu In.	Carburetor Type	Advertised Horsepower @ rpm■	Advertised Torque @ rpm (ft. lbs.)■	Bore and Stroke (in.)	Advertised Compression Ratio	Oil Pressure @ 2000 rpm
1976	8-350	4 bbl	165 @ 3800	260 @ 2400 ②	4.000 x 3.480	8.5:1	40
	8-400	4 bbl	175 @ 3600	290 @ 2800	4.125 x 3.750	8.5:1	40
	8-454	4 bbl	245 @ 3800	365 @ 2800	4.251 x 4.000	8.25:1	40
	8-454 HD	4 bbl	240 @ 3800 ③	370 @ 2800 ④	4.251 x 4.000	8.15:1	40
1977	6-250	1 bbl	110 @ 3800	195 @ 1600	3.875 x 3.530	8.3:1	40–60
	6-250 HD	1 bbl	100 @ 3600	175 @ 1800	3.875 x 3.530	8.0:1	40–60
	6-292	1 bbl	120 @ 3600	215 @ 2000	3.870 x 4.120	8.0:1	40–60
	8-305 ⑤	2 bbl	145 @ 3800	245 @ 2200	3.740 x 3.480	8.5:1	40
	8-305 HD ⑤	2 bbl	140 @ 3800	235 @ 2000	3.740 x 3.480	8.5:1	40
	8-350	4 bbl	165 @ 3800	260 @ 2400 ②	4.000 x 3.480	8.5:1	40
	8-400	4 bbl	175 @ 3600	290 @ 2800	4.125 x 3.750	8.5:1	40
	8-454	4 bbl	245 @ 3800	365 @ 2800	4.251 x 4.000	8.25:1	40
	8-454 HD	4 bbl	240 @ 3800 ③	370 @ 2800 ④	4.251 x 4.000	8.15:1	40
1978	6-250 LD	1 bbl	115 @ 3800	195 @ 1600	3.870 x 3.530	8.0:1	40–60
	6-250 Calif	1 bbl	100 @ 3800	185 @ 1600	3.870 x 3.530	8.1:1	40–60
	6-250 HD	1 bbl	100 @ 3600	175 @ 1800	3.870 x 3.530	8.1:1	40–60
	6-292	1 bbl	120 @ 3600	215 @ 2000	3.870 x 4.120	8.0:1	40–60
	8-305	2 bbl	145 @ 3800	245 @ 2400	3.740 x 3.480	8.4:1	45
	8-350 LD	4 bbl	165 @ 3800	260 @ 2400	4.000 x 3.480	8.2:1	45
	8-350 HD	4 bbl	165 @ 3800	255 @ 2800	4.000 x 3.480	8.3:1	45
	8-350 Diesel	FI	120 @ 3600	220 @ 1600	4.057 x 3.385	22.5:1	35
	8-400	4 bbl	175 @ 3600	290 @ 2800	4.125 x 3.750	8.3:1	40
	8-400 Calif	4 bbl	165 @ 3600	290 @ 2000	4.125 x 3.750	8.2:1	40
	8-454 LD	4 bbl	205 @ 3600	335 @ 2800	4.250 x 4.000	8.0:1	40
	8-454 HD	4 bbl	240 @ 3800	370 @ 2800	4.250 x 4.000	7.9:1	40
	8-454 HD Calif	4 bbl	250 @ 3800	385 @ 2800	4.250 x 4.000	7.9:1	40
1979	6-250 LD	2 bbl	130 @ 3800	210 @ 2400	3.870 x 3.530	8.3:1	40–60
	6-250 Calif	2 bbl	125 @ 4000	205 @ 2000	3.870 x 3.530	8.3:1	40–60
	6-250 HD	2 bbl	130 @ 4000	205 @ 2000	3.870 x 3.530	8.3:1	40–60
	6-292	1 bbl	115 @ 3400	215 @ 1600	3.870 x 4.120	7.8:1	40–60
	8-305	2 bbl	140 @ 4000	240 @ 2000	3.740 x 3.480	8.4:1	45
	8-350 LD	4 bbl	165 @ 3600	270 @ 2000	4.000 x 3.480	8.2:1	45
	8-350 Hi Alt	4 bbl	155 @ 3600	260 @ 2000	4.000 x 3.480	8.2:1	45
	8-350 HD	4 bbl	165 @ 3800	255 @ 2800	4.000 x 3.480	8.3:1	45
	8-350 Diesel	FI	120 @ 3600	220 @ 1600	4.057 x 3.385	22.5:1	35
	8-400 HD	4 bbl	180 @ 3600	310 @ 2400	4.125 x 3.750	8.2:1	40
	8-454 LD	4 bbl	205 @ 3600	335 @ 2800	4.250 x 4.000	8.0:1	40
	8-454 HD	4 bbl	210 @ 3800	340 @ 2800	4.250 x 4.000	7.9:1	40

General Engine Specifications (cont.)

Year	Engine No. Cyl Displacement Cu In.	Carburetor Type	Advertised Horsepower @ rpm ■	Advertised Torque @ rpm (ft. lbs.) ■	Bore and Stroke (in.)	Advertised Compression Ratio	Oil Pressure @ 2000 rpm
1980	6-250	2 bbl	130 @ 4000	210 @ 2000	3.870 x 3.530	8.3:1	40–60
	6-250 Calif	2 bbl	130 @ 4000	205 @ 2000	3.870 x 3.530	8.3:1	40–60
	6-292	1 bbl	115 @ 3400	215 @ 1600	3.870 x 4.120	7.8:1	40–60
	8-305	2 bbl	135 @ 4200	235 @ 2400	3.740 x 3.480	8.5:1	45
	8-350 LD	4 bbl	175 @ 4000	275 @ 2400	4.000 x 3.480	8.2:1	45
	8-350 LD Calif	4 bbl	170 @ 4000	275 @ 2000	4.000 x 3.480	8.2:1	45
	8-350 HD	4 bbl	165 @ 3800	255 @ 2800	4.000 x 3.480	8.3:1	45
	8-350	Diesel	125 @ 3600	225 @ 1600	4.057 x 3.385	22.5:1	35
	8-400 HD	4 bbl	180 @ 3600	310 @ 2400	4.125 x 3.750	8.3:1	40
	8-454 HD	4 bbl	210 @ 3800	340 @ 2800	4.250 x 4.000	7.9:1	40
1981	6-250	2 bbl	130 @ 4000	210 @ 200	3.870 x 3.530	8.3:1	40–60
	6-250 Calif	2 bbl	130 @ 4000	205 @ 2000	3.870 x 3.530	8.3:1	40–60
	6-292	1 bbl	115 @ 3400	215 @ 1600	3.870 x 4.120	7.8:1	40–60
	8-305	2 bbl	135 @ 4200	235 @ 2400	3.740 x 3.480	8.5:1	45
	8-305	4 bbl	155 @ 4400	252 @ 2400	3.740 x 3.480	9.2:1	45
	8-350 LD	4 bbl	175 @ 4000	275 @ 2000	4.000 x 3.480	8.2:1	45
	8-350 HD	4 bbl	165 @ 3800	255 @ 2800	4.000 x 3.480	8.3:1	45
	8-350	Diesel	125 @ 3600	225 @ 1600	4.057 x 3.385	22.5:1	35
	8-454	4 bbl	210 @ 3800	340 @ 2800	4.250 x 4.000	7.9:1	40
1982	6-250	2 bbl	130 @ 4000	210 @ 2000	3.870 x 3.530	8.3:1	40–60
	6-292	1 bbl	115 @ 3400	215 @ 1600	3.870 x 4.120	7.8:1	40–60
	8-305	4 bbl	140 @ 4200	240 @ 2400	3.740 x 3.480	8.5:1	45
	8-305	4 bbl	155 @ 4400	252 @ 2100	3.740 x 3.480	9.2:1	45
	8-350 LD	4 bbl	175 @ 4000	275 @ 2000	4.000 x 3.480	8.2:1	45
	8-350 HD	4 bbl	165 @ 3800	255 @ 2800	4.000 x 3.480	8.3:1	45
	8-379	Diesel	140 @ 3600	240 @ 2000	3.980 x 3.800	21.5:1	45
	8-454	4 bbl	210 @ 3800	340 @ 2800	4.250 x 4.000	7.9:1	40
1983–84	6-250	2 bbl	120 @ 4000	205 @ 2000	3.870 x 3.530	8.3:1	40–60
	6-292	1 bbl	115 @ 3600	215 @ 1600	3.870 x 4.120	7.8:1	40–60
	8-305 ⑥	4 bbl	160 @ 4400	235 @ 2000	3.740 x 3.480	8.5:1	45
	8-305 ⑦	4 bbl	155 @ 4000	245 @ 1600	3.740 x 3.480	9.2:1	45
	8-350 ⑥	4 bbl	165 @ 3800	275 @ 1600	4.000 x 3.480	8.2:1	45
	8-350 ⑦	4 bbl	155 @ 4000	240 @ 2800	4.000 x 3.480	8.2:1	45
	8-379	Diesel	140 @ 3600	240 @ 2000	3.980 x 3.800	21.5:1	45
	8-454	4 bbl	210 @ 3800	340 @ 2800	4.250 x 4.000	7.9:1	40

■Starting 1972, horsepower and torque are SAE net figures. They are measured at the rear of the transmission with all accessories installed and operating. Since the figures vary when a given engine is installed in different models, some are representative rather than exact.

① 375 @ 2800—Calif.   ④ 385 @ 2800—Calif.   ⑥ 49-states
② 255 @ 2800 HD   ⑤ Not available in California   ⑦ California
③ 250 @ 3800—Calif.

Camshaft Specifications
(All measurements in inches)

| Year | Engine | Journal Diameter | Lobe Lift | | Camshaft End Play |
			Intake	Exhaust	
1970	6-250	1.8682–1.8692	.2217	.2217	—
	6-292	1.8682–1.8692	.2315	.2315	—
	8-307	1.8682–1.8692	.2600	.2733	—
	8-350	1.8682–1.8692	.2600	.2733	—
	8-396	1.9487–1.9497	.2343	.2343	—
1971	6-250	1.8682–1.8692	.2217	.2217	—
	6-292	1.8682–1.8692	.2315	.2315	—
	8-307	1.8682–1.8692	.2600	.2733	—
	8-350	1.8682–1.8692	.2600	.2733	—
	8-402	1.9487–1.9497	.2343	.2343	—
1972	6-250	1.8682–1.8692	.2217	.2217	—
	6-292	1.8682–1.8692	.2315	.2315	—
	8-307	1.8682–1.8692	.2600	.2733	—
	8-350	1.8682–1.8692	.2600	.2733	—
	8-402	1.9487–1.9497	.2343	.2343	—
1973	6-250	1.8682–1.8692	.2217	.2217	.001–.005
	6-292	1.8682–1.8692	.2315	.2315	.001–.005
	8-307	1.8682–1.8692	.2600	.2733	—
	8-350	1.8682–1.8692	.2600	.2733	—
	8-454	1.9482–1.9492	.2343	.2343	—
1974	6-250	1.8682–1.8692	.2217	.2217	.001–.005
	6-292	1.8682–1.8692	.2315	.2315	.001–.005
	8-350	1.8682–1.8692	.2600	.2733	—
	8-454	1.9482–1.9492	.2343	.2343	—
1975	6-250	1.8682–1.8692	.2217	.2217	—
	6-292	1.8682–1.8692	.2315	.2315	—
	8-350	1.8682–1.8692	.2600	.2733	—
	8-400	1.9482–1.9492	.2600	.2733	—
	8-454	1.9482–1.9492	.2590	.2590	—
1976	6-250	1.8682–1.8692	.2217	.2217	—
	6-292	1.8682–1.8692	.2315	.2315	—
	8-350	1.8682–1.8692	.2600	.2733	—
	8-400	1.9482–1.9492	.2600	.2733	—
	8-454	1.9482–1.9492	.2590	.2590	—
1977	6-250	1.8677–1.8697	.2217	.2217	.001–.005
	6-292	1.8677–1.8697	.2315	.2315	.001–.005
	8-305	1.8682–1.8692	.2485	.2485	—
	8-350	1.8682–1.8692	.2600	.2733	—
	8-400	1.9482–1.9492	.2600	.2733	—
	8-454	1.9482–1.9492	.2343	.2343	—

Camshaft Specifications (cont.)
(All measurements in inches)

Year	Engine	Journal Diameter	Lobe Lift		Camshaft End Play
			Intake	Exhaust	
1978	6-250	1.8677–1.8697	.2217	.2315	.003–.008
	6-292	1.8677–1.8697	.2217	.2315	.003–.008
	8-305	1.8682–1.8692	.2484	.2667	.004–.012
	8-350	1.8682–1.8692	.2600	.2733	.004–.012
	8-350 Diesel	—	—	—	.011–.077
	8-400	1.9482–1.9492	.2600	.2733	.004–.012
	8-454	1.9482–1.9492	.2343	.2343	.004–.012
1979	6-250	1.8677–1.8697	.2217	.2315	.003–.008
	6-292	1.8677–1.8697	.2217	.2315	.003–.008
	8-305	1.8682–1.8692	.2484	.2667	.004–.012
	8-350	1.8682–1.8692	.2600	.2733	.004–.012
	8-350 Diesel	—	—	—	—
	8-400	1.9482–1.9492	.2600	.2733	.004–.012
	8-454	1.9482–1.9492	.2343	.2343	.004–.012
1980	6-250	1.8677–1.8697	.2217	.2315	.003–.008
	6-292	1.8677–1.8697	.2315	.2315	.003–.008
	8-305	1.8682–1.8692	.2484	.2667	.004–.012
	8-350	1.8682–1.8692	.2600	.2733	.004–.012
	8-350 Diesel	①	—	—	.011–.077
	8-400	1.8682–1.8692	.2600	.2733	.004–.012
	8-454	1.9482–1.9492	.2343	.2530	—
1981	6-250	1.8677–1.8697	.2217	.2315	.003–.008
	6-292	1.8677–1.8697	.2315	.2315	.003–.008
	8-305	1.8682–1.8692	.2484	.2667	.004–.012
	8-350	1.8682–1.8692	.2600	.2733	.004–.012
	8-350 Diesel	①	—	—	.011–.077
	8-454	1.9482–1.9492	.2343	.2530	—
1982–84	6-250	1.8677–1.8697	.2217 ③	.2315	.003–.008
	6-292	1.8677–1.8697	.2315	.2315	.003–.008
	8-305	1.8682–1.8692	.2484	.2667	.004–.012
	8-350	1.8682–1.8692	.2600	.2733	.004–.012
	8-379 Diesel	②	.2808	.2808	—
	8-454	1.9482–1.9492	.2343	.2530	—

① 1. 2.0357–2.0365
  2. 2.0157–2.0165
  3. 1.9957–1.9965
  4. 1.9757–1.9765
  5. 1.9557–1.9565
② 2#1,2,3,4: 2.1663–2.1643
  #5: 2.0088–2.0068
③ .2315 Calif.

Torque Specifications
(ft. lbs)

Engine No. Cyl Displacement (cu in.)	Cylinder Head Bolts	Rod Bearing Bolts	Main Bearing Bolts	Crank-shaft Bolt▲	Flywheel to Crank-shaft Bolts	Manifold	
						Intake	Exhaust
6-250	95 ⑤	35	65	—	60	—	30 ①
6-292	95	35	65	—	110	35	30
8-305	65	45	70	60	60	30	20
8-350	65	45	70	60	60	30	30 ①
8-350 Diesel	130 ②	42	120	200–310	60	40 ②	25
8-379 Diesel	100	48	④	150	—	31	22
8-396	80	50	110	—	65	30	20
8-400	65	45	70	60	60	30	30
8-402	80	50	110	—	65	30	20
8-454	80	50 ③	110	65	65	30	20

▲ Front of crankshaft
① End bolts: 20 ft. lbs.
② Dip in oil.
③ 7/16 in. bolts 70 ft. lbs.
④ inner: 111
   outer: 100
⑤ Left-hand front bolt: 85 ft. lbs.

f. CEC solenoid.

g. Coil.

h. Neutral safety switch.

8. Disconnect:

a. Accelerator linkage (hairpin at bell-crank, throttle and T.V. cables at intake manifold brackets on diesels. Position away from the engine.).

b. Choke cable at carburetor (if so equipped).

c. Fuel line to fuel pump.

d. Heater hoses at engine.

e. Air conditioning compressor with hoses attached. *Do not remove the hoses from the air conditioning compressor. Remove it as a unit and set it aside.* Its contents are under pressure, and can freeze body tissue on contact.

f. Transmission dipstick and tube on automatic transmission models, except for diesel. Plug the tube hole.

g. Oil dipstick and tube. Plug the hole.

h. Vacuum lines.

i. Oil pressure line to gauge, if so equipped.

j. Parking brake cable.

k. Power steering pump. This can be removed as a unit and set aside, without removing any of the hoses.

l. Engine ground straps.

m. Exhaust pipe (support if necessary).

9. Loosen and remove the fan belt, remove the fan blades and pulley. If you have the finned aluminum viscous drive fan clutch, keep it upright in its normal position. If the fluid leaks out, the unit will have to be replaced.

10. Remove the clutch cross-shaft.

11. Attach a lifting device to the engine. You may have to remove the carburetor. Take the engine weight off the engine mounts, and unbolt the mounts. On all models except the gas-engined ½ and ¾ ton, support and disconnect the transmission. With automatic transmission, remove the torque converter underpan and starter, unbolt the converter from the flywheel, detach the throttle linkage and vacuum modulator line, and unbolt the engine from the transmission. Be certain that the converter does not fall out. With manual transmission, unbolt the clutch housing from the engine. Further details are in Chapter 6.

12. On two wheel drive models, remove the driveshaft. See details in Chapter 7. Either drain the transmission or plug the driveshaft opening. Disconnect the speedometer cable at the transmission. Disconnect the TCS switch wire, if so equipped. Disconnect the shift linkage or lever, or the clutch linkage. Disconnect the transmission cooler lines, if so equipped. If you have an automatic or a four speed transmission, the rear crossmember must be removed. With the three speed, unbolt the transmission from the crossmember. Raise the engine/transmission assembly and pull it forward.

13. On diesels, remove the three bolts,

Crankshaft and Connecting Rod Specifications

All measurements are given in in.

Year	Engine No. Cyl Displacement (cu in.)	Crankshaft Main Brg Journal Dia.	Crankshaft Main Brg Oil Clearance	Crankshaft Shaft End-Play	Crankshaft Thrust on No.	Connecting Rod Journal Diameter	Connecting Rod Oil Clearance	Connecting Rod Side Clearance
1970	6-250	2.2983-2.2993	.0003-.0029	.002-.006	7	1.999-2.000	.0007-.0027	.009-.014
	6-292	2.2983-2.2993	.0008-.0034	.002-.006	7	1.999-2.100	.0007-.0028	.009-.014
	8-307, 350	2.4484-2.4493 ②	.0008-.0020 ⑤	.002-.006	5	2.199-2.200	.0007-.0028	.008-.014
	8-396	⑥	⑦	.006-.010	5	2.199-2.200	.0009-.0025	.008-.014
1971	6-250	2.2983-2.2993	.0003-.0029	.002-.006	7	1.999-2.000	.0007-.0027	.009-.014
	6-292	2.2983-2.2993	.0008-.0034	.002-.006	7	2.099-2.100	.0007-.0027	.009-.014
	8-307, 350	2.4484-2.4493 ②	.0008-.0015 ⑤	.002-.006	5	2.199-2.200	.0007-.0028	.008-.014
	8-402	⑥	⑧	.006-.010	5	2.1985-2.1995	.0009-.0025	.013-.023
1972	6-250	2.2983-2.2993	.0003-.0029	.002-.006	7	1.999-2.000	.0007-.0027	.009-.014
	6-292	2.2983-2.2993	.0008-.0034	.002-.006	7	2.099-2.100	.0007-.0027	.009-.014
	8-307, 350	2.4484-2.4493 ②	.0008-.0020 ⑤	.002-.006	5	2.199-2.200	.0007-.0028	.008-.014
	8-402	⑥	⑧	.006-.010	5	2.1985-2.1995	.0009-.0025	.013-.023
1973-77	6-250	2.2983-2.2993	.0003-.0029	.002-.006	7	1.999-2.000	.0007-.0027	.006-.017
	6-292	2.2983-2.2993	.0008-.0034	.002-.006	7	2.099-2.100	.0007-.0027	.006-.017
	8-305, 307, 350, 400	2.4484-2.4493 ② ⑪	.0008-.0020 ⑤	.002-.006	5	2.199-2.200	.0013-.0035	.008-.014
	8-454	⑨	⑩	.006-.010	5	2.1985-2.1995	.0009-.0025	.013-.023
1978-81	6-250	2.2979-2.2994	Nos. 1-6 .0010-.0024 No. 7 .0016-.0035	.002-.006	7	1.999-2.000	.0010-.0026	.006-.017
	6-292	2.2979-2.2994	Nos. 1-6 .0010-.0024 No. 7 .0016-.0035	.002-.006	7	2.099-2.100	.0010-.0026	.006-.017

Engine	Main brg journal dia.	Main brg oil clearance	Shaft end-play	Thrust on No.	Rod journal dia.	Rod oil clearance	Rod side clearance
8-305, 350, 400	⑪	.0008–.0020 ⑤	.002–.006	5	2.199–2.200 ⑫	.0013–.0035	.008–.014
8-454	⑨	⑩	.006–.010	5	2.1985–2.1995	.0009–.0025	.013–.023
8-350 Diesel	2.9993–3.0003	Nos. 1–4 .0005–.0021 No. 5 .0015–.0031	.0035–.0135	5	2.1238–2.1248	.0005–.0026	.006–.020
6-250 (1982–84)	2.2979–2.2994	Nos. 1–6 .0010–.0024 No. 7 .0016–.0035	.002–.006	7	1.999–2.000	.0010–.0026	.006–.017
6-292	2.2979–2.2994	Nos. 1–6 .0010–.0024 No. 7 .0016–.0035	.002–.006	7	2.099–2.100	.0010–.0026	.006–.017
8-305 8-350	⑪	.0008–.0020 ⑤	.002–.006	5	2.0988–2.0998	.0013–.0035	.008–.014
8-379 Diesel	⑭	⑮	.002–.007	5	2.398–2.399	—	.007–.024
8-454	⑬	⑩	.006–.010	5	2.200–2.199	.009–.0025	.013–.023

② No. 5—2.4479–2.4488
No. 2–4—.0011–.0023
No. 5—.0017–.0033

⑤ No. 5—2.7478–2.7488
Nos. 1–4—.0013–.0025
No. 5—.0024–.0040

⑥ Nos. 1–2—2.7487–2.7496
Nos. 3–4—2.7481–2.7490
No. 5—2.7478–2.7488

⑦ No. 1—.0007–.0019
Nos. 2–4—.0013–.0025
No. 5—.0024–.0040

⑧ No. 1—.0007–.0019
Nos. 2–4—.0013–.0025
No. 5—.0019–.0033

⑨ No. 1—2.7485–2.7494
Nos. 2–4—2.7481–2.7490

⑩ Nos. 1–4—.0013–.0025
No. 5—.0024–.0040

⑪ 1977–82 only: 305, 350—No. 1—2.4484–2.4493
Nos. 2–4—2.4481–2.4490
No. 5—2.4479–2.4488

⑫ 1978–80: 2.0988–2.0998

⑬ Nos. 1–4: 2.7481–2.7490
No. 5: 2.7476–2.7486

⑭ Nos. 1–4: 2.9494–2.9504
No. 5: 2.9492–2.9502

⑮ Nos. 1–4: .0018–.0032
No. 5: .0022–.0037

Valve Specifications

Year	Engine No. Cyl Displacement (cu in.)	Seat Angle (deg)	Face Angle (deg)	Spring Test Pressure (lbs. @ in.)	Spring Installed Height (in.) ①	Stem to Guide Clearance (in.)		Stem Diameter (in.)	
						Intake	Exhaust	Intake	Exhaust
1970	6-250	46	45	186 @ 1.27	1²¹⁄₃₂	0.0010–0.0027	0.0015–0.0032	0.3414	0.3414
	6-292	46	45	180 @ 1.30	1⁵⁄₈	0.0010–0.0027	0.0015–0.0032	0.3414	0.3414
	8-307	46	45	200 @ 1.25	1²³⁄₃₂	0.0010–0.0027	0.0010–0.0027	0.3414	0.3414
	8-350	46	45	200 @ 1.25	1²³⁄₃₂	0.0010–0.0027	0.0010–0.0027	0.3414	0.3414
	8-396	46	45	220 @ 1.40	1¹³⁄₁₆	0.0017–0.0020	0.0019–0.0022	0.3414	0.3414
1971	6-250	46	45	186 @ 1.27	1²¹⁄₃₂	0.0010–0.0027	0.0015–0.0032	0.3414	0.3414
	6-292	46	45	180 @ 1.30	1⁵⁄₈	0.0010–0.0027	0.0015–0.0032	0.3414	0.3414
	8-307	46	45	200 @ 1.25	1²³⁄₃₂	0.0010–0.0027	0.0010–0.0027	0.3414	0.3414
	8-350	46	45	200 @ 1.25	1²³⁄₃₂	0.0010–0.0027	0.0010–0.0027	0.3414	0.3414
	8-402	46	45	240 @ 1.38	1⁷⁄₈	0.0010–0.0027	0.0012–0.0029	0.3414	0.3414
1972	6-250	46	45	186 @ 1.27	1²¹⁄₃₂	0.0010–0.0027	0.0015–0.0032	0.3414	0.3414
	6-292	46	45	180 @ 1.30	1⁵⁄₈	0.0010–0.0027	0.0015–0.0032	0.3414	0.3414
	8-307	46	45	200 @ 1.25	1²³⁄₃₂	0.0010–0.0027	0.0010–0.0027	0.3414	0.3414
	8-350	46	45	200 @ 1.25	1²³⁄₃₂	0.0010–0.0027	0.0010–0.0027	0.3414	0.3414
	8-402	46	46	240 @ 1.38	1⁷⁄₈	0.0010–0.0027	0.0010–0.0029	0.3414	0.3414
1973	6-250	46	45	186 @ 1.27	1²¹⁄₃₂	0.0010–0.0027	0.0015–0.0032	0.3414	0.3414
	6-292	46	45	180 @ 1.30	1⁵⁄₈	0.0010–0.0027	0.0015–0.0032	0.3414	0.3414
	8-307	46	45	200 @ 1.25	1⁵⁄₈	0.0010–0.0027	0.0010–0.0027	0.3414	0.3414
	8-350	46	45	200 @ 1.25	1²³⁄₃₂	0.0010–0.0027	0.0010–0.0027	0.3414	0.3414
	8-454	46	45	300 @ 1.38	1⁷⁄₈	0.0010–0.0027	0.0012–0.0029	0.3414	0.3414
1974	6-250	46	45	186 @ 1.27	1²¹⁄₃₂	0.0010–0.0027	0.0015–0.0032	0.3414	0.3414
	6-292	46	45	180 @ 1.30	1⁵⁄₈	0.0010–0.0027	0.0015–0.0032	0.3414	0.3414
	8-350	46	45	200 @ 1.25	1²³⁄₃₂	0.0010–0.0027	0.0010–0.0027	0.3414	0.3414
	8-454	46	45	300 @ 1.38	1⁷⁄₈	0.0010–0.0027	0.0012–0.0029	0.3414	0.3414
1975–80	6-250	46	45	186 @ 1.27 ②	1²¹⁄₃₂	0.0010–0.0027	0.0015–0.0032	0.3414	0.3414
	6-292	46	45 ⑤	180 @ 1.30 ⑥	1⁵⁄₈ ⑦	0.0010–0.0027	0.0015–0.0032	0.3414	0.3414
	8-305	46	45	200 @ 1.25	③	0.0010–0.0027	0.0010–0.0027	0.3414	0.3414
	8-350	46	45	200 @ 1.25	③	0.0010–0.0027	0.0010–0.0027	0.3414	0.3414
	8-400	46	45	200 @ 1.25	③	0.0010–0.0027	0.0012–0.0029	0.3414	0.3414
	8-454	46	45	300 @ 1.38	1⁷⁄₈	0.0010–0.0027	0.0012–0.0029	0.3719	0.3719
	8-350 Diesel	⑧	④	151 @ 1.30	1⁴³⁄₆₄	0.0010–0.0027	0.0015–0.0032	—	—
1981	6-250	46	45	175 @ 1.26	1.66	0.0010–0.0027	0.0015–0.0032	0.3414	0.3414
	6-292	46	46	175 @ 1.26	1.66	0.0010–0.0027	0.0015–0.0032	0.3414	0.3414
	8-305	46	45	200 @ 1.25 ⑨	1²³⁄₃₂ ⑩	0.0010–0.0027	0.0010–0.0027	0.3414	0.3414
	8-350	46	45	200 @ 1.25 ⑨	1²³⁄₃₂ ⑩	0.0010–0.0027	0.0010–0.0027	0.3414	0.3414
	8-350 Diesel	⑧	④	205 @ 1.30	—	0.0010–0.0027	0.0015–0.0032	—	—
	8-454	46	45	220 @ 1.40	1⁵¹⁄₆₄	0.0010–0.0027	0.0012–0.0029	0.3719	0.3719

Valve Specifications (cont.)

Year	Engine No. Cyl Displacement (cu in.)	Seat Angle (deg)	Face Angle (deg)	Spring Test Pressure (lbs. @ in.)	Spring Installed Height (in.) ①	Stem to Guide Clearance (in.)		Stem Diameter (in.)	
						Intake	Exhaust	Intake	Exhaust
1982–84	6-250	46	45	175 @ 1.26	1.66	0.0010–0.0027	0.0015–0.0032	0.3414	0.3414
	6-292	46	45	175 @ 1.26	1.66	0.0010–0.0027	0.0015–0.0032	0.3414	0.3414
	8-305	46	45	200 @ 1.25 ⑨	1²³⁄₃₂ ⑩	0.0010–0.0027	0.0010–0.0027	0.3414	0.3414
	8-350	46	45	200 @ 1.25 ⑨	1²³⁄₃₂ ⑩	0.0010–0.0027	0.0010–0.0027	0.3414	0.3414
	8-379 Diesel	46	45	740 @ 1.40	1¹³⁄₁₆	0.0010–0.0027	0.0010–0.0027	—	—
	8-454	46	45	220 @ 1.40	1⁵¹⁄₆₄	0.0010–0.0027	0.0012–0.0029	0.3719	0.3719

① ± $\frac{1}{32}$ in.
② 172 @ 1.26 (1980)
③ Intake—1²³⁄₃₂
  Exhaust—1¹⁹⁄₃₂
④ Intake 44°
  Exhaust 30°
⑤ 1978–82: 46°
⑥ 185 @ 1.26 (1980)
⑦ 1978–82: 1²¹⁄₃₂
⑧ Intake 45°
  Exhaust 31°
⑨ 200 @ 1.16 exhaust
⑩ 1¹⁹⁄₃₂ exhaust

Ring Side Clearance—Compression Rings

(in.)

Year	Engine	Top Compression	Bottom Compression
1970–73	8-307	0.0012–0.0027	0.0012–0.0032
1970–84	6-250	0.0012–0.0027	0.0012–0.0032
1970–80	6-292	0.0020–0.0040	0.0020–0.0040
1970–84	8-350	0.0012–0.0032	0.0012–0.0032
1975–80	8-400	0.0012–0.0032	0.0012–0.0032
1970	8-396	0.0012–0.0032	0.0012–0.0032
1971–72	8-402	0.0017–0.0032	0.0017–0.0032
1973–84	8-454	0.0017–0.0032	0.0017–0.0032
1977–84	8-305	0.0012–0.0032	0.0012–0.0032
1978–81	8-350 Diesel	0.0040–0.0060 ①	0.0018–0.0038
1982–84	8-379 Diesel	0.0030–0.0070	0.0015–0.0031

Ring Side Clearance—Oil Rings

(in.)

Year	Engine	Oil Control	Year	Engine	Oil Control
1970–73	6-250, 8-307	0.0000–0.0050	1973–84	8-454	0.0005–0.0065
1974–84	6-250	0.0000–0.0050	1975–80	8-400	0.002–0.007
1970–84	8-350	0.002–0.007	1977–84	8-305	0.002–0.007
1970–84	6-292	0.0050–0.0055	1978–81	8-350 Diesel	0.001–0.005
1970	8-396	0.0012–0.0060	1982–84	8-379 Diesel	0.0016–0.0038
1971–72	8-402	0.0005–0.0065			

① .005–.007 (1980–82)

Ring Gap
(in.)

Year	Engine	Top Compression	Bottom Compression	Oil Control
1970–84	6-250	0.010–0.020	0.010–0.020	0.015–0.055
1970–84	6-292	0.010–0.020	0.010–0.020	0.015–0.055
1970–72	8-307	0.010–0.020	0.010–0.020	0.015–0.055
1970–84	8-350	0.010–0.020	0.013–0.025 ②	0.015–0.055
1975–80	8-400	0.010–0.020	0.010–0.025	0.010–0.035 ①
1970	8-396	0.010–0.020	0.010–0.020	0.010–0.030
1971–72	8-402	0.010–0.020	0.010–0.020	0.010–0.030
1973–84	8-454	0.010–0.020	0.010–0.020	0.010–0.030 ①
1977–84	8-305	0.010–0.020	0.010–0.025	0.015–0.055
1978–81	8-350 Diesel	0.015–0.025	0.015–0.025	0.015–0.055
1982–84	8-379 Diesel	0.0012–0.022	0.030–0.040	0.0098–0.0200

① 0.015–0.055—1977–80
② 0.010–0.025—1977–84

Piston Clearance

Year	Engine	Piston-to-Bore Production Clearance (in.)
1970	6-250	0.0005–0.0015
	6-292	0.0025–0.0031
	8-307	0.0005–0.0011
	8-350	0.0012–0.0022
	8-396	0.0018–0.0026
1971–72	6-250	0.0005–0.0015
	6-292	0.0025–0.0031
	8-307	0.0012–0.0018
	8-350	0.0007–0.0013
	8-402	0.0018–0.0026
1973	6-250	0.0005–0.0015
	6-292	0.0026–0.0036
	8-307	0.0012–0.0018
	8-350	0.0007–0.0013
	8-454	0.0018–0.0028
1974–76	6-250	0.0005–0.0015
	6-292	0.0026–0.0036
	8-350	0.0007–0.0013
	8-400	0.0014–0.0024
	8-454	0.0018–0.0028
1977–81	6-250	0.0005–0.0015 ①
	6-292	0.0026–0.0036
	8-305	0.0007–0.0017
	8-350	0.0007–0.0017
	8-350 Diesel	0.0050–0.0060 ②
	8-400	0.0014–0.0024
	8-454	0.0014–0.0024 ③

Piston Clearance (cont.)

Year	Engine	Piston-to-Bore Production Clearance (in.)
1982–84	6-250	0.0010–0.0020
	6-292	0.0026–0.0036
	8-305	0.0007–0.0017
	8-350	0.0007–0.0017
	8-379 Diesel	0.0040–0.0050
	8-454	0.0030–0.0040

① 0.0010–0.0020—1978–81
② Service clearance
③ .0030 .0040 (1980–81)

transmission, right side; disconnect the wires to the starter and remove the starter.

14. On four wheel drive, raise and pull the engine forward until it is free of the transmission. On diesels, slightly raise the transmission, remove the three left transmission to engine bolts, and remove the engine.

15. On all trucks, lift the engine out slowly, making certain as you go that all lines between the engine and the truck have been disconnected.

Installation is as follows:

1. On four wheel drive and diesels, lower the engine into place and align it with the transmission. Push the engine back gently and

ENGINE OVERHAUL

Most engine overhaul procedures are fairly standard. In addition to specific parts replacement procedures and complete specifications for your individual engine, this chapter also is a guide to accepted rebuilding procedures. Examples of standard rebuilding practice are shown and should be used along with specific details concerning your particular engine.

Competent and accurate machine shop services will ensure maximum performance, reliability and engine life. Procedures marked with the symbol shown above should be performed by a competent machine shop, and are provided so that you will be familiar with the procedures necessary to a successful overhaul.

In most instances it is more profitable for the do-it-yourself mechanic to remove, clean and inspect the component, buy the necessary parts and deliver these to a shop for actual machine work.

On the other hand, much of the rebuilding work (crankshaft, block, bearings, pistons, rods, and other components) is well within the scope of the do-it-yourself mechanic.

Tools

The tools required for an engine overhaul or parts replacement will depend on the depth of your involvement. With a few exceptions, they will be the tools found in a mechanic's tool kit (see Chapter 1). More in-depth work will require any or all of the following:
 • a dial indicator (reading in thousandths) mounted on a universal base
 • micrometers and telescope gauges
 • jaw and screw-type pullers
 • scraper
 • valve spring compressor
 • ring groove cleaner
 • piston ring expander and compressor
 • ridge reamer
 • cylinder hone or glaze breaker
 • Plastigage®
 • engine stand

Use of most of these tools is illustrated in this chapter. Many can be rented for a one-time use from a local parts jobber or tool supply house specializing in automotive work.

Occasionally, the use of special tools is called for. See the information on Special Tools and the Safety Notice in the front of this book before substituting another tool.

Inspection Techniques

Procedures and specifications are given in this chapter for inspecting, cleaning and assessing the wear limits of most major components. Other procedures such as Magnaflux and Zyglo can be used to locate material flaws and stress cracks. Magnaflux is a magnetic process applicable only to ferrous materials. The Zyglo process coats the material with a flourescent dye penetrant and can be used on any material. Check for suspected surface cracks can be more readily made using spot check dye. The dye is sprayed onto the suspected area, wiped off and the area sprayed with a developer. Cracks will show up brightly.

Overhaul Tips

Aluminum has become extremely popular for use in engines, due to its low weight. Observe the following precautions when handling aluminum parts:
 • Never hot tank aluminum parts (the caustic hot-tank solution will eat the aluminum)
 • Remove all aluminum parts (identification tag, etc.) from engine parts prior to hot-tanking.
 • Always coat threads lightly with engine oil or anti-seize compounds before installation, to prevent seizure.
 • Never over-torque bolts or spark plugs, especially in aluminum threads.

Stripped threads in any component can be repaired using any of several commercial repair kits (Heli-Coil, Microdot, Keenserts, etc.)

When assembling the engine, any parts that will be in frictional contact must be pre-lubed to provide lubrication at initial start-up. Any product specifically formulated for this purpose can be used, but engine oil is not recommended as a pre-lube.

When semi-permanent (locked, but removable) installation of bolts or nuts is desired, threads should be cleaned and coated with Loctite® or other similar, commercial non-hardening sealant.

Repairing Damaged Threads

Several methods of repairing damaged threads are available. Heli-Coil® (shown here), Keenserts® and Microdot® are among the most widely used. All involve basically the same principle—drilling out stripped threads, tapping the hole and installing a pre-wound insert—making welding, plugging and oversize fasteners unnecessary.

Two types of thread repair inserts are usually supplied—a standard type for most Inch Coarse, Inch Fine, Metric Coarse and Metric Fine thread sizes and a spark plug type to fit most spark plug port sizes. Consult the individual manufacturer's catalog to determine exact applications. Typical thread repair kits will contain a selection of pre-wound threaded inserts, a tap (corresponding to the outside diameter threads of the insert) and an installation tool. Spark plug inserts usually differ because they require a tap equipped with pilot threads and a combined reamer/tap section. Most manufacturers also supply blister-packed thread repair inserts separately in addition to a master kit containing a variety of taps and inserts plus installation tools.

Before effecting a repair to a threaded hole, remove any snapped, broken or damaged bolts or studs. Penetrating oil can be used to free frozen threads; the offending item can be removed with locking pliers or with a screw or stud extractor. After the hole is clear, the thread can be repaired, as follows:

Drill out the damaged threads with specified drill. Drill completely through the hole or to the bottom of a blind hole

With the tap supplied, tap the hole to receive the thread insert. Keep the tap well oiled and back it out frequently to avoid clogging the threads

Damaged bolt holes can be repaired with thread repair inserts

Standard thread repair insert (left) and spark plug thread insert (right)

Screw the threaded insert onto the installation tool until the tang engages the slot. Screw the insert into the tapped hole until it is ¼–½ turn below the top surface. After installation break off the tang with a hammer and punch

Standard Torque Specifications and Fastener Markings

In the absence of specific torques, the following chart can be used as a guide to the maximum safe torque of a particular size/grade of fastener.
- There is no torque difference for fine or coarse threads.
- Torque values are based on clean, dry threads. Reduce the value by 10% if threads are oiled prior to assembly.
- The torque required for aluminum components or fasteners is considerably less.

U.S. Bolts

SAE Grade Number	1 or 2			5			6 or 7		
Number of lines always 2 less than the grade number.									
Bolt Size (Inches)—(Thread)	Maximum Torque			Maximum Torque			Maximum Torque		
	Ft./Lbs.	Kgm	Nm	Ft./Lbs.	Kgm	Nm	Ft./Lbs.	Kgm	Nm
¼—20	5	0.7	6.8	8	1.1	10.8	10	1.4	13.5
—28	6	0.8	8.1	10	1.4	13.6			
5/16—18	11	1.5	14.9	17	2.3	23.0	19	2.6	25.8
—24	13	1.8	17.6	19	2.6	25.7			
⅜—16	18	2.5	24.4	31	4.3	42.0	34	4.7	46.0
—24	20	2.75	27.1	35	4.8	47.5			
7/16—14	28	3.8	37.0	49	6.8	66.4	55	7.6	74.5
—20	30	4.2	40.7	55	7.6	74.5			
½—13	39	5.4	52.8	75	10.4	101.7	85	11.75	115.2
—20	41	5.7	55.6	85	11.7	115.2			
9/16—12	51	7.0	69.2	110	15.2	149.1	120	16.6	162.7
—18	55	7.6	74.5	120	16.6	162.7			
⅝—11	83	11.5	112.5	150	20.7	203.3	167	23.0	226.5
—18	95	13.1	128.8	170	23.5	230.5			
¾—10	105	14.5	142.3	270	37.3	366.0	280	38.7	379.6
—16	115	15.9	155.9	295	40.8	400.0			
⅞—9	160	22.1	216.9	395	54.6	535.5	440	60.9	596.5
—14	175	24.2	237.2	435	60.1	589.7			
1—8	236	32.5	318.6	590	81.6	799.9	660	91.3	894.8
—14	250	34.6	338.9	660	91.3	849.8			

Metric Bolts

Relative Strength Marking	4.6, 4.8			8.8		
Bolt Markings						
Bolt Size Thread Size x Pitch (mm)	Maximum Torque			Maximum Torque		
	Ft./Lbs.	Kgm	Nm	Ft./Lbs.	Kgm	Nm
6 x 1.0	2–3	.2–.4	3–4	3–6	.4–.8	5–8
8 x 1.25	6–8	.8–1	8–12	9–14	1.2–1.9	13–19
10 x 1.25	12–17	1.5–2.3	16–23	20–29	2.7–4.0	27–39
12 x 1.25	21–32	2.9–4.4	29–43	35–53	4.8–7.3	47–72
14 x 1.5	35–52	4.8–7.1	48–70	57–85	7.8–11.7	77–110
16 x 1.5	51–77	7.0–10.6	67–100	90–120	12.4–16.5	130–160
18 x 1.5	74–110	10.2–15.1	100–150	130–170	17.9–23.4	180–230
20 x 1.5	110–140	15.1–19.3	150–190	190–240	26.2–46.9	160–320
22 x 1.5	150–190	22.0–26.2	200–260	250–320	34.5–44.1	340–430
24 x 1.5	190–240	26.2–46.9	260–320	310–410	42.7–56.5	420–550

CHECKING ENGINE COMPRESSION

A noticeable lack of engine power, excessive oil consumption and/or poor fuel mileage measured over an extended period are all indicators of internal engine wear. Worn piston rings, scored or worn cylinder bores, blown head gaskets, sticking or burnt valves and worn valve seats are all possible culprits here. A check of each cylinder's compression will help you locate the problems.

As mentioned in the "Tools and Equipment" section of Chapter 1, a screw-in type compression gauge is more accurate than the type you simply hold against the spark plug hole, although it takes slightly longer to use. It's worth it to obtain a more accurate reading. Follow the procedures below for gasoline and diesel-engined cars.

Gasoline Engines

1. Warm up the engine to normal operating temperature.
2. Remove all spark plugs.

The screw-in type compression gauge is more accurate

3. Disconnect the high-tension lead from the ignition coil.
4. On carbureted cars, fully open the throttle either by operating the carburetor throttle linkage by hand or by having an assistant "floor" the accelerator pedal. On fuel-injected cars, disconnect the cold start valve and all injector connections.
5. Screw the compression gauge into the No. 1 spark plug hole until the fitting is snug.

NOTE: *Be careful not to crossthread the plug hole. On aluminum cylinder heads use extra care, as the threads in these heads are easily ruined.*

6. Ask an assistant to depress the accelerator pedal fully on both carbureted and fuel-injected cars. Then, while you read the compression gauge, ask the assistant to crank the engine two or three times in short bursts using the ignition switch.

7. Read the compression gauge at the end of each series of cranks, and record the highest of these readings. Repeat this procedure for each of the engine's cylinders. Compare the highest reading of each cylinder to the compression pressure specifications in the "Tune-Up Specifications" chart in Chapter 2. The specs in this chart are maximum values.

A cylinder's compression pressure is usually acceptable if it is not less than 80% of maximum. The difference between each cylinder should be no more than 12–14 pounds.

8. If a cylinder is unusually low, pour a tablespoon of clean engine oil into the cylinder through the spark plug hole and repeat the compression test. If the compression comes up after adding the oil, it appears that that cylinder's piston rings or bore are damaged or worn. If the pressure remains low, the valves may not be seating properly (a valve job is needed), or the head gasket may be blown near that cylinder. If compression in any two adjacent cylinders is low, and if the addition of oil doesn't help the compression, there is leakage past the head gasket. Oil and coolant water in the combustion chamber can result from this problem. There may be evidence of water droplets on the engine dipstick when a head gasket has blown.

Diesel Engines

Checking cylinder compression on diesel engines is basically the same procedure as on gasoline engines except for the following:

1. A special compression gauge adaptor suitable for diesel engines (because these engines have much greater compression pressures) must be used.
2. Remove the injector tubes and remove the injectors from each cylinder.

NOTE: *Don't forget to remove the washer underneath each injector; otherwise, it may get lost when the engine is cranked.*

Diesel engines require a special compression gauge adaptor

3. When fitting the compression gauge adaptor to the cylinder head, make sure the bleeder of the gauge (if equipped) is closed.
4. When reinstalling the injector assemblies, install new washers underneath each injector.

turn the crankshaft until the manual transmission shaft and clutch engage. Bolt the transmission to the engine. With automatic transmission, align the converter with the flywheel, bolt the transmission to the engine, bolt the converter to the flywheel, replace the underpan and starter, and connect the throttle linkage and vacuum modulator line. See Chapter 6 for details.

2. On two wheel drive, lower the engine/transmission unit into place. Replace the rear crossmember if removed. Bolt the three speed transmission back to the crossmember. Replace the driveshaft.

3. Install the engine mounts.

4. Replace all transmission connections and the clutch cross-shaft. Replace the fan, pulley, and belts.

5. Replace all the items removed from the engine earlier. Connect all the wires which were detached.

6. Replace the radiator and fan shroud, air cleaner, and battery or battery cables. Fill the cooling system and check the automatic transmission fuel level. Fill the crankcase with oil. Check for leaks.

Valve Cover(s)

REMOVAL AND INSTALLATION

All Engines

1. Remove air cleaner.

2. Disconnect and reposition as necessary any vacuum or PCV hoses that obstruct the valve covers.

3. Disconnect electrical wire(s) (spark plug, etc.) from the valve cover clips.

4. Unbolt and remove the valve cover(s).

NOTE: *Do not pry the covers off if they seem stuck. Instead, gently tap around each cover with a rubber mallet until the old gasket or sealer breaks loose.*

Valve cover and rocker arm removal, gasoline V8 shown. Rocker arms are marked "L" and "R" for left and right

Apply a 3/32" bead of R. T. V. (room temperature vulcanizing) sealer on the valve cover as shown.

Apply sealer to all valve covers as shown. Always run the sealer bead on the inside edge of the bolt holes on the cover flange

5. To install, use a new valve cover gasket or RTV (or any equivalent) sealer. If using sealer, follow directions on the tube. Install valve cover and tighten cover bolts to 3 ft. lbs.

6. Connect and reposition all vacuum and PCV hoses, and reconnect electrical and/or spark plug wires at the cover clips. Install the air cleaner.

Rocker Arms

REMOVAL AND INSTALLATION

All Gasoline Sixes and V8s

1. Remove the valve cover.

2. Remove the rocker arm flanged bolts, and remove the rocker pivots.

3. Remove the rocker arms.

NOTE: *Remove each set of rocker arms (one set per cylinder) as a unit.*

4. To install, position a set of rocker arms (for one cylinder) in the proper location.

Six-cylinder rocker arm components—all gasoline V8s similar

NOTE: *Install the rocker arms for each cylinder only when the lifters are off the cam-lobe and both valves are closed.*

5. Coat the replacement rocker arm and pivot with SAE 90 gear oil and install the pivots.

6. Install the flanged bolts and tighten alternately. Torque the bolts to 25 ft. lbs.

350 Diesel

NOTE: *When the diesel engine rocker arms are removed or loosened, the lifters must be bled down to prevent oil pressure buildup inside each lifter, which could cause it to raise up higher than normal and bring the valves within striking distance of the pistons.*

1. Remove the valve cover.

2. Remove the rocker arm pivot bolts, the bridged pivot and rocker arms.

3. Remove each rocker set as a unit.

4. To install, lubricate the pivot wear point and position each set of rocker arms in its proper location. Do not tighten the pivot bolts for fear of bending the valves when the engine is turned.

5. The lifters can be bled down for six cylinders at once with the crankshaft in either of the following two positions:

   a. For cylinders number 3, 5, 7, 2, 4 and 8, turn the crankshaft so the saw slot on the harmonic balancer is at 0° on the timing indicator.

   b. For cylinders 1, 3, 7, 2, 4 and 6, turn the crankshaft so the saw slot on the harmonic balancer is at 4 o'clock.

6. Tighten the rocker arm pivot bolts VERY SLOWLY to 28 ft. lbs. It will take 45 minutes to completely bleed down the lifters in this position. If additional lifters must be bled, rotate the engine to the other position, tighten the rocker arm pivot bolts, and again wait 45 minutes before rotating the crankshaft. *Excess torque here can bend the pushrods, so be careful!*

7. Assemble the remaining components in the reverse of disassembly. The rocker covers do not use gaskets, but are sealed with a bead of RTV (Room Temperature Vulcanizing) silicone sealer.

379 (6.2L) Diesel

1. Remove the valve cover as previously explained.

2. The rocker assemblies on the 379 differ completely from those on the 350 diesel. The 379 arms are mounted on two short rocker shafts per cylinder head, with each shaft operating four rockers. Remove the two bolts which secure each rocker shaft assembly, and remove the shaft.

3. The rocker arms can be removed from the shaft by removing the cotter pin on the end of

ROCKER ARM/SHAFT

55 N·m (41 FT. LBS.)

6.2L diesel rocker shaft assemblies

each shaft. The rocker arms and springs slide off.

4. To install, make sure first that the rocker arms and springs go back on the shafts *in the exact order in which they were removed*.

NOTE: *Always install new cotter pins on the rocker shaft ends*.

5. Install the rocker shaft assemblies, torquing the bolts to 41 ft. lbs.

Intake Manifold

REMOVAL AND INSTALLATION

Inline Six Cylinder

1974 and earlier 250 and 292 six cylinder engines use a combined intake and exhaust manifold, both of which are removed together. 1976 and later engines have an intake manifold which is cast integrally with the cylinder head and cannot be removed.

1. Remove the air cleaner assembly and air ducts.

2. Tag and disconnect the throttle linkage at the carburetor. Tag and disconnect the fuel line, vacuum lines, hoses, and electrical connections.

3. Disconnect the transmission downshift linkage (if equipped), and remove the PCV valve from the rocker cover. On models equipped with air injection, disconnect the air supply hose from the check valve on the air injection manifold.

4. Remove the carburetor, with spacer and heat shield (if equipped).

5. Spray the nuts and bolts connecting the exhaust manifold to the exhaust pipe with a rust penetrant, as these are usually quite difficult to remove. Unbolt the exhaust manifold from the pipe.

NOTE: *It may be necessary to remove the generator rear bracket and/or A/C bracket on some models.*

6. Unbolt the manifold bolts and clamps, and remove the manifold assembly.

7. If you intend to separate the manifolds, remove the single bolt and two nuts at the center of the manifold assembly.

8. Installation is the reverse of removal. When assembling the manifolds, install the connecting bolts loosely first. Place the manifolds on a straight, flat surface and hold them securely during tightening—this assures the proper mating of surfaces when the manifold assembly is fastened to the head. *Stress cracking could occur if the manifolds are not assembled first in this manner.* On all manifolds, always use new gaskets between the manifolds and cylinder head.

V8 Except Diesel

1. Drain the cooling system.
2. Remove the air cleaner assembly.
3. Remove the thermostat housing and the bypass hose. It is not necessary to remove the top radiator hose from the thermostat housing.
4. Disconnect the heater hose at the rear of the manifold.
5. Disconnect all electrical connections and vacuum lines from the manifold. Remove the EGR valve if necessary.
6. On vehicles equipped with power brakes remove the vacuum line from the vacuum booster to the manifold.
7. Remove the distributor (if necessary).
8. Remove the fuel line to the carburetor.

305 and 350 V8 intake manifold bolt torque sequence

396 and 454 intake manifold bolt torque sequence

9. Remove the carburetor linkage.
10. Remove the carburetor.
11. Remove the intake manifold bolts. Remove the manifold and the gaskets. Remember to reinstall the O-ring seal between the intake manifold and timing chain cover during assembly, if so equipped.
12. Installation is the reverse of removal. Use plastic gasket retainers to prevent the manifold gasket from slipping out of place, if so equipped.

Typical gasoline V8 intake manifold installation showing related components

On small-blocks, run a ³⁄₁₆ in. bead of RTV sealer across the block and ½ in. up the sides of the block just prior to manifold installation

On the small-block V8s, place a ³⁄₁₆ in. bead of RTV type silicone sealer on the front and rear ridges of the cylinder block-to-manifold mating surfaces. Extend the bead ½ in. up each cylinder head to seal and retain the manifold side gaskets.

NOTE: *Before installing the intake manifold, be sure that the gasket surfaces are thoroughly clean.*

350 Diesel

1. Remove the air cleaner.
2. Drain the radiator. Loosen the upper bypass hose clamp, remove the thermostat housing bolts, and remove the housing and the thermostat from the intake manifold.
3. Remove the breather pipes from the rocker covers and the air crossover. Remove the air crossover.
4. Disconnect the throttle rod and the return spring. If equipped with cruise control, remove the servo.
5. Remove the hairpin clip at the bell-crank and disconnect the cables. Remove the throttle cable from the bracket on the manifold; position the cable away from the engine. Disconnect and label any wiring as necessary.
6. Remove the alternator bracket if necessary. If equipped with air conditioning, remove the compressor mounting bolts and move the compressor aside, without disconnecting any of the hoses. Remove the compressor mounting bracket from the intake manifold.
7. Disconnect the fuel line from the pump and the fuel filter. Remove the fuel filter and bracket.

350 diesel intake manifold installation. Note sealer application

350 V8 diesel intake manifold torque sequence

350 diesel intake manifold drain tube

8. Remove the fuel injection pump and lines. See Chapter 4, "Fuel System," for procedures.
9. Disconnect and remove the vacuum pump or oil pump drive assembly from the rear of the engine.
10. Remove the intake manifold drain tube.
11. Remove the intake manifold bolts and

VACUUM PUMP
(OIL PUMP DRIVE)

20 FT. LBS.
(27 N·m)

"O" RING
(APPLY LUBE TO
"O" RING BEFORE
INSTALLING)

NOTICE: DO NOT OPERATE ENGINE WITHOUT
VACUUM PUMP AS THIS IS THE DRIVE
FOR THE ENGINE OIL PUMP AND ENGINE
DAMAGE WOULD OCCUR.

**Oil pump drive and vacuum pump, 350 diesel shown.
379 diesel pump similar**

ADAPTER TO
MANIFOLD SEAL

FUEL INJECTION
PUMP ADAPTER

8 FT. LBS.   25 ft. lbs.

WASHER

ADAPTER STUD

INTAKE
MANIFOLD

SEAL

ADAPTER

Adapter and seal details, 350 diesel

PUMP DRIVEN GEAR

OFFSET

**The index mark on the injection pump driven gear
will be offset to the right when the No. 1 cylinder is
at TDC**

remove the manifold. Remove the adapter seal.
Remove the injection pump adapter.

12. Clean the mating surfaces of the cylinder heads and the intake manifold using a putty knife.

J-28425

ADAPTER
SEAL

ADAPTER

LUBRICATE SEAL, TOOL, ADAPTER & MANIFOLD

Adapter seal installation with the special tool

HOLD
TORQUE TO
50 FT. LBS.

J-26896

ADAPTER

TIMING
MARK

INJECTION PUMP FLANGE

Adapter timing mark application

13. Coat both sides of the gasket surface that seal the intake manifold to the cylinder heads with G.M. sealer #1050026 or the equivalent. Position the intake manifold gaskets on the cylinder heads. Install the end seals, making sure that the ends are positioned under the cylinder heads.

14. Carefully lower the intake manifold into place on the engine.

15. Clean the intake manifold bolts thoroughly, then dip them in clean engine oil. Install the bolts and tighten to 15 ft. lbs. in the sequence shown. Next, tighten all the bolts to 30 ft. lbs., in sequence, and finally tighten to 40 ft. lbs. in sequence.

16. Install the intake manifold drain tube and clamp.

17. Install injection pump adapter. See Chapter 4. If a new adapter is not being used, skip steps 4 and 9.

379 (6.2L) Diesel

1. Disconnect both batteries.
2. Remove the air cleaner assembly.
3. Remove the crankcase ventilator tubes, and disconnect the secondary fuel filter lines. Remove the secondary filter and adaptor.
4. Loosen the vacuum pump hold-down

379 diesel intake manifold gasket mounting and bolt torque sequence

clamp and rotate the pump to gain access to the nearest manifold bolt.

5. Remove the EPR/EGR valve bracket, if equipped.

6. Remove the rear air conditioning bracket, if equipped.

7. Remove the intake manifold bolts; the injection line clips are retained by these bolts.

8. Remove the intake manifold.

CAUTION: *If the engine is to be further serviced with the manifold removed, install protective covers over the intake ports.*

9. Clean the manifold gasket surfaces on the cylinder heads and install new gaskets before installing the manifold.

NOTE: *The gaskets have an opening for the EGR valve on light duty installations; an insert covers this opening on heavy-duty installations.*

10. Install the manifold. Torque the bolts in the sequence illustrated.

11. The secondary filter must be filled with clean diesel fuel before it is reinstalled.

12. Reverse the remaining removal procedures to complete the installation.

Exhaust Manifold

REMOVAL AND INSTALLATION

Inline Six Cylinder

NOTE: *1974 and earlier inline six cylinder exhaust manifold removal and installation procedures are covered under the "Intake Manifold" procedure (both manifolds are a unit). 1975 and later inline six procedures are covered below.*

1. Disconnect and remove the air cleaner

1975 and later inline six exhaust manifold torque sequence—engines with integral intake manifold/cylinder head

assembly, including the carburetor pre-heat tube.

2. Disconnect the exhaust pipe at the exhaust manifold. You will probably have to use a liquid rust penetrant to free the bolts.

3. Remove the engine oil dipstick bracket bolt.

4. Liberally coat the manifold nuts with a rust penetrating lubricant. Remove the exhaust manifold bolts and remove the manifold.

5. To install, mount the manifold on the cylinder head and start all bolts.

6. Torque the bolts to specification using the torque sequence illustrated. Complete the installation by reversing the removal procedure.

Gasoline V8s

Tab locks are used on the front and rear pairs of bolts on each exhaust manifold. When removing the bolts, straighten the tabs from beneath the car using a suitable tool. When installing the tab locks, bend the tabs against the sides of the bolt, not over the top of the bolt.

1. Remove the air cleaner.

2. Remove the hot air shroud, (if so equipped).

PLASTIC GASKET
RETAINERS

GASKET

Plastic manifold gasket retainers, gasoline V8s

INNER
SHROUD

EXHAUST
MANIFOLD

7 FT. LBS.
(9 N·m)

25 FT. LBS.
(34 N·m)

UPPER
SHROUD
PLATE
(EXC. CALIF.)

UPPER SHROUD
(EXC. CALIF.)

7 FT. LBS.
(9 N·m)

UPPER
SHROUD
(CALIF.)

LOWER
SHROUD

15 FT. LBS.
(20 N·m)

Typical gasoline V8 exhaust manifold with hot air shrouds

3. Loosen the alternator and remove its lower bracket.

4. Jack up your car and support it with jack stands.

5. Disconnect the crossover pipe from both manifolds.

NOTE: *On models with air conditioning it may be necessary to remove the compressor, and tie it out of the way. Do not disconnect the compressor lines.*

6. Remove the manifold bolts and remove the manifold(s). Some models have lock tabs on the front and rear manifold bolts which must be removed before removing the bolts. These tabs can be bent with a drift pin.

7. Installation is the reverse of removal.

350 Diesel V8

LEFT SIDE

1. Remove the air cleaner and cover the air crossover with a protective plate, screen or cover.

2. Remove the lower generator bracket.

3. Jack up the truck and safely support it with jackstands.

4. Remove the exhaust pipe at the manifold flange.

5. Lower the truck.

6. Remove the exhaust manifold from above.

7. Reverse the above procedure to install. Torque the manifold nuts and bolts according to the illustration.

RIGHT SIDE

1. Jack up the truck and safely support it with jackstands.

2. Disconnect the exhaust pipe at the manifold flange.

3. Remove the manifold.

4. Reverse the above procedure to install, torquing the manifold bolts according to the accompanying illustration.

R. H. EXHAUST MANIFOLD

WASHER

25 FT. LBS.

BOLT
LOCK

GASKET

FUEL PUMP

WASHER

30 FT. LBS.

BOLT
LOCK

25 FT. LBS.

L. H. EXHAUST MANIFOLD

25 FT. LBS.

AFTER BOLTS ARE TORQUED TO
SPECIFICATIONS, BEND LOCK
TABS AROUND BOLT HEADS

25 FT. LBS.

350 diesel exhaust manifold installation

379 Diesel V8

RIGHT SIDE

1. Disconnect the batteries.

2. Jack up the truck and safely support it with jackstands.

3. Disconnect the exhaust pipe from the manifold flange and lower the truck.

4. Disconnect the glow plug wires.

5. Remove the air cleaner duct bracket.

6. Remove the glow plug wires.

7. Remove the manifold bolts and remove the manifold.

8. To install, reverse the above procedure and torque the bolts to 25 ft. lbs.

LEFT SIDE

1. Disconnect the batteries.

2. Remove the dipstick tube nut, and remove the dipstick tube.

3. Disconnect the glow plug wires.

4. Jack up the truck and safely support it with jackstands.

5. Disconnect the exhaust pipe at the manifold flange.

6. Remove the manifold bolts. Remove the manifold from underneath the truck.

7. Reverse the above procedure to install. Start the manifold bolts while the truck is jacked up first. Torque the bolts to 25 ft. lbs.

250 and 292 six cylinder head bolt torque sequence

Cylinder Head

REMOVAL AND INSTALLATION

Inline Six Cylinder

1. Drain the cooling system and remove the air cleaner assembly. Disconnect the PCV hose.

2. Tag and disconnect the throttle linkage at the carburetor. Tag and disconnect the fuel line, vacuum lines, and any electrical connections at the carburetor.

3. Remove the top radiator hose, and the battery ground strap. Disconnect the wires from the temperature sending unit, leaving the harness clear of the clips on the rocker cover.

4. Disconnect the coil wires after tagging them, and remove the coil. Tag and disconnect the spark plug wires from the plugs.

5. Remove the intake and exhaust manifolds.

6. Remove the rocker arm cover. Back off the rocker arm nuts, and pivot the rocker arms so the pushrods will clear.

7. Take a piece of heavy cardboard and cut 12 holes in it the same diameter as the pushrod stem. Number the holes in relation to the pushrods being removed. This cardboard holder will keep the pushrods in order (and hopefully out of harms way) while they are out of the engine. Remove the pushrods one at a time.

NOTE: *Pushrods MUST be returned to their original locations.*

8. Remove the cylinder head bolts one at a time, and mark them or keep them in order,

as they should go back in their original locations. You may need a flex bar on your socket, or a piece of pipe on your ratchet, as the bolts are under a lot of torque.

9. Remove the cylinder head, along with the gasket. If the head seems tuck to the block, gently tap around the edge of the head with a rubber mallet until the joint breaks. NEVER pry between the head and block as you may gouge one or the other. Often it is necessary to carefully scrape the top of the engine block and the cylinder head to completely remove the gasket.

10. Clean the bottom of the head and top of block throughly before reinstalling the head. Place a new gasket over the dowel pin in the top of the block.

NOTE: *Different types of head gaskets are available. If you are using a steel-asbestos composition gasket, do not use gasket sealer.*

11. Lower the cylinder head carefully onto the block, over the dowel pins and gasket.

12. Coat the heads and threads of the cylinder head bolts with sealing compound, GM part No. 1052080 or equivalent, and install finger tight.

13. Tighten the head bolts gradually in three stages, following the sequence illustrated, to the specification listed under "Torque Specifications."

14. Install the pushrods in the exact location from which they were removed. Make sure they are seated in their lifter sockets.

15. Swing the rocker arms over into the cor-

Small-block V8 cylinder head torque sequence

Big-block V8 torque sequence

Typical Chevrolet gasoline V8 cylinder head installation, all engines similar rect position. Tighten the rocker arms until all pushrod play is taken up.

16. Install the manifold assembly, using new gaskets. Torque the manifold(s) to the specified torque.

17. Reverse the remainder of the removal procedure for installation. Adjust the valves, following the procedure in this chapter. Use a new gasket or high-temperature sealer when installing the rocker arm cover.

Gasoline V8s

1. Disconnect the battery.
2. Drain the coolant and save it if still fresh.
3. Remove the air cleaner.
4. Remove the air conditioning compressor, *but do not disconnect any A/C lines.* Secure the compressor to one side.
5. Disconnect the AIR hose at the check valve.
6. Remove the intake manifold.
7. When removing the right cylinder head, loosen the alternator belt, disconnect the wiring and remove the alternator.
8. When removing the left cylinder head, remove the dipstick, power steering pump and air pump if so equipped.
9. Label the spark plug wires and disconnect them.
10. Disconnect the exhaust manifold from the head being removed.
11. Remove the valve cover. Scribe the rocker arms with an identifying mark for reassembly; *it is important that the rocker assembly is reinstalled in the same position as it was removed.* Remove the rocker arm bolts, rocker arms and pivots.
12. Take a piece of heavy cardboard and cut 16 holes (or 8 holes if you are only removing one head) in it the same diameter as the pushrod stem. Number the holes in relation to the pushrods being removed. This cardboard holder will keep the pushrods in order (and hopefully out of harm's way) while they are out of the engine. Remove the pushrods.

NOTE: *Pushrods MUST be returned to their original locations.*

13. On models equipped with power brakes, it is necessary to disconnect the brake booster and turn it sideways to remove the No. 7 pushrod.
14. Remove the cylinder head bolts, and remove the cylinder head and gasket. If the head seems stuck to the block, gently tap around the edge of the head with a rubber mallet until the joint breaks.
15. Install in the reverse order of removal. NEW head gasket(s) should be used. On all engines, the head bolts should be dipped in clean oil before installing. Tighten all head bolts in

sequence to 60–70 ft. lbs., then again in sequence to the specified torque (see Torque Specifications chart in this chapter). Re-torque the bolts after the engine is warmed up.

NOTE: *When installing the intake manifold remember to use new gaskets.*

Diesel Engines

1. Remove the intake manifold, using the procedure outlined above.
2. Remove the rocker arm cover(s), after removing any accessory brackets which interfere with cover removal.
3. Disconnect and label the glow plug wiring.
4. If the right cylinder head is being removed, remove the ground strap from the head.
5. On the 350, remove the rocker arms bolts, the bridged pivots, the rocker arms, and the pushrods, keeping all the parts in order so that they can be returned to their original positions. On the 379, remove the rocker shaft assemblies. It is a good practice to number or mark the parts to avoid interchanging them.
6. Remove the fuel return lines from the nozzles.
7. Remove the exhaust manifold(s), using the procedure outlined earlier in this chapter.
8. On the 350, remove the engine block drain plug on the side of the engine from which the cylinder head is being removed.
9. Remove the head bolts. Remove the cylinder head.

350 diesel cylinder head torque sequence

379 diesel cylinder head installation and torque sequence

10. To install, first clean the mating surfaces thoroughly. Install new head gaskets on the engine block. Do NOT coat the gaskets with any sealer on either engine. The gaskets have a special coating that eliminates the need for sealer. The use of sealer will interfere with this coating and cause leaks. Install the cylinder head onto the block.

11. Clean the head bolts thoroughly. On the 350, dip the bolts in clean engine oil and install them into the cylinder block until the heads of the bolts lightly contact the cylinder head. On the 379, the left rear head bolt must be installed into the head prior to head installation. Coat the threads of the 379 cylinder head bolts with sealing compound (GM part #1052080 or equivalent) before installation.

12. On the 350, tighten the bolts in the illustrated sequence to 100 ft. lbs. When all the bolts have been tightened to this figure, begin the tightening sequence again, and torque all bolts to 130 ft. lbs. On the 379, tighten each bolt gradually in the sequence shown until the final torque specified (100 ft. lbs.) is met.

13. Install the engine block drain plugs on the 350, the exhaust manifolds, the fuel return lines, the glow plug wiring, and the ground strap for the right cylinder head.

14. Install the valve train assembly. Refer to the "Diesel Engine Rocker Arm Replacement" in this chapter for the valve lifter bleeding procedures.

15. Install the intake manifold.

16. Install the valve covers. These are sealed with RTV-type silicone sealer instead of a gasket. See the "Valve Cover" procedure for proper sealer application. Install the cover to the head within 10 minutes, while the sealer is still wet.

Valves and Springs

REMOVAL AND INSTALLATION

Cylinder Heads Removed

1. Remove the head(s), and place on a clean surface.

2. Using a suitable spring compressor (for pushrod-type overhead valve engines), compress the valve spring and remove the valve spring cap key. Release the spring compressor and remove the valve spring and cap (and valve rotator on some engines).

NOTE: *Use care in removing the keys; they are easily lost.*

3. Remove the valve seals from the intake valve guides. Throw these old seals away, as you'll be installing new seals during reassembly.

4. Slide the valves out of the head from the combustion chamber side.

5. Make a holder for the valves out of a piece

Typical valve train, all gasoline engines similar

Use care not to lose the valve keys when compressing the valve springs. A dab of grease on the keys holds them in place during installation

Compressing valve springs on the 379 diesel V8

VALVE SPRING COMPRESSOR

Removing the valve springs

of wood or cardboard, as outlined for the push-rods in gasoline engine "Cylinder Head Removal." Make sure you number each hole in the cardboard to keep the valves in proper order. Slide the valves out of the head from the combustion chamber side; they MUST be installed as they were removed.

Cylinder Head(s) Installed

It is often not necessary to remove the cylinder head(s) in order to service the valve train. Such is the case when valve seals need to be replaced. Valve seals can be easily replaced with the head(s) on the engine; the only special equipment needed for this job are an air line adapter (sold in most auto parts stores), which screws a compressed air line into the spark plug hole of the cylinder on which you are working, and a valve spring compressor. A source of compressed air is needed, of course.

J-5892

J-23590
ADAPTER

Replacing valve stem seals using compressed air, an adapter for the spark plug holes, and a valve spring compressor

1. Remove the valve cover as previously detailed.
2. Remove the spark plug, rocker arm and push rod on the cylinder(s) to be serviced.
3. Install the air line adapter (GM tool #J-23590 or equivalent) into the spark plug hole. Turn on the air compressor to apply compressed air into the cylinder. This keeps the valves up in place.
NOTE: *Set the regulator of the air compressor at least 50 pounds to ensure adequate pressure.*
4. Using the valve spring compressor, compress the valve spring and remove the valve keys and keepers, the valve spring and damper.
5. Remove the valve stem seal.
6. To reassemble, oil the valve stem and new seal. Install a new seal over the valve stem. Set the spring, damper and keeper in place. Compress the spring. Coat the keys with grease to hold them onto the valve stem and install the keys, making sure they are seated fully in the keeper. Reinstall the valve cover after adjusting the valves, as outlined in this chapter.

INSPECTION

Inspect the valve faces and seats (in the head) for pits, burned spots and other evidence of poor seating. If a valve face is in such bad shape that the head of the valve must be ground in order to true up the face, discard the valve because the sharp edge will run too hot. The correct angle for valve faces is 45 degrees. We recommend the re-facing be done at a reputable machine shop.

Check the valve stem for scoring and burned spots. If not noticeably scored or damaged, clean the valve stem with solvent to remove all gum and varnish. Clean the valve guides using solvent and an expanding wire-type valve guide cleaner. If you have access to a dial indicator for measuring valve stem-to-guide clearance, mount it so that the stem of the indicator is at 90° to the valve stem, and as close to the valve guide as possible. Move the valve off its seat, and measure the valve guide-to-stem clearance by rocking the stem back and forth to actuate the dial indicator. Measure the valve stems using a micrometer, and compare to specifications to determine whether stem or guide wear is responsible for the excess clearance. If a dial indicator and micrometer are not available to you, take your cylinder head and valves to a reputable machine shop for inspection.

Some of the engines covered in this guide are equipped with valve rotators, which double as valve spring caps. In normal operation the rotators put a certain degree of wear on the tip of the valve stem; this wear appears as con-

FOR DIMENSIONS, REFER TO SPECIFICATIONS

CHECK FOR BENT STEM

DIAMETER

VALVE FACE ANGLE

1/32″ MINIMUM

THIS LINE PARALLEL WITH VALVE HEAD

Critical valve dimensions

DIAL INDICATOR

VALVE STEM

Checking the valve stem-to-guide clearance

Cutaway of a knurled valve guide

Proper Tip Pattern	No Rotation Pattern	Partial Rotation Tip Pattern
Rotator Functioning Properly	Replace Rotator and check rotation	Replace Rotator and check rotation

Valve stem wear

centric rings on the stem tip. However, if the rotator is not working properly, the wear may appear as straight notches or "X" patterns across the valve stem tip. Whenever the valves are removed from the cylinder head, the tips should be inspected for improper pattern, which could indicate valve rotator problems. Valve stem tips will have to be ground flat if rotator patterns are severe.

Valve Guides

The engines covered in this guide use integral valve guides; that is, they are a part of the cylinder head and cannot be replaced. The guides can, however, be reamed oversize if they are found to be worn past an acceptable limit. Occasionally, a valve guide bore will be oversize as manufactured. These are marked on the inboard side of the cylinder heads on the machined surface just above the intake manifold.

If the guides must be reamed (this service is available at most machine shops), then valves with oversize stems must be fitted. Valves are usually available in 0.001, 0.003 and 0.005 in. stem oversizes. Valve guides which are not excessively worn or distorted may, in some cases, be knurled rather than reamed. Knurling is a process in which the metal on the valve guide

bore is displaced and raised, thereby reducing clearance. Knurling also provides excellent oil control. The option of knurling rather than reaming valve guides should be discussed with a reputable machinist or engine specialist.

Cylinder Head
CLEANING AND INSPECTION
Gasoline Engines

NOTE: *Any diesel cylinder head work should be handled by a reputable machine shop familiar with diesel engines. Disassembly, valve lapping, and assembly can be completed by following the gasoline engine procedures.*

Once the complete valve train has been removed from the cylinder head(s), the head itself can be inspected, cleaned and machined (if necessary). Set the head(s) on a clean work space, so the combustion chambers are facing up. Begin cleaning the chambers and ports with a hardwood chisel or other non-metallic tool (to avoid nicking or gouging the chamber, ports, and especially the valve seats). Chip away the

Use a wire brush and electric drill to remove carbon from the combustion chambers and exhaust ports

major carbon deposits, then remove the remainder of carbon with a wire brush fitted to an electric drill.

NOTE: *Be sure that the carbon is actually removed, rather than just burnished.*

After decarbonizing is completed, take the head(s) to a machine shop and have the head "hot tanked." In this process, the head is lowered into a hot chemical bath that very effectively cleans all grease, corrosion, and scale from all internal and external head surfaces. Also have the machinist check the valve seats and re-cut them if necessary. When you bring the clean head(s) home, place them on a clean surface. Completely clean the entire valve train with solvent.

CHECKING FOR HEAD WARPAGE

Lay the head down with the combustion chambers facing up. Place a straight-edge across the gasket surface of the head, both diagonally and straight across the center. Using a flat feeler gauge, determine the clearance at the center of the straight-edge. If warpage exceeds .003 in. in a 6 in. span, or .006 in. over the total length, the cylinder head must be resurfaced (which is akin to planing a piece of wood). Resurfacing can be performed at most machine shops.

NOTE: *When resurfacing the cylinder head(s) of V8 engines, the intake manifold*

Have the valve seat concentricity checked at a machine shop

mounting position is altered, and must be corrected by machining a proportionate amount from the intake manifold flange.

LAPPING THE VALVES

When valve faces and seats have been re-faced and re-cut, or if they are determined to be in good condition, the valves must be "lapped in" to ensure efficient sealing when the valve closes against the seat.

1. Invert the cylinder head so that the combustion chambers are facing up.

2. Lightly lubricate the valve stems with clean oil, and coat the valve seats with valve grinding compound. Install the valves in the head as numbered.

3. Attach the suction cup of a valve lapping tool to a valve head. *You'll probably have to moisten the cup to securely attach the tool to the valve.*

4. Rotate the tool between the palms, changing position and lifting the tool often to

1 & 3 CHECK DIAGONALLY
2 CHECK ACROSS CENTER

Check the cylinder head mating surface for warpage with a precision straight edge

Lapping the valves by hand

Home-made valve lapping tool

Check the valve spring free length and squareness

prevent grooving. Lap the valve until a smooth, polished seat is evident (you may have to add a bit more compound after some lapping is done).

5. Remove the valve and tool, and remove ALL traces of grinding compound with solvent-soaked rag, or rinse the head with solvent.

NOTE: *Valve lapping can also be done by fastening a suction cup to a piece of drill rod in a hand "eggbeater" type drill. Proceed as above, using the drill as a lapping tool. Due to the higher speeds involved when using the hand drill, care must be exercised to avoid grooving the seat. Lift the tool and change direction of rotation often.*

Valve Springs

HEIGHT AND PRESSURE CHECK

1. Place the valve spring on a flat, clean surface next to a square.

2. Measure the height of the spring, and rotate it against the edge of the square to measure distortion (out-of-roundness). If spring height varies between springs by more than $\frac{1}{16}$ in. or if the distortion exceeds $\frac{1}{16}$ in. replace the spring.

A valve spring tester is needed to test spring test pressure, so the valve springs must usually be taken to a professional machine shop for this test. Spring pressure at the installed and compressed heights is checked, and a tolerance of plus or minus 5 lbs. is permissible on the springs covered in this guide.

VALVE INSTALLATION

NOTE: *For installing new valve stem seals without removing the cylinder head(s), see the procedure under "Valves and Springs— Cylinder Head(s) Installed" earlier in this chapter.*

Have the valve spring test pressure checked professionally

Check valve spring installed height

New valve seals must be installed when the valve train is put back together. Certain seals slip over the valve stem and guide boss, while others require that the boss be machined. In some applications Teflon guide seals are avail-

Installing valve stem seals

Diesel 350 V8 valve location

6.2L (379) diesel valve arrangement

able. Check with a machinist and/or automotive parts store for a suggestion on the proper seals to use.

NOTE: *Remember that when installing valve seals, a small amount of oil must be able to pass the seal to lubricate the valve guides; otherwise, excessive wear will result.*

To install the valves and rocker assembly:

1. Lubricate the valve stems with clean engine oil.

2. Install the valves in the cylinder head, one at a time, as numbered.

3. Lubricate and position the seals and valve springs, again a valve at a time.

4. Install the spring retainers, and compress the springs.

5. With the valve key groove exposed above the compressed valve spring, wipe some wheel bearing grease around the groove. This will retain the keys as you release the spring compressor.

6. Using needlenose pliers (or your fingers), place the keys in the key grooves. The grease should hold the keys in place. Slowly release the spring compressor; the valve cap or rotator will raise up as the compressor is released, retaining the keys.

7. Install the rocker assembly, and install the cylinder head(s).

VALVE ADJUSTMENT

All gasoline and diesel engines in this guide use hydraulic valve lifters, which require no periodic maintenance or adjustment. However, in

Valve location, Chevrolet-built 305, 350 V8

the event of cylinder head removal or any operation that requires disturbing or removing the rocker arms, the rocker arms have to be adjusted.

Inline Six Cylinder

PRELIMINARY ADJUSTMENT

1. After rocker arm or cylinder head disassembly, proceed as follows:

2. Remove the valve cover if it is not already removed.

3. Remove the distributor cap and crank the engine until the rotor points at number one plug terminal in the cap. It is easier to do this if you mark the location of number one plug wire before you remove the cap. The points should be open (pre-1975) and timing marks should be aligned. (the 0° mark on the timing tab). Number one cylinder should now be at TDC.

4. With the number one cylinder of the six in this position, adjust: Intake valves 1,2,4, and exhaust valves 1,3,5 (numbered from the front of the engine). The adjustment is performed as follows: Turn the adjusting nut until all lash is removed from this particular valve train. This is determined by checking pushrod sideplay while turning the adjusting nut. When all play has been removed, turn the adjusting nut *one more turn.* This will place the lifter plunger in the center of its travel.

5. Crank the engine over through one complete revolution until number six cylinder is in the firing (TDC, timing pointer at 0°) position. At this point, you can adjust the following valves

on the 250 six: Intake valves 3,5, and 6; exhaust valves 2,4 and six.

6. After the engine is running, readjust the valves following the procedure under "Engine Running." Install the valve covers using new gaskets or sealer.

ENGINE RUNNING ADJUSTMENT

1. Run the engine until normal operating temperature is attained. Remove the valve cover. To prevent oil splashing, install oil deflector clips, which are available at auto supply stores.

2. With the engine at idle, back off the rocker arm nut until the rocker arm begins to clatter.

3. Slowly tighten the rocker arm nut until the clatter just stops. This is zero lash.

4. Tighten the nut another quarter turn and then wait about ten seconds until the engine is running smoothly. Tighten the nut another quarter turn and wait another ten seconds. Repeat the procedure until the nut has been turned down one full turn from zero lash.

NOTE: *Pausing ten seconds each time allows the lifter to adjust itself. Failing to pause might cause interference between the intake valve and the piston top causing internal damage and bent pushrods.*

5. Adjust the remaining valves in the same manner.

6. Replace the valve cover.

Typical valve adjustment, all except 6.2L diesel

V8 Including 350 Diesel

NOTE: *After the 350 diesel valves are adjusted (following rocker arm or cylinder head removal and installation), the hydraulic lifters must be bled down. See the lifter bleeding procedure under "Rocker Arm Removal and Installation—350 Diesel" earlier in this chapter.*

1. Remove the valve covers and crank the engine until the mark on the damper aligns with the TDC or 0° mark on the timing tab and the engine is in the No. 1 firing position. This can be determined by placing the fingers on the No. 1 cylinder valves as the marks align. If the valves do not move, it is in the No. 1 firing position. If the valves move, it is in the No. 6 firing position and the crankshaft should be rotated one more revolution to the No. 1 firing position.

2. Back out the adjusting nut until lash is felt at the pushrod, then turn the adjusting nut in until all lash is removed. This can be determined by checking pushrod end-play while turning the adjusting nut. When all play has been removed, turn the adjusting nut in 1 full turn.

3. With the engine in the No. 1 firing position, the following valves can be adjusted:
  - V8-Exhaust—1,3,4,8
  - V8-Intake—1,2,5,7

4. Crank the engine 1 full revolution until the marks are again in alignment. This is the No. 6 firing position. The following valves can now be adjusted:
  - V8-Exhaust—2,5,6,7
  - V8-Intake—3,4,6,8

5. Install the valve covers using new gaskets or sealer as required.

Valve Lifters

REMOVAL AND INSTALLATION

Inline Six

1. Remove the rocker arm cover.

2. Loosen the rocker arm until you can rotate it away from the pushrod, giving clearance to the top of the pushrod.

3. Remove the pushrod. If you are replacing all of the lifters, it is wise to make a pushrod holder as mentioned under "Cylinder Head Removal." This will help keep the pushrods in order, as they MUST go back in their original positions.

4. Remove the pushrod covers on the side of the block.

5. Remove the lifter(s). A hydraulic lifter removal tool (GM part #J-3049 or equivalent) is available at dealers and most parts stores, and is quite handy for this procedure.

6. Before installing new lifters, all sealer coating must be removed from the inside. This can be done with kerosene or carburetor cleaning solvent. Also, the new lifters *must* be primed before installation, as *dry lifters will seize when the engine is started.* Submerge the lifters in clean engine oil and work the lifter plunger up and down.

Valve lifter, exploded view

Roller lifter, all 379 and 1981 350 diesel engines. 1980 and earlier 350s have a conventional lifter

Removing hydraulic valve lifter

7. Install the lifter(s) and pushrod(s) into the cylinder block in their original positions.

8. Pivot the rocker arm back into its original position. With the lifter on the base circle of the camshaft (valve closed), tighten the rocker arm nut to 20 ft. lbs. Do not over torque. You will have to rotate the crankshaft to do the individual valves.

9. Replace the pushrod covers using new gaskets. Replace the rocker arm cover, using a new gasket or sealer.

Gasoline V8 and 350 Diesel

NOTE: *Valve lifters and pushrods should be kept in order so they can be reinstalled in*

Diesel valve lifter guide and retainer

their original position. Some engines will have both standard size and .010 in. oversize valve lifters as original equipment. The oversize lifters are etched with an "O" on their sides; the cylinder block will also be marked with an "O" if the oversize lifter is used.

1. Remove the intake manifold and gasket.

2. Remove the valve covers, rocker arm assemblies and pushrods.

3. If the lifters are coated with varnish, apply carburetor cleaning solvent to the lifter body. The solvent should dissolve the varnish in about 10 minutes.

4. Remove the lifters. On diesels, remove the lifter retainer guide bolts, and remove the guides. A special tool for removing lifters is available, and is helpful for this procedure.

5. New lifter MUST be primed before installation, *as dry lifters will seize when the engine is started.* Submerge the lifters in clean engine oil and work the lifter plunger up and down.

6. Install the lifters and pushrods into the cylinder block in their original order. On diesels, install the lifter retainer guide.

7. Install the intake manifold gaskets and manifold.

8. Position the rocker arms, pivots and bolts on the cylinder head.

9. Install the valve covers, connect the spark plug wires and install the air cleaner.

379 Diesel

1. Remove the valve covers as previously detailed.

2. Remove the rocker shaft assemblies.

3. Remove the cylinder head(s).

4. Remove the guide clamps and guide plates. It may be necessary to use mechanical fingers to remove the guide plates.

379 diesel lifer and guide plate access through hole

Applying sealer front cover mounting on the 250 inline six

CUT THIS PORTION
FROM NEW SEAL

Oil pan front seal modification

Cut the oil pan seal flush with the front of the block

CRANKSHAFT DAMPER
CENTERING TOOL

Installing timing cover, inline six cylinder

5. Using GM tool #J-29834 or another suitable lifter removal tool and a magnet, remove the lifter(s) through the access in the block.

6. Coat the lifters with clean engine oil before installation. If installing new lifters, they must be primed first by working the lifter plunger while the lifter is submerged in clean kerosene or diesel fuel. *Lifters that have not been primed will seize when the engine is started.*

7. Install the lifters in their original positions in the block. A lifter installation tool can be fabricated out of welding rod or similar gauge wire and may help.

8. Install the lifter guide plate and guide plate clamp. The crankshaft must be turned two full rotations (720°) after assembly of the lifter guide plate clamp to insure free movement of the lifters in the guide plates.

9. Install the remainder of components in reverse order of removal.

NOTE: *The pushrods must be installed with their painted ends facing "UP".*

Timing Chain Cover and Front Oil Seal

REMOVAL AND INSTALLATION

Inline Six

1. Drain the engine coolant, remove the radiator hoses, and remove the radiator.

2. Remove the fan belt and any accessory belts. Remove the fan pulley.

3. A harmonic balancer puller is necessary to pull the balancer. Install the puller and remove the balancer.

4. Remove the two screws which attach the oil pan to the front cover. Remove the screws which attach the front cover to the block. Do not remove the cover yet.

5. Before the front cover is removed, it is necessary to cut the oil pan front seal. Pull the cover forward slightly.

6. Using a sharp knife or razor knife, cut the oil pan front seal flush with the cylinder block on both sides of the cover.

7. Remove the front cover and the attached portion of oil pan front seal. Remove the front cover gasket from the block.

8. To install the front cover, first obtain an oil pan front seal. Cut the tabs from the new seal.

9. Install the seal in the front cover, pressing the tips into the holes provided in the cover. Coat the mating area of the front cover with a room temperature vulcanizing (RTV) sealer first.

10. Coat the new front cover gasket with sealer and install it on the cover.

11. Apply a ⅛ in. bead of RTV sealer to the joint formed at the oil pan and cylinder block.

12. Install the front cover.

13. Install the harmonic balancer. Make sure the front cover seal is positioned evenly around the balancer. If you do not have access to a balancer installation tool (and you probably don't), you can either fabricate one using the illustration as a guide, or you can tap the balancer on using a brass or plastic mallet. If you use the last method, *make sure the balancer goes on evenly.*

14. The rest of the installation is in the reverse order of removal.

Gasoline V8s

1. Drain the cooling system.

2. Remove the crankshaft pulley and damper. Remove the water pump. Remove the screws holding the timing case cover to the block and remove the cover and gaskets.

3. Use a suitable tool to pry the old seal out of the front face of the cover.

Removing harmonic balancer from end of crankshaft, all gasoline engines similar

Seal installation with the cover removed

Front cover/water pump assembly, gasoline V8s

Seal installation with cover installed, V8s

TRIM PAN GASKET FLUSH WITH BLOCK

R.T.V. SEALER

Sealer application

GUIDE PAN SEAL WITH SMALL SCREW DRIVER

Guiding front cover into place. Be careful seal remains in place

4. Install the new seal so that the open end is toward the inside of the cover.

NOTE: *Coat the lip of the new seal with oil prior to installation.*

5. Check that the timing chain oil slinger is in place against the crankshaft sprocket.

6. Apply sealer to the front cover as shown in the accompanying illustration. Install the cover carefully onto the locating dowels.

7. Tighten the attaching screws to 6–8 ft. lbs.

350 Diesel

1. Drain the cooling system and disconnect the radiator hoses.

2. Remove all belts, fan and pulley, crankshaft pulley and balancer, using a balancer puller.

CAUTION: *The use of any other type of puller, such as a universal claw type which pulls on the outside of the hub, can destroy the balancer. The outside ring of the balancer is bonded in rubber to the hub. Pulling on the outside will break the bond. The timing mark is on the outside ring. If it is suspected that the bond is broken, check that the center of the keyway is 16° from the center of the timing slot. In addition, there are chiseled aligning marks between the weight and the hub.*

3. Unbolt and remove the cover, timing indicator and water pump.

4. It may be necessary to grind a flat on the cover for gripping purposes.

5. Grind a chamfer on one end of each dowel pin.

6. Cut the excess material from the front end of the oil pan gasket on each side of the block.

7. Clean the block, oil pan and front cover mating surfaces with solvent.

8. Trim about ⅛ in. off each end of a new front pan seal.

9. Install a new front cover gasket on the block and a new seal in the front cover.

10. Apply sealer to the gasket around the coolant holes.

11. Apply sealer to the block at the junction of the pan and front cover.

12. Place the cover on the block and press down to compress the seal. Rotate the cover left and right and guide the pan seal into the cavity using a small screwdriver. Oil the bolt threads and install two bolts to hold the cover in place. Install both dowel pins (chamfered end first), then install the remaining front cover bolts.

CHAMFER

Grinding chamfer o 350 diesel dowel pin

Trimming pan seal with razor blade

45 N·m
(33 FT. LBS.)

BAFFLE

45 N·m
(33 FT. LBS.)

FRONT COVER

VIEW A

BAFFLE

45 N·m
(33 FT. LBS.)

PUMP
DRIVE
GEAR

CAM CHAIN

SEALING
SURFACE

Front cover assembly showing sealer application, 379 diesel

13. Apply a lubricant, compatible with rubber, on the balancer seal surface.

14. Install the balancer and bolt. Torque the bolt to 200–300 ft. lbs.

15. Install the other parts in the reverse order of removal.

379 Diesel

1. Drain the cooling system.

2. Remove the water pump as outlined elsewhere in this chapter.

3. Rotate the crankshaft to align the marks on the injection pump driven gear and the camshaft gear as shown in the illustration.

4. Scribe a mark aligning the injection pump flange and the front cover.

5. Remove the crankshaft pulley and torsional damper.

6. Remove the front cover-to-oil pan bolts (4).

7. Remove the two fuel return line clips.

8. Remove the injection pump drive gear. Remove the injection pump retaining nuts from the front cover.

9. Remove the baffle. Remove the remaining cover bolts, and remove the front cover.

10. If the front cover oil seal is to be replaced, it can now be pried out of the cover with a suitable prying tool. Press the new seal into the cover evenly.

NOTE: *The oil seal can also be replaced with the front cover installed. Remove the torsional damper first, then pry the old seal out*

PUMP GEAR

25 N·m
(20 FT. LBS.)

ALIGNMENT
MARK

CAM GEAR

Injection pump and cam gear alignment, 379 diesel

of the cover using a suitable prying tool. Use care not to damage the surface of the crankshaft. Install the new seal evenly into the cover and install the damper.

11. To install the front cover, first clean both sealing surfaces until all traces of old sealer are gone. Apply a 2mm bead of sealant (GM sealant #1052357 or equivalent) to the sealing surface as shown in the illustration. Apply a bead of RTV-type sealer to the bottom portion of the front cover which attaches to the oil pan. Install the front cover.

12. Install the baffle.

13. Install the injection pump, making sure the scribe marks on the pump and front cover are aligned.

14. Install the injection pump driven gear, making sure the marks on the cam gear and pump gear are aligned. Be sure the dowel pin and the three holes on the pump flange are also aligned.

15. Install the fuel line clips, the front cover-to-oil pan bolts, and the torsional damper and crankshaft pulley. Torque the pan bolts to 4–7 ft. lbs., and the damper bolt to 140–162 ft. lbs.

205 N·m
(150 FT. LBS.)

379 diesel crankshaft (torsional) damper. Note key

Timing Gears

REMOVAL AND INSTALLATION

Inline Sixes

The camshaft in these engines is gear-driven, unlike the chain-driven cams in V8s. The removal of the timing gear requires removal of the camshaft.

1. After the cam is removed, place the camshaft and gear in an arbor press and remove the gear from the cam. Many well-equipped machine shops have this piece of equipment if you need the gear pressed off.

2. Installation is in the reverse order of removal. The clearance between the camshaft and the thrust plate should be 0.001–0.005 in. on both engines. If less than 0.0015 in. clearance exists, the spacer ring should be replaced. If more than 0.005 in. clearance, the thrust plate should be replaced.

CAUTION: *The thrust plate must be positioned so that the Woodruff key in the shaft does not damage it when the shaft is pressed out of the gear. Support the hub of the gear or the gear will be seriously damaged.*

NOTE: *The six-cylinder crankshaft gear may*

Access holes in the inline six cylinder camshaft gear for the camshaft thrust plate screws

Crankshaft gear puller, inline sixes

Inline six-cylinder timing gear alignment

Installing camshaft timing gear and checking thrust plate end clearances, inline sixes

be removed with a gear puller while in place on the block.

Timing Chain

REMOVAL AND INSTALLATION

Gasoline V8

To replace the chain, remove the radiator core, water pump, the harmonic balancer and the crankcase front cover. This will allow access to the timing chain. Crank the engine until the

Gasoline V8 timing sprocket alignment, 1970–78

#1 CYLINDER AT T.D.C.

#6 CYLINDER AT T.D.C.

Timing sprocket alignment, 1979 and later gasoline V8s

Gasoline V8 crankshaft sprocket removal

timing marks on both sprockets are nearest each other and in line between the shaft centers. Then take out the three bolts that hold the camshaft gear to the camshaft. This gear is a light press fit on the camshaft and will come off easily. It is located by a dowel.

The chain comes off with the camshaft gear.

A gear puller will be required to remove the crankshaft gear.

Without disturbing the position of the engine, mount the new crankshaft gear on the shaft, and mount the chain over the camshaft gear. Arrange the camshaft gear in such a way that the timing marks will line up between the shaft centers and the camshaft locating dowel will enter the dowel hole in the cam sprocket.

Place the cam sprocket, with its chain mounted over it, in position on the front of the car and pull up with the three bolts that hold it to the camshaft.

After the gears are in place, turn the engine two full revolutions to make certain that the

timing marks are in correct alignment between the shaft centers.

End-play of the camshaft is zero.

350 Diesel

1. Remove the crankshaft pulley, the harmonic balancer and the front cover as previously detailed.

2. Align the timing marks on the cam and crankshaft.

3. Remove the oil slinger and camshaft sprocket retaining nut.

4. Remove the crankshaft sprocket. The sprocket-to-crankshaft fit is such that a puller may be necessary. If possible, the crankshaft key should be removed before using the puller. If this is not possible, align the puller so that the fingers of the tool do not overlap the end of the key when the sprocket is removed. The keyway is machined only partway in the crankshaft sprocket, and breakage can occur if the sprocket is improperly removed.

5. Remove the timing chain and camshaft sprocket.

6. The fuel pump eccentric is behind the crankshaft sprocket, and may be removed if necessary.

7. Install the key in the crankshaft, if removed. Install the fuel pump eccentric, if removed.

8. Install the camshaft sprocket, crankshaft sprocket, and the timing chain together, with the timing marks aligned. Tighten the camshaft sprocket retaining bolt to 65 ft. lbs.

NOTE: *When the two timing marks are in alignment and closest together, the No. 6 cylinder is at TDC. To obtain TDC for No.*

65 FT. LBS.

ALIGN TIMING MARKS

350 diesel timing sprocket alignment

1 cylinder, slowly rotate the crankshaft one full revolution. This will move the camshaft sprocket timing mark to the top. No. 1 cylinder will then be at TDC.

9. Install the oil slinger.

10. The injection pump must be re-timed. See Chapter 2.

11. Install the front cover, harmonic balancer, and the crankshaft pulley.

379 Diesel

1. Remove the front cover as previously detailed.

2. Remove the bolt and washer attaching the camshaft gear. Remove the injection pump gear.

3. Remove the camshaft sprocket, timing chain, and crankshaft sprocket as a unit.

4. To install, the cam sprocket, timing chain and crankshaft sprocket as a unit, aligning the timing marks on the sprockets as shown in the illustration.

5. Rotate the crankshaft 360° so that the camshaft gear and the injection pump gear are aligned as shown in the illustration (accompanying the 379 Diesel Front Cover Removal Procedure).

6. Install the front cover as previously detailed. The injection pump must be retimed since the timing chain assembly was removed. See Chapter 2 for this procedure.

379 diesel timing chain assembly

Camshaft

REMOVAL AND INSTALLATION

Inline Six Cylinder

1. Remove the grille. Remove the radiator hoses and remove the radiator.

2. Remove the timing gear cover.

3. Remove the valve cover and gasket, loosen all the rocker arm nuts, and pivot the rocker arms clear of the pushrods.

4. Remove the distributor and the fuel pump.

5. Remove the pushrods. Remove the coil

and then remove the side cover. Remove the valve lifters.

6. Remove the two camshaft thrust plate retaining screws by working through the holes in the camshaft gear.

7. Remove the camshaft and gear assembly by pulling it out through the front of the block.

8. If either the camshaft or the camshaft gear is being renewed, the gear must be pressed off the camshaft. The replacement parts must be assembled in the same way. When placing the gear on the camshaft, press the gear onto the shaft until it bottoms against the gear spacer ring. The end clearance of the thrust plate should be .001 to .005 in.

9. Pre-lube the camshaft lobes with clean engine oil and then install the camshaft assembly in the engine. Be careful not to damage the bearings.

10. Turn the crankshaft and the camshaft

Checking camshaft gear runout, inline six engines

Removing camshaft. Slowly turn the cam as you remove it

gears so that the timing marks align. Push the camshaft into position and install and torque the thrust plate bolts to 7 ft. lbs.

11. Check camshaft and crankshaft gear run-out with a dial indicator. Camshaft gear run-out should not exceed .004 in. and crankshaft gear run-out should not be above .003 in.

12. Using a dial indicator, check the backlash at several points between the camshaft and crankshaft gear teeth. Backlash should be .004–.006 in.

13. Install the timing gear cover. Install the harmonic balancer.

14. Install the valve lifters and the pushrods. Install the side cover. Install the coil and the fuel pump.

15. Install the distributor and set the timing. Pivot the rocker arms over the pushrods and adjust the valves.

16. Install the radiator, hoses and grille.

Gasoline V8

1. Disconnect the battery.

2. Drain and remove the radiator.

3. Disconnect the fuel line at the fuel pump. Remove the pump on 1978 and later models.

4. Disconnect the throttle cable and the air cleaner.

5. Remove the alternator belt, loosen the alternator bolts and move the alternator to one side.

6. Remove the power steering pump from its brackets and move it out of the way.

7. Remove the air conditioning compressor from its brackets and move the compressor out of the way without disconnecting the lines.

8. Disconnect the hoses from the water pump.

9. Disconnect the electrical and vacuum connections.

10. Mark the distributor as to location in the block. Remove the distributor.

11. Raise the car and drain the oil pan.

12. Remove the exhaust crossover pipe and starter motor.

13. Disconnect the exhaust pipe at the manifold.

14. Remove the harmonic balancer and pulley.

15. Support the engine and remove the front motor mounts.

16. Remove the flywheel inspection cover.

17. Remove the engine oil pan.

18. Support the engine by placing wooden blocks between the exhaust manifolds and the front crossmember.

19. Remove the engine front cover.

20. Remove the valve covers.

21. Remove the intake manifold, oil filler pipe, and temperature sending switch.

22. Mark the lifters, pushrods, and rocker arms as to location so that they may be installed in the same position. Remove these parts.

23. If the car is equipped with air conditioning, discharge the A/C system and remove the condenser.

24. Remove the fuel pump eccentric, camshaft gear, oil slinger, and timing chain. Remove the camshaft thrust plate (on front of camshaft) if equipped.

25. Carefully remove the camshaft from the engine.

26. Inspect the shaft for signs of excessive wear or damage.

27. Liberally coat camshaft and bearings with heavy engine oil or engine assembly lubricant and insert the cam into the engine.

28. Align the timing marks on the camshaft and crankshaft gears. See Timing Chain Replacement for details.

29. Install the distributor using the locating marks made during removal. If any problems are encountered, see "Distributor Installation."

30. To install, reverse the removal procedure but pay attention to the following points:

    a. Install the timing indicator before installing the power steering pump bracket.

    b. Install the flywheel inspection cover after installing the starter.

    c. Replace the engine oil and radiator coolant.

350 Diesel

NOTE: *If equipped with air conditioning, the system must be discharged by an air conditioning specialist before the camshaft is removed. The condenser must also be removed from the car.*

Removal of the camshaft also requires removal of the injection pump drive and driven gears, removal of the intake manifold, disassembly of the valve lifters, and retiming of the injection pump.

Camshaft and oil gallery plugs at rear of block

350 diesel injection pump drive gear installation

1. Disconnect the negative battery cables.
2. Remove the intake manifold and gasket and the front and rear intake manifold seals. Refer to the intake manifold removal and installation procedure.
3. Remove the balancer pulley and the balancer. See "Caution" under diesel engine front cover removal and installation, above. Remove the engine front cover using the appropriate procedure.
4. Remove the valve covers. Remove the rocker arms, pushrods and valve lifters; see the procedure earlier in this section. Be sure to keep the parts in order so that they may be returned to their original positions.
5. Remove the camshaft sprocket retaining bolt, and remove the timing chain and sprockets, using the procedure outlined earlier.
6. Position the camshaft dowel pin at the 3 o'clock position.
7. Push the camshaft rearward and hold it there, being careful not to dislodge the oil gallery plug at the rear of the engine. Remove the fuel injection pump drive gear by sliding it from the camshaft while rocking the pump driven gear.
8. To remove the fuel injection pump driven gear, remove the pump adapter, the snap ring, and remove the selective washer. Remove the driven gear and spring.
9. Remove the camshaft by sliding it out the front of the engine. Be extremely careful not to allow the cam lobes to contact any of the bearings, or the journals to dislodge the bearings during camshaft removal. *Do not force the camshaft, or bearing damage will result.*
10. If either the injection pump drive or driven gears are to be replaced, replace both gears.
11. Coat the camshaft and the cam bearings with a heavy-weight engine oil, GM lubricant #1052365 or the equivalent.
12. Carefully slide the camshaft into position in the engine.
13. Fit the crankshaft and camshaft sprock-

ets, aligning the timing marks as shown in the timing chain removal and installation procedure, above. Remove the sprockets without disturbing the timing.
14. Install the injection pump driven gear, spring, shim, and snap ring. Check the gear end play. If the end play is not within 0.002–0.006 in. on V8s through 1979, and .002 to .015 in. on 1980 and later, replace the shim to obtain the specified clearance. Shims are available in 0.003 in. increments, from 0.080 to 0.115 in.
15. Position the camshaft dowel pin at the 3 o'clock position. Align the zero marks on the pump drive gear and pump driven gear. Hold the camshaft in the rearward position and slide the pump drive gear onto the camshaft. Install the camshaft bearing retainer.
16. Install the timing chain and sprockets, making sure the timing marks are aligned.
17. Install the lifters, pushrods and rocker arms. See "Rocker Arm Replacement, Diesel Engine" for lifter bleed down procedures. *Failure to bleed down the lifters could bend valves when the engine is turned over.*
18. Install the injection pump adapter and injection pump. See the appropriate sections under "Fuel System" above for procedures.
19. Install the remaining components in the reverse order of removal.

379 Diesel

1. Disconnect both batteries.
2. Jack up the truck and safely support it with jackstands.
3. Drain the cooling system, including the block.
4. Disconnect the exhaust pipes at the manifolds. Remove the fan shroud.
5. Lower the truck.
6. Remove the radiator and fan.
7. Remove the vacuum pump, and remove the intake manifold as previously detailed.
8. Remove the injection pump and lines as outlined in Chapter 4. Make sure you cap all injection lines to prevent dirt from entering the system, and tag the lines for later installation.
9. Remove the water pump.
10. Remove the injection pump drive gear.
11. Scribe a mark aligning the line on the injection pump flange to the front cover.
12. Remove the injection pump from the cover.
13. Remove the power steering pump and the generator and lay them aside.
14. If the truck is equipped with air conditioning, remove the compressor (with the lines attached) and position it out of the way.
CAUTION: *DO NOT disconnect the air*

conditioning lines unless you are familiar with this procedure.

15. Remove the valve covers.

16. Remove the rocker shaft assemblies and pushrods. Place the pushrods in order in a rack (easily by punching holes in a piece of heavy cardboard and numbering the holes) so that they can be installed in correct order.

17. Remove the thermostat housing and the crossover from the cylinder heads.

18. Remove the cylinder heads as previously detailed, with the exhaust manifolds attached.

19. Remove the valve lifter clamps, guide plates and valve lifters. Place these parts in a rack so they can be installed in the correct order.

20. Remove the front cover.

21. Remove the timing chain assembly.

22. Remove the fuel pump.

23. Remove the camshaft retainer plate.

24. If the truck is equipped with air conditioning, remove the A/C condenser mounting bolts. Have an assistant help in lifting the condenser out of the way.

25. Remove the camshaft by carefully sliding it out of the block.

INSTALLATION

Whenever a new camshaft is installed, GM recommends replacing all the valve lifters, as well as the oil filter. The engine oil must be changed. These measures will help ensure proper wear characteristics of the new camshaft.

1. Coat the camshaft lobes with "Molykote®" or an equivalent lube. Liberally lube the camshaft journals with clean engine oil and install the camshaft carefully.

2. Install the camshaft retainer plate and torque the bolts to 20 ft. lbs.

3. Install the fuel pump.

4. Install the timing chain assembly as previously detailed.

5. Install the front cover as previously detailed.

6. Install the valve lifters, guide plates and clamps, and rotate the crankshaft as previously outlined so that the lifters are free to travel.

7. Install the cylinder heads.

8. Install the pushrods in their original order. Install the rocker shaft assemblies, then install the valve covers.

9. Install the injection pump to the front cover, making sure the lines on the pump and the scribe line on the front cover are aligned.

10. Install the injection pump driven gear, making sure the gears are aligned. Retime the injection pump.

11. Install the remaining engine components in the reverse order of removal. Make the necessary adjustments (drive belts, etc.) and refill the cooling system.

CAMSHAFT INSPECTION

Completely clean the camshaft with solvent, paying special attention to cleaning the oil holes. Visually inspect the cam lobes and bearing journals for excessive wear. If a lobe is questionable, have the cam checked at a reputable machine shop; if a journal or lobe is worn, the camshaft must be reground or replaced. Also have the camshaft checked for straightness on a dial indicator.

NOTE: *If a cam journal is worn, there is a good chance that the bushings are worn.*

Camshaft Bearings

REMOVAL AND INSTALLATION

If excessive camshaft wear is found, or if the engine is being completely rebuilt, the camshaft bearings should be replaced.

NOTE: *The front and rear bearings should be removed last, and installed first. Those bearings act as guides for the other bearings and pilot.*

1. Drive the camshaft rear plug from the block.

2. Assemble the removal puller with its shoulder on the bearing to be removed. Gradually tighten the puller nut until the bearing is removed.

3. Remove the remaining bearings, leaving the front and rear for last. To remove these, reverse the position of the puller, so as to pull the bearings towards the center of the block. Leave the tool in this position, pilot the new front and rear bearings on the installer, and pull them into position.

4. Return the puller to its original position and pull the remaining bearings into position.

Camshaft bearing removal and installation tool

NOTE: *You must make sure that the oil holes of the bearings and block align when installing the bearings. If they don't align, the camshaft will not get proper lubrication and may seize or at least be seriously damaged. To check for correct oil hole alignment, use a piece of brass rod with a 90° bend in the end as shown in the illustration. Check all oil hole openings; the wire must enter each hole, or the hole is not properly aligned.*

5. Replace the camshaft rear plug, and stake it into position. On the 379 diesel, coat the outer diameter of the new plug with GM sealant #1052080 or equivalent, and install it flush to $\frac{1}{32}$ in. deep.

Installing front cam bearing on 379 diesel. Bearing tool is illustrated inset. Method is similar on other engines

Make this simple tool to check camshaft bearing oil hole alignment

Pistons and Connecting Rods

REMOVAL AND INSTALLATION

Before removing the pistons, the top of the cylinder bore must be examined for a ridge. A ridge at the top of the bore is the result of nor-

RIDGE CAUSED BY CYLINDER WEAR

CYLINDER WALL

TOP OF PISTON

Ridge formed by piston rings at the top of their travel

mal cylinder wear, caused by the piston rings only travelling so far up the bore in the course of the piston stroke. The ridge can be felt by hand; it must be removed before the pistons are removed.

A ridge reamer is necessary for this operation. Place the piston at the bottom of its stroke, and cover it with a rag. Cut the ridge away with the ridge reamer, using extreme care to avoid cutting too deeply. Remove the rag, and remove the cuttings that remain on the piston with a magnet and a rag soaked in clean oil. *Make sure the piston top and cylinder bore are absolutely clean before moving the piston.*

1. Remove intake manifold and cylinder head or heads.

2. Remove oil pan.

3. Remove oil pump assembly if necessary.

4. Match-mark the connecting rod cap to the connecting rod with a scribe; each cap must be reinstalled on its proper rod in the proper direction. Remove the connecting rod bearing cap and the rod bearing. Number the top of each piston with silver paint or a felt-tip pen for later assembly.

5. Cut lengths of $\frac{3}{8}$ in. diameter hose to use as rod bolt guides. Install the hose over the threads of the rod bolts, to prevent the bolt threads from damaging the crankshaft journals and cylinder walls when the piston is removed.

6. Squirt some clean engine oil onto the cylinder wall from above, until the wall is coated. Carefully push the piston and rod assembly up and out of the cylinder by tapping on the bottom of the connecting rod with a wooden hammer handle.

7. Place the rod bearing and cap back on the connecting rod, and install the nuts temporarily. Using a number stamp or punch, stamp the cylinder number on the side of the connecting rod and cap; this will help keep the

Match the connecting rods to their caps with a scribe mark

USE A SHORT PIECE OF 3/8" HOSE AS A GUIDE

Connecting rod bolt guide

Match the connecting rods to their cylinders with a number stamp

proper piston and rod assembly on the proper cylinder.

NOTE: *On all V8s, starting at the front the right bank cylinders are 2-4-6-8 and the left bank 1-3-5-7.*

8. Remove remaining pistons in similar manner.

On all gasoline engines, the notch on the piston will face the front of the engine for assembly. The chamfered corners of the bearing caps should face toward the front of the left bank and toward the rear of the right bank, and the boss on the connecting rod should face toward the front of the engine for the right bank and to the rear of the engine on the left bank.

On the 350 diesel, install each piston and rod in its respective cylinder bore so the valve depression in the top of the piston is towards the inner side of the engine. On the forward half of the engine (cylinders 1,2,3,4) the large valve depression goes to the front. On the rear half, the large valve depression goes to the rear. On the 379 diesel, install the piston and rod assemblies with the rod bearing tang slots on the side opposite the camshaft.

Push the piston and rod out with a hammer handle

PISTON AND CONNECTING ROD. INSTALL IN CYLINDER BORES #5, #6, #7 & #8

42 FT. LBS.

LARGER VALVE DEPRESSION

CONNECTING ROD BEARING

CONNECTING ROD CAP

PISTON AND CONNECTING ROD. INSTALL IN CYLINDER BORES #1, #2, #3 & #4

350 diesel piston positioning

On various engines, the piston compression rings are marked with a dimple, a letter "T", a letter "O," "GM" or the word "TOP" to identify the side of the ring which must face toward the top of the piston.

Piston Ring and Wrist Pin

REMOVAL

Some of the engines covered in this guide utilize pistons with pressed-in wrist pins; these must be removed by a special press designed for this purpose. Other pistons have their wrist pins secured by snap rings, which are easily removed with snap ring pliers. Separate the piston from the connecting rod.

A piston ring expander is necessary for removing piston rings without damaging them; any other method (screwdriver blades, pliers, etc.) usually results in the rings being bent, scratched or distorted, or the piston itself being damaged. When the rings are removed, clean the ring grooves using an appropriate ring groove cleaning tool, using care not to cut too deeply. Thoroughly clean all carbon and varnish from the piston with solvent.

CAUTION: *Do not use a wire brush or caustic solvent (acids, etc.) on pistons.*

Inspect the pistons for scuffing, scoring,

250 and 292 six cylinder piston and rod positioning

Small-block V8 piston and rod positioning

Big-block (Mark IV) V8 piston and rod positioning

Piston ring and wrist pin assembly, 350 diesel shown. Gas engines similar

cracks, pitting, or excessive ring groove wear. If these are evident, the piston must be replaced.

The piston should also be checked in relation to the cylinder diameter. Using a telescoping gauge and micrometer, or a dial gauge, measure the cylinder bore diameter perpendicular (90°) to the piston pin, 2½ in. below the cylinder block deck (surface where the block mates with the heads). Then, with the micrometer, measure the piston perpendicular to its

Remove the piston rings

Cylinder bore measuring points

Install the piston lock-rings, if used

Measuring cylinder bore with a dial gauge

Clean the piston ring grooves using a ring groove cleaner

Cylinder bore cross-hatching after honing

Measuring the piston prior to fitting

larger piston to bring clearance to within specifications. If this is not possible, obtain the first oversize piston and hone (or if necessary, bore) the cylinder to size. Generally, if the cylinder bore is tapered .005 in. or more or is out-of-round .003 in. or more, it is advisable to rebore for the smallest possible oversize piston and rings.

After measuring, mark pistons with a felt-tip pen for reference and for assembly.

NOTE: *Cylinder honing and/or boring should be performed by a reputable, professional*

wrist pin on the skirt. The difference between the two measurements is the piston clearance. If the clearance is within specifications or slightly below (after the cylinders have been bored or honed), finish honing is all that is necessary. If the clearance is excessive, try to obtain a slightly *mechanic with the proper equipment. In some cases, "clean-up" honing can be done with the cylinder block in the car, but most excessive honing and all cylinder boring must be done with the block stripped and removed from the car.*

PISTON RING END GAP

Piston ring end gap should be checked while the rings are removed from the pistons. Incorrect end gap indicates that the wrong size rings are being used; *ring breakage could occur.*

Compress the piston rings to be used in a cylinder, one at a time, into that cylinder. Squirt clean oil into the cylinder, so that the rings and the top 2 inches of cylinder wall are coated. Using an inverted piston, press the rings approximately 1 in. below the deck of the block (on diesels, measure ring gap clearance with

the ring positioned at the *bottom* of ring travel in the bore). Measure the ring end gap with a feeler gauge, and compare to the "Ring Gap" chart in this chapter. Carefully pull the ring out of the cylinder and file the ends squarely with a fine file to obtain the proper clearance.

PISTON RING SIDE CLEARANCE CHECK AND INSTALLATION

Check the pistons to see that the ring grooves and oil return holes have been properly cleaned. Slide a piston ring into its groove, and check the side clearance with a feeler gauge. On gasoline engines, make sure you insert the gauge between the ring and its lower land (lower edge of the groove), because any wear that occurs forms a step at the inner portion of the lower land. On diesels, insert the gauge between the ring and the *upper* land. If the piston grooves have worn to the extent that relatively high steps exist on the lower land, the piston grooves have worn to the extent that relatively high steps exist on the lower land, the piston should be replaced, because these will interfere with the operation of the new rings and ring clearances will be excessive. Piston rings are not fur-

Checking piston ring end gap with a feeler gauge

ENGINE LEFT   ENGINE FRONT   ENGINE RIGHT

2-4-6-8 cyl.

1-3-5-7 cyl.

"SMALL V8"

"A" OIL RING SPACER GAP
(Tang in Hole or Slot within Arc)

"B" OIL RING RAIL GAPS

"C" 2ND COMPRESSION RING CAP

"D" TOP COMPRESSION RING GAP

Ring gap location—all gasoline engines. Inline sixes same on all cylinders also

Checking piston ring side clearance

379 diesel piston ring gap positioning

nished in oversize widths to compensate for ring groove wear.

Install the rings on the piston, *lowest ring first*, using a piston ring expander. There is a high risk of breaking or distorting the rings, or scratching the piston, if the rings are installed by hand or other means.

Position the rings on the piston as illustrated; *spacing of the various piston ring gaps is crucial to proper oil retention and even cylinder wear.* When installing new rings, refer to the installation diagram furnished with the new parts.

Connecting Rod Bearings

Connecting rod bearings for the engines covered in this guide consist of two halves or shells which are interchangeable in the rod and cap. When the shells are placed in position, the ends extend slightly beyond the rod and cap surfaces so that when the rod bolts are torqued the shells will be clamped tightly in place to insure positive seating and to prevent turning. A tang holds the shells in place.

NOTE: *The ends of the bearing shells must never be filed flush with the mating surface of the rod and cap.*

If a rod bearing becomes noisy or is worn so that its clearance on the crank journal is sloppy, a new bearing of the correct undersize must be selected and installed since there is a provision for adjustment.

CAUTION: *Under no circumstances should the rod end or cap be filed to adjust the bearing clearance, nor should shims of any kind be used.*

Inspect the rod bearings while the rod assemblies are out of the engine. If the shells are scored or show flaking, they should be replaced. If they are in good shape check for proper clearance on the crank journal (see below). Any scoring or ridges on the crank journal means the crankshaft must be replaced, or reground and fitted with undersized bearings.

CHECKING BEARING CLEARANCE AND REPLACING BEARINGS

NOTE: *Make sure connecting rods and their caps are kept together, and that the caps are installed in the proper direction.*

Replacement bearings are available in standard size, and in undersizes for reground crankshafts. Connecting rod-to-crankshaft bearing clearance is checked using Plastigage® at either the top or bottom of each crank journal. The Plastigage® has a range of .001 in. to .003 in.

1. Remove the rod cap with the bearing shell. Completely clean the bearing shell and the crank

FLATTENED GAGING PLASTIC

Checking rod bearing clearance with Plastigage® or equivalent

TANG

GM M 400

8943

UNDERSIZE STAMP IN THOUSANDS

Undersize marks are stamped on the bearing shells. Tangs fit in the notches in the rod and cap

journal, and blow any oil from the oil hole in the crankshaft; Plastigage® is soluble in oil.

2. Place a piece of Plastigage® lengthwise along the bottom center of the lower bearing shell, then install the cap with shell and torque the bolt or nuts to specification. DO NOT turn the crankshaft with Plastigage® in the bearing.

3. Remove the bearing cap with the shell. The flattened Plastigage® will be found sticking to either the bearing shell or crank journal. *Do not remove it yet.*

4. Use the scale printed on the Plastigage® envelope to measure the flattened material at its widest point. The number within the scale which most closely corresponds to the width of the Plastigage® indicates bearing clearance in thousandths of an inch.

5. Check the specifications chart in this chapter for the desired clearance. It is advisable to install a new bearing if clearance exceeds .003 in.; however, if the bearing is in good condition and is not being checked because of

bearing noise, bearing replacement is not necessary.

6. If you are installing new bearings, try a standard size, then each undersize in order until one is found that is within the specified limits when checked for clearance with Plastigage®. Each undersize shell has its size stamped on it.

7. When the proper size shell is found, clean off the Plastigage®, oil the bearing thoroughly, reinstall the cap with its shell and torque the rod bolt nuts to specification.

NOTE: *With the proper bearing selected and the nuts torqued, it should be possible to move the connecting rod back and forth freely on the crank journal as allowed by the specified connecting rod end clearance. If the rod cannot be moved, either the rod bearing is too far undersize or the rod is misaligned.*

Piston and Connecting Rod

ASSEMBLY AND INSTALLATION

Install the connecting rod to the piston, making sure piston installation notches and any marks on the rod are in proper relation to one another. Lubricate the wrist pin with clean engine oil, and install the pin into the rod and piston assembly, either by hand or by using a wrist pin press as required. Install snap rings if equipped, and rotate them in their grooves to make sure they are seated. To install the piston and connecting rod assembly:

1. Make sure connecting rod big-end bearings (including end cap) are of the correct size and properly installed.

2. Fit rubber hoses over the connecting rod bolts to protect the crankshaft journals, as in the "Piston Removal" procedure. Coat the rod bearings with clean oil.

3. Using the proper ring compressor, insert the piston assembly into the cylinder so that the notch in the top of the piston faces the front of the engine (this assumes that the dimple(s) or other markings on the connecting rods are in correct relation to the piston notch(s)).

4. From beneath the engine, coat each crank journal with clean oil. Pull the connecting rod, with the bearing shell in place, into position against the crank journal.

5. Remove the rubber hoses. Install the bearing cap and cap nuts and torque to specification.

NOTE: *When more than one rod and piston assembly is being installed, the connecting rod cap attaching nuts should only be tightened enough to keep each rod in position until all have been installed. This will ease the installation of the remaining piston assemblies.*

RING COMPRESSOR

Using a wooden hammer handle, tap the piston down through the ring compressor and into the cylinder

Checking connecting rod side clearance with a feeler gauge. Use a small pry bar to carefully spread the connecting rods

6. Check the clearance between the sides of the connecting rods and the crankshaft using a feeler gauge. Spread the rods slightly with a screwdriver to insert the gauge. If clearance is below the minimum tolerance, the rod may be machined to provide adequate clearance. If clearance is excessive, substitute an unworn rod, and recheck. If clearance is still outside specifications, the crankshaft must be welded and reground, or replaced.

7. Replace the oil pump if removed and the oil pan.

8. Install the cylinder head(s) and intake manifold.

Crankshaft and Main Bearings

CRANKSHAFT REMOVAL

1. Drain the engine oil and remove the engine from the car. Mount the engine on a work

stand in a suitable working area. Invert the engine, so the oil pan is facing up.

2. Remove the engine front (timing) cover.
3. Remove the timing chain and gears.
4. Remove the oil pan.
5. Remove the oil pump.
6. Stamp the cylinder number on the machined surfaces of the bolt bosses of the connecting rods and caps for identification when reinstalling. If the pistons are to be removed eventually from the connecting rod, mark the cylinder number on the pistons with silver paint or felt-tip pen for proper cylinder identification and cap-to-rod location.
7. Remove the connecting rod caps. Install lengths of rubber hose on each of the connecting rod bolts, to protect the crank journals when the crank is removed.
8. Mark the main bearing caps with a number punch or punch so that they can be reinstalled in their original positions.
9. Remove all main bearing caps.
10. Note the position of the keyway in the crankshaft so it can be installed in the same position.
11. Install rubber bands between a bolt on each connecting rod and oil pan bolts that have been reinstalled in the block (see illustration). This will keep the rods from banging on the block when the crank is removed.
12. Carefully lift the crankshaft out of the block. The rods will pivot to the center of the engine when the crank is removed.

MAIN BEARING INSPECTION AND REPLACEMENT

Like connecting rod big-end bearings, the crankshaft main bearings are shell-type inserts that do not utilize shims and cannot be adjusted. The bearings are available in various standard and undersizes; if main bearing clearance is found to be too sloppy, a new bearing (both upper and lower halves) is required.

NOTE: *Factory-undersized crankshafts are marked, sometimes with a "9" and/or a large spot of light green paint; the bearing caps also will have the paint on each side of the undersized journal.*

Generally, the lower half of the bearing shell (except No. 1 bearing) shows greater wear and fatigue. If the lower half only shows the effects of normal wear (no heavy scoring or discoloration), it can usually be assumed that the upper half is also in good shape; conversely, if the lower half is heavily worn or damaged, both halves should be replaced. *Never replace one bearing half without replacing the other.*

CHECKING CLEARANCE

Main bearing clearance can be checked both with the crankshaft in the car and with the engine out of the car. If the engine block is still in the car, the crankshaft should be supported both front and rear (by the damper and to remove clearance from the upper bearing.) Total clearance can then be measured between the lower bearing and journal. If the block has been removed from the car, and is inverted, the crank will rest on the upper bearings and the total clearance can be measured between the lower

350 diesel crankshaft, exploded view. Gasoline V8 engines and 6.2L (379) diesel similar configuration

1. Rubber hose
2. #4 rod
3. #3 rod
4. Oil pan bolt
5. Note overlap of adjacent rods
6. Rubber bands

Crankshaft removal showing hose lengths on rod bolts

bearing and journal. Clearance is checked in the same manner as the connecting rod bearings, with Plastigage®.

NOTE: *Crankshaft bearing caps and bearing shells should NEVER be filed flush with the cap-to-block mating surface to adjust for wear in the old bearings. Always install new bearings.*

1. If the crankshaft has been removed, install it (block removed from car). If the block is still in the car, remove the oil pan and oil pump. Starting with the rear bearing cap, remove the cap and wipe all oil from the crank journal and bearing cap.

2. Place a strip of Plastigage® the full width of the bearing (parallel to the crankshaft), on the journal.

CAUTION: *Do not rotate the crankshaft while the gaging material is between the bearing and the journal.*

3. Install the bearing cap and evenly torque the cap bolts to specification.

4. Remove the bearing cap. The flattened Plastigage® will be sticking to either the bearing shell or the crank journal.

5. Use the graduated scale on the Plastigage® envelope to measure the material at its widest point.

NOTE: *If the flattened Plastigage® tapers towards the middle or ends, there is a difference in clearance indicating the bearing or journal has a taper, low spot or other irregularity. If this is indicated, measure the crank journal with a micrometer.*

6. If bearing clearance is within specifications, the bearing insert is in good shape. Replace the insert if the clearance is not within specifications. *Always replace both upper and lower inserts as a unit.*

7. Standard, .001 in. or .002 in. undersize bearings should produce the proper clearance. If these sizes still produce too sloppy a fit, the crankshaft must be reground for use with the next undersize bearing. Recheck all clearances after installing new bearings.

8. Replace the rest of the bearings in the same manner. After all bearings have been checked, rotate the crankshaft to make sure there is no excessive drag. When checking the No. 1 main bearing, loosen the accessory drive belts (engine in car) to prevent a tapered reading with the Plastigage.®

MAIN BEARING REPLACEMENT

Engine out of Car

1. Remove and inspect the crankshaft.

2. Remove the main bearings from the bearing saddles in the cylinder block and main bearing caps.

Home-made bearing roll-out pin

Roll-out pin installed for removing upper half of main bearing

3. Coat the bearing surfaces of the new, correct size main bearings with clean engine oil and install them in the bearing saddles in the block and in the main bearing caps.

4. Install the crankshaft. See "Crankshaft Installation."

Engine in Car

1. With the oil pan, oil pump and spark plugs removed, remove the cap from the main bearing needing replacement and remove the bearing from the cap.

2. Make a bearing roll-out pin, using a bent cotter pin as shown in the illustration. Install the end of the pin in the oil hole in the crankshaft journal.

3. Rotate the crankshaft clockwise as viewed from the front of the engine. This will roll the upper bearing out of the block.

4. Lube the new upper bearing with clean engine oil and insert the plain (unnotched) end between the crankshaft and the indented or notched side of the block. Roll the bearing into place, making sure that the oil holes are aligned. Remove the roll pin from the oil hole.

5. Lube the new lower bearing and install the main bearing cap. Install the main bearing

cap, making sure it is positioned in proper direction with the matchmarks in alignment.

6. Torque the main bearing cap bolts to specification.

NOTE: *See "Crankshaft Installation" for thrust bearing alignment.*

CRANKSHAFT END PLAY AND INSTALLATION

When main bearing clearance has been checked, bearings examined and/or replaced, the crankshaft can be installed. Thoroughly clean the upper and lower bearing surfaces, and lube them with clean engine oil. Install the crankshaft and main bearing caps.

Dip all main bearing cap bolts in clean oil, and torque all main bearing caps, excluding the thrust bearing cap, to specifications (see the "Crankshaft and Connecting Rod" chart in this chapter to determine which bearing is the thrust bearing). Tighten the thrust bearing bolts finger tight. To align the thrust bearing, pry the crankshaft the extent of its axial travel several times, holding the last movement toward the front of the engine. Add thrust washers if re-

quired for proper alignment. Torque the thrust bearing cap to specifications.

To check crankshaft end-play, pry the crankshaft to the extreme rear of its axial travel, then to the extreme front of its travel. Using a feeler gauge, measure the end-play at the front of the rear main bearing. End play may also be measured at the thrust bearing. Install a new rear main bearing oil seal in the cylinder block and main bearing cap. Continue to reassemble the engine.

Oil Pan

REMOVAL AND INSTALLATION

Gasoline Engines

NOTE: *Pan removal may be easier if the engine is turned to No. 1 cylinder firing position. This positions the crankshaft in the path of least resistance for pan removal.*

1. Disconnect the negative battery terminal.

2. Remove the fan shroud-to-radiator tie bar screws.

3. Remove the air cleaner and disconnect the throttle linkage.

4. Raise the truck and support it on jackstands.

5. Drain the oil.

6. Remove the lower flywheel housing, re-

Measuring crankshaft end play at the front of the rear main bearing

Oil pan installation; gaskets and seals may differ among engines

Aligning the crankshaft thrust bearing

move the shift linkage attaching bolt and swing it out of the way, and disconnect the exhaust crossover pipe at the engine.

7. Remove the front engine mounting bolts.

8. Raise the engine by placing a jack under the crankshaft pulley mounting.

CAUTION: *On air conditioned cars, place a support under the right-side of the transmission before raising the engine. If you don't do this, the engine and transmission will cock to the right due to the weight of the air conditioning equipment.*

9. Remove the oil pan bolts and remove the pan.

10. Installation is the reverse of removal. Use gasket sealer and new gaskets (if gaskets are used). Tighten the pan bolts to 14 ft. lbs.

Diesel Engines

1. Remove the vacuum pump and drive (with A/C) or the oil pump drive (without A/C).

2. Disconnect the batteries and remove the dipstick.

3. Remove the upper radiator support and fan shroud.

4. Raise and support the truck. Drain the oil.

5. Remove the flywheel cover.

6. Disconnect the exhaust and crossover pipes.

7. Remove the oil cooler lines at the filter base.

8. Remove the starter assembly. Support the engine with a jack.

9. Remove the engine mounts from the block.

10. Raise the front of the engine and remove the oil pan.

11. Installation is the reverse of removal.

Oil Pump

REMOVAL AND INSTALLATION

Gasoline and Diesel

The oil pump is mounted to the bottom of the block and is accessible only by removing the oil pan.

On all engines, including diesel, remove the oil pan, then unbolt and remove the oil pump and screen as an assembly. On the inline sixes, remove the flange mounting bolts and nut from the elongated number 6 main bearing cap bolt, then remove the pump.

To install, align the oil pump drive shaft on six cylinder engines to match with the distributor tang and position the pump flange over the distributor lower bushing. Install the pump mounting bolts. On V8 engines, insert the drive shaft extension through the opening in the main bearing cap until the shaft mates with the dis-

tributor drive gear. *You may have to turn the drive shaft extension* one way or the other to get the two to mesh. Position the pump on the cap and install the attaching bolts. Install the oil pans on all engines.

Oil pump installation, typical

Oil pump exploded view

CHECK CLEARANCE BETWEEN STRAIGHT EDGE & GASKET SURFACE

Checking oil pump end clearance

OVERHAUL

Inline Sixes

1. With the pump removed from the block, remove the 4 cover attaching screws, the cover, idler gear and drive gear and shaft.

2. Remove the pressure regulator valve and related valve parts.

CAUTION: *Do not disturb the oil pickup pipe on the screen or body.*

3. Inspect the pump body for excessive wear or cracks, and inspect the pump gears for excessive wear, cracks or damage. Check the shaft for looseness in the housing; it should not be a sloppy fit. Check the inside of the cover for wear that would permit oil to leak past the ends of the gears. Remove any debris from the surface of the screen, and check the screen for damage. Check the pressure regulator valve plunger for fit in the pump body.

4. Assemble the pump as previously described. Tighten the cover screws to 8 ft. lbs.

V8 Including Diesel

1. Remove the oil pump drive shaft extension.

2. Remove the cotter pin, spring and the pressure regulator valve.

NOTE: *Place your thumb over the pressure regulator bore before removing the cotter pin, as the spring is under pressure.*

3. Remove the oil pump cover attaching screws and remove the oil pump cover and gasket. Clean the pump in solvent or kerosene, and wash out the pick-up screen.

4. Remove the drive gear and idler gear from the pump body.

5. Check the gears for scoring and other damage. Install the gears if in good condition, or replace them if damaged. Check gear end clearance by placing a straight edge over the gears and measure the clearance between the straight edge and the gasket surface with a feeler gauge. End clearance for the 350 diesel is .0005 in. to .0075 in.; and for gasoline V8s is .002 in. to .0065 in. If end clearance is excessive, check

for scores in the cover that would bring the total clearance over the specs.

6. Check gear side clearance by inserting the feeler gauge between the gear teeth and the side wall of the pump body. Clearance should be between .002 in. and .005 in.

7. Pack the inside of the pump completely with petroleum jelly. DO NOT use engine oil. The pump MUST be primed this way or it won't produce any oil pressure when the engine is started.

8. Install the cover screws and tighten alternately and evenly to 8 ft. lbs.

9. Position the pressure regulator valve into the pump cover, closed end first, then install the spring and retaining pin.

NOTE: *When assembling the drive shaft extension to the drive shaft, the end of the extension nearest the washers must be inserted into the drive shaft.*

10. Insert the drive shaft extension through the opening in the main bearing cap and block until the shaft mates into the distributor drive gear.

11. Install the pump onto the rear main bearing cap and install the attaching bolts. Torque the bolts to 35 ft. lbs.

12. Install the oil pan.

Rear Main Oil Seal

REMOVAL AND INSTALLATION

Inline Sixes

The rear main bearing oil seal, both halves, can be removed without removal of the crankshaft. *Always replace the upper and lower halves together.*

1. Remove the oil pan.

2. Remove the rear main bearing cap.

3. Remove the old oil seal from its groove in the cap, prying from the bottom using a small screwdriver.

4. Coat a new seal-half completely with clean engine oil, and insert it into the bearing cap groove. Keep oil off of the parting line surface, as this surface is treated with glue. Gradually push the seal with a hammer handle until the seal is rolled into place.

5. To remove the upper half of the old seal, use a small hammer and a soft, blunt punch to tap one end of the oil seal out until it protrudes far enough to be removed with needlenose pliers. Push the new seal into place with the lip toward the front of the engine.

6. Install the bearing cap and torque the bolts to a loose fit—*do not final torque*. With the cap fitted loosely, move the crankshaft first to the rear and then to the front with a rubber mallet. This will properly position the thrust bearing.

FEELER GAUGE

Measuring oil pump side clearance, typical

Torque the bearing cap to a final torque of 65 ft. lbs. Install the oil pan.

Gasoline V8s

The rear main bearing seal on these engines can also be replaced without removing the crankshaft. Extreme care should be exercised when installing the seal to protect the sealing bead (located in the channel on the outside diameter of the seal). Use of a seal installation tool, as described in the above procedures, is recommended.

1. Remove the oil pan, oil pump and rear main bearing cap.

2. Remove the old oil seal from the cap by carefully prying from the bottom with a small pry bar or old screwdriver.

3. Using a small hammer and brass pin punch, tap on one end of the oil upper seal until it protrudes far enough on the other side to be removed with needle nose pliers.

4. Clean all sealant and foreign material from the bearing cap, crankshaft journal and all mating surfaces using a solvent. Inspect the components for nicks, scratches and burrs.

Typical rear main seal half, bearing cap side

Make a rear main bearing seal packing tool from a wooden dowel. The upper tool dimensions are for engines up to 400 cu. in.; the bottom is for 454s

Remove the seal half from the bearing cap without scratching the cap

Removing the upper seal half from the block

Packing the oil seal

CUT OFF SECTION OF
OLD ROPE SEAL

USE BEARING CAP
AS HOLDING FIXTURE

Cutting the lower (bearing cap) seal ends

APPLY
SEALANT
TO SHADED
AREAS ONLY

Sealing the bearing cap before final torquing. Apply
a bit of oil to the crank journal just before installing
the cap

5. Coat the lips of the new upper seal with clean engine oil, keeping the oil off of the seal mating ends.

6. Position the tip of the oil seal mating tool between the crank journal and the seal seat in the cylinder block. Position the new seal between the crankshaft and the tip of the tool so that the seal bead contacts the tip of the tool.

NOTE: *Make sure the oil seal lip is positioned toward the front of the engine.*

7. Rotate the seal around the crank journal, using the tool as a "shoehorn" to protect the seal bead from the sharp corner of the seal seat surface in the cylinder block.

NOTE: *Keep the installation tool in position until the seal is properly positioned with both ends flush with the block.*

8. Remove the tool, being careful not to withdraw the seal.

9. Thoroughly lubricate the new lower seal-half (for the bearing cap) with clean engine oil. Install the seal into the cap, feeding the seal in with thumb and finger.

10. Install the bearing cap onto the cylinder block, using sealant applied to the cap-to-block mating surfaces. Be careful to keep the sealant off the seal split line.

11. Install the bearing cap bolts and torque to 70 ft. lbs. Install the oil pump and oil pan in the reverse order of removal.

350 and 379 Diesel V8s

The crankshaft need not be removed to replace the rear main bearing upper oil seal. The lower seal is installed in the bearing cap.

1. Drain the crankcase oil and remove the oil pan and rear main bearing cap.

2. Using a special main seal tool or a tool that can be made from a dowel (see illustration), drive the upper seal into its groove on each side until it is tightly packed. This is usually ¼–¾ in.

3. Measure the amount the seal was driven up on one side; add ¹⁄₁₆ in., then cut this length

from the old seal that was removed from the main bearing cap. Use a single-edge razor blade. Measure the amount the seal was driven up on the other side; add ¹⁄₁₆ in. and cut another length from the old seal. Use the main bearing cap as a holding fixture when cutting the seal as illustrated. Carefully trim protruding seal.

4. Work these two pieces of seal up into the cylinder block on each side with two nail-sets or small screwdrivers. Using the packing tool again, pack these pieces into the block, then trim them flush with a razor blade or hobby knife as shown. *Do not scratch the bearing surface with the razor.*

NOTE: *It may help to use a bit of oil on the short pieces of the rope seal when packing it into the block.*

5. Apply Loctite® #496 sealer or equivalent to the rear main bearing cap and install the rope seal. Cut the ends of the seal flush with the cap.

6. Check to see if the rear main cap with the new seal will seat properly on the block. Place a piece of Plastigage® on the rear main journal, install the cap and torque to 70 ft. lbs. Remove the cap and check the Plastigage® against specifications. If out of specs, recheck the ends of the seal for fraying that may be preventing the cap from seating properly.

7. Make sure all traces of Plastigage® are removed from the crankshaft journal. Apply a thin film of sealer (GM part #1052357 or equivalent) to the bearing cap. Keep the sealant off of both the seal and bearing.

8. Just before assembly, apply a light coat of clean engine oil on the crankshaft surface that will contact the seal.

9. Install the bearing cap and torque the bolts to specifications.

10. Install the oil pump and oil pan.

Flywheel and Ring Gear
REMOVAL AND INSTALLATION

The ring gear is an integral part of the flywheel and is not replaceable.

1. Remove the transmission.
2. Remove the six bolts attaching the flywheel to the crankshaft flange. Remove the flywheel.
3. Inspect the flywheel for cracks, and inspect the ring gear for burrs or worn teeth. Replace the flywheel if any damage is apparent. Remove burrs with a mill file.
4. Install the flywheel. The flywheel will only attach to the crankshaft in one position, as the bolt holes are unevenly spaced. Install the bolts and torque to specification.

ENGINE COOLING

The cooling system consists of a radiator, belt-driven fan, thermostat, and a mechanical water pump. Air conditioned and diesel engines are equipped with a clutch type drive fan. This fan restricts operation at 1500 rpm in cold weather and 3500 rpm during warmer temperatures. This fan requires less horsepower to drive during high rpm operation and reduces under-hood noise. 1977 and later models are equipped with a special pressure relief radiator cap. Be sure any replacement cap used is the same.

Refer to Chapter 1 for the coolant level checking procedure and to the Appendix for "Antifreeze" charts. The coolant should periodically be drained and the system flushed with clean water, at the intervals specified in Chapter 1. Service stations have reverse flushing equipment available; there are also permanently-installed do-it-yourself reverse flushing attachments available.

There is a coolant drain cock at the bottom of most radiators. Six-cylinder engines have a coolant drain plug on the left side of the engine block; V8s have one on each side. Some engines don't have any.

The coolant should always be maintained at a minimum of $-20°F$ freezing protection, regardless of the prevailing temperature. This concentration assures rust protection and the highest possible boiling point. It also prevents the heater core from freezing on air-conditioned models.

The common causes of corrosion are air suction and exhaust gas leakage. Air may be drawn into the system due to low coolant level in the radiator, a leaky water pump, loose hose connections, a defective radiator pressure cap, or a leaky overflow hose connection to the radiator on the coolant recovery bottle. Exhaust gas may be blown into the cooling system past the cylinder head gasket or through cracks in the cylinder head and block.

Radiator

All pick-up trucks are equipped with cross-flow type radiators.

REMOVAL AND INSTALLATION
1970–72

1. Drain the radiator and remove the hoses.
2. Disconnect and plug the transmission cooler line (if equipped).
3. On six cyl. engines, remove the finger guard.
4. Remove the upper retainers with the fan shroud attached (V8 movels) and rest the fan shroud over the engine.
5. Lift the radiator out of the lower retainers.
6. Installation is the reverse of removal. Fill the cooling system, check the automatic transmission fluid level and run the engine, checking for leaks.

1973 and Later

1. Drain the radiator. On some 1973 models, you will have to siphon the coolant out of the filler neck or detach the lower radiator hose. 1974 and later models are equipped with a drain cock.
CAUTION: *Do not attempt to start the siphoning process with your mouth. The coolant is poisonous and can cause death.*
2. Disconnect the hoses and automatic transmission cooler line (if equipped). Plug the cooler lines. Diesels have transmission cooler and oil cooler lines.
3. Disconnect the coolant recovery system hose.
4. If the vehicle is equipped with a fan shroud, detach the shroud and hang it over the fan to provide clearance.
5. On six cylinder engines, remove the finger guard.
6. Remove the mounting panel from the radiator support and remove the upper mounting pads.
7. Lift the radiator up and out of the truck. Lift the shroud out if necessary.
8. Installation is the reverse of removal. Fill the cooling system and check the automatic transmission fluid level, and run the engine, checking for leaks.

Water Pump
REMOVAL AND INSTALLATION
All Engines Except 379 (6.2L) Diesel

1. Drain the radiator and loosen the fan pulley bolts.

Typical radiator mounting

Typical radiator, shroud, and finger guard. The finger guard is usually found on trucks with six cylinder engines

2. Disconnect the heater hose and radiator. Disconnect the lower radiator hose at the water pump.

3. Loosen the alternator swivel bolt and remove the fan belt. Remove the fan bolts, fan and pulley.

4. Remove the water pump attaching bolts and remove the pump and gasket from the engine. On inline engines, remove the water pump straight out of the block to avoid damaging the impeller.

NOTE: *Do not store viscous drive (thermostatic) fan clutches in any other position than the normal installed position. They should be supported so that the clutch disc remains vertical; otherwise, silicone fluid may leak out.*

5. Check the water pump shaft bearings for end play or roughness in operation. Water pump bearings usually emit a squealing sound with the engine running when the bearings need to be replaced. Replace the pump with a rebuilt or new pump (usually on an exchange basis) if the bearings are not in good shape or have been noisy.

6. Installation is the reverse of removal. Clean the gasket surfaces and install new gaskets. Coat the gasket with sealer. A $5/16$ in. x 24 x 1 in. guide stud installed in one hole of the fan will make installing the fan onto the hub easier. It can be removed after the other 3 bolts are started. Fill the cooling system and adjust the fan belt tension.

379 Diesel

1. Disconnect the batteries.
2. Remove the fan and fan shroud.
3. Drain the radiator.
4. If the truck is equipped with air conditioning, remove the A/C hose bracket nuts.
5. Remove the oil fill tube.

Coolant recovery tank

379 diesel water pump assembly. Note sealer application surface

6. Remove the generator pivot bolt and remove the generator belt.

7. Remove the generator lower bracket.

8. Remove the power steering belt. Remove the power steering belt and secure it out of the way.

9. Remove the air conditioning belt if equipped.

10. Disconnect the by-pass hose and the lower radiator hose.

11. Remove the water pump bolts. Remove the water pump plate and gasket and water pump. If the pump gasket is to be replaced, remove the plate attaching bolts to the water pump and remove (and replace) the gasket.

12. When installing the pump, the flanges must be free of oil. Apply an anaerobic sealer (GM part #1052357 or equivalent) as shown in the accompanying illustration.

NOTE: *The sealer must be wet to the touch when the bolts are torqued.*

13. Attach the water pump and plate assembly. Torque the pump bolts to specifications.

14. Assemble the remaining components in the reverse order of removal. Fill the cooling system, start the engine and check for leaks.

Thermostat

The factory installed thermostat is a 195°F unit.

NOTE: *Poor heater output and slow warmup is often caused by a thermostat stuck in the open position; occasionally one sticks shut causing immediate overheating. Do not attempt to correct a chronic overheating condition by permanently removing the thermostat. Thermostat flow restriction is designed into the system; without it, localized overheating due to turbulence may occur.*

REMOVAL AND INSTALLATION

1. Drain approximately ⅓ of the coolant. This will reduce the coolant level to below the level of the thermostat housing.

The 379 diesel thermostat is located in the coolant reservoir pipe

Typical V8 thermostat installation, gasoline and 350 diesel engines

2. It is not necessary to remove the upper radiator hose from the thermostat housing. Remove the 2 retaining bolts from the thermostat housing (located on the front top of V8 intake manifolds and directly in front of the valve cover on six cylinder engines) and remove the thermostat. On 379 diesels, the thermostat is

Typical thermostat installation

mounted in the coolant crossaver pipe located at the front of the engine.

3. To test the thermostat, place it in hot water or a solution of 33% glycol, 25° above the temperature stamped on the valve. Submerge the valve and agitate the solution. The valve should open fully. Remove the thermostat and place it in the same solution 10° below the temperature stamped on the valve. The valve should close completely.

4. Installation is the reverse of removal. Use a new gasket and sealer. Refill the cooling system and run the engine, checking for leaks.

Emission Controls and Fuel System

GASOLINE ENGINE EMISSION CONTROLS

The emission control devices required in Chevrolet and GMC pick-ups are determined by weight classification. Light duty emission models use the same controls as cars. These are all 1970–74 trucks; all 1975–78 two wheel drive trucks under 6000 lbs. Gross Vehicle Weight; all 1979 trucks under 8500 lbs. GVW; and all 1980 trucks under 8600 lbs. GVW. Heavy duty models use fewer emission controls and include all four wheel drive trucks, 1970–74; all trucks over 6000 lbs. GVW, 1975–78; all trucks over 8500 lbs. GVW, 1979; and all trucks over 8600 lbs. GVW, 1980 and later.

The CEC (Combined Emission Control) and TCS (Transmission Controlled Spark) have been used since 1970 and basically do not allow distributor vacuum advance in Low gear.

In 1973, the EGR (Exhaust Gas Recirculation) system was developed in response to more stringent Federal exhaust emission standards regarding NO_x (oxides of nitrogen). Oxides of nitrogen are formed at higher combustion chamber temperatures and increase with higher temperatures. The EGR system is designed to reduce combustion temperature thereby reducing the formation of NO_x.

In addition to controlling the engine emissions, the ECS (Evaporative Control System) is designed to control fuel vapors that escape from the fuel tank through evaporation. When the fuel vapors combine with the atmosphere and sunlight they form photochemical smog. This system seals the fuel tank to retain vapors in a charcoal canister. The canister is purged and the vapors burned during engine operation.

In 1975, a catalytic converter was added to the emission control system on some light duty models, and its use has slowly spread through the line in succeeding years. Through catalytic action (that is, causing a chemical reaction without taking part in the reaction itself) the platinum and palladium coated beads in the converter oxidize unburnt hydrocarbons (HC) and carbon monoxide (CO) into carbon dioxide (CO_2) and water (H_2O). The converter itself is a muffler-shaped device installed in the exhaust system of the truck. Converter-equipped trucks require the use of unleaded fuel.

With emission level maintenance standards getting stricter on state and Federal levels, proper testing and service of each system becomes more important. Much confusion results from the variety and combinations of systems used in any year. The following sections are devoted to the description and service of each separate system.

FRESH AIR

PCV CONTROL VALVE

CRANKCASE BLOW-BY GASES

⟹ FRESH-AIR

⟺ MIXTURE OF FRESH-AIR AND BLOW-BY GAS

➡ CRANKCASE BLOW-BY GASES

PCV system

Positive Crankcase Ventilation

This system draws crankcase vapors that are formed through normal combustion into the intake manifold and subsequently into the combustion chambers to be burned. Fresh air is introduced to the crankcase by way of a hose connected to the carburetor air cleaner. Manifold vacuum is used to draw the vapors from the crankcase through a PCV valve and into the intake manifold.

SERVICE

The PCV system should be inspected as stated in the "Maintenance Interval" chart in Chapter 1. Other than checking and replacing the PCV valve and associated hoses, there is no other service required.

1. Remove the PCV valve from the intake manifold or valve cover.
2. Allow the engine to idle.

3. Place your thumb over the end of the valve to check for vacuum. If there is no vacuum at the valve, check for plugged hoses or valve.
4. Remove the valve and shake it. If it rattles the valve is still good, if not, replace it.
5. After installation of a PCV valve or hoses adjust the idle if necessary.

Air Injector Reactor (A.I.R.)

The AIR system injects compressed air into the exhaust system, near enough to the exhaust valves to continue the burning of the normally unburned segment of the exhaust gases. To do this it employs an air injection pump and a system of hoses, valves, tubes, etc., necessary to carry the compressed air from the pump to the exhaust manifolds. Carburetors and distributors for AIR engines have specific modifications to adapt them to the air injection system. These components should not be interchanged with those intended for use on engines that do not have the system.

A diverter valve is used to prevent backfiring. The valve senses sudden increases in manifold vacuum and ceases the injection of air during fuel-rich periods. During coasting, this valve diverts the entire air flow through a muffler and during high engine speeds, expels it through a relief valve. Check valves in the system prevent exhaust gases from entering the pump.

TESTING

Check Valve

To test the check valve, disconnect the hose at the diverter valve. Blow into the hose and suck on it. Air should flow only into the engine.

Diverter Valve

Pull off the vacuum line to the top of the valve with the engine running. There should be vac-

Closed and positive PCV systems, 6-cylinder shown

V8 PCV valve location

AIR system operation

Inline six air pump mounting

uum in the line. Replace the line. No air should be escaping with the engine running at a steady idle. Open and quickly close the throttle. A blast of air should come out of the valve muffler for at least one second. If the valve must be replaced, use a new gasket at the valve mounting on the pump and torque the bolts to 85 in. lbs.

Air Pump

Disconnect the hose from the diverter valve. Start the engine and accelerate it to about 1,500 rpm. The airflows should increase as the engine is accelerated. If no airflow is noted or it remains constant, check the following:

1. Drive belt tension.
2. Listen for a leaking pressure relief valve. If it is defective, replace the whole relief/diverter valve.
3. Foreign matter in pump filter openings. If the pump is defective or excessively noisy, it must be replaced.

SERVICE

The AIR system's effectiveness depends on correct engine idle speed, ignition timing, and dwell. These settings should be strictly adhered to and checked frequently. All hoses and fittings should be inspected for condition and

Air pump system, V8

tightness of connections. Check the drive belt for wear and tension every 12 months or 12,000 miles (4 months/6,000 miles 1974–75). If, after completion of a tune-up and/or individual inspection of components, a malfunction still exists, the vehicle should be serviced by qualified mechanics.

The AIR system is not completely noiseless. Under normal conditions, noise rises in pitch as engine speed increases. To determine if excessive noise is the fault of the AIR system, operate the engine with the pump drive belt removed. If the noise does not exist with the belt removed:

1. Check for a seized pump.
2. Check hoses, tubes and connections for leaks or kinks.
3. Check the diverter valve.
4. Check the pump for proper mounting.

CAUTION: *Do not oil AIR pump.*

If no irregularities exist and the AIR pump noise is still excessive, replace the pump.

COMPONENT REMOVAL

Air Pump

CAUTION: *Do not pry on the pump housing or clamp the pump in a vise: the housing is soft and may become distorted.*

1. Disconnect the air hoses at the pump.
2. Hold the pump pulley from turning and loosen the pulley bolts.
3. Loosen the pump mounting bolt and adjustment bracket bolt. Remove the drive belt.
4. Remove the mounting bolts, and then remove the pump.
5. Install the pump using a reverse of the removal procedure.

Pump Filter

1. Remove the drive belt and pump pulley.
2. Using needle-nose pliers, pull the fan from the pump hub.

NOTE: *Use care to prevent any dirt or fragments from entering the air intake hole. DO NOT insert a screwdriver between the pump and the filter, and do not attempt to remove the metal hub. It is seldom possible to remove the filter without destroying it.*

3. To install a new filter, draw it on with the pulley and pulley bolts. Do not hammer or press the filter on the pump.
4. Draw the filter down evenly by torquing the bolts alternately. Make sure the outer edge of the filter slips into the housing. A slight amount of interference with the housing bore is normal.

NOTE: *The new filter may squeal initially until the sealing lip on the pump outer diameter has worn in.*

Diverter (Anti-afterburn) Valve

1. Detach the vacuum sensing line from the valve.
2. Remove the other hose(s) from the valve.
3. Unfasten the diverter valve from the elbow or the pump body.

Installation is performed in the reverse order of removal. Always use a new gasket. Tighten the valve securing bolts to 85 in. lbs.

Air Management System

The Air Management System is used on 198 and later to provide additional oxygen to continue the combustion process after the exhaust gases leave the combustion chamber; much the same as the AIR system described earlier in this chapter. Air is injected into either the exhaust port(s), the exhaust manifold(s) or the catalytic converter by an engine driven air pump. The system is in operation at all times and will bypass air only momentarily during deceleration and at high speeds. The bypass function is performed by the Air Management Valve, while the check valve protects the air pump by preventing any backflow of exhaust gases.

The AIR system helps to reduce HC and CO

AIR filter removal

Air management system—typical

content in the exhaust gases by injecting air into the exhaust ports during cold engine operation. This air injection also helps the catalytic converter to reach the proper temperature quicker during warm-up. When the engine is warm (closed loop), the AIR system injects air into the beds of a three-way converter to lower the HC and CO content in the exhaust.

The Air Management System utilizes the following components:

1. An engine driven air pump.
2. Air management valves (Air Control and Air Switching)
3. Air flow and control hoses
4. Check valves
5. A dual-bed, three-way catalytic converter

The belt driven, vane-type air pump is located at the front of the engine and supplies clean air to the system for purposes already stated. When the engine is cold, the Electronic Control Module (ECM) energizes an air control solenoid. This allows air to flow to the air switching valve. The air switching valve is then energized to direct air into the exhaust ports.

When the engine is warm, the ECM de-energizes the air switching valve, thus directing the air between the beds of the catalytic converter. This then provides additional oxygen for the oxidizing catalyst in the second bed to decrease HC and CO levels, while at the same time keeping oxygen levels low in the first bed, enabling the reducing catalyst to effectively decrease the levels of NO_x.

If the air control valve detects a rapid increase in manifold vacuum (deceleration), certain operating modes (wide open throttle, etc.) or if the ECM self-diagnostic system detects any problems in the system, air is diverted to the air cleaner or directly into the atmosphere.

The primary purpose of the ECM's divert mode is to prevent backfiring. Throttle closure at the beginning of deceleration will temporarily create air/fuel mixtures which are too rich to burn completely. These mixtures will become burnable when they reach the exhaust if they are combined with injection air. The next firing of the engine will ignite the mixture causing an exhaust backfire. Momentary diverting of the injection air from the exhaust prevents this.

The Air Management System check valves and hoses should be checked periodically for any leaks, cracks or deterioration.

REMOVAL AND INSTALLATION
Air Pump

1. Remove the valves and/or adapter at the air pump.
2. Loosen the air pump adjustment bolt and remove the drive belt.
3. Unscrew the three mounting bolts and then remove the pump pulley.
4. Unscrew the pump mounting bolts and then remove the pump.
5. Installation is in the reverse order of removal. Be sure to adjust the drive belt tension after installing it.

Check valve and hoses—1981 and later air management system

Check Valve

1. Release the clamp and disconnect the air hoses from the valve.

2. Unscrew the check valve from the air injection pipe.

3. Installation is in the reverse order of removal.

Air Management Valve

1. Disconnect the negative battery cable.

2. Remove the air cleaner.

3. Tag and disconnect the vacuum hose from the valve.

4. Tag and disconnect the air outlet hoses from the valve.

5. Bend back the lock tabs and then remove the bolts holding the elbow to the valve.

6. Tag and disconnect any electrical connections at the valve and then remove the valve from the elbow.

7. Installation is in the reverse order of removal.

Pulse Air Injection

The PAIR system is used on some 1979 and later 250 six cylinder engines. The system utilizes exhaust system pulses to siphon fresh air into the exhaust manifold. The injected air supports continued combustion of the hot exhaust gases in the exhaust manifold, reducing exhaust emissions.

Air is drawn into the PAIR plenums through a hose connected to the air cleaner case. There are two plenums, mounted on the rocker arm cover. The air passes through a check valve (there are four check valves—two at each plenum), then through a manifold pipe to the exhaust manifold. All manifold pipes are the same length, to prevent uneven pulsation. The check valves open during pulses of negative exhaust back pressure, admitting air into the manifold pipe and the exhaust manifold. During pulses of positive exhaust back pressure, the check valves close, preventing backfiring into the plenums and air cleaner.

REMOVAL AND INSTALLATION

1. Remove the air cleaner. Disconnect the rubber hose from the plenum connecting pipe.

Disconnect the four manifold pipes at the exhaust manifold. Remove the check valves from the plenum grommets.

3. Unbolt the check valve from the manifold pipe, if necessary.

4. To install, assemble the check valves to the pipes before the pipes are installed on the exhaust manifold.

5. Install the manifold pipe fittings to the exhaust manifold, but tighten the fittings only finger tight.

6. Use a 1 inch open end wrench, or something similar, as a lever to align the check valve on the "A" pipe assemblies (see the illustration) with the plenum grommet. Use the palm of your hand to press the check valve into the

Pulse air system

grommet. A rubber lubricant can be used to ease assembly.

7. Repeat this operation on the "B" pipe assembly.

8. After all the check valves have been installed in the rubber grommets, tighten the manifold pipe-to-exhaust manifold fittings to 28 ft. lbs. Connect the rubber hose to the plenum pipe and install the air cleaner.

Controlled Combustion System

The CCS system is a combination of systems and calibrations. Many of these are not visible or serviceable, but are designed into the engine. Originally the system was comprised of special carburetion and distributor settings, higher engine operating temperatures and a thermostatically-controlled air cleaner. In later years, the thermostatically-controlled air cleaner was used independently of the other settings on some engines. Likewise, some engines used the special settings without Thermac. In 1970, the TCS system was incorporated and the entire system was renamed CEC in 1971. The name reverted to TCS in 1972. In 1973, EGR was also added to the system.

The various systems, TCS, CEC and EGR are all part of the Controlled Combustion System.

SERVICE

Refer to the TCS, CEC or EGR Sections for maintenance and service (if applicable). In addition be sure that the ignition timing, dwell and carburetor settings are correct.

Thermostatic Air Cleaner

The thermostatic air cleaner (Thermac) is on all gasoline engines. This system uses a damper assembly in the air cleaner inlet, controlled by a vacuum motor to mix preheated and cold air entering the air cleaner. This is necessary to maintain a controlled air temperature into the carburetor. The vacuum motor is controlled by a temperature sensor in the air cleaner. The preheating of the air cleaner inlet air allows leaner carburetor and choke settings, which result in lower emissions, while maintaining good driveability.

SERVICE

1. Either start with a cold engine or remove the air cleaner from the engine for at least half an hour. While cooling the air cleaner, leave the engine compartment hood open.

2. Tape a thermometer, of known accuracy, to the inside of the air cleaner so that it is near the temperature sensor unit. Install the air

Thermostatically-controlled air cleaner case

cleaner on the engine but do not fasten its securing nut.

3. Start the engine. With the engine cold and the outside temperature less than 90°F., the door should be in the "heat on" position (closed to outside air).

NOTE: *Due to the position of the air cleaner on some trucks, a mirror may be necessary when observing the position of the air door.*

4. Operate the throttle lever rapidly to ½–¾ of its opening and release it. The air door should open to allow outside air to enter and then close again.

5. Allow the engine to warm up to normal temperature. Watch the door. When it opens to the outside air, remove the cover from the air cleaner. The temperature should be over 90°F and no more than 130°F; 115°F is about normal. If the door does not work within these temperature ranges, or fails to work at all, check for linkage or door binding.

If binding is not present and the air door is not working, proceed with the vacuum tests, given below. If these indicate no faults in the vacuum motor and the door is not working, the temperature sensor is defective and must be replaced.

Vacuum Motor Test

NOTE: *Be sure that the vacuum hose which runs between the temperature switch and the vacuum motor is not pinched by the retaining clip under the air cleaner. This could prevent the air door from closing.*

1. Check all of the vacuum lines and fittings for leaks. Correct any leaks. If none are found, proceed with the test.

2. Remove the hose which runs from the sensor to the vacuum motor. Run a hose directly from the manifold vacuum source to the vacuum motor.

3. If the motor closes the air door, it is func-

tioning properly and the temperature sensor is defective.

4. If the motor does *not* close the door and no binding is present in its operation, the vacuum motor is defective and *must* be replaced.

NOTE: *If an alternate vacuum source is applied to the motor, insert a vacuum gauge in the line by using a T-fitting. Apply at least 9 in. Hg of vacuum in order to operate the motor.*

Transmission Controlled Spark

Introduced in 1970, this system controls exhaust emissions by eliminating vacuum advance in the lower forward gears.

The 1970 system consists of a transmission switch, solenoid vacuum switch, time delay relay, and a thermostatic water temperature switch. The solenoid vacuum switch is deenergized in the lower gears via the transmission switch and closes off distributor vacuum. The two-way transmission switch is activated by the shifter shaft on manual transmissions, and by oil pressure on automatic transmissions. The switch energizes the solenoid in High gear, the plunger extends and uncovers the vacuum port, and the distributor receives full vacuum. The temperature switch overrides the system, until the engine temperature reaches 82°F. This allows vacuum advance in all gears, thereby preventing stalling after starting. A time delay relay opens fifteen seconds after the ignition is switched on. Full vacuum advance during this delay eliminated the possibility of stalling.

The 1971 system is similar, except that the vacuum solenoid (now called a Combination Emissions Control solenoid) serves two functions. One function is to control distributor vacuum; the added function is to act as a deceleration throttle stop in High gear. This cuts down on emissions when the vehicle is coming to a stop in High gear. Two throttle settings are necessary; one for curb idle and one for emission control on coast. Both settings are described in the tune-up section.

The 1972 six cyl. system is similar to that used in 1971, except that an idle stop solenoid has been added to the system and the name is changed back to TCS. In the energized position, the solenoid maintains engine speed at a predetermined fast idle. When deenergized the solenoid allows the throttle plates to close beyond the normal idle position; thus cutting off the air supply and preventing engine run-on. The 6 is the only 1972 engine with a CEC valve, which serves the same deceleration function as in 1971. The time delay relay now delays full vacuum twenty seconds after the transmission is shifted into High gear. 1972 V8 engines use

a vacuum advance solenoid similar to that used in 1970. The solenoid controls distributor vacuum advance and performs no throttle positioning function. The idle stop solenoid used on V8s operates in the same manner as the one on six cyl. engines. All air conditioned cars have an additional antidiesel (run-on) solenoid which engages the compressor clutch for three seconds after the ignition is switched off.

The 1973 TCS system on the six cyl. engine is identical to that on 1972 6, except for recalibration of the temperature switch. The system used on small block 1973 engines changed slightly from 1972. In place of the CEC solenoid on the 6, the V8 continues to use a vacuum advance solenoid. The other differences are: the upshift delay relay, previously located under the instrument panel has been done away with; a 20 second time delay relay identical to the one on six cyl. engines is now used; small block V8s use manifold vacuum with TCS and ported vacuum without TCS.

The six cyl. TCS system was revised for 1974–75 by replacing the CEC solenoid with a vacuum advance solenoid. Otherwise the system remains the same as 1973.

TESTING

If there is a TCS system malfunction, first connect a vacuum gauge in the hose between the solenoid valve and the distributor vacuum unit. Drive the vehicle or raise it on a frame lift and observe the vacuum gauge. If full vacuum is available in all gears, check for the following:

1. Blown fuse.
2. Disconnected wire at solenoid-operated vacuum valve.
3. Disconnected wire at transmission switch.
4. Temperature override switch energized due to low engine temperature.
5. Solenoid failure.

If no vacuum is available in any gear, check the following:

1. Solenoid valve vacuum lines switched.
2. Clogged solenoid vacuum valve.
3. Distributor or manifold vacuum lines leaking or disconnected.
4. Transmission switch or wire grounded.

Test for individual components are as follows:

Idle Stop Solenoid

This unit may be checked simply by observing it while an assistant switches the ignition on and off. It should extend further with the current switched on. The unit is not repairable.

Solenoid Vacuum Valve

Check that proper manifold vacuum is available. Connect the vacuum gauge in the line between the solenoid valve and the distributor. Apply 12 volts to the solenoid. If vacuum is still not available, the valve is defective, either mechanically or electrically. The unit is not repairable. If the valve is satisfactory, check the relay next.

Relay

1. With the engine at normal operating temperature and the ignition on, ground the solenoid vacuum valve terminal with the black lead. The solenoid should energize (no vacuum) if the relay is satisfactory.

2. With the solenoid energized as in Step 1, connect a jumper from the relay terminal with the green/white stripe lead to ground. The solenoid should deenergize (vacuum available) if the relay is satisfactory.

3. If the relay worked properly in Steps 1 and 2, check the temperature switch. The relay unit is not repairable.

Temperature Switch

The vacuum valve solenoid should be deenergized (vacuum available) with the engine cold. If it is not, ground the green/white stripe wire from the switch. If the solenoid now deenergizes, replace the switch. If the switch was satisfactory, check the transmission switch.

Transmission Switch

With the engine at normal operating temperature and the transmission in one of the no-vacuum gears, the vacuum valve solenoid should be energized (no vacuum). If not, remove and ground the switch electrical lead. If the solenoid energizes, replace the switch.

Exhaust Gas Recirculation

The EGR system and valve were introduced in 1973. Its purpose is to control oxides of nitrogen which are formed during the peak combustion temperatures. The end products of combustion are relatively inert gases derived from the exhaust gases which are directed into the EGR valve to help lower peak combustion temperatures.

The EGR valve contains a vacuum diaphragm operated by manifold vacuum. The vacuum signal port is located in the carburetor body and is exposed to engine vacuum in the off-idle, part-throttle, and wide-open throttle operation. In 1974, a thermo-delay switch was added to delay operation of the valve during engine warm-up, when NO_x levels are already at a minimum.

There are actually three types of EGR systems: Vacuum Modulated, Positive Exhaust Backpressure Modulated, and Negative Ex-

Six cylinder EGR valve

NOTE: INDENTIFY NEGATIVE PRESSURE MODULATED EGR VALVE BY DIAPHRAGM PLATE DESIGN.

DIAPHRAGM PLATE ASSEMBLY

NOTE: INDENTIFY POSITIVE PRESSURE MODULATED EGR VALVE BY DIAPHRAGM PLATE DESIGN.

DIAPHRAGM PLATE ASSEMBLY

Negative (top) and positive backpressure EGR valves

haust Backpressure Modulated. The principle of all the systems is the same; the only difference is in the method used to control how far the EGR valve opens.

In the Vacuum Modulated system, which is used on all trucks through 1976, and some models thereafter, the amount of exhaust gas admitted into the intake manifold depends on a ported vacuum signal. A ported vacuum sig-

NOTE: INDENTIFY VACUUM MODULATED EGR VALVE BY DIAPHRAGM PLATE DESIGN

DIAPHRAGM PLATE ASSEMBLY

Vacuum-modulated EGR valve

nal is one taken from the carburetor above the throttle plates. Thus, the vacuum signal (amount of vacuum) is dependent on how far the throttle plates are opened. When the throttle is closed (idle or deceleration) there is no vacuum signal. Thus, the EGR valve is closed, and no exhaust gas enters the intake manifold. As the throttle is opened, a vacuum is produced, which opens the EGR valve, admitting exhaust gas into the intake manifold.

In the Exhaust Backpressure Modulated system, a transducer is installed in the EGR valve body, reacting to either positive or negative backpressure, depending on design. The vacuum used is still ported vacuum, but the transducer uses exhaust gas backpressure to control an air bleed within the valve to modify this vacuum signal. Backpressure valves are used on all light duty emissions California and High Altitude engines in 1976 and 1978, and on most engines, 1979 and later. The choice of either a

positive or negative back-pressure valve is determined by measurement of the engine's normal backpressure output. Negative valves are used on engines with relatively low backpressure; positive valves are used on engines with relatively high backpressure. The choice of valve usage is made at the factory, and is nothing for the backyard mechanic to worry about; however, if the valve is replaced, it is important to install the same type as the original. The difference between the three valves (ported, positive, or negative) can be determined by the shape of the diaphragm plate; your Chevrolet or GMC dealer will be able to match the old valve to a new one.

On six cylinder engines, the EGR valve is located on the intake manifold adjacent to the carburetor. On small block V8 engines, the valve is located on the right rear side of the intake manifold adjacent to the rocker arm cover. Mark IV V8 EGR valves are located in the left front corner of the intake manifold in front of the carburetor.

SERVICE

The EGR valve is not serviceable, except for replacement. To check the ported vacuum signal valve, proceed as follows:

1. Connect a tachometer to the engine.
2. With the engine running at normal operating temperature, with the choke valve fully open, set the engine rpm at 2,000. The transmission should be in Park (automatic) or Neutral (manual) with the parking brake on and the wheels blocked.
3. Disconnect the vacuum hose at the valve. Make sure that vacuum is available at the valve and look at the tachometer to see if the engine speed increases. If it does, a malfunction of the valve is indicated.
4. If necessary, replace the valve.

A back pressure EGR valve is used on all light duty emissions California and High Altitude six and V8 engines in 1977 and 1978, and most 1979 and later models.

The system can be tested as follows:

1. Remove air cleaner so that the EGR valve diaphragm movement can be observed. The choke secondary vacuum break TVS can be unclipped and removed from the air cleaner body, rather than removing hoses.
2. Plug the intake manifold air cleaner vacuum fitting. Connect a tachometer.
3. Start the engine and warm to operating temperature. Open the throttle part way and release. Watch or feel the EGR diaphragm for movement. The valve should open slightly when the throttle is opened and close when it is released.

(15-22 FT-LBS)

VALVE

GASKET

SPACER

GASKET

Typical EGR valve mounting, V8s

4. Remove the EGR hose from the EGR valve and plug the hose. Place the carburetor cam follower on the second step of the fast idle cam and note the speed.

5. Attach a vacuum hose between the air cleaner vacuum fitting and the EGR valve. Note the speed change. The speed should drop at least 200 rpm with automatic transmissions, or at least 150 with manuals.

If the EGR valve does not meet the criteria specified in these tests, it must be replaced.

Evaporation Control System

Introduced on California vehicles in 1970, and nationwide in 1971, this system reduces the amount of escaping gasoline vapors. Float bowl emissions are controlled by internal carburetor modifications. Redesigned bowl vents, reduced bowl capacity, heat shields, and improved intake manifold-to-carburetor insulation serve to reduce vapor loss into the atmosphere. The venting of fuel tank vapors into the air has been stopped. Fuel vapors are now directed through lines to a canister containing an activated charcoal filter. Unburned vapors are trapped here until the engine is started. When the engine is running, the canister is purged by air drawn in by manifold vacuum. The air and fuel vapors are directed into the engine to be burned.

SERVICE

Replace the filter in the engine compartment canister as specified in the "Maintenance Intervals Chart" in Chapter 1. If the fuel tank cap requires replacement, ensure that the new cap is the correct part for your truck.

Early Fuel Evaporation

The six cylinder and 1975 Mark IV (big block) V8 EFE systems consist of an EFE valve mounted at the flange of the exhaust manifold, and actuator, a thermal vacuum switch (TVS) and a vacuum solenoid. The TVS is located on the right-hand side of the engine forward of the oil pressure switch on six cyl. engines and directly above the oil filter on the Mark IV V8. The TVS is normally closed and sensitive to oil temperature.

The small block V8 and 1976 and later Mark IV EFE system consists of an EFE valve at the flange of the exhaust manifold, an actuator, and a thermal vacuum switch. The TVS is located

Evaporation Control System (ECS)

Typical EFE valve installation

EFE valve, installation, 250 six cylinder

in the coolant outlet housing and directly controls vacuum.

In both systems, manifold vacuum is applied to the actuator, which in turn, closes the EFE valve. This routes hot exhaust gases to the base of the carburetor. When coolant or oil temperatures reach a set limit, vacuum is denied to the actuator allowing an internal spring to return the actuator to its normal position, opening the EFE valve.

Throttle Return Control

Two different throttle return control systems are used. The first is used from 1975 to 1978. It consists of a control valve and a throttle lever actuator. When the truck is coasting against the engine, the control valve is open to allow vacuum to operate the throttle lever actuator. The throttle lever actuator then pushes the throttle lever slightly open reducing the HC (hydrocarbon) emission level during coasting. When manifold vacuum drops below a predeter-

Throttle return control valve through 1978

TRC system schematic

mined level, the control valve closes, the throttle lever retracts, and the throttle lever closes to the idle position.

The second TRC system is used in 1979 and later. It consists of a throttle lever actuator, a solenoid vacuum control valve, and an electronic speed sensor. The throttle lever actuator, mounted on the carburetor, opens the primary throttle plates a preset amount, above normal engine idle speed, in response to a signal from the solenoid vacuum control valve. The valve, mounted at the left rear of the engine above the intake manifold on the six cylinder, or on the thermostat housing mounting stud on the V8, is held open in response to a signal from the electronic speed sensor. When open, the valve allows a vacuum signal to be sent to the throttle lever actuator. The speed sensor monitors engine speed at the distributor. It supplies an electrical signal to the solenoid valve, as long as a preset engine speed is exceeded. The object of this system is the same as that of the earlier system.

SERVICE

Control Valve

1975–76

1. Disconnect the valve-to-carburetor hose and connect it to an external vacuum source with a vacuum gauge.

2. Disconnect the valve-to-actuator hose at the connector and connect it to a vacuum gauge.

3. Place a finger firmly over the end of the bleed fitting.

4. Apply a minimum of 23 in. Hg vacuum to the control valve and seal off the vacuum source. The gauge on the actuator side should read the same as the gauge on the source side. If not, the valve needs adjustment. If vacuum drops off on either side (with the finger still on the bleed fitting), the valve is defective and should be replaced.

5. With a minimum of 23 in. Hg vacuum in the valve, remove the finger from the bleed fitting. The vacuum level in the actuator side will drop to zero and the reading on the source side will drop to a value that will be the value

TRS Control Valve
Set Points

Engine	Set Point (in. Hg)
292	22.5
305	22.5
350	21.5
400	21.5
454 (1975–76)	21.0
454 (1977–78)	23.0

TRC Speed

Engine	Setting (rpm)
292	1600
305	1600
350	1500
400	1500
454 (1975–76)	1400
454 (1977–78)	1500

set point. If the value is not within ½ in. Hg vacuum of the specified valve set point, adjust the valve.

6. Gently pry off the plastic cover.

7. Turn the adjusting screw in (clockwise) to raise the set point or out (counterclockwise) to lower the set point.

8. Recheck the valve set point.

9. If necessary, repeat the adjustment until the valve set point is attained ± ½ in. Hg. vacuum.

1977–78

1. Disconnect the valve-to-carburetor hose at the carburetor. Connect the hose to an external vacuum source, with an accurate vacuum gauge connected into the line near the valve.

2. Apply a minimum of 25 in. Hg. of vacuum to the control valve vacuum supply fitting while sealing off the vacuum supply between the gauge and the vacuum source. The vacuum gauge will indicate the set point value of the valve.

3. If the gauge reading is not within 0.5 in. Hg. of the specified value (see the chart), the valve must be adjusted. If the trapped vacuum drops off faster than 0.1 in. Hg. per second, the valve is leaking and must be replaced.

4. To adjust the valve set point, follow Steps 6–9 of the 1975–76 adjustment procedure.

Throttle Valve

1975–78

1. Disconnect the valve-to-actuator hose at the valve and connect it to an external vacuum source.

2. Apply 20 in. Hg vacuum to the actuator and seal the vacuum source. If the vacuum gauge reading drops, the valve is leaking and should be replaced.

3. Check the throttle lever, shaft, and linkage for freedom of operation.

4. Start the engine and warm it to operating temperature.

5. Note the idle rpm.

6. Apply 20 in. Hg vacuum to the actuator and manually operate the throttle. Allow it to

close against the extended actuator plunger. Note the engine rpm.

7. Release and reapply 20 in. Hg vacuum to the actuator and note the rpm at which the engine speed increases (do not assist the actuator).

8. If the engine speed obtained in Step 7 is not within 150 rpm of that obtained in Step 6, then the actuator may be binding. If the binding cannot be corrected, replace the actuator.

9. Release the vacuum from the actuator and the engine speed should return to within 50 rpm of the speed noted in Steps 4 and 5.

To adjust the actuator:

10. Turn the screw on the actuator plunger until the specified TRC speed range is obtained.

THROTTLE LEVER ACTUATOR

1979 and Later

The checking procedure is the same as for earlier years. Follow Steps 1–9 of the "Throttle Valve" procedure. Adjustment procedures are covered in the carburetor adjustments section, later in this chapter.

TRC SYSTEM CHECK

1979 and Later

1. Connect a tachometer to the distributor "TACH" terminal. Start the engine and raise the engine speed to 1890 rpm. The throttle lever actuator on the carburetor should extend.

2. Reduce the engine speed to 1700 rpm. The lever actuator should retract.

3. If the actuator operates outside of the

TRC valve assembly—inline six

TRC valve assembly—V8s

speed limits, the speed switch is faulty and must be replaced. It cannot be adjusted.

4. If the actuator does not operate at all:

a. Check the voltage at the vacuum solenoid and the speed switch with a voltmeter. Connect the negative probe of the voltmeter to the engine ground and the positive probe to the voltage source wire on the component. The positive probe can be inserted on the connector body at the wire side; it is not necessary to unplug the connector. Voltage should be 12 to 14 volts in both cases.

b. If the correct voltage is present at one component but not the other, the engine wiring harness is faulty.

c. If voltage is not present at all, check the engine harness connections at the distributor and the bulkhead connector and repair as necessary.

d. If the correct voltage is present at both components, check the solenoid operation: ground the solenoid-to-speed switch connecting wire terminal at the solenoid connector with a jumper wire. This should cause the throttle lever actuator to extend, with the engine running.

e. If the lever actuator does not extend, remove the hose from the solenoid side port which connects to the actuator hose. Check the port for obstructions or blockage. If the port is not plugged, replace the solenoid.

f. If the actuator extends in Step d, ground the solenoid-to-speed switch wire terminal at the switch. If the actuator does not extend, the wire between the speed switch and the solenoid is open and must be repaired. If the actuator does extend, check the speed switch ground wire for a ground; it should read zero volts with the engine running. Check the speed switch-to-distributor wire for a proper connection. If the ground and distributor wires are properly connected and the actuator still does not extend when the engine speed is above 1890 rpm, replace the speed switch.

5. If the actuator is extended at all speeds:

a. Remove the connector from the vacuum solenoid.

b. If the actuator remains extended, check the solenoid side port orifice for blockage. If plugged, clear and reconnect the system and recheck. If the actuator is still extended, remove the solenoid connector; if the actuator does not retreat, replace the vacuum solenoid.

c. If the actuator retracts with the solenoid connector off, reconnect it and remove the speed switch connector. If the actuator retracts, the problem is in the speed switch, which should be replaced. If the actuator does not retract, the solenoid-to-speed switch wire is shorted to ground in the wiring harness. Repair the short.

Oxygen Sensor

1983 and Later

The oxygen sensor is a spark plug-shaped device that is screwed into the exhaust manifold on V8s and into the exhaust pipe on inline sixes. It monitors the oxygen content of the exhaust gases and sends a voltage signal to the Electronic Control Module (ECM). The ECM monitors this voltage and, depending on the value of the received signal, issues a command to the mixture control solenoid on the carburetor to adjust for rich or lean conditions.

The proper operation of the oxygen sensor depends upon four basic conditions:

1. Good electrical connections—since the sensor generates low currents, good clean electrical connections at the sensor are a must.

2. Outside air supply—air must circulate to the internal portion of the sensor. When servicing the sensor, do not restrict the air passages.

3. Proper operating temperatures—the ECM will not recognize the sensor's signals until the sensor reaches approximately 600°F.

4. Non-leaded fuel—the use of leaded gasoline will damage the sensor very quickly.

NOTE: *No attempt should be made to measure the output voltage of the sensor. The current drain of any conventional voltmeter would be enough to permanently damage the sensor. No jumpers, test leads, or other electrical connections should ever be made to the sensor. Use these tools ONLY on the ECM side of the harness connector AFTER the oxygen sensor has been disconnected.*

REMOVAL AND INSTALLATION

CAUTION: *The sensor uses a permanently attached pig-tail and connector. This pig-tail should not be removed from the sensor. Damage or removal of the pig-tail or connector could affect the proper operation of the sensor. Keep the electrical connector and louvered end of the sensor clean and free of grease. NEVER use cleaning solvents of any type on the sensor.*

1 OXYGEN SENSOR - V8

1 OXYGEN SENSOR - L6

Oxygen sensor locations

NOTE: *The oxygen sensor may be difficult to remove when the temperature of the engine is below 120°F. Excessive force may damage the threads in the exhaust manifold or exhaust pipe.*

1. Disconnect the electrical connector and any attaching hardware.

2. Remove the sensor.

3. Coat the threads of the sensor with a GM anti-seize compound (#5613695) before installation. New· sensors are pre-coated with this compound.

NOTE: *The GM anti-seize compound is NOT a conventional anti-seize paste. The use of a regular paste may electrically insulate the sensor, rendering it useless. The threads MUST be coated with the proper electrically-conductive anti-seize compound.*

4. Install the sensor and torque to 30 ft. lbs. Use care in making sure the silicone boot is in the correct position to avoid melting it during operation.

5. Connect the electrical connector and attaching hardware if used.

Catalytic Converter

Starting 1975 an underfloor catalytic converter is used to control hydrocarbon and carbon monoxide emissions on some models. Control is accomplished by placing a catalyst in the exhaust system in such a way as to enable all exhaust gas flow from the engine to pass through it and undergo a chemical reaction before passing into the atmosphere. The chemical reaction involved is the oxidizing of hydrocarbons and carbon monoxide into water vapor and carbon dioxide.

REMOVAL AND INSTALLATION

Warning; *Catalytic converter operating temperatures are extremely high. Outside converter temperatures can go well over 1,000°F. Use extreme care when working on the catalytic converter or when working anywhere around it.* ·

1. Jack up your truck and support it with jack stands.

2. Remove the clamps at the front and rear of the converter.

3. Cut the converter pipes at the front and rear of the converter and remove it.

4. Remove the support from the transmission or transfer case.

5. Remove the converter pipe-to-exhaust pipe and the converter pipe-to-tailpipe.

6. Installation is the reverse of removal.

Trapped Vacuum Spark

This system is used to prevent a drop in vacuum to the distributor vacuum advance during cold engine operation, when the engine is accelerating. A thermal vacuum switch (TVS) is used to sense engine coolant temperature. A check valve is installed in the vacuum line to the distributor. The other side of the check valve has two connections: one to manifold vacuum (at the carburetor base), and the other to the thermal vacuum switch.

When the engine is cold, the TVS vacuum ports are closed. Manifold vacuum is routed through the check valve to the distributor. The check valve keeps the vacuum to the distributor at a high vacuum level, so that when the engine is accelerated, the vacuum to the dis-

Typical catalytic converter mounting

tributor does not drop. This results in a constant spark advance.

When the engine temperature reaches a predetermined value, the TVS ports open to allow manifold vacuum to the distributor, and the check valve operates only as a connector.

DIESEL ENGINE EMISSIONS CONTROLS

Crankcase Ventilation

A Crankcase Depression Regulator Valve (CDRV) is used to regulate (meter) the flow of crankcase gases back into the engine to be burned. The CDRV is designed to limit vacuum in the crankcase as the gases are drawn from the valve covers through the CDRV and into the intake manifold (air crossover).

Fresh air enters the engine through the combination filter, check valve and oil fill cap. The fresh air mixes with blow-by gases and enters both valve covers. The gases pass through a filter installed on the valve covers and are drawn into connecting tubing.

Intake manifold vacuum acts against a spring loaded diaphragm to control the flow of crankcase gases. Higher intake vacuum levels pull the diaphragm closer to the top of the outlet tube. This reduces the amount of gases being drawn from the crankcase and decreases the vacuum level in the crankcase. As the intake

CRANKCASE VENTILATION SYSTEM SCHEMATIC V-TYPE DIESEL ENGINE WITH DEPRESSION REGULATOR VALVE

1. Crankcase depression regulator
2. Ventilation filter
3. Breather cap

Diesel crankcase ventilation system flow, 350 shown

vacuum decreases, the spring pushes the diaphragm away from the top of the outlet tube allowing more gases to flow to the intake manifold.

NOTE: *Do not allow any solvent to come in contact with the diaphragm of the Crankcase Depression Regulator Valve because the diaphragm will fail.*

379 diesel emissions components

1. Crankcase depression regulator (CDR)
2. Ventilation filter
3. Brace clip
4. Ventilation pipes
5. Crankcase depression regulator (CDR)

6. L.H. valve cover
7. Bracket
8. Air crossover
9. Air crossover to regulator valve pipe

Crankcase ventilation system components, diesels

Exhaust Gas Recirculation (EGR)

To lower the formation of nitrogen oxides (NO_x) in the exhaust, it is necessary to reduce combustion temperatures. This is done in the diesel, as in the gasoline engine, by introducing exhaust gases into the cylinders through the EGR valve.

On the 379 diesel, an Exhaust Pressure Regulator (EPR) valve and solenoid operate in conjunction with the EGR valve. The EPR valve's job is to increase exhaust backpressure in order to increase EGR flow (to reduce nitrous oxide emissions). The EPR valve is usually open, and

the solenoid is normally closed. When energized by the B+ wire from the Throttle Position Switch (TPS), the solenoid opens, allowing vacuum to the EPR valve, closing it. This occurs at idle. As the throttle is opened, at a calibrated throttle angle, the TPS de-energizes the EPR solenoid, cutting off vacuum to the EPR valve, closing the valve.

FUNCTIONAL TESTS OF COMPONENTS

Vacuum Regulator Valve (VRV)

The Vacuum Regulator Valve is attached to the side of the injection pump and regulates vacuum in proportion to throttle angle. Vacuum

Exhaust Pressure Regulator valve and solenoid, 379 diesels

Diesel vacuum regulator valve (VRV), mounted to injection pump

VACUUM PUMP

EGR VALVE

EPR SOLENOID

ASSEMBLY

EGR SOLENOID

FRT

Diesel EGR valve location; 379 (6.2L) shown, 350 similar

from the vacuum pump is supplied to port A and vacuum at port B is reduced as the throttle is opened. At closed throttle, the vacuum is 15 inches; at half throttle—6 inches; at wide open throttle there is zero vacuum.

Exhaust Gas Recirculation (EGR) Valve

Apply vacuum to vacuum port. The valve should be fully open at 10.5″ and closed below 6″.

Response Vacuum Reducer (RVR)

Connect a vacuum gauge to the port marked "To EGR valve or T.C.C. solenoid." Connect a hand operated vacuum pump to the VRV port. Draw a 50.66 kPa (15 inch) vacuum on the pump

and the reading on the vacuum gauge should be lower than the vacuum pump reading as follows:

- .75″ Except High Altitude
- 2.5″ High Altitude

Torque Converter Clutch Operated Solenoid

When the torque converter clutch is engaged, an electrical signal energizes the solenoid allowing ports 1 and 2 to be interconnected. When the solenoid is not energized, port 1 is closed and ports 2 and 3 are interconnected.

Solenoid Energized

- Ports 1 and 3 are connected.

EGR System Diagnosis—Diesel Engine

Condition	Possible Causes	Correction
EGR valve will not open. Engine stalls on deceleration. Engine runs rough on light throttle.	Binding or stuck EGR valve. No vacuum to EGR valve. Control valve blocked or air flow restricted.	Replace EGR valve. Replace EGR valve. Check VRV, RVR, solenoid, T.C.C. Operation, Vacuum Pump and connecting hoses.
EGR valve will not close. (Heavy smoke on acceleration).	Binding or stuck EGR valve. Constant high vacuum to EGR valve.	Replace EGR valve. Check VRV, RVR, solenoid, and connecting hoses.
EGR valve opens partially.	Binding EGR valve. Low vacuum at EGR valve.	Replace EGR valve. Check VRV, RVR, solenoid, vacuum pump, and connecting hoses.

Solenoid De-Energized
- Ports 2 and 3 are connected.

Engine Temperature Sensor (ETS)

OPERATION

The engine temperature sensor has two terminals. Twelve volts are applied to one terminal and the wire from the other terminal leads to the fast idle solenoid and Housing Pressure Cold Advance solenoid that is part of the injection pump.

The switch contacts are closed below 125°F. At the calibration point, the contacts are open which turns off the solenoids.

TWO ELECTRICAL TERMINALS:

1. TO FAST IDLE AND H.P.C.A.

2. 12 VOLTS

Engine Temperature Sensor (ETS), 350 diesel

Above Calibration
- Open Circuit.

Below Calibration
- Closed Circuit.

Vacuum Pump Diesel Engines

Since the air crossover and intake manifold in a diesel engine is unrestricted (unlike a gasoline engine which has throttle plates creating a venturi effect) there is no vacuum source. To provide vacuum, a vacuum pump is mounted in the location occupied by the distributor in a gasoline engine. This pump supplies the air conditioning servos, the cruise control servos, and the transmission vacuum modulator where required.

The pump is a diaphragm-type which needs no maintenance. It is driven by a drive gear on its lower end which meshes with gear teeth on the end of the engine's camshaft.

REMOVAL AND INSTALLATION

350 and 379 Diesels

1. Disconnect the batteries.
2. Remove the air cleaner, and cover the intake manifold.
3. Remove the vacuum pump clamp, disconnect the vacuum line and remove the pump.
4. Install a new gasket. Install the pump and reverse the removal procedures for installation.

GASOLINE ENGINE FUEL SYSTEM

Mechanical Fuel Pump

The fuel pump is a single action AC diaphragm type. All fuel pumps used on inline and V8 engines in trucks are diaphragm type and because of design are serviced by replacement only. No adjustments or repairs are possible.

The pump is operated by an eccentric on the camshaft on gasoline engines. On six cylinder engines, the eccentric acts directly on the pump rocker arm. On V8 engines, a pushrod between the camshaft eccentric and the fuel pump operates the pump rocker arm.

Some trucks have a fuel pump which has a metering outlet for a vapor return system. Any vapor which forms is returned to the fuel tank along with hot fuel through a separate line. This greatly reduces any possibility of vapor lock by keeping cool fuel from the tank constantly circulating through the fuel pump.

TESTING THE FUEL PUMP

Fuel pumps should always be tested on the vehicle. The larger line between the pump and tank is the suction side of the system and the smaller line, between the pump and carburetor is the pressure side. A leak in the pressure side would be apparent because of dripping fuel. A leak in the suction side is usually only apparent because of a reduced volume of fuel delivered to the pressure side.

1. Tighten any loose line connections and look for any kinks or restrictions.
2. Disconnect the fuel line at the carburetor. Disconnect the distributor-to-coil pri-

Vacuum pump mounting, 379 diesel. 350 diesel engine similar

mary wire. Place a container at the end of the fuel line and crank the engine a few revolutions. If little or no fuel flows from the line, either the fuel pump is inoperative or the line is plugged. Blow through the lines with compressed air and try the test again. Reconnect the line.

3. If fuel flows in good volume, check the fuel pump pressure to be sure.

4. Attach a pressure gauge to the pressure side of the fuel line. On trucks equipped with a vapor return system, squeeze off the return hose.

5. Run the engine at idle and note the reading on the gauge. Stop the engine and compare the reading with the specifications listed in the "Tune-Up Specifications" chart. If the pump is operating properly, the pressure will be as specified and will be constant at idle speed. If pressue varies sporadically or is too high or low, the pump should be replaced.

6. Remove the pressure gauge.

The following flow test can also be performed:

1. Disconnect fuel line from carburetor. Run fuel line into a suitable measuring container.

2. Run the engine at idle until there is one pint of fuel in the container. One pint should be pumped in 30 seconds or less.

3. If flow is below minimum, check for a restriction in the line.

The only way to check fuel pump pressure is by connecting an accurate pressure gauge to the fuel line at the carburetor level. Never replace a fuel pump without performing this simple test. If the engine seems to be starving out, check the ignition system first. Also check for a plugged fuel filter or a restricted fuel line before replacing the pump.

REMOVAL AND INSTALLATION

NOTE: *When you connect the fuel pump outlet fitting, always use two wrenches to avoid damaging the pump.*

1. Disconnect the fuel intake and outlet lines at the pump and plug the pump intake line.

2. On small-block V8 engines, remove the upper bolt from the right front mounting boss. Insert a long bolt ($3/8$–16 x 2 in.) in this hole to hold the fuel pump pushrod.

3. Remove the two pump mounting bolts and lockwashers; remove the pump and its gasket.

4. If the rocker arm pushrod is to be removed from V8s, remove the two adapter bolts and lockwashers and remove the adapter and its gasket from small blocks and remove the pipe plug and pushrod from 454 cu. in. engines.

5. Install the fuel pump with a new gasket reversing the removal procedure. Coat the mating surfaces with sealer.

6. Connect the fuel lines and check for leaks.

Big-block (Mark IV) fuel pump installation; other engines similar

Carburetor

REMOVAL AND INSTALLATION

1. Remove the air cleaner and its gasket.

2. Disconnect the fuel and vacuum lines from the carburetor.

3. Disconnect the choke coil rod or heated air line tube.

4. Disconnect the throttle linkage.

5. On automatic transmission trucks, disconnect the throttle valve linkage.

6. Remove the CEC valve vacuum hose and electrical connector.

7. Remove the idle stop electrical wiring from the idle stop solenoid, if so equipped.

8. Remove the carburetor attaching nuts and/or bolts, gasket or insulator, and remove the carburetor.

9. Install the carburetor using a reverse of the removal procedure. Use a new gasket and fill the float bowl with gasoline to ease starting the engine.

IDENTIFICATION

Carburetor identification numbers will generally be found in the following locations:

1 MV, ME: Stamped on the vertical portion of the float bowl, adjacent to the fuel inlet nut.

2 GV, GC: Stamped on the flat section of the float bowl next to the fuel inlet nut.

E2SE, 2SE: Stamped on the vertical surface of the float bowl adjacent to the vacuum tube.

M2MC: Stamped on the vertical surface of the left rear corner of the float bowl.

E4ME, 4 MV, M4MC, M4ME: Stamped on the vertical section of the float bowl, near the secondary throttle lever.

OVERHAUL

Efficient carburetion depends greatly on careful cleaning and inspection during overhaul, since dirt, gum, water, or varnish in or on the carburetor parts are often responsible for poor performance.

Overhaul your carburetor in a clean, dust-free area. Carefully disassemble the carburetor, referring often to the exploded views and directions packaged with the rebuilding kit. Keep all similar and look-alike parts segregated during disassembly and cleaning to avoid accidental interchange during assembly. Make a note of all jet sizes.

When the carburetor is disassembled, wash all parts (except diaphragms, electric choke units, pump plunger, and any other plastic, leather, fiber, or rubber parts) in clean carburetor solvent. Do not leave parts in the solvent any longer than is necessary to sufficiently loosen the deposits. Excessive cleaning may remove the special finish from the float bowl and choke valve bodies, leaving these parts unfit for service. Rinse all parts in clean solvent, and blow them dry with compressed air or allow them to air dry. Wipe clean all cork, plastic, leather, and fiber parts with a clean, lint-free cloth.

Blow out all passages and jets with compressed air and be sure that there are no restrictions or blockages. Never use wire or similar tools to clean jets, fuel passages, or air bleeds. Clean all jets and valves separately to avoid accidental interchange.

Check all parts for wear or damage. If wear or damage is found, replace the defective parts. Especially check the following:

1. Check the float needle and seat for wear. If wear is found, replace the complete assembly.

2. Check the float hinge pin for wear and the float(s) for dents or distortion. Replace the float if fuel has leaked into it.

3. Check the throttle and choke shaft bores for wear or an out-of-round condition. Damage or wear to the throttle arm, shaft, or shaft bore will often require replacement of the throttle body. These parts require a close tolerance of it; wear may allow air leakage, which could affect starting and idling.

NOTE: *Throttle shafts and bushings are not included in overhaul kits. They can be purchased separately.*

4. Inspect the idle mixture adjusting needles for burrs or grooves. Any such condition requires replacement of the needle, since you will not be able to obtain a satisfactory idle.

5. Test the accelerator pump check valves. They should pass air one way but not the other. Test for proper seating by blowing and sucking on the valve. Replace the valve as necessary. If the valve is satisfactory, wash the valve again to remove breath moisture.

6. Check the bowl cover for warped surfaces with a straightedge.

7. Closely inspect the valves and seats for wear and damage, replacing as necessary.

8. After the carburetor is assembled, check the choke valve for freedom of operation.

Carburetor overhaul kits are recommended for each overhaul. These kits contain all gaskets and new parts to replace those which deteriorate most rapidly. Failure to replace all parts supplied with the kit (especially gaskets) can result in poor performance later.

Some carburetor manufacturers supply overhaul kits of three basic types: minor repair; major repair; and gasket kits.

After cleaning and checking all components, reassemble the carburetor, using new parts and referring to the exploded view. When reassembling, make sure that all screws and jets are tight in their seats, but do not overtighten as the tips will be distorted. Tighten all screws gradually, in rotation. Do not tighten needle valves into their seats; uneven jetting will result. Always use new gaskets. Be sure to adjust the float level when reassembling.

Carburetor Adjustments

PRELIMINARY CHECKS (ALL CARBURETORS)

The following should be observed before attempting any adjustments.

1. Run the engine to normal operating temperature.

2. Check the torque of all carburetor mounting nuts. Also check the intake manifold-to-cylinder head bolts. If air is leaking at any of these points, you will not get a proper adjustment.

3. Check the manifold heat control valve (if used) to be sure that it is free.

4. Check and adjust the choke as necessary.

5. Adjust the idle speed and mixture. If any adjustments are performed that might possibly change the idle speed or mixture, adjust the idle and mixture again when you are finished.

ROCHESTER MV (1970–74)

Fast Idle

NOTE: *The fast idle adjustment must be made with the transmission in Neutral.*

Carburetor Specifications

ROCHESTER MV (1970–74)

	1970	1971	1972	1973	1974
Float Level (in.)	¼	¼	¼	¼	¼ ⑮
Fast Idle Mechanical (in.)	0.100	0.100	—	—	—
Running (rpm)	2400	2400	2400	2400	1800 ⑯
Choke Rod (in.)	0.180 ①	0.180 ④	⑦	⑪	.0245 ⑰
Vacuum Break (in.)	0.260 ②	0.350 ⑤	0.190 ⑧	0.430 ⑫	0.300 ⑱
Choke Unloader (in.)	0.350	0.350	0.500	0.600 ⑬	0.500 ⑲
Thermostat Choke Rod (in.)	③	—	—	—	—
Metering Rod (in.)	0.070	0.070 ⑥	0.070 ⑨	0.070 ⑭	0.080 ⑳
CEC Valve (rpm)	NA	㉑	⑩	⑩	—

—Not applicable
① W/292 cu in. engine—0.275 in.
② W/292 cu in. engine—0.350 in.
③ Bottom of the rod even with top of hole
④ 0.300 in. w/carb No. 7021022
   0.275 inn. w/carb No. 7041026
⑤ 0.230 in. w/carb No. 7041021
   0.260 in. w/carb No. 7041025
⑥ 0.080 in. w/carb No. 7041021
⑦ 0.150 in. w/carb No. 7042021, 7042921
   0.125 in. w/carb No. 7042022, 7042922
   0.180 in. w/carb No. 7042025
   0.275 in. w/carb No. 7042026
⑧ 0.225 in. w/carb No. 7042021, 7042921
   0.260 in. w/carb No. 7042025
   0.350 in. w/carb No. 7042026
⑨ 0.076 in. w/carb No. 7042991
   0.078 in. w/carb No. 7042021
   0.079 in. w/carb No. 7042022
⑩ 250 cu in. only—1000 (manual/Neutral)
   —650 (automatic/Drive)

⑪ 0.245 in. w/carb No. 7043022
   0.275 in. w/carb No. 7043021
   0.350 in. w/carb No. 7043025
   0.375 in. w/carb No. 7043026
⑫ 0.300 in. w/carb No. 7043022
   0.350 in. w/carb No. 7043021
⑬ 0.500 in. w/carb No. 7043022, 3021
⑭ 0.080 in. w/carb No. 7043022, 3021
⑮ 0.295 in. w/carb No. 7044021, 4022, 4321
⑯ 2400 rpm w/carb No. 7044025, 4026
⑰ 0.275 in. w/carb No. 7044021, 4026
   0.300 in. w/carb No. 7044321
⑱ 0.350 in. w/carb No. 7044021, 4026
   0.375 in. w/carb No. 7044321
⑲ 0.521 in. w/carb No. 7044025, 4026
   measured at top of choke blade
⑳ 0.070 in. w/carb No. 7044025, 4026
㉑ 250, 292, 307 Manual—1000 rpm
   350V8 Manual—900 rpm
   402V8 Manual—850 rpm
   250, 292 Automatic—750
   350, 307V8 Automatic—650
   402V8 Automatic—650

ROCHESTER MV (1975)

Float Level (in.)	11⁄32	Primary Vacuum Break (in.)	0.300 ②
Metering Rod (in.)	0.080	Auxiliary Vacuum Break (in.)	③
Choke Rod (in.)	①	Choke Unloader (in.)	0.325 ④

① 0.245 w/carb No. 7045004, 302, 304
   0.260 w/carb No. 7045002
   0.275 w/carb No. 7045003, 005, 303, 305
② 0.350 w/carb No. 7045005, 303, 305

③ 0.150 w/carb No. 7045004, 302
   0.170 w/carb No. 7045303
   0.290 w/carb No. 7045002, 003, 005, 304, 305
④ 0.275 w/carb No. 7045302, 303

Carburetor Specifications (cont.)

ROCHESTER MV (1976)

Carburetor Number	Float Level (in.)	Metering Rod (in.)	Choke Rod (Fast Idle Cam) (in.)	Primary Vacuum Break (in.)	Auxiliary Vacuum Break (in.)	Choke Unloader (in.)
17056002	11/32	0.080	0.130	0.165	0.265	0.335
6003	11/32	0.080	0.145	0.180	W.O.	0.335
6302	11/32	0.080	0.155	0.190	W.O.	0.325
6303	11/32	0.080	0.180	0.225	W.O.	0.325
6004	11/32	0.080	0.130	0.165	0.265	0.335
6006	1/4	0.080	0.130	0.165	—	0.270
6007	1/4	0.070	0.130	0.165	—	0.275
6008, 6009, 6308, 6309	1/4	0.070	0.150	0.190	—	0.275

ROCHESTER ME (1977)

Carburetor Number	Float Level (in.)	Metering Rod (in.)	Choke Rod (Fast Idle Cam) (in.)	Primary Vacuum Break (in.)	Auxiliary Vacuum Break (in.)	Choke Unloader (in.)
17057001	3/8	0.080	0.125	0.150	—	0.325
7002, 7004, 7101, 7302	3/8	0.080	0.110	0.135	—	0.325
7005	3/8	0.080	0.125	0.180	—	0.325
7006, 7007	5/16	0.070	0.150	0.180	—	0.275
7008, 7009, 7308, 7309	5/16	0.065	0.150	0.180	—	0.275
7303	3/8	0.090	0.125	0.150	—	0.325

ROCHESTER ME (1978)

Carburetor Number	Float Level (in.)	Metering Rod (in.)	Choke Rod (Fast Idle Cam) (in.)	Primary Vacuum Break (in.)	Auxiliary Vacuum Break (in.)	Choke Unloader (in.)
17058008, 8009, 8308, 8309, 8358, 8359	5/16	0.065	0.275	0.275	—	0.520
8006, 8007	5/16	0.070	0.275	0.275	—	0.520
8310, 8312, 8320, 8322	5/16	0.080	0.190	0.250	—	0.600
8311, 8313, 8323	5/16	0.100	0.190	0.250	—	0.600
8021, 8022, 8024, 8081, 8082, 8084	5/16	—	0.200	0.250	—	0.450

ROCHESTER ME (1979)

Carburetor Number	Float Level (in.)	Metering Rod (in.)	Choke Rod (Fast Idle Cam) (in.)	Primary Vacuum Break (in.)	Auxiliary Vacuum Break (in.)	Choke Unloader (in.)
17059009, 9309, 9359	5/16	0.065	0.275	0.400	—	0.521

Carburetor Specifications (cont.)

ROCHESTER MV (1980–84)

Carburetor Number	Float Level (in.)	Metering Rod (in.)	Choke Rod (Fast Idle Cam) (in.)	Primary Vacuum Break (in.)	Auxiliary Vacuum Break (in.)	Choke Unloader (in.)

ROCHESTER ME (1980–84)

Carburetor Number	Float Level (in.)	Metering Rod (in.)	Choke Rod (Fast Idle Cam) (in.)	Primary Vacuum Break (in.)	Auxiliary Vacuum Break (in.)	Choke Unloader (in.)
17080009, 0309, 0359, 1309 1009, 1329	$^{11}/_{32}$	0.090	0.275	0.400	—	0.520

ROCHESTER 2GV, 2GC

	(2GV) 1970	(2GV) 1971	(2GV) 1972	(2GV) 1973	(2GV) 1974	(2GC) 1975	(2GC) 1976	(2GC) 1977–78
Float Level (in.)	$^{23}/_{32}$ ⑦	$^{21}/_{32}$ ①	$^{21}/_{32}$ ㉒	$^{21}/_{32}$ ⑬	$^{19}/_{32}$	$^{21}/_{32}$	$^{21}/_{32}$	$^{19}/_{32}$
Float Drop (in.)	$1^{3}/_{4}$	$1^{3}/_{4}$ ②	$1^{9}/_{32}$	$1^{9}/_{32}$	$1^{9}/_{32}$	$^{31}/_{32}$	$1^{9}/_{32}$	$1^{9}/_{32}$
Pump Rod (in.)	—	$1^{3}/_{64}$ ③	$1^{5}/_{16}$ ㉓	$1^{5}/_{16}$ ⑭	$1^{9}/_{32}$ ⑱	$1^{5}/_{8}$	$1^{11}/_{16}$	$1^{21}/_{32}$
Choke Rod (in.) (Fast Idle Cam)	0.060	0.040 ④	0.040 ⑩	0.150 ⑮	0.200 ⑲	0.400	0.260	0.260
Vacuum Break (in.)	0.140 ⑧	0.080 ⑤	0.080 ⑪	0.080 ⑯	0.140 ⑳	0.130	0.130	0.130 ㉕㉖
Choke Unloader (in.)	0.215	0.215 ⑥	0.210 ㉔	0.215 ⑰	0.250 ㉑	0.350	0.325	0.325
Thermostatic Choke Rod	⑨	—	—	—	—	—	—	—
CEC Valve (rpm)	⑫	⑫	—	—	—	—	—	—
Fast Idle (rpm)	2200– 2400	—	1850 (1¼) 2200 (1½)	1600	1600	—	—	—

① $^{23}/_{32}$ in. w/carb No. 7041138, 139
② 1¼ in. w/carb No. 7041138, 139
③ $1^{5}/_{32}$ in. w/carb No. 7041138, 139
④ 0.100 in. w/carb No. 7041138, 139
⑤ 0.170 in. w/carb No. 7041138
   0.180 in. w/carb No. 7041139
⑥ 0.325 in. w/carb No. 7041138, 139
⑦ $^{27}/_{32}$ in. w/carb No. 7040108
⑧ 0.130 in. w/carb No. 7040108
⑨ Bottom of rod even with top of hole
⑩ 0.075 in. w/carb No. 7042824, 825
   0.100 in. w/carb No. 7042108
⑪ 0.110 in. w/carb No. 7042824, 825
   0.170 in. w/carb No. 7042108
⑫ 1000 w/Manual
   650 w/Automatic

⑬ $^{25}/_{32}$ in. w/carb No. 7043108
⑭ $1^{7}/_{16}$ in. w/carb No. 7043108
⑮ 0.200 in. w/carb No. 7043108
⑯ 0.140 in. w/carb No. 7043108
⑰ 0.250 in. w/carb No. 7043108
⑱ $1^{3}/_{16}$ in. w/carb No. 7044114
⑲ 0.245 in. w/carb No. 7044114
⑳ 0.130 in. w/carb No. 7044114
㉑ 0.325 in. w/carb No. 7044114
㉒ $^{25}/_{32}$ in. w/carb No. 7042108
㉓ 1½ in. w/carb No. 7042108
㉔ 0.325 in. w/carb No. 7042108
㉕ Below 22,500 mi
   0.160 above 22,500 mi
㉖ 0.190 in. w/carb No. 17056137
— Not applicable

NOTE: 2 versions of the 2GV are available: 1½ in. diameter and 1¼ in. diameter venturi.

Carburetor Specifications (cont.)

ROCHESTER 2SE (1979–82)

Carburetor Identification	Float Level (in.)	Pump Rod (in.)	Fast Idle (rpm)	Choke Coil Lever (in.)	Fast Idle Cam (deg./in.)	Air Valve Rod (in.)	Primary Vacuum Break (deg./in.)	Secondary Vacuum Break (deg./in.)	Choke Unloader (deg./in.)	Secondary Lockout (in.)
17059640	1/8	9/16	2000	0.085	17/.090	0.040	20/.110	37/.234	49/.341	.011–.040
17059641	1/8	9/16	1800	0.085	17/.090	0.040	23.5/.132	37/.234	49/.341	.011–.040
17059643	1/8	9/16	1800	0.085	17/.090	0.040	23.5/.132	37/.234	49/.341	.011–.040
17059740	1/8	9/16	2000	0.085	17/.090	0.040	20/.110	37/.234	49/.341	.011–.040
17059741	1/8	9/16	2100	0.085	17/.090	0.040	20/.110	37/.234	49/.341	.011–.040
17058764	1/8	9/16	2100	0.085	17/.090	0.040	20/.110	37/.234	49/.341	.011–.040
17059765	1/8	9/16	2100	0.085	17/.090	0.040	23.5/.132	37/.234	49/.341	.011–.040
17059767	1/8	9/16	2100	0.085	17/.090	0.040	23.5/.132	37/.234	49/.341	.011–.040
17080621	1/8	9/16	2000	0.085	17/.090	0.010	22/.123	35/.220	41/.269	.011–.040
17080622	1/8	9/16	2200	0.085	17/.090	0.010	22/.123	35/.220	41/.269	.011–.040
17080623	1/8	9/16	2000	0.085	17/.090	0.010	22/.123	35/.220	41/.269	.011–.040
17080626	1/8	9/16	2200	0.085	17/.090	0.010	22/.123	35/.220	41/.269	.011–.040
17080720	1/8	9/16	2200	0.085	17/.090	0.010	20/.110	35/.220	41/.269	.011–.040
17080721	1/8	9/16	2000	0.085	17/.090	0.010	23.5/.132	35/.220	41/.269	.011–.040
17080722	1/8	9/16	2200	0.085	17/.090	0.010	20/.110	35/.220	41/.269	.011–.040
17080723	1/8	9/16	2000	0.085	17/.090	0.010	23.5/.132	35/.220	41/.269	.011–.040
17081621	3/16	5/8	①	—	15/.077	②	26/.149	38/.243	38/.243	—
17081622	3/16	5/8	①	—	15/.077	②	26/.149	38/.243	38/.243	—
17081623	3/16	5/8	①	—	15/.077	②	26/.149	38/.243	38/.243	—
17081624	3/16	5/8	①	—	15/.077	②	26/.149	38/.243	38/.243	—
17081625	3/16	5/8	①	—	15/.077	②	26/.149	38/.243	38/.243	—
17081626	3/16	5/8	①	—	15/.077	②	26/.149	38/.243	38/.243	—
17081627	3/16	5/8	①	—	15/.077	②	26/.149	38/.243	38/.243	—
17081629	3/16	5/8	①	—	15/.077	②	24/.136	34/.211	41/.269	—
17081630	3/16	5/8	①	—	15/.077	②	26/.149	38/.243	38/.243	—
17081633	3/16	5/8	①	—	15/.077	②	26/.149	38/.243	38/.243	—
17081720	3/16	5/8	①	—	15/.077	②	30/.179	37/.234	41/.269	—
17081721	3/16	5/8	①	—	15/.077	②	30/.179	37/.234	41/.269	—
17081725	3/16	5/8	①	—	15/.077	②	30/.179	37/.234	41/.269	—
17081726	3/16	5/8	①	—	15/.077	②	30/.179	37/.234	41/.269	—
17081727	3/16	5/8	①	—	15/.077	②	30/.179	37/.234	41/.269	—

① See underhood specifications sticker
② 1° all carburetors

ROCHESTER M2MC (1979–81)

Carburetor Identification	Float Level (in.)	Choke Rod (in.)	Choke Unloader (in.)	Front Vacuum Break (in.)	Pump Rod (in.)	Choke Coil Lever (in.)	Automatic Choke (notches)
All 1979	$15/32$	0.243	0.243	0.171	$13/32$ ①	0.120	1 Lean
All 1980	$7/16$	0.243	0.243	0.171	$9/32$ ①	0.120	②
All 1981	$13/32$	0.243	0.243	0.142	$5/16$	—	—

① Inner hole
② Riveted cover; replacement kits contain setting instructions

Carburetor Specifications (cont.)

ROCHESTER 4MV

	1970	1971	1972	1973	1974	1975
Float Level (in.)	$1/4$	$1/4$ ④	⑥	⑨	⑫	⑯
Accelerator Pump (in.)	$5/16$	$5/16$	$3/8$	$13/32$	$13/32$	0.275
Fast Idle (rpm)	2400	2400	⑦	1600	1600 ⑬	1600
Choke Rod (in.)	0.100	0.100	0.100	0.430	0.430	0.430
Choke Vacuum Break (in.)	0.245 ①	0.260	0.215 ⑧	0.215 ⑩	0.215 ⑭	⑰
Choke Unloader (in.)	0.450	0.450	0.450	0.450	0.450	0.450
Thermostatic Choke Rod Setting	②	②	—	—	—	—
Air Valve Spring (in.)	$7/16$ ③	—	—	$1/2$ ⑪	$7/8$ ⑮	⑱
Air Valve Dashpot	0.020	0.020	0.020	—	—	0.015
CEC Valve (rpm)	—	⑤	—	—	—	—

—Not applicable
① 0.275 in. w/carb No. 7040511 and manual trans
  No. 7040509 and manual trans
② Top of rod should be even with bottom of hole
③ $13/16$ in. w/all 396 cu in. V8
④ $11/32$ in. w/carb No. 7041209
⑤ 350 V8 w/manual trans—900 rpm
  402 V8 w/manual trans—850 rpm
  350 V8 w/automatic trans—650 rpm
  402 V8 w/automatic trans—650 rpm
⑥ $1/4$ in. w/carb No. 7042206, 218
  $3/16$ in. w/carb No. 7042208, 210, 211, 910, 911
  $11/32$ in. w/carb No. 7042207, 219
⑦ 1350—Manual transmission
  1500—Automatic transmission
⑧ 0.250 in. w/carb No. 7042206, 207, 218, 219
⑨ $7/32$ in. w/carb No. 7043202, 203
  $5/16$ in. w/carb No. 7043208, 215
  $1/4$ in. w/carb No. 7043200, 216, 207, 507
⑩ 0.250 in. w/carb No. 7043200, 216
  0.275 in. w/carb No. 7043507
⑪ $11/16$ in. w/carb No. 7043200, 216, 207, 507

⑫ $1/4$ in. w/carb No. 7044202, 502, 203, 503, 218, 518, 219, 519
  $11/32$ in. w/carb No. 7044213, 513
  0.675 in. w/carb No. 7044212, 217, 512, 517, 500, 520
⑬ 1700 rpm in. w/carb No. 7044212, 217, 512, 517
⑭ 0.220 in. w/carb No. 7044223, 227
  0.230 in. w/carb No. 7044212, 217, 512, 517
  0.250 in. w/carb No. 7044500, 520
⑮ $7/16$ in. w/carb No. 7044223, 227, 212, 217, 512, 517, 500, 520
⑯ $3/8$ in. w/carb No. 7045212
  $11/32$ in. w/carb No. 7045213, 229, 583, 589
  $15/32$ in. w/carb No. 7045229
⑰ 0.225 in. w/carb No. 7045212
  0.210 in. w/carb No. 7045213
  0.200 in. w/carb No. 7045229
  0.230 in. w/carb No. 7045583, 589
⑱ $7/16$ in. w/carb No. 7045212
  $7/8$ in. w/carb No. 7045213, 583
  $3/4$ in. w/carb No. 7045229, 589

Carburetor Specifications (cont.)

ROCHESTER 4MV (1976)

Carburetor Number	Float Level (in.)	Vacuum Break (in.)	Air Valve Spring Windup (in.)
7045231	11/32	0.145	7/8
7045229	11/32	0.138	3/4
7045583	11/32	0.155	7/8
7045588	11/32	0.155	3/4
17056212	3/8	0.155	7/16

ROCHESTER 4MV (1977)

Carburetor Number	Float Level (in.)	Vacuum Break (in.)	Air Valve Spring Windup (in.)
7045583	11/32	0.120	7/8
17056212	3/8	0.120	7/16
17057213	11/32	0.115	7/8

NOTE: Pump Rod: 9/32 in. in all applications
Air Valve Dashpot: 0.015 in. in all applications
Choke Unloader: 0.295 in. except
17057213: 0.205 in.
Choke Rod (Fast Idle Cam): 0.290 in. except
17057213: 0.220 in.

ROCHESTER M4MC, M4MCA (1975)

Carburetor Number	Float Level (in.)	Choke Rod (Fast Idle Cam) (in.)	Front Vacuum Break (in.)	Rear Vacuum Break (in.)	Choke Unloader (in.)	Choke Setting
7045202, 203	15/32	0.300	0.180	0.170	0.325	*
7045220	17/32	0.300	0.200	0.550	0.325	*
7045512	17/32	0.300	0.180	0.550	0.325	*

ROCHESTER M4MC (1976)

Carburetor Number	Float Level (in.)	Choke Rod (Fast Idle Cam) (in.)	Front Vacuum Break (in.)	Rear Vacuum Break (in.)	Choke Unloader (in.)	Choke Setting
17056208, 508	**	0.325	0.185	—	0.325	2 NL
17056209	**	0.325	0.185	—	0.325	3 NL
17056509	**	0.325	0.185	—	0.325	1 NL
17056512	7/16	0.325	0.185	—	0.275	Index

ROCHESTER M4MC (1977)

Carburetor Number	Float Level (in.)	Choke Rod (Fast Idle Cam) (in.)	Front Vacuum Break (in.)	Rear Vacuum Break (in.)	Choke Unloader (in.)	Choke Setting
17057202, 204	15/32	0.325	0.160	—	0.280	2 NL
17057209	7/16	0.325	0.160	—	0.325	3 NL
17057229	11/32	0.285	0.160	—	0.280	2 NL
17057502, 504	15/32	0.325	0.165	—	0.280	2 NL
17057503	15/32	0.325	0.165	—	0.280	1 NL
17057512	7/16	0.285	0.165	—	0.240	Index
17057529	11/32	0.285	0.175	—	0.280	2 NL
17057582, 584	15/32	0.385	0.180	—	0.280	2 NL

ROCHESTER M4ME (1976–77)

Carburetor Number	Float Level (in.)	Choke Rod (Fast Idle Cam) (in.)	Front Vacuum Break (in.)	Rear Vacuum Break (in.)	Choke Unloader (in.)	Choke Setting
17056221	7/16	0.300	—	0.160	0.325	2 NR
17057221	3/8	0.385	—	0.160	0.280	2 Notches Counter-clockwise

Inner Pump Rod Setting: 0.275 in.—1975;
9/32 in.—1976; 9/32 in.—1977 except:
17057582, 584: 3/8 in. Outer Pump Rod only
Choke Coil Lever: 0.120 in. all years
Air Valve Dashpot: 0.015 in. all years
Air Valve Spring Windup: 7/8 in. all years except:

7045220, 512: 9/16 in. 1975 only
NL: Notches Lean
NR: Notches Rich
* Choke valve setting is at the top of the valve
** Needle seat with groove at upper edge: 5/16 in.
Needle seat without groove at upper edge: 7/16 in.

Carburetor Specifications (cont.)

ROCHESTER M4MC, 4MV (1978)

Float Adjustment: (in.)	
17058212, 8218, 8219, 8222, 8525	7/16
8500, 8501, 8520, 8521	3/8
8512	13/32
All others	15/32

Pump Adjustment: (in.)	
17058509, 8510, 8586, 8588	11/32 Outer
All others	9/32 Inner

Choke Coil: (in.)	
All	0.120

Choke Setting	
17058512	Index
8201, 8219, 8500, 8501, 8520, 8521	3 NL
8218, 8222, 8509, 8510, 8586, 8588	2 NL
All others	1 NL

Air Valve Spring Windup:	
17058525	3/4 turn
All others	7/8 turn

ROCHESTER M4MC (1979)

Float Adjustment: (in.)	
17059212	7/16
512	13/32
520, 521	3/8
All others	15/32

Pump Adjustment: (in.)	
17059212, 213, 215, 229, 510, 512, 513, 515, 520, 521, 529	9/32 Inner
377, 378, 527, 528	9/32 Outer
All others	13/32 Inner

Choke Coil Lever: (in.)	
All	0.120

Choke Rod: (in.)	
17059213, 215, 229, 513, 515, 529	0.234
All others	0.314

Air Valve Rod: (in.)	
All	0.015

Unloader Adjustment: (in.)	
17059212, 213, 215, 229, 512, 513, 515, 529	0.260
All others	0.277

Front Vacuum Break: (in.)	
17059213, 215, 229, 513, 515, 529	0.129
212, 512	0.136
501, 520, 521	0.164
509, 510, 586, 588	0.179

Rear Vacuum Break: (in.)	
17059363, 366, 368, 377, 378, 503, 506, 508, 527, 528	0.149
All others	0.129

Air Valve Spring: (turns)	
17059212, 512	¾
213, 215, 229, 513, 515, 529	1
All others	⅞

Choke Setting:	
17059061, 201	Index
509, 510, 586, 588	2 Lean
520, 521, 501	3 Lean
212, 213, 215, 229, 512, 513, 515, 529	1 Rich
All others	1 Lean

ROCHESTER M4MC (1980)

Float Adjustment: (in.)	
17080213, 215, 513, 515, 229, 529	⅜
All others	¹⁵⁄₃₂

Pump Adjustment: (in.)	
All	⁹⁄₃₂ Inner

Choke Coil Lever (in.)	
All	0.120

Choke Rod: (in.)	
17080213, 215, 513, 515, 229, 529	0.234
All others	0.314

Air Valve Rod: (in.)	
All	0.015

Unloader Adjustment: (in.)	
17080212, 213, 215, 512, 513, 515, 229, 529	0.260
All others	0.277

Front Vacuum Break: (in.)	
17080212, 512	0.136
All others	0.129

Rear Vacuum Break: (in.)	
17080290, 291, 292, 503, 506, 508	0.149
212, 213, 215, 512, 513, 515, 229, 529	0.179
All others	0.129

Air Valve Spring: (turns)	
17080212, 512	¾
213, 215, 513, 515, 229, 529	1
All others	⅞

Choke Setting:
All models have a riveted choke cover; replacement kits contain setting instructions.

NOTE: *All other adjustments require special angle gauge.*

Carburetor Specifications (cont.)

ROCHESTER M4MC–M4ME (1981–82)

Carburetor Identification	Float Adjustment: (in.)	Pump Adjustment: (in.)	Choke Rod: (in.)	Air Valve Rod: (in.)	Unloader Adjustment: (in.)	Front Vacuum Break: (in.)	Rear Vacuum Break: (in.)	Air Valve Spring: (turns)	Choke Setting:
17080212	3/8	9/32	.314	.025	.260	.136	.179	3/4	①
17080213	3/8	9/32	.234	.025	.260	.129	.179	1	①
17080215	3/8	9/32	.234	.025	.260	.129	.179	1	①
17080298	3/8	9/32	.234	.025	.260	.129	.179	1	①
17080507	3/8	9/32	.234	.025	.260	.129	.179	1	①
17080512	3/8	9/32	.314	.025	.260	.136	.179	3/4	①
17080513	3/8	9/32	.234	.025	.260	.129	.179	3/4	①
17081200	15/32	9/32	.314	.025	.277	.136	.129	7/8	①
17081201	15/32	9/32	.314	.025	.277	.129	.129	7/8	①
17081205	15/32	9/32	.314	.025	.277	.129	.129	7/8	①
17081206	15/32	9/32	.314	.025	.277	.129	.129	7/8	①
17081220	15/32	9/32	.314	.025	.277	.129	.129	7/8	①
17081226	15/32	9/32	.314	.025	.277	.136	.129	7/8	①
17081227	15/32	9/32	.314	.025	.277	.136	.129	7/8	①
17081290	13/32	9/32	.314	.025	.277	.129	.136	7/8	①
17081291	13/32	9/32	.314	.025	.277	.129	.136	7/8	①
17081292	13/32	9/32	.314	.025	.277	.129	.136	7/8	①
17081506	13/32	9/32	.314	.025	.227	.129	.227	7/8	①
17081508	13/32	9/32	.314	.025	.227	.129	.227	7/8	①
17081524	13/32	5/16	.314	.025	.243	.142	.227	7/8	①
17081526	13/32	5/16	.314	.025	.243	.142	.227	7/8	①

① All models have a riveted choke cover; replacement kit contains setting instructions.

Carburetor Specifications (cont.)

ROCHESTER E2SE (1983–84)

Carburetor Identification	Float Level (in.)	Air Valve Spring (turns)	Fast Idle (rpm)	Choke Coil Lever (in.)	Fast Idle Cam (deg./in.)	Air Valve Rod (deg.)	Primary Vacuum Break (deg./in.)	Secondary Vacuum Break (deg./in.)	Choke Unloader (deg./in.)
17083430	11/32	1	①	.085	15/.077	1	26/.149	38/.243	42/.277
17083431	11/32	1	①	.085	15/.077	1	26/.149	38/.243	42/.277
17083434	11/32	1	①	.085	15/.077	1	26/.149	38/.243	42/.277
17083435	11/32	1	①	.085	15/.077	1	26/.149	38/.243	42/.277

① See Underhood Specifications Sticker

Carburetor Specifications (cont.)

ROCHESTER E4ME (1983–84)

Carburetor Number	Float Level (in.)	Choke Rod (Fast Idle Cam) (deg./in.)	Front Vacuum Break (deg./in.)	Rear Vacuum Break (deg./in.)	Air Valve Spring (turns)	Choke Unloader (deg./in.)
17083202	$^{11}/_{32}$	20/.110	—	27/.157	$^{7}/_{8}$	38/.243
17083203	$^{11}/_{32}$	38/.243	—	27/.157	$^{7}/_{8}$	38/.243
17083204	$^{11}/_{32}$	20/110	—	27/.157	$^{7}/_{8}$	38/.243
17083207	$^{11}/_{32}$	38/.243	—	27/.157	$^{7}/_{8}$	38/.243
17083216	$^{11}/_{32}$	20/.110	—	27/.157	$^{7}/_{8}$	38/.243
17083218	$^{11}/_{32}$	20/.110	—	27/.157	$^{7}/_{8}$	38/.243
17083236	$^{11}/_{32}$	20/.110	—	27/.157	$^{7}/_{8}$	38/.243
17083506	$^{7}/_{16}$	20/.110	27/.157	36/.227	$^{7}/_{8}$	36/.227
17083508	$^{7}/_{16}$	20/.110	27/.157	36/.227	$^{7}/_{8}$	36/.227
17083524	$^{7}/_{16}$	20/.110	25/.142	36/.227	$^{7}/_{8}$	36/.227
17083526	$^{7}/_{16}$	20/.110	25/.142	36/.227	$^{7}/_{8}$	36/.227

1. Position the fast idle lever on the high step of the fast idle cam.

2. Be sure that the choke is properly adjusted and in the wide open position with the engine warm. Disconnect the vacuum advance on 1974 manual transmission models.

3. Bend the fast idle lever until the specified speed is obtained.

Choke Rod (Fast Idle Cam)

NOTE: *Adjust the fast idle before making choke rod adjustments.*

1. Place the fast idle cam follower on the second step of the fast idle cam and hold it firmly against the rise to the high step.

2. Rotate the choke valve in the direction of a closed choke by applying force to the choke coil lever.

3. Bend the choke rod, to give the specified opening between the lower edge of the choke valve and the inside air horn wall.

NOTE: *Measurement must be made at the center of the choke valve.*

Choke Vacuum Break

The adjustment of the vacuum break diaphragm unit insures correct choke valve opening after engine starting.

1. Remove the air cleaner on vehicles with Therm AC air cleaner; plug the sensor's vacuum take off port.

2. Using an external vacuum source, apply vacuum to the vacuum break diaphragm until the plunger is fully seated.

3. When the plunger is seated, push the choke valve toward the closed position.

4. Holding the choke valve in this position, place the specified gauge between the lower edge of the choke valve and the air horn wall.

5. If the measurement is not correct, bend the vacuum break rod.

Choke Unloader

1. Apply pressure to the choke valve and hold it in the closed position.

2. Open the throttle valve to the wide open position.

3. Check the dimension between the lower edge of the choke plate and the air horn wall; if adjustment is needed, bend the unloader tang on the throttle lever to adjust to specification.

Choke Coil Rod

1. Disconnect the coil rod from the upper choke lever and hold the choke valve closed.

2. Push down on the coil rod to the end of its travel.

3. The top of the rod should be even with the bottom hole in the choke lever.

4. To make adjustments, bend the rod as needed.

Float

1. Hold the float retainer in place and the float arm against the top of the float needle by pushing down on the float arm at the outer end toward the float bowl casting.

2. Using an adjustable T scale, measure the distance from the toe of the float to the float bowl gasket surface.

NOTE: *The float bowl gasket should be re-*

*moved and the gauge held on the index point
on the float for accurate measurement.*

3. Adjust the float level by bending the float
arm up or down at the float arm junction.

Metering Rod

1. Hold the throttle valve wide-open and
push down on the metering rod against spring
tension, then remove the rod from the main
metering jet.

2. In order to check adjustment, the slow
idle screw must be backed out and the fast idle
cam rotated so that the fast idle cam follower
does not contact the steps on the cam.

3. With the throttle valve closed, push down
on the power piston until it contacts its stop.

4. With the power piston depressed, swung
the metering rod holder over the flat surface of
the bowl casting next to the carburetor bore.

5. Insert a specified size drill between the
bowl casting sealing bead and the lower surface
of the metering rod holder. The drill should
slide smoothly between both surfaces.

6. If adjustment is needed, carefully bend
the metering rod holder up or down. After adjustment, reinstall the metering rod.

C.E.C. Solenoid Adjustment

Do not set the C.E.C. valve to the idle rpm.
This adjustment should only be made after replacement of the solenoid, carburetor overhaul, or after the throttle body is replaced.

1. With the engine running, and transmission in Neutral (manual) or Drive (Automatic),
air conditioner OFF, distributor vacuum hose
removed and plugged, and fuel tank vapor hose
disconnected, manually extend the C.E.C. valve
plunger to contact the throttle lever.

2. Adjust the plunger length to obtain the
C.E.C. valve rpm.

3. Reconnect the vapor hose and vacuum
hose.

*ROCHESTER MV (1975–76), ME (1977
AND LATER)*

Fast idle

1. Check and adjust the idle speed.

2. With the engine at normal operating
temperature, air cleaner ON, EGR valve signal line disconnected and plugged and the air
conditioning OFF, connect a tachometer.

3. Disconnect the vacuum advance hose at
the distributor and plug the line.

4. With the transmission in Neutral, start the
engine and set the fast idle cam follower on the
high step of the cam.

5. Bend the tang in or out to obtain the fast
idle speed.

MV fast idle adjustment

Fast Idle Cam

1. Check and adjust the fast idle speed.

2. Set the fast idle cam follower on the second step of the cam.

3. Apply force to the choke coil rod and hold
the choke valve toward the closed position.

4. Measure the clearance between the lower
edge of the choke valve and the inside of the
air horn wall. For 1976–77, insert the gauge
between the upper edge of the choke valve and
the inside of the air horn wall.

5. Bend the cam to choke rod to obtain
clearance.

MV fast idle cam adjustment

Choke Unloader

1. Hold the choke valve down by applying
light force to the choke coil lever.

2. Open the throttle valve to wide open.

3. Measure the clearance between the upper edge of the choke valve and the air horn
wall. Measure at the lower edge of the choke
valve on 1978 and later models only.

4. If adjustment is necessary, bend the tang
on the throttle lever.

MV choke unloader adjuster

Choke Coil Rod

1975

1. Pull the rod up to the end of its travel to completely close the choke valve.
2. The bottom of the rod should be even with the top of the lever.
3. If adjustment is necessary, bend the rod.

1976

1. Disconnect the upper end of the choke coil rod at the choke valve.
2. Completely close the choke valve.
3. Push up on the choke coil rod to its end of travel.
4. Bottom of rod should be even with the top of the lever.
5. Bend the rod for adjustment.
6. Connect rod to choke valve.

1977 AND LATER

1. Place the cam follower on the high step of the cam.
2. Hold the choke valve completely closed.

MV choke coil rod adjustment—1975

3. A .120 in. plug gauge must pass through the hole in the lever attached to the choke coil housing and enter the hole in the casting.
4. Bend link to adjust.

Primary Vacuum Break

1975

1. With an outside vacuum source, apply vacuum to the primary vacuum break diaphragm until the plunger is fully seated.
2. Measure the clearance between the choke valve and the air horn wall.
3. Bend the vacuum break rod to adjust the clearance. Be sure that there is no binding or interference.

1976 AND LATER

1. Place cam follower on high step of cam.
2. Plug purge bleed hole with masking tape over vacuum break end cover. Not all 1977 and later models will have this hole.
3. Using an outside vacuum source, apply vacuum to primary vacuum break diaphragm until the plunger is fully seated.
4. Push up on choke coil lever rod in the end of the slot. Push down on the choke valve for 1978 and later.
5. Insert a specified gauge between the upper edge of the choke valve and the air horn wall. Measure at the lower edge of the choke valve, 1978 and later only.
6. Bend vacuum break rod for adjustment.
7. After adjustment, check for binding or interference. Remove tape.

MV primary vacuum break adjustment—1975

Auxiliary Vacuum Break (1975–76 Only)

1. With an outside vacuum source, apply vacuum to the auxiliary vacuum break diaphragm until the plunger is seated.
2. Place the cam follower on the high step of the fast idle cam.
3. Measure the clearance between the upper edge of the choke valve and the air horn

MV auxiliary vacuum break adjustment

MV and ME float level adjustment

MV metering rod adjustment—1975-76

wall. Bend the link between the vacuum break and the choke valve to adjust.

Metering Rod Adjustment—1977 and Later

1. Remove metering rod by holding throttle valve wide open. Push downward on metering rod against spring tension, then slide metering rod out of slot in holder and remove from main metering jet.

2. Back out idle stop solenoid—hold throttle valve completely closed.

3. Hold power piston down and swing metering rod holder over flat surface (gasket removed) of bowl casting next to carburetor bore.

4. Insert specified gauge.

5. Bend the metering rod holder as necessary.

ROCHESTER 2GV (1970–74)

These procedures are for both the 1¼ and 1½ models. Where there are differences these are noted. The 1½ model has larger throttle bores and an additional fuel feed circuit to make it suitable for use on the 350 V8.

Fast Idle Cam

1. Turn the idle screw onto the second step of the fast idle cam.

2. Hold the choke valve toward the closed position and check the clearance between the upper edge of the choke valve and the air horn wall.

3. If this measurement varies from specifications, bend the tang on the choke lever.

Choke Vacuum Break

1. Apply vacuum to the diaphragm to fully seat the plunger.

2. Push the choke valve in toward the closed position and hold it there.

3. Check the distance between the lower edge of the choke valve and the air horn wall.

4. If this dimension is not within specifications, bend the vacuum break rod to adjust.

Choke Unloader

1. Hold the throttle valves wide-open and use a rubber band to hold the choke valve toward the closed position.

2. Measure the distance between the upper edge of the choke valve and the air horn wall.

3. If this measurement is not within specifications, bend the unloader tang on the throttle lever to correct it.

Choke Coil Rod

1. Hold the choke valve completely open.

2. With the choke coil rod disconnected from the upper lever, push downward on the end of the rod to the end of its travel.

3. With the rod pushed fully downward, the bottom of the rod should be even with the bottom of the slotted hole in the lever.

4. To adjust the lever, bend the lever as needed.

Accelerator Pump Rod

1. Back the idle stop screw out and close the throttle valves in their bores.

2. Measure the distance from the top of the air horn to the top of the pump rod.

3. Bend the pump rod at a lower angle to correct this dimension.

Float Level

Invert the air horn, and with the gasket in place and the needle seated, measure the level as follows:

On nitrophyl floats, measure from the air horn gasket to the lip on the toe of the float.

On brass floats, measure from the air horn gasket to the lower edge of the float seam.

Bend the float tang to adjust the level.

Float Drop

Holding the air horn right side up, measure float drop as follows:

On nitrophyl floats, measure from the air horn gasket to the lip at the toe of the float.

On brass floats, measure from the air horn gasket to the bottom of the float.

Bend the float tang to adjust either type float.

ROCHESTER 2GC (1975–78)

Pump Rod

1. Back out the idle speed adjusting screw.
2. Hold the throttle valve completely closed.
3. Measure the distance from the top of the air horn ring to the top of the pump rod.
4. If necessary, bend the pump rod to adjust.

Fast Idle Cam

1. Turn the idle speed screw in until it contacts the low step of the fast idle cam. Then turn the screw in one full turn.
2. Place the idle speed screw on the second step of the fast idle cam against the highest step.
3. Measure the clearance between the upper edge of the choke valve and the air horn wall.
4. Bend the choke lever tang to adjust.

2GC pump rod adjustment

2GC fast idle cam adjustment

Choke Unloader

1. With the throttle valves wide open, place the choke valve in the closed position.
2. Measure the clearance between the upper edge of the choke valve and the air horn casting.
3. Bend the throttle lever tang to adjust.

2GC choke unloader adjustment

Intermediate Choke Rod

1. Remove the thermostatic cover coil, gasket, and inside baffle plate.
2. Place the idle screw on the high step of the fast idle cam.
3. Close the choke valve by pushing up on the intermediate choke lever.
4. The edge of the choke lever inside the choke housing must align with the edge of the plug gauge.
5. Bend the intermediate choke lever to adjust.
6. Replace the cover and set as in the following adjustment.

2GC intermediate choke rod adjustment

2GC vacuum break adjustment

Automatic Choke Coil

1. Place the idle screw on the high step of the fast idle cam.

2. Loosen the thermostatic choke coil cover retaining screws.

3. Rotate the choke cover against coil tension until the choke valve begins to close. Continue rotating it until the index mark aligns with the specified point on the choke housing. On models with slotted coil pick-up lever, make sure coil tang is installed in slot in lever. This will have to be checked with the choke coil cover removed.

4. Tighten the choke cover retaining screws.

Vacuum Break

1. Disconnect the vacuum hose. Using an outside vacuum source, seat the vacuum diaphragm.

2. Cover the vacuum break bleed hole with a small piece of tape so that the diaphragm will be held inward.

3. Place the idle speed screw on the high step of the fast idle cam.

4. 1975–76: Remove the thermostatic coil and cover; hold the choke coil lever inside the choke coil housing towards the closed choke position. 1977–78: Pull out the stem from the vacuum diaphragm to the vacuum break rod until seated.

5. Measure the clearance between the upper edge of the choke valve and the air horn wall.

2GC float level adjustment

2GC float drop adjustment

6. Bend the vacuum break rod to adjust.

7. After adjustment, remove the piece of tape and reconnect the vacuum hose.

ROCHESTER 2SE (1979 AND LATER)

Float Adjustment

1. Remove the air horn from the throttle body.

2. Use your fingers to hold the retainer in place, and to push the float down into light contact with the needle.

3. Measure the distance from the toe of the float (furthest from the hinge) to the top of the carburetor (gasket removed).

4. To adjust, remove the float and gently bend the arm to specification. After adjust-

2GC automatic choke coil adjustment

① HOLD RETAINER FIRMLY IN PLACE

③ GAUGE AT TOE OF FLOAT AT POINT FURTHEST AWAY FROM FLOAT HINGE PIN (SEE INSET).

(INSET)

④ REMOVE FLOAT AND BEND FLOAT ARM UP OR DOWN TO ADJUST

② PUSH FLOAT DOWN LIGHTLY AGAINST NEEDLE

⑤ VISUALLY CHECK FLOAT ALIGNMENT AFTER ADJUSTING

2SE float adjustment

ment, check the float alignment in the chamber.

Pump Adjustment

1. With the throttle closed and the fast idle screw off the steps of the fast idle cam, measure the distance from the air horn casting to the top of the pump stem.

2. To adjust, remove the retaining screw and washer and remove the pump lever. Bend the end of the lever to correct the stem height. Do not twist the lever or bend it sideways.

3. Install the lever, washer and screw and

check the adjustment. When correct, open and close the throttle a few times to check the linkage movement and alignment.

NOTE: *1981 and later models do not require this adjustment.*

Fast Idle Adjustment

1. Set the ignition timing and curb idle speed, and disconnect and plug hoses as directed on the emission control decal.

2. Place the fast idle screw on the highest step of the cam.

3. Start the engine and adjust the engine speed to specification with the fast idle screw.

Choke Coil Lever Adjustment

1. Remove the three retaining screws and remove the choke cover and coil. On models with a riveted choke cover, drill out the three rivets and remove the cover and choke coil.

NOTE: *A choke stat cover retainer kit is required for reassembly.*

2. Place the fast idle screw on the high step of the cam.

3. Close the choke by pushing in on the intermediate choke lever. The intermediate choke lever is behind the choke vacuum diaphragm.

4. Insert a drill or gauge of the specified size (.085) into the hole in the choke housing. The

NOTE:
THE PUMP ADJUSTMENT SHOULD NOT BE CHANGED FROM ORIGINAL FACTORY SETTING UNLESS GAUGING SHOWS OUT OF SPECIFICATION. THE PUMP LEVER IS MADE FROM HEAVY DUTY, HARDENED STEEL MAKING BENDING DIFFICULT. DO NOT REMOVE PUMP LEVER FOR BENDING UNLESS ABSOLUTELY NECESSARY.

② GAUGE FROM AIR HORN CASTING SURFACE TO TOP OF PUMP STEM. DIMENSION SHOULD BE AS SPECIFIED.

① THROTTLE VALVES COMPLETELY CLOSED. MAKE SURE FAST IDLE SCREW IS OFF STEPS OF FAST IDLE CAM.

③ IF NECESSARY TO ADJUST, REMOVE PUMP LEVER RETAINING SCREW AND WASHER AND REMOVE PUMP LEVER BY ROTATING LEVER TO REMOVE FROM PUMP ROD. PLACE LEVER IN A VISE, PROTECTING LEVER FROM DAMAGE, AND BEND END OF LEVER (NEAREST NECKED DOWN SECTION).

NOTE: DO NOT BEND LEVER IN A SIDEWAYS OR TWISTING MOTION.

⑤ OPEN AND CLOSE THROTTLE VALVES CHECKING LINKAGE FOR FREEDOM OF MOVEMENT AND OBSERVING PUMP LEVER ALIGNMENT.

④ REINSTALL PUMP LEVER, WASHER AND RETAINING SCREW. RECHECK PUMP ADJUSTMENT ① AND ②. TIGHTEN RETAINING SCREW SECURELY AFTER THE PUMP ADJUSTMENT IS CORRECT.

2SE pump adjustment

choke lever in the housing should be up against the side of the gauge.

5. If the lever does not just touch the gauge, bend the intermediate choke rod to adjust.

Fast Idle Cam (Choke Rod) Adjustment

NOTE: *A special angle gauge should be used.*
1. Adjust the choke coil lever and fast idle first.
2. Rotate the degree scale until it is zeroed.
3. Close the choke and install the degree scale onto the choke plate. Center the leveling bubble.
4. Rotate the scale so that the specified degree is opposite the scale pointer.
5. Place the fast idle screw on the second step of the cam (against the high step). Close the choke by pushing in the intermediate lever.
6. Push on the vacuum break lever in the direction of opening choke until the lever is against the rear tang on the choke lever.
7. Bend the fast idle cam rod at the U to adjust angle to specifications.

Air Valve Rod Adjustment

1. Seat the vacuum diaphragm with an outside vacuum source. Tape over the purge bleed hole if present.
2. Close the air valve.
3. Insert the specified gauge between the rod and the end of the slot in the air valve.
4. Bend the rod to adjust the clearance.

2SE air valve rod adjustment

Primary Side Vacuum Break Adjustment

1. Follow Steps 1–4 of the Fast Idle Cam Adjustment.
2. Seat the choke vacuum diaphragm with an outside vacuum source.
3. Push in on the intermediate choke lever to close the choke valve, and hold closed during adjustment.
4. Adjust by bending the vacuum break rod until the bubble is centered.

Secondary Vacuum Break Adjustment

1. Follow Steps 1–4 of the Fast Idle Cam Adjustment.
2. Seat the choke vacuum diaphragm with an outside vacuum source.
3. Push in on the intermediate choke level to close the choke valve, and hold closed during adjustment. Make sure the plunger spring is compressed and seated, if present.
4. Bend the vacuum break rod at the U next to the diaphragm until the bubble is centered.

Electric Choke Setting

This procedure is only for those carburetors with choke covers retained by screws. Riveted choke covers are preset and nonadjustable.
1. Loosen the three retaining screws.
2. Place the fast idle screw on the high step of the cam.
3. Rotate the choke cover to align the cover mark with the specified housing mark.

Choke Unloader Adjustment

1. Follow Steps 1–4 of the Fast Idle Cam Adjustment.
2. Install the choke cover and coil, if removed, aligning the marks on the housing and cover as specified.
3. Hold the primary throttle wide open.
4. If the engine is warm, close the choke valve by pushing in on the intermediate choke lever.
5. Bend the unloader tang until the bubble is centered.

2SE unloader adjustment

Secondary Lockout Adjustment

1. Pull the choke wide open by pushing out on the intermediate choke lever.
2. Open the throttle until the end of the secondary actuating lever is opposite the toe of the lockout lever.
3. Gauge clearance between the lockout lever and secondary lever should be as specified.

2SE secondary lockout adjustment

M2MC fast idle adjustment on the bench

4. To adjust, bend the lockout lever where it contacts the fast idle cam.

ROCHESTER M2MC M2ME (1979 AND LATER)

Float Adjustment

NOTE: *The M2ME carburetor is the same as the M2MC except that the choke is now electrically operated.*

1. Remove the air horn from the throttle body.

2. Use your fingers to hold the retainer in place, and to push the float down into light contact with the needle.

3. Gauge from the top of the casting to the top of the float, at a point 9/16 in. back from the end of the toe of the float (gasket removed).

4. To adjust, remove the float and gently bend the arm to specification. After adjustment, check the float alignment in the chamber.

M2MC float adjustment

Fast Idle Speed

1. Place the fast idle lever on the high step of the fast idle cam.

2. Turn the fast idle screw out until the throttle valves are closed.

3. Turn the screw in to contact the lever, then turn it in two more turns. Check this preliminary setting against the sticker figure.

Fast Idle Cam Adjustment

1. Adjust the fast idle speed.

2. Place the cam follower lever on the second step of the fast idle cam, holding it firmly against the rise of the high step.

3. Close the choke valve by pushing upward on the choke coil lever inside the choke housing.

4. Gauge between the upper edge of the choke valve and the inside of the air horn wall.

5. Bend the tang on the fast idle cam to adjust.

M2MC fast idle cam adjustment

Pump Adjustment

1. With the fast idle cam follower off the steps of the fast idle cam, back out the idle speed screw until the throttle valves are completely closed.

2. Place the pump rod in the proper hole of the lever.

M2MC pump adjustment

3. Measure from the top of the choke valve wall, next to the vent stack, to the top of the pump stem.

4. Bend the pump lever to adjust.

Choke Coil Lever Adjustment

1. Remove the choke cover and thermostatic coil from the choke housing.

2. Push up on the coil tang (counterclockwise) until the choke valve is closed. The top of the choke rod should be at the bottom of the slot in the choke valve lever. Place the fast idle cam follower on the high step of the cam.

3. Insert a 0.120 in. plug gauge in the hole in the choke housing.

4. The lower edge of the choke coil lever should just contact the side of the plug gauge.

5. Bend the choke rod to adjust.

M2MC choke coil lever adjustment

Front Vacuum Break Adjustment

1. Seat the choke vacuum diaphragm, using an outside vacuum source. If there is an air bleed hole on the diaphragm, tape it over.

2. Remove the choke cover and coil. Rotate the inside coil lever counterclockwise.

3. Check that the specified gap is present between the top of the choke valve and the air horn wall.

4. Turn the vacuum break adjusting screw to adjust.

Automatic Choke Coil Adjustment

1. Place the cam follower on the highest step of the fast idle cam.

2. Loosen the three choke cover retaining screws.

3. Rotate the cover and coil assembly counterclockwise until the choke valve just closes.

4. Align the mark on the choke cover with the specified mark on the housing. Make sure the slot in the lever is engaged with the coil tang. Tighten the cover retaining screws.

Unloader Adjustment

1. With the choke valve completely closed, hold the throttle valves wide open.

M2MC unloader adjustment

2. Measure between the upper edge of the choke valve and the air horn wall.

3. Bend the tang on the fast idle lever to obtain the proper measurement.

Air Conditioning Idle Speed-Up Solenoid Adjustment

1. With the engine at normal operating temperature and automatic transmissions in drive, manual transmissions in neutral, adjust the curb idle to specifications by means of the idle speed screw (air conditioning off).

2. Turn the air conditioning on and disconnect the compressor clutch electrical lead at the connector. The solenoid should be energized. Open the throttle slightly to allow the solenoid plunger to fully extend.

3. Turn the solenoid screw (plunger) to adjust the engine idle to the specified rpm. See your underhood specifications sticker for proper idle speed.

M2MC A/C idle speed-up solenoid adjustment

ROCHESTER 4MV (1970–78)

Fast Idle

1. Position the fast idle lever on the high step of the fast idle cam.

2. Be sure that the choke is wide-open and the engine warm. On 1974 models, with manual transmission, disconnect the vacuum advance. On 1976 California 454s and all 1977–78 models, disconnect and plug vacuum hose at EGR valve.

3. Turn the fast idle screw to gain the proper fast idle rpm.

Choke Rod (Fast Idle Cam)

1. Place the cam follower on the second step of the fast idle cam.

2. Close the choke valve by exerting counterclockwise pressure on the external choke lever.

3. Insert a gauge of the proper size between the lower edge of the choke valve and the inside air horn wall. For 1976–78, measure between the upper edge of the choke valve and the inside air horn wall.

4. To adjust, bend the choke rod.

Vacuum Break

1. Fully seat the vacuum break diaphragm using an outside vacuum source.

2. Open the throttle valve enough to allow the fast idle cam follower to clear the fast idle cam.

3. The end of the vacuum break rod should be at the outer end of the slot in the vacuum break diaphragm plunger.

4. The specified clearance should register from the lower end of the choke valve to the inside air horn wall. For 1976–78, measure between the upper edge of the choke valve to the inside air horn wall.

5. If the clearance is not correct, bend the vacuum break line at the point shown in the illustration.

Secondary Vacuum Break (1970–75 Only)

1. Using an outside vacuum source, seat the auxiliary vacuum break diaphragm plunger.

2. Rotate the choke lever in the closed position until the spring-loaded diaphragm plunger is fully extended.

3. Holding the choke valve closed, check the distance between the lower edge of the choke valve and the air horn wall.

4. To adjust to specifications, bend the vacuum break link.

Choke Unloader

1. Push up on the vacuum break lever and fully open the throttle valves. (1976–78; push up or down to close choke).

2. Measure the distance from the lower edge of the choke valve to the air horn wall (1976–78: measure from upper edge of choke valve).

3. To adjust, bend the tang on the fast idle lever.

Choke Coil Rod

Before making this adjustment, check choke mechanism for free operation. Any binding caused by gum on shaft or linkage should be cleaned off. Do not oil linkage.

1. Close the choke valve by rotating the choke coil lever counterclockwise.

2. Disconnect the thermostatic coil rod from the upper lever.

3. Push down on the rod until it contacts the bracket of the coil.

4. The rod must fit in the notch of the upper lever.

5. If it does not, it must be bent on the curved portion just below the upper lever.

Secondary Closing Adjustment

This adjustment assures proper closing of the secondary throttle plates.

1. Set the slow idle as per instructions in Chapter 2. Make sure that the fast idle cam follower is not resting on the fast idle cam. The choke valve should be wide open.

2. There should be the specified clearance between the secondary throttle actuating rod and the front of the slot on the secondary throttle lever with the closing tang on the throttle lever resting against the actuating lever.

3. Bend the tang on the primary throttle actuating rod to adjust.

Secondary Opening Adjustment

1. Open the primary throttle valves until the actuating link contacts the upper tang on the secondary lever.

2. With two point linkage, the bottom of the link should be in the center of the secondary lever slot.

3. With three point linkage, there should be the specified clearance between the link and the middle tang.

4. Bend the upper tang on the secondary lever to adjust as necessary.

Float Level

With the air horn assembly upside down, measure the distance from the air horn gasket surface (gasket removed) to the top of the float at the toe.

NOTE: *Make sure that the retaining pin is firmly held in place and that the tang of the float is firmly against the needle and seat assembly.*

Accelerator Pump

1. Close the primary throttle valves by backing out the slow idle screw and making sure that the fast idle cam follower is off the steps of the fast idle cam.

2. Bend the secondary throttle closing tang away from the primary throttle lever, if necessary.

3. With the pump in the appropriate hole in the pump lever, measure from the top of the choke valve wall to the top of the pump stem.

4. To adjust, bend the pump lever.

5. After adjusting, readjust the secondary throttle tank and the slow idle screw.

Air Valve Spring Adjustment

To adjust the air valve spring windup, loosen the allen head lockscrew and turn the adjusting screw counterclockwise to remove all spring tension. Hold the air valve closed, and turn the adjusting screw clockwise the specified number of turns after the torsion spring contacts the pin on the shaft. Hold the adjusting screw in this position and tighten the lockscrew.

Secondary Lockout Adjustment

For 1970–75, see the illustration in this section. For 1976–78, refer to the secondary throttle lock-out adjustment in the next section.

ROCHESTER M4MC AND M4MCA (1975) M4MC AND M4ME (1976–1978)

NOTE: *The illustrations in this section apply to all M4MC, M4MCA, and M4ME carburetors unless otherwise indicated.*

Pump Rod

1. Take the fast idle cam follower off the fast idle cam steps.
2. Back out the idle speed screw until the throttle valves are completely closed.
3. Be sure that the secondary actuating rod is not preventing the throttle from closing completely. If the primary throttle valves do not close completely, bend the secondary closing tang out of position, then readjust later.
4. Place the pump rod in the specified hole in the lever.
5. Measure the clearance from the top of the choke valve wall, next to the vent stack, and the top of the pump stem.
6. To adjust the dimension, support the pump lever and bend the pump lever.
7. Adjust the idle speed.
8. If necessary, readjust the secondary actuating rod.

Fast Idle—1975–77

NOTE: *This procedure is to be used only when the carburetor is off the truck, as a means of roughly setting the fast idle speed before the carburetor is reinstalled. For normal adjustment of fast idle speed, refer to the idle adjustment section in Chapter 2.*

1. Hold the cam follower on the high step of the fast idle cam.
2. Turn the fast idle screw out until the primary throttle valves are closed (1975), or until it pulls away from the fast idle cam follower (1976–77).
3. Turn the fast idle screw in to contact the lever, then turn the screw in three turns.
4. Recheck the fast idle speed.

M4MC and M4ME fast idle adjustment

Choke Coil Lever

1. Loosen the three retaining screws and remove the cover and coil assembly from the choke housing. On the 1978 and later models, also place the fast idle cam follower on the high step of the cam.
2. Push up on the thermostatic coil tang (counterclockwise) until the choke valve closes.
3. Insert the specified gauge into the hole in the choke housing.

M4MC and M4ME pump rod adjustment

M4MC and M4ME choke coil lever adjustment

4. The lower edge of the choke coil lever should just contact the side of the gauge.

5. Bend the choke rod to adjust.

Choke Rod

The choke coil lever adjustment must be made before making the following adjustment. The thermostatic cover and coil will remain off for this adjustment.

1. Adjust the fast idle.

2. Place the cam follower on the second step of the fast idle cam firmly against the rise of the high step.

3. Close the choke valve by pushing up on the choke coil lever inside the choke housing.

4. Measure the clearance between the upper edge of the choke valve and the inside of the air horn wall.

5. Bend the tang on the fast idle cam to adjust the clearance. Be sure that the tang lies against the cam after bending it.

6. Recheck the fast idle.

M4MC and M4ME choke rod adjustment

Air Valve Dashpot

1. Seat the front vacuum diaphragm using an outside vacuum source. Plug the purge bleed hole with masking tape on models where used. Remove tape after making adjustment.

2. The air valves must be completely closed.

3. Measure the clearance between the air valve dashpot and the end of the slot in the air valve lever.

4. Bend the air valve dashpot rod to adjust the clearance.

Front Vacuum Break

1. Remove the thermostatic cover and coil assembly from the choke housing.

2. Place the cam follower on the high step of the fast idle cam.

3. Seat the front vacuum diaphragm using an outside vacuum source.

4. Push up on the inside choke coil lever until the tang on the vacuum break lever contacts the tang on the vacuum break plunger.

5. Measure the clearance between the upper edge of the choke valve and the air horn wall.

6. Turn the adjusting screw on the vacuum break plunger lever to adjust.

7. Reconnect the vacuum hose after adjustment.

M4MC and M4ME front vacuum break adjustment

Rear Vacuum Break (All 1975; 1976–78 M4ME; 1979 and Later M4MC)

1. Remove the thermostatic cover and coil assembly from the choke housing.

2. Place the cam follower on the high step of the fast idle cam.

3. Plug the bleed hose in the vacuum break unit cover with tape.

4. Seat the rear vacuum diaphragm using an outside vacuum source.

5. Push up the choke coil lever inside the choke housing toward the closed position. Diaphragm should be pulled out until seated, bucking spring compressed (where used) on 1976 and later.

6. With the choke rod in the bottom slot of the choke lever, measure the clearance between the upper edge of the choke valve and air horn wall.

7. Bend the vacuum break rod if necessary to adjust.

M4MC and M4ME air valve dashpot adjustment

NOTE: HOLD GAUGE VERTICALLY

⑤ GAUGE BETWEEN AIR HORN WALL & UPPER EDGE OF CHOKE VALVE

CLOSING ASSIST SPRING

④ ROD IN BOTTOM OF SLOT

NOTE: PLUG PURGE BLEED HOLE WITH A PIECE OF MASKING TAPE

⑥ BEND ROD TO ADJUST

③ PUSH UP ON CHOKE COIL LEVER TOWARDS CLOSED CHOKE

② SEAT REAR VACUUM BREAK DIAPHRAGM USING OUTSIDE VACUUM SOURCE

① PLACE CAM FOLLOWER LEVER ON HIGHEST STEP OF FAST IDLE CAM

(ALL EXCEPT 454 ENGINE)

⑤ CHOKE VALVE SHOULD BE WIDE OPEN (VERTICAL)

④ ROD IN BOTTOM OF SLOT

⑥ BEND ROD TO ADJUST

③ PUSH UP ON CHOKE COIL LEVER TOWARDS CLOSED CHOKE

② SEAT REAR VACUUM BREAK DIAPHRAGM USING OUTSIDE VACUUM SOURCE

① PLACE CAM FOLLOWER LEVER ON HIGHEST STEP OF FAST IDLE CAM

(454 ENGINE)

M4MC and M4MCA rear vacuum break adjustment. Refer to the upper illustration for 1976–78 M4ME

8. After adjustment, remove the tape and install the vacuum hose.

Automatic Choke Coil, M4MC

1. Install the thermostatic coil and cover with a gasket between the choke cover and choke housing. On all models except the 1976 454 cu. in. V8, the thermostatic coil must be installed in the slot in the inside of the choke coil lever pick-up arm.

2. Place the fast idle cam follower on the high step of the fast idle cam.

② ROTATE COVER AND COIL ASSEMBLY COUNTERCLOCKWISE UNTIL CHOKE VALVE JUST CLOSES

③ ALIGN INDEX MARKS AS SPECIFIED

① PLACE CAM FOLLOWER ON HIGHEST STEP OF CAM

M4MC automatic choke coil adjustment

3. Rotate the cover and coil assembly counterclockwise until the choke valve just closes.

4. Align the index point on the cover with the specified mark on the choke housing.

5. Tighten the retaining screws.

Automatic Choke Coil, M4ME

1. Install the electric choke assembly in choke housing, making sure coil tang contacts bottom side of inside choke coil lever pick-up arm.

2. Place fast idle cam follower on high step of cam.

3. Rotate cover and coil assembly counterclockwise until choke valve just closes.

4. Align index point on cover with specified mark on housing.

5. Install cover retainers and screws.

NOTE: *Ground contact for the electric choke is provided by a metal plate located at the rear of the choke assembly. Do not install a choke cover gasket between the electric choke assembly and the choke housing. Do not immerse the electric choke assembly in any cleaning solution. Severe damage can result.*

Unloader

1. Perform Step 1 of the appropriate automatic choke coil procedure.

2. Hold the throttle valves wide open with the choke valve completely closed. On a warm engine, close the choke valve by pushing on the tang of the intermediate choke lever which contacts the fast idle cam. A rubber band will hold it in position.

3. Measure the distance between the upper edge of the choke valve and the air horn wall.

4. Bend the tang on the fast idle lever to adjust the clearance. Check to be sure that the tang on the fast idle cam lever is contacting the center of the fast idle cam after adjustment.

Secondary Throttle Lock-Out

SECONDARY LEVER CLEARANCE

1. Hold the choke valve and secondary throttle valves closed.

2. Measure the clearance between the lock-out pin and the lock-out lever.

3. If necessary, bend the lock-out pin to adjust to .015 in.

OPENING CLEARANCE

4. Hold the choke valve wide open by pushing down on the fast idle cam.

5. Hold the secondary throttle valves slightly open.

6. Measure the clearance between the end of the lock-out pin and the toe of the lock-out lever.

7. If necessary, file off the end of the lock-out pin to obtain .015 in. clearance.

M4MC and M4ME choke unloader adjustment

M4MC and M4ME secondary throttle lock-out adjustment

Secondary Closing

1. Set the idle speed to specification.

2. Hold the choke valve wide open with the cam follower lever off the steps of the fast idle cam.

3. Measure the clearance between the slot in the secondary throttle valve pickup lever and the secondary actuating rod.

4. Bend the secondary closing tang on the primary throttle lever to adjust to .020 in. clearance.

M4MC and M4ME secondary closing adjustment

Secondary Opening

1. Lightly, crack the primary throttle lever until the link just contacts the tang on the secondary lever.

2. With the link against the tang, the link should be in the center of the slot in the secondary lever.

3. Bend the tang on the secondary lever to adjust.

M4MC and M4ME secondary opening adjustment

Air Valve Spring Wind-Up

1. Remove the front vacuum break diaphragm and the air valve dashpot rod.

2. Loosen the lockscrew.

3. Turn the tension adjusting screw counterclockwise until the air valve opens partway.

4. Turn the tension adjusting screw clockwise while tapping lightly on the casting with the handle of a screwdriver.

5. When the air valve just closes, turn the tension adjusting screw clockwise the specified number of turns after the spring contacts the pin.

6. Tighten the lockscrew and reinstall the diaphragm and dashpot rod.

Deceleration Throttle Stop

1. Adjust the idle speed.

2. Push the hex end of the throttle stop plunger in (toward the throttle lever) until the

M4MC and M4ME air valve spring windup

M4MC and M4ME deceleration throttle stop

M4MC and M4ME float level adjustment

plunger stem hits the stop inside the diaphragm.

3. With the plunger against the stop, turn the plunger adjusting screw in or out to obtain the specified deceleration rpm.

ROCHESTER E2SE 2-bbl.

The model E2SE, introduced on Chevrolet pickup trucks in 1983, is designed as a part of the GM Computer Command Control system (C^3). An electrically-operated mixture control solenoid differentiates the E2SE from the conventional 2SE series.

A plunger in the end of the above-mentioned solenoid is submerged in fuel in the fuel chamber of the float bowl. The plunger is controlled, or "pulsed," by electrical signals received from the Electronic Control Module (ECM). The solenoid system is used to control the air/fuel mixture in the primary bore of the carburetor.

The model E2SE also has a Throttle Position Sensor (TPS) mounted in the float bowl and is used to signal the ECM as throttle position changes occur. As throttle position changes, a tang on the pump lever moves the TPS plunger, modifying an electrical signal to the ECM. This signal is used in conjunction with signals from various other engine sensors by the ECM to control various engine operating modes.

(1) **HOLD RETAINER IN PLACE.**

(2) **PUSH FLOAT DOWN LIGHTLY AGAINST NEEDLE.**

(3) **GAGE AT LARGE TOE OF FLOAT, AT POINT FARTHEST FROM FLOAT HINGE.**

(4) **REMOVE FLOAT AND BEND FLOAT ARM UP OR DOWN TO ADJUST.**

(SOME MODELS HAVE FLOAT STABILIZER SPRING. USE CARE IN REMOVING.)

(5) **VISUALLY CHECK FLOAT ALIGNMENT.**

FLOAT STABILIZING SPRING

E2SE 2-bbl. float adjustment

NOTE: ON MODELS USING A CLIP TO RETAIN PUMP ROD IN PUMP LEVER, NO PUMP ADJUSTMENT IS REQUIRED. ON MODELS USING THE "CLIPLESS" PUMP ROD, THE PUMP ADJUSTMENT SHOULD NOT BE CHANGED FROM ORIGINAL FACTORY SETTING UNLESS GAUGING SHOWS OUT OF SPECIFICATION. THE PUMP LEVER IS MADE FROM HEAVY DUTY, HARDENED STEEL MAKING BENDING DIFFICULT. DO NOT REMOVE PUMP LEVER FOR BENDING UNLESS ABSOLUTELY NECESSARY.

(1) THROTTLE VALVES COMPLETELY CLOSED. MAKE SURE FAST IDLE SCREW IS OFF STEPS OF FAST IDLE CAM.

(3)

IF NECESSARY TO ADJUST. REMOVE PUMP LEVER RETAINING SCREW AND WASHER AND REMOVE PUMP LEVER BY ROTATING LEVER TO REMOVE FROM PUMP ROD. PLACE LEVER IN A VISE, PROTECTING LEVER FROM DAMAGE, AND BEND END OF LEVER (NEAREST NECKED DOWN SECTION).

NOTE: DO NOT BEND LEVER IN A SIDEWAYS OR TWISTING MOTION.

(2) GAUGE FROM AIR HORN CASTING SURFACE TO TOP OF PUMP STEM. DIMENSION SHOULD BE AS SPECIFIED.

(5) OPEN AND CLOSE THROTTLE VALVES CHECKING LINKAGE FOR FREEDOM OF MOVEMENT AND OBSERVING PUMP LEVER ALIGNMENT.

(4) REINSTALL PUMP LEVER, WASHER AND RETAINING SCREW. RECHECK PUMP ADJUSTMENT (1) AND (2). TIGHTEN RETAINING SCREW SECURELY AFTER THE PUMP ADJUSTMENT IS CORRECT.

E2SE 2-bbl. pump adjustment

Float Adjustment

1. Remove the air horn from the throttle body.

2. Use your fingers to hold the retainer in place, and to push the float down into light contact with the needle.

3. Measure the distance from the toe of the float (furthest from the hinge) to the top of the carburetor (gasket removed).

4. To adjust, remove the float and gently bend the arm to specification. After adjustment, check the float alignment in the chamber.

Pump Adjustment

1. With the throttle closed and the fast idle screw off the steps of the fast idle cam, measure the distance from the air horn casting to the top of the pump stem.

2. To adjust, remove the retaining screw and washer and remove the pump lever. Bend the end of the lever to correct the stem height. *Do not twist the lever or bend it sideways.*

3. Install the lever, washer and screw and check the adjustment. When correct, open and close the throttle a few times to check the linkage movement and alignment.

NOTE: *No pump adjustment is required on 1981 and later models.*

Fast Idle Adjustment

1. Set the ignition timing and curb idle speed, and disconnect and plug hoses as directed on the emission control decal.

2. Place the fast idle screw on the highest step of the cam.

3. Start the engine and adjust the engine speed to specification with the fast idle screw.

Choke Coil Lever Adjustment

1. Remove the three retaining screws and remove the choke cover and coil. On models with a riveted choke cover, drill out the three rivets and remove the cover and choke coil.

NOTE: *A choke stat cover retainer kit is required for reassembly.*

Fast idle adjustment, E2SE 2-bbl.

E2SE 2-bbl. choke coil lever adjustment

2. Place the fast idle screw on the high step of the cam.

3. Close the choke by pushing in on the intermediate choke lever. On front wheel drive models, the intermediate choke lever is behind the choke vacuum diaphragm.

4. Insert a drill or gauge of the specified size into the hole in the choke housing. The choke lever in the housing should be up against the side of the gauge.

5. If the lever does not just touch the gauge, bend the intermediate choke rod to adjust.

Air Valve Rod Adjustment

Refer to the accompanying illustration for this procedure.

Primary Side Vacuum Break Adjustment

Refer to the illustration for this procedure.

Electric Choke Setting

This procedure is only for those carburetors with choke covers retained by screws. Riveted choke covers are preset and nonadjustable.

③ ROTATE AIR VALVE IN THE DIRECTION OF OPEN AIR VALVE BY APPLYING LIGHT PRESSURE TO AIR VALVE LEVER.

④ TO ADJUST, SUPPORT AT "4-S" AND BEND AIR VALVE ROD ("A" OR "B") UNTIL BUBBLE IS CENTERED.

① SET UP ANGLE GAGE ON AIR VALVE AND SET ANGLE TO SPECIFICATIONS.

② USE VACUUM SOURCE, AT LEAST 18" HG., TO SEAT VACUUM BREAK PLUNGER.

Air valve rod adjustment, 2-bbl. E2SE

⑤ AIR VALVE ROD MUST NOT RESTRICT PLUNGER FROM RETRACTING FULLY. IF NECESSARY, SUPPORT AT "5-S" AND BEND ROD (SEE ARROW) TO PERMIT FULL PLUNGER TRAVEL. FINAL ROD CLEARANCE MUST BE SET AFTER VACUUM BREAK SETTING HAS BEEN MADE. WHERE APPLICABLE, PLUNGER STEM MUST BE EXTENDED FULLY TO COMPRESS BUCKING SPRING.

⑥ TO CENTER BUBBLE, EITHER:
A ADJUST WITH 1/8" (3.175 mm) HEX WRENCH (VACUUM STILL APPLIED).
-OR-
B SUPPORT AT "6-S" AND BEND WIRE-FORM VACUUM BREAK ROD. (VACUUM STILL APPLIED).

① ATTACH RUBBER BAND TO INTERMEDIATE CHOKE LEVER.

② OPEN THROTTLE TO ALLOW CHOKE VALVE TO CLOSE.

③ SET UP ANGLE GAGE AND SET ANGLE TO SPECIFICATION.

④ RETRACT VACUUM BREAK PLUNGER USING VACUUM SOURCE, AT LEAST 18" HG. PLUG AIR BLEED HOLES WHERE APPLICABLE.

E2SE primary vacuum break adjustment

1. ATTACH RUBBER BAND TO INTER-MEDIATE CHOKE LEVER.

2. OPEN THROTTLE TO ALLOW CHOKE VALVE TO CLOSE.

3. SET UP ANGLE GAGE AND SET ANGLE TO SPECIFICATIONS.

4. HOLD THROTTLE LEVER IN WIDE OPEN POSITION.

5. PUSH ON CHOKE SHAFT LEVER TO OPEN CHOKE VALVE AND TO MAKE CONTACT WITH BLACK CLOSING TANG.

6. ADJUST BY BENDING TANG UNTIL BUBBLE IS CENTERED.

E2SE choke unloader adjustment

1. Loosen the three retaining screws.

2. Place the fast idle screw on the high step of the cam.

3. Rotate the choke cover to align the cover mark with the specified housing mark.

Choke Unloader Adjustment

Refer to the accompanying illustrations for this procedure.

ROCHESTER E4ME AND E4MC QUADRAJET 4-bbl.

These 4-bbl. carburetors feature an electrically-operated mixture control solenoid, and are designed as part of the GM Computer Command Control (C^3) system. As with the E2SE 2-bbl., the electric mixture control solenoid is mounted in the float bowl, and is used to control the air/fuel mixture in the primary bores of the carburetor. The plunger in the solenoid is controlled, or "pulsed," by electrical signals received from the Electronic Control Module.

An Idle Speed Control (ISC) assembly, monitored by the ECM, controls engine idle speed. The curb (base) idle is programmed into the ECM and is not adjustable. When the throttle lever is resting against the ISC plunger, the ISC acts as a "dashpot" on throttle closing. An Idle Speed Solenoid or Idle Load Compensator is used on some models to position the primary throttle valve, providing engine idle speed requirements.

On E4MC models, an Idle Load Compensator (ILC) mounted on the float bowl is used to control curb idle speeds. The ILC uses manifold vacuum to sense changes in engine load (the A/C compressor clutch engaged, for example) and compensates by adjusting throttle angle for the curb idle speed. The ILC uses a spring-loaded vacuum-sensitive diaphragm whose plunger either extends (vacuum decrease) or retracts (vacuum increase) to adjust throttle angle for curb idle speeds. Both the ISC and ILC are factory-adjusted.

Float Level

With the air horn assembly removed, measure the distance from the air horn gasket surface (gasket removed) to the top of the float at the toe ($1/16$ in. back from the toe).

NOTE: *Make sure the retaining pin is firmly held in place and that the tang of the float is lightly held against the needle and seat assembly.*

Remove the float and bend the float arm to adjust except on carburetors used with the computer controlled systems (E4MC and E4ME). For those carburetors, if the float level is too high, hold the retainer firmly in place and push down on the center of the float to adjust. If the float level is too low on models with the computer controlled system, lift out the metering rods. Remove the solenoid connector screw. Turn the lean mixture solenoid screw in clockwise, counting and recording the exact number of turns until the screw is lightly bottomed in the bowl. Then turn the screw out clockwise and remove. Lift out the solenoid and connector. Remove the float and bend the arm up to adjust. Install the parts, turning the mixture solenoid screw in until it is lightly bot-

③ GAUGE FROM TOP OF CASTING TO TOP OF FLOAT - GAUGING POINT 3/16" BACK FROM END OF FLOAT AT TOE (SEE INSET)

① HOLD RETAINER FIRMLY IN PLACE

—TOE

(INSET)

GAUGING POINT (3/16" BACK FROM TOE)

② PUSH FLOAT DOWN LIGHTLY AGAINST NEEDLE

E4ME/MC float level adjustment

tomed, then unscrewing it the exact number of turns counted earlier.

Accelerator Pump

The accelerator pump is not adjustable on computer controlled carburetors (E4MC and E4ME).

1. Close the primary throttle valves by backing out the slow idle screw and making sure that the fast idle cam follower is off the steps of the fast idle cam.

2. Bend the secondary throttle closing tang away from the primary throttle lever, if necessary, to insure that the primary throttle valves are fully closed.

3. With the pump in the appropriate hole in the pump lever, measure from the top of the choke valve wall to the top of the pump stem.

4. To adjust, bend the pump lever.

5. After adjusting, readjust the secondary throttle tang and the slow idle screw.

③ GAUGE FROM TOP OF CHOKE VALVE WALL, NEXT TO VENT STACK, TO TOP OF PUMP STEM AS SPECIFIED

⑤ BEND PUMP LEVER TO ADJUST

② ROD IN SPECIFIED HOLE OF PUMP LEVER

④ SUPPORT LEVER WITH SCREWDRIVER WHILE BENDING LEVER

① THROTTLE VALVES COMPLETELY CLOSED NOTE: MAKE SURE FAST IDLE CAM FOLLOWER LEVER IS OFF STEPS ON FAST IDLE CAM

BEND SECONDARY CLOSING TANG AWAY TO CLOSE PRIMARY VALVES, THEN RE-ADJUST

Accelerator pump adjustment, E4ME/MC 4-bbl.

NOTE: HOLD GAUGE VERTICALLY

④ PLACE GAUGE BETWEEN UPPER EDGE OF CHOKE VALVE AND INSIDE WALL OF AIR HORN — ROD IN BOTTOM OF SLOT.

⑤ TURN SCREW TO ADJUST

② SEAT DIAPHRAGM USING OUTSIDE VACUUM SOURCE

① PLACE CAM FOLLOWER ON HIGHEST STEP OF FAST IDLE CAM

③ PUSH INSIDE CHOKE COIL LEVER COUNTERCLOCK WISE UNTIL TANG ON VACUUM BREAK LEVER CONTACTS TANG ON VACUUM BREAK PLUNGER.

E4ME/MC front vacuum break adjustment

④ GAUGE BETWEEN UPPER EDGE OF CHOKE VALVE & INSIDE AIR HORN WALL

NOTE: HOLD GAUGE VERTICAL

⑤ BEND TANG ON FAST IDLE CAM TO ADJUST

FAST IDLE CAM

③ CLOSE CHOKE BY PUSHING UPWARD ON CHOKE COIL LEVER

② PLACE CAM FOLLOWER ON SECOND STEP OF CAM NEXT TO HIGH STEP

① MAKE FAST IDLE ADJUSTMENT

Choke rod (fast idle cam) adjustment—E4ME/MC

① ATTACH RUBBER BAND TO GREEN TANG OF INTERMEDIATE CHOKE SHAFT.

② OPEN THROTTLE TO ALLOW CHOKE VALVE TO CLOSE.

③ SET UP ANGLE GAGE AND SET ANGLE TO SPECIFICATION.

④ RETRACT VACUUM BREAK PLUNGER, USING VACUUM SOURCE, AT LEAST 18" HG. PLUG AIR BLEED HOLES WHERE APPLICABLE.

④A ON QUADRAJETS, AIR VALVE ROD MUST NOT RESTRICT PLUNGER FROM RETRACTING FULLY. IF NECESSARY. BEND ROD HERE TO PERMIT FULL PLUNGER TRAVEL. WHERE APPLICABLE, PLUNGER STEM MUST BE EXTENDED FULLY TO COMPRESS PLUNGER BUCKING SPRING.

⑤ TO CENTER BUBBLE, EITHER:
A. ADJUST WITH 1/8" HEX WRENCH (VACUUM STILL APPLIED)

-OR-

B. SUPPORT AT "S" AND BEND VACUUM BREAK ROD (VACUUM STILL APPLIED)

E4ME/MC rear vacuum break adjustment

55 WAYS TO IMPROVE FUEL ECONOMY

CHILTON'S
FUEL ECONOMY
& TUNE-UP TIPS

Tune-up • Spark Plug Diagnosis • Emission Controls

Fuel System • Cooling System • Tires and Wheels

General Maintenance

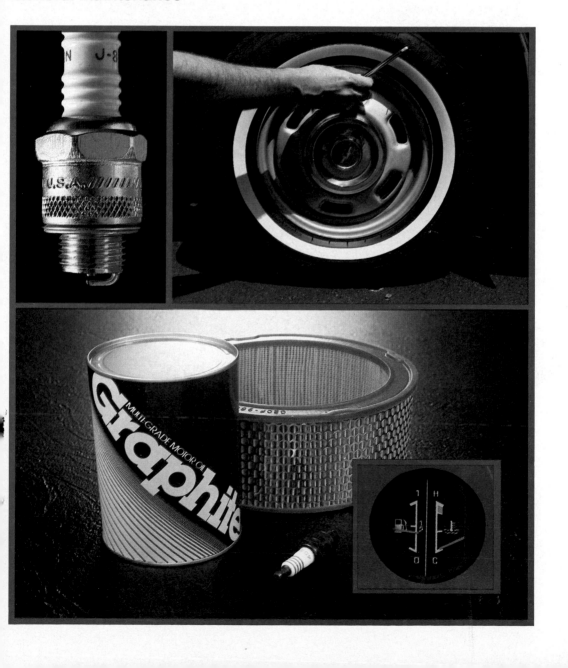

CHILTON'S FUEL ECONOMY & TUNE-UP TIPS

Fuel economy is important to everyone, no matter what kind of vehicle you drive. The maintenance-minded motorist can save both money and fuel using these tips and the periodic maintenance and tune-up procedures in this Repair and Tune-Up Guide.

There are more than 130,000,000 cars and trucks registered for private use in the United States. Each travels an average of 10-12,000 miles per year, and, and in total they consume close to 70 billion gallons of fuel each year. This represents nearly ⅔ of the oil imported by the United States each year. The Federal government's goal is to reduce consumption 10% by 1985. A variety of methods are either already in use or under serious consideration, and they all affect you driving and the cars you will drive. In addition to "down-sizing", the auto industry is using or investigating the use of electronic fuel delivery, electronic engine controls and alternative engines for use in smaller and lighter vehicles, among other alternatives to meet the federally mandated Corporate Average Fuel Economy (CAFE) of 27.5 mpg by 1985. The government, for its part, is considering rationing, mandatory driving curtailments and tax increases on motor vehicle fuel in an effort to reduce consumption. The government's goal of a 10% reduction could be realized — and further government regulation avoided — if every private vehicle could use just 1 less gallon of fuel per week.

How Much Can You Save?

Tests have proven that almost anyone can make at least a 10% reduction in fuel consumption through regular maintenance and tune-ups. When a major manufacturer of spark plugs sur-

TUNE-UP

1. Check the cylinder compression to be sure the engine will really benefit from a tune-up and that it is capable of producing good fuel economy. A tune-up will be wasted on an engine in poor mechanical condition.

2. Replace spark plugs regularly. New spark plugs alone can increase fuel economy 3%.

3. Be sure the spark plugs are the correct type (heat range) for your vehicle. See the Tune-Up Specifications.

Heat range refers to the spark plug's ability to conduct heat away from the firing end. It must conduct the heat away in an even pattern to avoid becoming a source of pre-ignition, yet it must also operate hot enough to burn off conductive deposits that could cause misfiring.

The heat range is usually indicated by a number on the spark plug, part of the manufacturer's designation for each individual spark plug. The numbers in bold-face indicate the heat range in each manufacturer's identification system.

Manufacturer	Typical Designation
AC	R **45** TS
Bosch (old)	WA **145** T30
Bosch (new)	HR **8** Y
Champion	RBL **15** Y
Fram/Autolite	4**15**
Mopar	P-**62** PR
Motorcraft	BRF-**42**
NGK	BP **5** ES-15
Nippondenso	W **16** EP
Prestolite	14GR **5** 2A

Periodically, check the spark plugs to be sure they are firing efficiently. They are excellent indicators of the internal condition of your engine.

On AC, Bosch (new), Champion, Fram/Autolite, Mopar, Motorcraft and Prestolite, a higher number indicates a hotter plug. On Bosch (old), NGK and Nippondenso, a higher number indicates a colder plug.

4. Make sure the spark plugs are properly gapped. See the Tune-Up Specifications in this book.

5. Be sure the spark plugs are firing efficiently. The illustrations on the next 2 pages show you how to "read" the firing end of the spark plug.

6. Check the ignition timing and set it to specifications. Tests show that almost all cars have incorrect ignition timing by more than 2°.

veyed over 6,000 cars nationwide, they found that a tune-up, on cars that needed one, increased fuel economy over 11%. Replacing worn plugs alone, accounted for a 3% increase. The same test also revealed that 8 out of every 10 vehicles will have some maintenance deficiency that will directly affect fuel economy, emissions or performance. Most of this mileage-robbing neglect could be prevented with regular maintenance.

Modern engines require that all of the functioning systems operate properly for maximum efficiency. A malfunction anywhere wastes fuel. You can keep your vehicle running as efficiently and economically as possible, by being aware of your vehicle's operating and performance characteristics. If your vehicle suddenly develops performance or fuel economy problems it could be due to one or more of the following:

PROBLEM	POSSIBLE CAUSE
Engine Idles Rough	Ignition timing, idle mixture, vacuum leak or something amiss in the emission control system.
Hesitates on Acceleration	Dirty carburetor or fuel filter, improper accelerator pump setting, ignition timing or fouled spark plugs.
Starts Hard or Fails to Start	Worn spark plugs, improperly set automatic choke, ice (or water) in fuel system.
Stalls Frequently	Automatic choke improperly adjusted and possible dirty air filter or fuel filter.
Performs Sluggishly	Worn spark plugs, dirty fuel or air filter, ignition timing or automatic choke out of adjustment.

Check spark plug wires on conventional point type ignition for cracks by bending them in a loop around your finger.

Be sure that spark plug wires leading to adjacent cylinders do not run too close together. (Photo courtesy Champion Spark Plug Co.)

7. If your vehicle does not have electronic ignition, check the points, rotor and cap as specified.

8. Check the spark plug wires (used with conventional point-type ignitions) for cracks and burned or broken insulation by bending them in a loop around your finger. Cracked wires decrease fuel efficiency by failing to deliver full voltage to the spark plugs. One misfiring spark plug can cost you as much as 2 mpg.

9. Check the routing of the plug wires. Misfiring can be the result of spark plug leads to adjacent cylinders running parallel to each other and too close together. One wire tends to

pick up voltage from the other causing it to fire "out of time".

10. Check all electrical and ignition circuits for voltage drop and resistance.

11. Check the distributor mechanical and/or vacuum advance mechanisms for proper functioning. The vacuum advance can be checked by twisting the distributor plate in the opposite direction of rotation. It should spring back when released.

12. Check and adjust the valve clearance on engines with mechanical lifters. The clearance should be slightly loose rather than too tight.

SPARK PLUG DIAGNOSIS

Normal

APPEARANCE: This plug is typical of one operating normally. The insulator nose varies from a light tan to grayish color with slight electrode wear. The presence of slight deposits is normal on used plugs and will have no adverse effect on engine performance. The spark plug heat range is correct for the engine and the engine is running normally.

CAUSE: Properly running engine.

RECOMMENDATION: Before reinstalling this plug, the electrodes should be cleaned and filed square. Set the gap to specifications. If the plug has been in service for more than 10-12,000 miles, the entire set should probably be replaced with a fresh set of the same heat range.

Oil Deposits

APPEARANCE: The firing end of the plug is covered with a wet, oily coating.

CAUSE: The problem is poor oil control. On high mileage engines, oil is leaking past the rings or valve guides into the combustion chamber. A common cause is also a plugged PCV valve, and a ruptured fuel pump diaphragm can also cause this condition. Oil fouled plugs such as these are often found in new or recently overhauled engines, before normal oil control is achieved, and can be cleaned and reinstalled.

RECOMMENDATION: A hotter spark plug may temporarily relieve the problem, but the engine is probably in need of work.

Incorrect Heat Range

APPEARANCE: The effects of high temperature on a spark plug are indicated by clean white, often blistered insulator. This can also be accompanied by excessive wear of the electrode, and the absence of deposits.

CAUSE: Check for the correct spark plug heat range. A plug which is too hot for the engine can result in overheating. A car operated mostly at high speeds can require a colder plug. Also check ignition timing, cooling system level, fuel mixture and leaking intake manifold.

RECOMMENDATION: If all ignition and engine adjustments are known to be correct, and no other malfunction exists, install spark plugs one heat range colder.

Photos Courtesy Fram Corporation

Carbon Deposits

APPEARANCE: Carbon fouling is easily identified by the presence of dry, soft, black, sooty deposits.

CAUSE: Changing the heat range can often lead to carbon fouling, as can prolonged slow, stop-and-start driving. If the heat range is correct, carbon fouling can be attributed to a rich fuel mixture, sticking choke, clogged air cleaner, worn breaker points, retarded timing or low compression. If only one or two plugs are carbon fouled, check for corroded or cracked wires on the affected plugs. Also look for cracks in the distributor cap between the towers of affected cylinders.

RECOMMENDATION: After the problem is corrected, these plugs can be cleaned and reinstalled if not worn severely.

MMT Fouled

APPEARANCE: Spark plugs fouled by MMT (Methycyclopentadienyl Maganese Tricarbonyl) have reddish, rusty appearance on the insulator and side electrode.

CAUSE: MMT is an anti-knock additive in gasoline used to replace lead. During the combustion process, the MMT leaves a reddish deposit on the insulator and side electrode.

RECOMMENDATION: No engine malfunction is indicated and the deposits will not affect plug performance any more than lead deposits (see Ash Deposits). MMT fouled plugs can be cleaned, regapped and reinstalled.

High Speed Glazing

APPEARANCE: Glazing appears as shiny coating on the plug, either yellow or tan in color.

CAUSE: During hard, fast acceleration, plug temperatures rise suddenly. Deposits from normal combustion have no chance to fluff-off; instead, they melt on the insulator forming an electrically conductive coating which causes misfiring.

RECOMMENDATION: Glazed plugs are not easily cleaned. They should be replaced with a fresh set of plugs of the correct heat range. If the condition recurs, using plugs with a heat range one step colder may cure the problem.

Ash (Lead) Deposits

APPEARANCE: Ash deposits are characterized by light brown or white colored deposits crusted on the side or center electrodes. In some cases it may give the plug a rusty appearance.

CAUSE: Ash deposits are normally derived from oil or fuel additives burned during normal combustion. Normally they are harmless, though excessive amounts can cause misfiring. If deposits are excessive in short mileage, the valve guides may be worn.

RECOMMENDATION: Ash-fouled plugs can be cleaned, gapped and reinstalled.

Detonation

APPEARANCE: Detonation is usually characterized by a broken plug insulator.

CAUSE: A portion of the fuel charge will begin to burn spontaneously, from the increased heat following ignition. The explosion that results applies extreme pressure to engine components, frequently damaging spark plugs and pistons.

Detonation can result by over-advanced ignition timing, inferior gasoline (low octane) lean air/fuel mixture, poor carburetion, engine lugging or an increase in compression ratio due to combustion chamber deposits or engine modification.

RECOMMENDATION: Replace the plugs after correcting the problem.

Photos Courtesy Champion Spark Plug Co.

EMISSION CONTROLS

13. Be aware of the general condition of the emission control system. It contributes to reduced pollution and should be serviced regularly to maintain efficient engine operation.

14. Check all vacuum lines for dried, cracked or brittle conditions. Something as simple as a leaking vacuum hose can cause poor performance and loss of economy.

15. Avoid tampering with the emission control system. Attempting to improve fuel econ-

FUEL SYSTEM

Check the air filter with a light behind it. If you can see light through the filter it can be reused.

Extremely clogged filters should be discarded and replaced with a new one.

18. Replace the air filter regularly. A dirty air filter richens the air/fuel mixture and can increase fuel consumption as much as 10%. Tests show that ⅓ of all vehicles have air filters in need of replacement.

19. Replace the fuel filter at least as often as recommended.

20. Set the idle speed and carburetor mixture to specifications.

21. Check the automatic choke. A sticking or malfunctioning choke wastes gas.

22. During the summer months, adjust the automatic choke for a leaner mixture which will produce faster engine warm-ups.

COOLING SYSTEM

29. Be sure all accessory drive belts are in good condition. Check for cracks or wear.

30. Adjust all accessory drive belts to proper tension.

31. Check all hoses for swollen areas, worn spots, or loose clamps.

32. Check coolant level in the radiator or expansion tank.

33. Be sure the thermostat is operating properly. A stuck thermostat delays engine warm-up and a cold engine uses nearly twice as much fuel as a warm engine.

34. Drain and replace the engine coolant at least as often as recommended. Rust and scale

TIRES & WHEELS

38. Check the tire pressure often with a pencil type gauge. Tests by a major tire manufacturer show that 90% of all vehicles have at least 1 tire improperly inflated. Better mileage can be achieved by over-inflating tires, but never exceed the maximum inflation pressure on the side of the tire.

39. If possible, install radial tires. Radial tires deliver as much as ½ mpg more than bias belted tires.

40. Avoid installing super-wide tires. They only create extra rolling resistance and decrease fuel mileage. Stick to the manufacturer's recommendations.

41. Have the wheels properly balanced.

omy by tampering with emission controls is more likely to worsen fuel economy than improve it. Emission control changes on modern engines are not readily reversible.

16. Clean (or replace) the EGR valve and lines as recommended.

17. Be sure that all vacuum lines and hoses are reconnected properly after working under the hood. An unconnected or misrouted vacuum line can wreak havoc with engine performance.

---

23. Check for fuel leaks at the carburetor, fuel pump, fuel lines and fuel tank. Be sure all lines and connections are tight.

24. Periodically check the tightness of the carburetor and intake manifold attaching nuts and bolts. These are a common place for vacuum leaks to occur.

25. Clean the carburetor periodically and lubricate the linkage.

26. The condition of the tailpipe can be an excellent indicator of proper engine combustion. After a long drive at highway speeds, the inside of the tailpipe should be a light grey in color. Black or soot on the insides indicates an overly rich mixture.

27. Check the fuel pump pressure. The fuel pump may be supplying more fuel than the engine needs.

28. Use the proper grade of gasoline for your engine. Don't try to compensate for knocking or "pinging" by advancing the ignition timing. This practice will only increase plug temperature and the chances of detonation or pre-ignition with relatively little performance gain.

Increasing ignition timing past the specified setting results in a drastic increase in spark plug temperature with increased chance of detonation or preignition. Performance increase is considerably less. (Photo courtesy Champion Spark Plug Co.)

---

that form in the engine should be flushed out to allow the engine to operate at peak efficiency.

35. Clean the radiator of debris that can decrease cooling efficiency.

36. Install a flex-type or electric cooling fan, if you don't have a clutch type fan. Flex fans use curved plastic blades to push more air at low speeds when more cooling is needed; at high speeds the blades flatten out for less resistance. Electric fans only run when the engine temperature reaches a predetermined level.

37. Check the radiator cap for a worn or cracked gasket. If the cap does not seal properly, the cooling system will not function properly.

---

42. Be sure the front end is correctly aligned. A misaligned front end actually has wheels going in differed directions. The increased drag can reduce fuel economy by .3 mpg.

43. Correctly adjust the wheel bearings. Wheel bearings that are adjusted too tight increase rolling resistance.

Check tire pressures regularly with a reliable pocket type gauge. Be sure to check the pressure on a cold tire.

GENERAL MAINTENANCE

Check the fluid levels (particularly engine oil) on a regular basis. Be sure to check the oil for grit, water or other contamination.

A vacuum gauge is another excellent indicator of internal engine condition and can also be installed in the dash as a mileage indicator.

44. Periodically check the fluid levels in the engine, power steering pump, master cylinder, automatic transmission and drive axle.

45. Change the oil at the recommended interval and change the filter at every oil change. Dirty oil is thick and causes extra friction between moving parts, cutting efficiency and increasing wear. A worn engine requires more frequent tune-ups and gets progressively worse fuel economy. In general, use the lightest viscosity oil for the driving conditions you will encounter.

46. Use the recommended viscosity fluids in the transmission and axle.

47. Be sure the battery is fully charged for fast starts. A slow starting engine wastes fuel.

48. Be sure battery terminals are clean and tight.

49. Check the battery electrolyte level and add distilled water if necessary.

50. Check the exhaust system for crushed pipes, blockages and leaks.

51. Adjust the brakes. Dragging brakes or brakes that are not releasing create increased drag on the engine.

52. Install a vacuum gauge or miles-per-gallon gauge. These gauges visually indicate engine vacuum in the intake manifold. High vacuum = good mileage and low vacuum = poorer mileage. The gauge can also be an excellent indicator of internal engine conditions.

53. Be sure the clutch is properly adjusted. A slipping clutch wastes fuel.

54. Check and periodically lubricate the heat control valve in the exhaust manifold. A sticking or inoperative valve prevents engine warm-up and wastes gas.

55. Keep accurate records to check fuel economy over a period of time. A sudden drop in fuel economy may signal a need for tune-up or other maintenance.

© 1980 Chilton Book Company, Radnor, PA 19089

① PLACE CAM FOLLOWER ON HIGH STEP OF FAST IDLE CAM

② CLOSE PRIMARY THROTTLE VALVES

③ TURN SCREW IN TO SPECIFIED FAST IDLE RPM TO ADJUST

Fast idle adjustment, E4ME/MC

DIESEL ENGINE FUEL SYSTEM

Fuel Supply Pump

REMOVAL AND INSTALLATION

The diesel fuel supply pump is serviced in the same manner as the fuel pump on the gasoline engines.

Fuel Filter

See "Diesel Fuel Filter" in Chapter 1 for service procedures.

WATER IN FUEL (DIESEL)

Water is the worst enemy of the diesel fuel injection system. The injection pump, which is designed and constructed to extremely close tolerances, and the injectors can be easily damaged if enough water is forced through them in the fuel. Engine performance will also be drastically affected, and engine damage can occur.

Diesel fuel is much more susceptible than gasoline to water contamination. Diesel-engined cars are equipped with an indicator lamp system that turns on an instrument panel lamp

ANTI-WATER MEASURES
(CHASSIS INSTALLED)

INJECTOR PUMP

4. SECONDARY FILTER

3. PRIMARY FUEL STRAINER (MOUNTS TO FRONT OF DASH)

2. WATER DRAIN SYPHON VALVE

5. HEATER

1. FUEL TANK

379 diesel-equipped pickups have this anti-water system built into the fuel system. Siphoning valve is located either at mid-frame, or to the rear of the fuel tank, depending on model

if water (1 to 2½ gallons) is detected in the fuel tank. The lamp will come on for 2 to 5 seconds each time the ignition is turned on, assuring the driver the lamp is working. If there is water in the fuel, the light will come back on after a 15 to 20 second off delay, and then remain on.

PURGING THE FUEL TANK

350 cu. in. Diesels

Trucks which have a "Water in Fuel" light may have the water removed from the tank with a siphon pump. The pump hose should be hooked up to the ¼ in. fuel return hose (the smaller of the two hoses) above the rear axle or under the hood near the fuel pump. Siphoning should continue until all water is removed from the tank. Use a clear plastic hose or observe the filter bowl on the siphon pump (if equipped) to determine when clear fuel begins to flow. Be sure to remove the cap on the fuel tank while purging. Replace the cap when finished. Discard the fuel filter and replace with a new filter.

379 cu. in. Diesels

The 379 (6.2L) diesel-equipped trucks also have a water-in-fuel warning system. The fuel tank is equipped with a filter which screens out the water and lets it lay in the bottom of the tank below the fuel pickup. When the water level reaches a point where it could be drawn into the system, a warning light flashes in the cab. A built-in siphoning system—starting at the fuel tank and going to the rear spring hanger on some models, and at the midway point of the right frame rail on other models permits you to attach a hose at the shut-off and siphon out the water.

If it becomes necessary to drain water from the fuel tank, also check the primary fuel filter for water. This procedure is covered under "Diesel Fuel Filter" in Chapter 1.

Fuel Injection Pump

REMOVAL AND INSTALLATION

350 cu. in.

NOTE: *For more illustrations on injection pump removal, see "Diesel Intake Manifold Removal" in Chapter 3.*

1. Remove the air cleaner.

2. Remove the filters and pipes from the valve covers and air crossover.

3. Remove the air crossover and cap and intake manifold with screened covers (tool J-26996-1).

4. Disconnect the throttle rod and return spring.

ELECTRIC SHUT-OFF
FUEL RETURN
PRE-SET DO NOT ADJUST
LOW IDLE ADJUSTMENT SCREW
PRESSURE TAP PLUG SCREW SEAL
FUEL RETURN PRESSURE TAP PLUG
INLET
THROTTLE LEVER

350 diesel injection pump

20 FT. LBS. (27 N·m)
18 FT. LBS. (24 N·m)
25 FT. LBS. (34 N·m)
18 FT. LBS. (24 N·m)
CLIP
25 FT. LBS. (34 N·m) (USE BACK-UP WRENCH ON UPPER INJECTION NOZZLE HEX)

TIMING MARK
INJECTION PUMP
ADAPTER

BOTH EDGES OF THE PUMP TIMING MARK MUST BE INSIDE THE EDGES OF THE PUMP ADAPTER MARK

VIEW A

350 diesel timing marks and injection pump lines

5. Remove the bellcrank.

6. Remove the throttle and transmission cables from the intake manifold brackets.

7. Disconnect the fuel lines from the filter and remove the filter.

8. Disconnect the fuel inlet line at the pump.

9. Remove the rear A/C compressor brace and remove the fuel line.

10. Disconnect the fuel return line from the injection pump.

11. Remove the clamps and pull the fuel return lines from each injection nozzle.

12. Using two wrenches, disconnect the high pressure lines at the nozzles.

13. Remove the three injection pump retaining nuts with tool J-26987 or its equivalent.

14. Remove the pump and cap all lines and nozzles.

To install:

15. Remove the protective caps.

16. Line up the offset tang on the pump driveshaft with the pump driven gear and install the pump.

17. Install, but do not tighten the pump retaining nuts.

18. Connect the high pressure lines at the nozzles.

19. Using two wrenches, torque the high pressure line nuts to 25 ft. lbs.

20. Connect the fuel return lines to the nozzles and pump.

21. Align the timing mark on the injection pump with the line on the timing mark adaptor and torque the mounting nuts to 35 ft. lbs.

NOTE: *A ¾ in. open end wrench on the boss at the front of the injection pump will aid in rotating the pump to align the marks.*

22. Adjust the throttle rod:

a. remove the clip from the cruise control rod and remove the rod from the bellcrank.

b. loosen the locknut on the throttle rod a few turns, then shorten the rod several turns.

c. rotate the bellcrank to the full throttle stop, then lengthen the throttle rod until the injection pump lever contacts the injection

PUMP DRIVEN GEAR

OFFSET

Offset on 350 diesel injection pump driven gear

THROTTLE CABLE
THROTTLE ROD
BELLCRANK
SOLENOID AND BRACKET ASSEMBLY
HAIRPIN CLIP
17 FT LBS
5 FT LBS
BRACKET
17 FT LBS

350 diesel throttle assembly

pump full throttle stop, then release the bellcrank.

d. tighten the throttle rod locknut.

23. Install the fuel inlet line between the transfer pump and the filter.

24. Install the rear A/C compressor brace.

25. Install the bellcrank and clip.

26. Connect the throttle rod and return spring.

27. Adjust the transmission cable:

a. push the snap-lock to the disengaged position.

b. rotate the injection pump lever to the full throttle stop and hold it there.

c. push in the snap-lock until it is flush.

d. release the injection pump lever.

28. Start the engine and check for fuel leaks.

29. Remove the screened covers and install the air crossover.

30. Install the tubes in the air flow control valve in the air crossover and install the ventilation filters in the valve covers.

31. Install the air cleaner.

32. Start the engine and allow it to run for two minutes. Stop the engine, let it stand for two minutes, then restart. This permits the air to bleed off within the pump.

379 cu. in.

1. Disconnect both batteries.

2. Remove the fan and fan shroud.

3. Remove the intake manifold as described in Chapter 3.

4. Remove the fuel lines as described in this chapter.

5. Disconnect the alternator cable at the injection pump, and the detent cable (see illustration) where applicable.

6. Tag and disconnect the necessary wires and hoses at the injection pump.

7. Disconnect the fuel return line at the top of the injection pump.

8. Disconnect the fuel feed line at the injection pump.

Rotate the crankshaft so the injection pump drive gear bolts become accessable through the hole

DETENT ROD

379 diesel accelerator cable linkage

9. Remove the air conditioning hose retainer bracket if equipped with A/C.

10. Remove the oil fill tube, including the crankcase depression valve vent hose assembly.

11. Remove the grommet.

INJECTION PUMP GEAR

ALIGNMENT MARK

CAM GEAR

45 N·m (35 FT. LBS.)

379 diesel injection pump mounting

Injection pump locating pin, 379 diesel

12. Scribe or paint a match mark on the front cover and on the injection pump flange.

13. The crankshaft must be rotated in order to gain access to the injection pump drive gear bolts through the oil filler neck hole.

14. Remove the injection pump-to-front cover attaching nuts. Remove the pump and cap all open lines and nozzles.

INSTALLATION

1. Replace the gasket. *This is important.*

2. Align the locating pin on the pump hub with the slot in the injection pump driven gear. At the same time, align the timing marks.

3. Attach the injection pump to the front cover, aligning the timing marks before torquing the nuts to 30 ft. lbs.

4. Install the drive gear to injection pump bolts, torquing the bolts to 20 ft. lbs.

5. Install the remaining components in the reverse order of removal. Torque the fuel feed line at the injection pump to 20 ft. lbs. Start the engine and check for leaks.

Injection Pump Fuel Lines

REMOVAL AND INSTALLATION

379 cu. in.

NOTE: *When the fuel lines are to be removed, clean all fuel line fittings thoroughly before loosening. Immediately cap the lines, nozzles and pump fittings to maintain cleanliness.*

1. Disconnect both batteries.

2. Disconnect the air cleaner bracket at the valve cover.

3. Remove the crankcase ventilator bracket and move it aside.

4. Disconnect the secondary filter lines.

5. Remove the secondary filter adapter.

6. Loosen the vacuum pump hold-down clamp and rotate the pump in order to gain access to the intake manifold bolt. Remove the

AT NOZZLE 25 N·m (20 FT. LBS.)

AT PUMP 25 N·m (20 FT. LBS.)

AT BRACKET 20 N·m (15 FT. LBS.)

AT INTAKE 40 N·m (30 FT. LBS.)

CLAMPS 3 N·m (26 IN. LBS.)

Torque specifications and fuel line routing, 379 diesel

Fuel line connections, 379 diesel

INLET FITTING TO BODY TORQUE
DIESEL EQUIPMENT – 45 FT. LBS. (60 N·m)
C.A.V. LUCAS – 25 FT. LBS. (34 N·m)

DIESEL EQUIPMENT   **C.A.V. LUCAS**

350 diesel injection nozzles. Note visual differences between manufacturers

intake manifold bolts. The injection line clips are retained by the same bolts.

7. Remove the intake manifold. Install a protective cover (GM part #J-29664-1 or equivalent) so no foreign material falls into the engine.

8. Remove the injection line clips at the loom brackets.

9. Remove the injection lines at the nozzles and cover the nozzles with protective caps.

10. Remove the injection lines at the pump and tag the lines for later installation.

11. Remove the fuel line from the injection pump.

12. Install all components in the reverse order of removal. Follow the illustrations for injection line connection.

Injector and glow plug installation, 350 diesel

Fuel Injectors

REMOVAL AND INSTALLATION

350 cu. in.

1. Remove the fuel return line from the injector.

2. Remove the nozzle hold-down clamp and spacer using tool J-26952.3. Cap the high pressure line and nozzle tip.

NOTE: *The nozzle tip is highly susceptible to damage and must be protected at all times.*

3. If an old injector is to be reinstalled, a new compression seal and carbon stop seal must be installed after removal of the used seals.

4. Remove the caps and install the injector spacer and clamp. Torque to 25 ft. lbs.

5. Replace return line, start the engine and check for leaks.

379 cu. in.

1. Disconnect the truck's batteries.

2. Disconnect the fuel line clip, and remove the fuel return hose.

3. Remove the fuel injection line as previously detailed.

4. Using GM special tool #J-29873, remove the injector. Always remove the injector by turning the 30mm hex portion of the injector; turning the round portion will damage the injector. Always cap the injector and fuel lines when disconnected, to prevent contamination.

5. Install the injector with new gasket and torque to 50 ft. lbs. Connect the injection line and torque the nut to 20 ft. lbs. Install the fuel return hose, fuel line clips, and connect the batteries.

Injector installation, 379 diesel

Injection Timing Adjustment

350 Cu. In.

For the engine to be properly timed, the lines on the top of the injection pump adapter and the flange of the injection pump must be aligned.

1. The engine must be off for resetting the timing.

2. Loosen the three pump retaining nuts with tool J-26987, an injection pump intake manifold wrench, or its equivalent.

3. Align the mark on the injection pump with the marks on the adapter and tighten the nuts. Torque to 35 ft. lbs. Use a ¾ in. open-end wrench on the boss at the front of the injection pump to aid in rotating the pump to align the marks.

4. Adjust the throttle rod. See step 22, "Fuel Injection Pump Removal and Installation."

CHECKING

For the engine to be properly timed, the marks on the top of the engine front cover and the injection pump flange must be aligned. The engine must be off when the timing is reset. On 49-states models, align the scribe marks. On California models, align the half-circles.

ADJUSTING

If the marks mentioned above are not aligned, adjustment is necessary. Loosen the three pump retaining nuts. Align the mark on the injection pump with the mark on the front cover, and tighten the nuts to 30 ft. lbs. Adjust the throttle rod (see step 22, "Fuel Injection Pump Removal and Installation").

Fuel Tank

DRAINING

CAUTION: *Disconnect the battery before beginning the draining operation.*

If the vehicle is not equipped with a drain plug, use the following procedure to remove the gasoline.

1. Using a 10 foot piece of ⅜ in. hose cut a flap slit 18 in. from one end.

2. Install a pipe nipple, of slightly larger diameter than the hose, into the opposite end of the hose.

3. Install the nipple end of the hose into the fuel tank with the natural curve of the hose pointing downward. Keep feeding the hose in until the nipple hits the bottom of the tank.

4. Place the other end of the hose in a suitable container and insert an air hose pointing it in the downward direction of the slit and inject air into the line.

NOTE: *If the vehicle is to be stored, always drain the gasoline from the complete fuel system including the carburetor, fuel pump, fuel lines, and tank.*

REMOVAL AND INSTALLATION

Cab-Mounted Tanks

1. Remove the seat back hold-down bolts and tilt the seat back forward.

2. If equipped, remove the tank cover.

3. Drain the tank.

4. Disconnect the fuel line, meter wire, and ground wire.

5. Remove the lug wrench and lug wrench mount.

6. Remove the bolts and fasteners securing the tank in place.

7. Remove the tank from the cab, and at the

same time, disengage the filler neck from the rubber grommet in the cab opening.

8. Remove the meter assembly from the tank.

9. Installation is the reverse of removal.

All Other Tanks

1. Drain the tank.

2. Jack up your vehicle and support it with jack stands.

3. Remove the clamp on the filler neck and the vent tube hose.

4. Remove the gauge hose which is attached to the frame.

5. While supporting the tank securely, remove the support straps.

6. Lower the tank until the gauge wiring can be removed.

7. Remove the tank.

8. Install the unit by reversing the removal procedure. Make certain that the anti-squeak material is replaced during installation.

9. Lower the vehicle.

TORQUE AT 12 FT. LBS.

TORQUE AT 12 FT. LBS.

ANTI-SQUEAK

CEMENT

STRAP

VIEW A

ANTI-SQUEAK

CEMENT

Tighten lower nut after upper nut has been tightened.

NOTE Hook must be assembled forward.

Fuel tank installation, typical of most models

Chassis Electrical

HEATER

Blower

REMOVAL AND INSTALLATION

1. Disconnect the negative battery terminal, open the hood, and securely support it.

2. On 1970–72 models, scribe the hood and fender location of the right hood hinge. Remove the hinge.

3. Mark the position of the blower motor in relation to its case. Remove the electrical connection at the motor.

4. Remove the blower attaching screws and remove the assembly. Pry gently on the flange if the sealer sticks.

5. The blower wheel can be removed from the motor shaft by removing the nut at the center.

Heater blower assembly

1	INSULATION
2	BLOWER MOTOR
3	FAN

Blower motor assembly. Later models have the insulator shield

6. Installation is the reverse of removal. Apply a bead of sealer to the mounting flange before installation.

Core

REMOVAL AND INSTALLATION

1970–72 Without Air Conditioning.

1. Drain the cooling system and disconnect the negative battery terminal.
2. Remove the electrical connection at the blower.
3. Remove the heater hoses at the core tubes.
4. Remove the right front fender skirt. Remove enough screws so that the fender can be moved outward.
5. Working from under the instrument panel, remove the seal on the temperature door cable and disconnect the cable from the temperature door.
6. Pull the case away from the mounting studs after removing the retaining bolts.
7. Remove the core retainers and remove the core.

The installation procedure is the reverse of removal.

1970–72 With Factory Installed Air Conditioning

NOTE: *Models with dealer installed air conditioning use the same procedure as those without air conditioning.*

1. Drain the coolant. Disconnect the battery ground cable.
2. Detach the heater hoses from the core tubes at the firewall.
3. Remove the stud nuts on the engine side of the firewall.
4. Remove the glove box.
5. Unplug the relay connector and remove the right ball outlet hose.
6. Remove the screw holding the panel outlet air distributor to the heater case. Remove the heater case retaining screws.
7. Pull the heater case away from the firewall; reach in and disconnect the resistor connector. Remove the resistor harness grommet and remove the harness.
8. Remove the heater case. Remove the core mounting straps. Reverse the procedure for installation.

1973 and Later

1. Disconnect the battery ground cable.
2. Disconnect the heater hoses at the core tubes and drain the engine coolant. Plug the core tubes to prevent spillage.
3. Remove the nuts from the distributor air ducts in the engine compartment.

Heater blower assembly, 1973 and later

Heater distributor, 1973 and later

4. Remove the glove compartment and door.
5. Disconnect the "Air-Defrost" and "Temperature" door cables.
6. Remove the floor outlet and remove the defroster duct-to-heater distributor screw.
7. Remove the heater distributor-to-instrument panel screws. Pull the assembly rearward to gain access to the wiring harness and disconnect the wires attached to the unit.
8. Remove the heater distributor from the truck.
9. Remove the heater core retaining straps and remove the core from the truck.
10. Installation is the reverse of removal. Be sure that the core-to-case and case-to-dash panel sealer is intact. Fill the cooling system and check for leaks.

RADIO

REMOVAL AND INSTALLATION

CAUTION: *Make certain that the speaker is attached to the radio before the unit is turned ON. If it is not, the output transistors will be damaged.*

SPEAKER

POWER   **VIEW A**   RECEIVER ASM.

Radio installation, 1972–72

1970–72

1. Disconnect the negative battery cable and remove the flex hoses from the heater distributor duct under the dashboard.

2. Remove the heater control head by removing the attaching screws and pushing the unit back and down.

3. Remove the ash tray and the ash tray retainer.

4. Remove the electrical connections from the rear of the radio and also the front attaching screws and knobs.

5. Remove the mounting screw on the side of the radio chassis. Push the radio back and up before slipping it down and out of the instrument panel.

6. To install the radio, reverse the removal procedure.

1973 and Later

1. Remove the negative battery cable and the control knobs and the bezels from the radio control shafts.

2. On AM radios, remove the support bracket stud nut and its lockwasher.

3. On AM/FM radios, remove the support bracket-to-instrument panel screws.

4. Lifting the rear edge of the radio, push

AM/FM

AM   AM/FM   AM

VIEW A   VIEW B

Radio installation, 1973 and later

the radio forward until the control shafts clear the instrument panel. Then lower the radio far enough so that the electrical connections can be disconnected.

5. Remove the power lead, speaker, and antenna wires and then pull out the unit.

6. Installation is the reverse of removal.

WINDSHIELD WIPERS

Motor

REMOVAL AND INSTALLATION

1970-72

1. Disconnect the battery ground cable. Be sure the wipers are in the parked position.

2. Remove the wiper arms and blades.

3. Remove the plenum chamber grille.

4. Disconnect wiper drive rods from crank arm; remove crank arm nut and arm from motor shaft.

5. Working under the instrument panel, disconnect the wiper motor and washer wiring connections. Remove the parking brake assembly if it is in the way.

Removing the 1970–72 drive rod retainer

Wiper installation, 1970–72

6. Remove the left hand defroster hose. Remove the washer hoses from the pump.

7. Remove the motor attaching screws and the motor.

8. To install, reverse the removal procedure.

1973 and Later

1. Make sure the wipers are parked.

2. Disconnect the ground cable from the battery.

3. Disconnect the wiring harness at the wiper motor and the hoses from the washer pump.

4. Reach down through the access hole in the plenum and loosen the wiper drive rod attaching screws. Remove the drive rod from the wiper motor crank arm.

5. Remove the wiper motor attaching screws and the motor assembly.

6. To install, reverse the removal procedure.

NOTE: *Lubricate the wiper motor crank arm pivot before reinstallation. Failure of the washers to operate or to shut off is often caused by grease or dirt on the electromagnetic contacts. Simply unplug the wire and pull off the plastic cover for access. Likewise, failure of the wipers to park is often caused by grease or dirt on the park switch contacts. The park switch is under the cover behind the pump.*

Wiper motor installation, 1973 and later

INSTRUMENT CLUSTER

REMOVAL AND INSTALLATION

1970-72

1. Disconnect the negative battery terminal. If equipped, remove the choke knob.

2. Remove the windshield wiper knob, the light switch rod, and the bezel. If equipped,

Standard instrument cluster, 1970–72

disconnect and plug the oil pressure line to the gauge.

3. Disconnect the speedometer cable and the chassis wiring harness which is located at the rear of the instrument panel. Protect the mast jacket with a rag or other covering so that it doesn't become scratched.

4. Remove the cluster retaining screws and remove the cluster.

5. To install the cluster, reverse the removal procedure.

1973–76

1. Remove the negative battery cable.

2. Remove the steering column cover and the cluster bezel.

3. Remove the knob from the clock (if equipped).

4. Remove the lens retaining screws and the lens.

5. Remove the transmission gear indicator (PRNDL) and the cluster retainer.

6. Disconnect the speedometer cable by depressing the spring clip and pulling the cable out of the speedometer head. Disconnect and plug the oil pressure line, if so equipped.

7. Disconnect the cluster wiring harness and remove the cluster retaining screws and pull out the cluster.

8. To install the cluster, reverse the removal procedure.

1977 and Later

1. Disconnect the battery ground cable.

2. Remove the headlamp switch control knob and radio control knobs.

3. Remove eight screws and remove instrument bezel. Remove the steering column cover.

4. Reach under the dash, depress the speedometer cable tang, and remove the cable.

5. Disconnect oil pressure gauge line at fitting in engine compartment, if so equipped.

6. Pull instrument cluster out just far enough to disconnect line from oil pressure gauge.

7. Remove the cluster.

8. Installation is the reverse of removal.

Speedometer Cable

REMOVAL AND INSTALLATION

1970 and Later

1. Disconnect the negative battery terminal.

2. Disconnect the cable from the back of the speedometer.

3. Remove the old core by pulling it out at the speedometer end. If the core is broken, it will be necessary to remove the broken half from the transmission end, of the cable.

4. Lubricate the entire length of the core before installation.

5. Installation is the reverse of removal.

Ignition Switch

REMOVAL AND INSTALLATION

1970–72

NOTE: *See Chapter 8 for 1973 and later Ignition Switch Removal and Installation.*

1973–76 instrument cluster; 1977 and later similar

1. Disconnect the battery ground cable.
2. Remove the lock cylinder by positioning the switch in "ACC" position and inserting a thin piece of wire in the small hole in the cylinder face. Push in on the wire and turn the key counterclockwise until the lock cylinder can be removed.
3. Remove the metal ignition switch nut.
4. Remove the ignition switch from under the dash and remove the wiring connector.
5. To remove the "theft-resistant" connector, the switch must be removed from under the dash. Use a small screwdriver, unsnap the locking tangs on the connector, and unplug the connector.
6. Installation is the reverse of removal.

LIGHTING

Headlights

REMOVAL AND INSTALLATION

1. Remove the headlight bezel.
2. Remove the retaining ring screws and the

Typical headlight mounting, 170–72; later models similar

VERTICAL ADJUSTMENT

HORIZONTAL ADJUSTMENT

Headlight adjustment slots, earlier models

retaining ring. Do not disturb the adjusting screws.

3. Unplug the headlight from the electrical connector and remove it.

4. Installation is the reverse of removal.

NOTE: *The number molded into the lens face must be at the top.*

HEADLIGHT AIMING

The headlights must be properly aimed to provide the best, safest road illumination. The lights should be checked for proper aim, and adjusted if necessary, after installing a new sealed beam unit or if the front end sheet metal has been replaced. Certain state and local authorities have requirements for headlight aiming and you should check these before adjusting.

1. Horizontal adj. screw-RH
2. Vertical adj. screw
3. Horizontal adj. screw-LH

Headlight aiming. Round headlight models similar

NOTE: *The truck's fuel tank should be about half full when adjusting the headlights. Tires should be properly inflated, and if a heavy load is carried in the pick-up bed, it should remain there.*

Horizontal and vertical aiming of each sealed beam unit is provided by two adjusting screws, which move the mounting ring in the body against the tension of the coil spring. There is no adjustment for focus; this is done during headlight manufacturing.

FUSES AND FLASHERS

Fuses are located in the junction box below the instrument panel to the left of the steering column. The turn signal flasher and the hazard-warning flasher also plug into the fuse block. Each fuse receptacle is marked as to the circuit it protects and the correct amperage of the fuse. In-line fuses are also used on the following circuits: 1970–75, ammeter; auxiliary heater and air conditioning 1973–74; and underhood lamp and air conditioning 1975 and later.

NOTE: *A special heavy duty turn signal flasher is required to properly operate the turn signals when a trailer's lights are connected to the system.*

CIRCUIT BREAKERS

A circuit breaker is an electrical switch which breaks the circuit in case of an overload. All models have a circuit breaker in the headlight switch to protect the headlight and parking light systems. An overload may cause the lamps to flicker or flash on and off, or in some cases, to remain off. 1974–and later windshield wiper motors are protected by a circuit breaker at the motor.

FUSIBLE LINKS

In addition to circuit breakers and fuses, the wiring harness incorporates fusible links to protect the wiring. Links are used rather than a fuse, in wiring circuits that are not normally fused, such as the ignition circuit. Fusible links are color coded red in the charging and load circuits to match the color coding of the circuits they protect. Each link is four gauges smaller than the cable it protects, and is marked on the insulation with the gauge size because the insulation makes it appear heavier than it really is.

The engine compartment wiring harness has several fusible links. The same size wire with a

FIGURE 1

REMOVE BATTERY CABLE & FUSIBLE LINK FROM STARTER SOLENOID AND CUT OFF DEFECTIVE WIRE AS SHOWN TWO PLACES.

FIGURE 2

STRIP INSULATION FROM WIRE ENDS. PLACE HEAT SHRINK TUBE OVER REPLACEMENT LINK. INSERT WIRE ENDS INTO CRIMP SPLICE AS SHOWN. NOTE: PUSH WIRES IN FAR ENOUGH TO ENGAGE WIRE ENDS.

FIGURE 3

CRIMP SPLICE WITH CRIMPING TOOL TWO PLACES TO BIND BOTH WIRES.

FIGURE 4

SLIDE TUBE OVER SPLICE WITH SPLICE CENTERED IN TUBE. APPLY LOW TEMPERATURE HEAT TO SHRINK TUBE AROUND WIRES & SPLICE. REASSEMBLE LINKS & BATTERY CABLE.

Fusible link repair

special hypalon insulation must be used when replacing a fusible link.

The links are located in the following areas:

1. A molded splice at the starter solenoid "Bat" terminal, a 14 gauge red wire.

2. A 16 gauge red fusible link at the junction block to protect the unfused wiring of 12 gauge or larger wire. This link stops at the bulkhead connector.

3. The alternator warning light and field circuitry is protected by a 20 gauge red wire fusible link used in the "battery feed to voltage regulator #3 terminal." The link is installed as a molded splice in the circuit at the junction block.

4. The ammeter circuit is protected by two 20 gauge fusible links installed as molded splices in the circuit at the junction block and battery to starter circuit.

Fusible Link Repair

1. Determine the circuit that is damaged.
2. Disconnect the negative battery terminal.
3. Cut the damaged fuse link from the harness and discard it.
4. Identify and procure the proper fuse link and butt connectors.
5. Strip the wire about ½ inch on each end.
6. Connect the fusible link and crimp the butt connectors making sure that the wires are secure.

Fusible links work like a fuse

7. Solder each connection with resin core solder, and wrap the connections with plastic electrical tape.
8. Reinstall the wire in the harness.
9. Connect the negative battery terminal and test the system for proper operation.

Speedometer Cable Core
REPLACEMENT

1. Disconnect the battery ground cable.
2. Disconnect the speedometer cable from the speedometer head by reaching up under the instrument panel, depressing the spring clip and pulling the cable from the head.
3. Remove the old core by pulling it out at

Various speedometer cable routings

the end of the speedometer cable casing. If the old cable core is broken it will be necessary to remove the lower piece from the transmission end of the casing. It is also important to replace both the casing and the core.

4. Lubricate the entire length of cable core with speedometer cable lubricant.

5. Install the new cable by reversing steps 1 through 3 above. Use care not to kink the cable core during installation.

LIGHT BULBS

Your local automotive parts store has light bulb lists covering your make and model truck.

WIRING DIAGRAMS

Wiring diagrams have been omitted from this book. As trucks have become more complex, and available with longer and longer option lists, wiring diagrams have grown in size and complexity as well. It has become impossible to provide a readable reproduction in a reasonable number of pages. Information on ordering wiring diagrams from Chevrolet or GMC can be found in the owner's manual.

Clutch and Transmission

![6]

MANUAL TRANSMISSION

Most three speed transmissions used are the very similar Saginaw and Muncie side cover units. These may be told apart by the shape of the side cover. The Saginaw has a single bolt centered at the top edge of the side cover, while the Muncie has two bolts along the top edge. Some 1976–80 models use the top cover Tremec three speed. All three speed transmissions use side mounted external linkage, with provision for linkage adjustment, and a column shaft.

The Muncie CH465 with synchronized 2nd, 3rd and 4th gears is the standard four speed transmission for 1970–and later. The transmission is distinguished by its top cover and the absence of external linkage. In addition, the New Process 435CR close ratio four speed transmission was available on all ½ and ¾ ton models in 1970. It was also available in 1971 in those trucks, but only with the 350 engine. The 435CR is also a top cover unit, with no provision for linkage adjustment. 1981 and later models have a 4 speed overdrive transmission as an option.

Three speed column shift controls, 1970–72

This unit uses external linkage which is adjustable.

LINKAGE ADJUSTMENT
3-Speed Column Shift

1. Place the column lever in the neutral position.
2. Under the truck, loosen the shift rod clamps. These are at the bottom of the column on 1970–72 models, and at the transmission for 1973–and later.
3. Make sure that the two levers on the transmission are in their center, neutral positions.
4. Install a ³⁄₁₆ to ⁷⁄₃₂ in. pin or drill bit through the alignment holes in the levers at the bottom of the steering column. This holds these levers in the neutral position.
5. Tighten the shift rod clamps.
6. Remove the pin and check the shifting operation.

Three and Four Speed Floor Shift Linkages

Place the shift lever in "neutral". A .249–.250 in. gage pin must fit freely through the shifter levers (see illustration) in the neutral position. A ¼ in. (.250) or "D" size (.249) drill bit will work here. Adjust the linkage at the point shown until the gage pin fits properly. Check adjustment by operating the shift lever through every gear shift combination.

REMOVAL AND INSTALLATION
Two Wheel Drive
3 AND 4 SPEED

1. Jack up your vehicle and support it with jack stands.
2. Drain the transmission.
3. Disconnect the speedometer cable, and back-up lamp wire at transmission.
4. Disconnect the shift control lever or shift

Three-speed column shift linkage adjustment. Note gage pin for aligning the shift levers

Three and four speed floor shift linkages, showing gage pin holes for adjustment

Transmission-to-bell housing mounting, manual transmissions

control from the transmission. On 4-speeds, remove the gearshift lever by pressing down firmly on the slotted collar plate with a pair of channel lock pliers and rotating counterclockwise. Plug the opening to keep out dirt.

5. Remove driveshaft after making the position of the shaft to the flange.

6. Position a transmission jack or its equivalent under the transmission to support it.

7. Remove the crossmember. Visually inspect to see if other equipment, brackets or lines, must be removed to permit removal of transmission.

NOTE: *Mark position of crossmember when removing to prevent incorrect installation. The tapered surface should face the rear.*

8. Remove the flywheel housing underpan.

9. Remove the top two transmission to housing bolts and insert two guide pins.

NOTE: *The use of guide pins will not only support the transmission but will prevent damage to the clutch disc. Guide pins can be made by taking two bolts, the same as those just removed only longer, and cutting off the heads. Slot for a screwdriver. Be sure to support the clutch release bearing and support assembly during removal of the transmission. This will prevent the release bearing from falling out of the flywheel housing.*

10. Remove two remaining bolts and slide transmission straight back from engine. Use care to keep the transmission drive gear straight in line with clutch disc hub.

11. Remove the transmission from beneath your vehicle.

12. Installation is the reverse of removal. Torque the mounting bolts to 55 ft. lbs., through 1972, 75 ft. lbs. 1973 and later.

NOTE: *Place transmission in gear and rotate transmission flange or output yoke to aid entry of main drive gear into disc's splines.*

Make sure clutch release bearing is in position.

CAUTION: *Do not force the transmission into the clutch disc hub. Do not let the transmission hang unsupported in the splined portion of the clutch disc.*

Four Wheel Drive

3-SPEED

1. Jack up the vehicle and support it on jack stands. Remove the skid plate, if so equipped.

2. Drain the transmission and transfer case. Remove the speedometer cable and the TCS switch, if so equipped, from the side of the transmission.

3. Disconnect the driveshafts and secure them out of the way.

4. Remove the shifter lever by removing the pivot bolt to the adapter assembly. You can then push the shifter up out of the way.

5. On 1978 and later models, remove the bolts attaching the strut to the right side of the transfer case and the rear of the engine, and remove the strut.

6. While supporting the transfer case, remove the attaching bolts to the adapter.

7. Remove the transfer case securing bolts from the frame and lower and remove the transfer case. (The case is attached to the right side of the frame.)

8. Disconnect the shift rods from the transmission.

9. While holding the rear of the engine with a jack, remove the adapter mounting bolts.

10. Remove the upper transmission bolts and insert two guide pins to keep the assembly aligned. See the two wheel drive procedure for details on making these.

205-series transfer case linkage

WITH "AUTOMATIC" TRANSMISSION

VIEW A

VIEW B

WITH "MANUAL" TRANSMISSION

Transfer case mounting, 205-series

11. Remove the flywheel pan and the lower transmission bolts.

12. Pull the transmission and the adapter straight back on the guide pins until the input shaft is free of the clutch disc.

13. The transmission and the adapter are removed as on assembly. The adapter can be separated once the assembly is out.

14. Installation is the reverse of removal. Place the transmission in gear and turn the output shaft to align the clutch splines. Transmission bolt torque is 55 ft. lbs. through 1972,

WITH AUTOMATIC TRANSMISSION

WITH MANUAL TRANSMISSION

208-series transfer case mounting

and 75 ft. lbs. for 1973–and later. See Transfer Case Removal and Installation for adapter bolt torques.

4-SPEED

1. Remove the shifter boots and retainers.

2. Remove the transmission shift lever. See the two wheel drive procedure for details on removing the lever. It may be necessary to remove the center floor outlet from the heater to complete the next step. Remove the center console, if so equipped.

3. Remove the transmission cover after releasing the attaching screws. It will be necessary to rotate the cover 90° to clear the transfer case shift lever.

4. Disconnect the transfer case shift lever link assembly and the lever from the adapter. Remove the skid plate, if any.

5. Remove the back-up light, the TCS switch, and the speedometer cable from the transmission.

6. Raise and support the truck with jack stands. Support the engine. Drain the transmission and the transfer case. Detach both drive shafts and secure them out of the way.

7. Remove the transmission-to-frame bolts. To do this, it will be necessary to open the locking tabs. Remove the transfer case-to-frame bracket bolts.

8. While supporting the transmission and transfer case, remove the crossmember bolts and the crossmember. It will be necessary to rotate the crossmember to remove it from the frame.

9. Remove the lower clutch housing cover.

NOTE: *On V8 engines it is necessary to remove the exhaust crossover pipe.*

10. Remove the transmission-to-clutch-housing bolts. Remove the upper bolts first and install guide pins. See the two wheel drive procedure for details.

11. Slide the transmission back until the input shaft clears the clutch assembly and then lower the unit.

12. Installation is the reverse of removal. The transfer case and transmission is installed as an assembly. Put the transmission in gear and turn the output shaft to align the clutch splines. Torque the transmission bolts to 55 ft. lbs. through 1972, to 75 ft. lbs. 1973–and later.

CLUTCH

Two types of clutches are used. Six cylinder engines use a single disc clutch with coil spring or diaphragm type pressure plates. V8 engines generally use a single disc with a coil spring pressure. Diaphragm type pressure plates operate with light pedal pressure, while coil spring pressure plates combine operating case with high torque capacity.

The operating controls are mechanical.

REMOVAL AND INSTALLATION

Diaphragm Clutch

NOTE: *Before removing the bell housing (1973 and later) the engine must be supported. This can be done by placing a hydraulic jack, with a board on top, under the oil pan.*

1. Remove the transmission.

2. Disconnect the clutch fork pushrod and spring. Remove the clutch housing.

3. Remove the clutch fork by pressing it away from the ball mounting with a screwdriver until the fork snaps loose from the ball or remove the ball stud from the clutch housing. Remove the throwout bearing from the clutch fork.

4. Install a pilot tool (an old mainshaft makes a good pilot tool) to hold the clutch while you are removing it.

NOTE: *Before removing the clutch from the flywheel, mark the flywheel, clutch cover and one pressure plate lug, so that these parts may be assembled in their same relative positions. They were balanced as an assembly.*

5. Loosen the clutch attaching bolts one turn at a time to prevent distortion of the clutch cover until the tension is released.

6. Remove the clutch pilot tool and the clutch from the vehicle.

Check the pressure plate and flywheel for signs of wear, scoring, overheating, etc. If the clutch plate, flywheel, or pressure plate is oil-soaked, inspect the engine rear main seal and the transmission input shaft seal, and correct leakage as required. Replace any damaged parts.

To install:

7. Install the pressure plate in the cover assembly, aligning the notch in the pressure plate with the notch in the cover flange. Install pressure plate retracting springs, lockwashers and drive strap to pressure plate bolts. Tighten to 11 ft. lbs. The clutch is now ready to be installed.

8. Turn the flywheel until the X mark is at the bottom.

9. Install the clutch disc, pressure plate and cover, using an old mainshaft as an aligning tool.

10. Turn the clutch until the X mark or painted white letter on the clutch cover aligns with the X mark on the flywheel.

11. Install the attaching bolts and tighten them a little at a time in a crossing pattern until the spring pressure is taken up.

12. Remove the aligning tool.

FLYWHEEL

DRIVEN PLATE ASSY.

PRESSURE PLATE
AND COVER ASSY.

THROWOUT BRG.

CLUTCH HOUSING
COVER

CLUTCH FORK

CLUTCH HOUSING

CLUTCH FORK
BALL STUD

Exploded view of a typical diaphragm clutch

13. Pack the clutch ball fork seat with a small amount of high temperature grease and install a new retainer in the groove of the clutch fork.

CAUTION: *Be careful not to use too much grease. Excessive amounts will get on the clutch fingers and cause clutch slippage.*

COAT THIS GROOVE

PACK
THIS
RECESS

Lubrication points of the throwout bearing

14. Install the retainer with the high side up with the open end on the horizontal.

15. If the clutch fork ball was removed reinstall it in the clutch housing and snap the clutch fork onto the ball.

16. Lubricate the inside of the throwout bearing collar and the throwout fork groove with a small amount of graphite grease.

17. Install the throwout bearing. Install the clutch housing.

18. Install the transmission.

19. Further installation is the reverse of removal. Adjust the clutch.

Coil Spring Clutch

Basically, the same procedures apply to diaphragm clutch removal as to coil spring clutch removal.

1. Before removing the clutch, punch-mark the flywheel, clutch cover and one pressure plate lug so that the components can be reassembled in their original locations.

2. Loosen the attaching screws one turn at a time to prevent distortion.

3. When the clutch plate is removed, be sure to mark the flywheel side.

4. Place ⅜ in. wood or metal spacers between the clutch levers and the cover to hold the levers down as the holding screws are removed.

Free Pedal Travel Adjustment

1970–72

Only one adjustment is necessary to assure that the clutch operates efficiently. This adjustment is for the amount of free clutch pedal travel before the throwout bearing contacts the clutch fingers. The pedal should be adjusted at periodic intervals to provide ¾–1 in. of free pedal travel.

1. Disconnect the clutch fork return spring at the fork.
2. Loosen the nut (A) and back it off approximately ½ in. from the swivel.
3. Hold the clutch fork pushrod against the fork to move the throwout bearing against the clutch fingers. The pushrod will slide through the swivel at the cross-shaft.
4. Rotate the lever until the clutch pedal contacts the bumper mounted on the parking brake support.
5. Adjust nut (B) to obtain ³⁄₁₆–¼ in. clearance between nut (B) and the swivel.
6. Release the pushrod, connect the return spring and tighten nut (A) to lock the swivel against nut (B).
7. Check the free pedal travel at the pedal and readjust as necessary.

Clutch pedal free-play adjustment, 1970–72

rearward until the throwout bearing lightly contacts the pressure plate levers.
4. Loosen the locknut and adjust the rod length so that the swivel slips freely into the gauge hole. Increase the rod length until all lash is removed.
5. Remove the swivel from the gauge hole. Insert the swivel in the lower hole in the lever. Install two washers and the cotter pin. Tighten the locknut, being careful not to change the rod length. Reinstall the spring and check the pedal free travel. It should be 1⅜–1⅝ in.

NOTE: *If you have a problem with driveline chatter in reverse on an early 1973 model, this can be corrected with a service kit (no. 340607) containing a new clutch cross shaft and relocated clutch fork springs. The kit components were installed at the factory in later models.*

Clutch linkage adjustment, 1973 and later. Clutch pedal free play at the pedal should be about ¾ to 1 in.

1973 and Later

1. Disconnect the return spring at the clutch fork.
2. Rotate the clutch lever and shaft assembly until the clutch pedal is firmly against the rubber bumper on the brake pedal bracket.
3. Push the outer end of the clutch fork

AUTOMATIC TRANSMISSION

Three automatic transmissions are used. The aluminum Powerglide was used from 1970 through 1971, when it was discontinued for use in trucks. The Turbo Hydra-Matic 350 and 400 have been in use from 1970–82. Some 1980 and later transmissions use the Torque Converter Clutch system. 1982 models are available with a 4 speed automatic which incorporates the torque converter clutch. No band adjustments are necessary or possible on Turbo Hydra-Matic transmissions; they use clutches instead of bands. Pan removal, fluid and filter changes for all three transmissions are covered in Chapter 1.

Powerglide

LOW BAND ADJUSTMENT

1. Raise and support the vehicle with jack stands.

2. Place the selector lever in Neutral.

3. Remove the protective cap from the low band adjusting screw.

4. Loosen the adjusting screw locknut ¼ turn and hold it in this position with a wrench.

5. Using an in. lb. torque wrench, adjust the band adjusting screw to 70 in. lbs., and back the screw off 4 complete turns for a band that has been in operation 6,000 miles or more; or 3 complete turns for a band that has been in operation less than 6,000 miles.

NOTE: *The back-off figure is not approximate; it must be exact.*

6. Tighten the adjusting screw locknut.

7. Lower the vehicle and road test.

SHIFT LINKAGE

The shift tube and selector linkage must be free in the mast jacket.

1. Set the transmission lever in Drive (D). Do not be guided by the position of the needle. Determine Drive by shifting the lever all the way to the right of the Low (L) detent. Rotate it back to the left, one detent, to Drive (D).

Powerglide low band adjustment

C   10, 20

Powerglide control rod adjustment

2. Attach the control rod to the lever and inner lever of the shaft assembly with the retainers.

3. Assemble the swivel, clamp, grommet, bushing, washers and nut loosely on the selector lever.

4. Attach the control rod to the outer lever of the shaft assembly with the retainer.

5. Place the selector lever tang in the Neutral drive gate of the selector plate assembly and insert the control rod into the swivel.

6. Rotate the lever clockwise viewed looking down the steering column, until the tang contacts the drive side of the Neutral drive gate.

7. Tighten the nut.

THROTTLE VALVE LINKAGE ADJUSTMENT

Six Cylinder Engines

1. With the accelerator depressed, the bell-crank on the engine must be in the wideopen throttle position.

2. The dash lever must be ¹⁄₆₄–¹⁄₁₆ in. off the lever stop and the transmission lever must be against the transmission internal stop.

V8 Engines

1. Remove the air cleaner.

2. Disconnect the accelerator linkage at the carburetor.

3. Disconnect the accelerator return spring and throttle valve rod return springs.

4. Pull the throttle valve rod forward until the transmission is through the detent. Open the carburetor to the wide-open throttle position. The carburetor must reach the wide-open throttle position at the same time that the ball stud contacts the end of the slot in the upper throttle valve rod.

5. Adjust the swivel on the end of the upper throttle valve rod as per Step 4. The allowable tolerance is approximately ¹⁄₃₂ in.

6. Connect and adjust the accelerator linkage.

7. Check for freedom of operation. Install the air cleaner.

NEUTRAL SAFETY SWITCH ADJUSTMENT (1970–71)

1. Align the slot in the contact support with the hole in the switch and insert a ³⁄₃₂ in. pin to hold it in this position.

2. The switch is now in the drive position.

3. Place the contact support drive slot over the shifter tube drive tang and tighten the screws.

4. Remove the clamp pin.

5. Check the operation of the switch. The

Powerglide throttle valve adjustment

engine should not be able to be started in any drive gear.

Turbo Hydra-Matic 350 and 400

SHIFT LINKAGE ADJUSTMENT

1970–72

1. The shift tube and levers located in the mast jacket of the steering column must move freely and must not bind.

2. Pull the shift lever toward the steering wheel and allow the lever to be positioned in Drive by the transmission detent. The pointer may be out of adjustment, so don't use the pointer on the column as a reference for positioning the lever. The pointer must be adjusted last.

3. Release the selector lever. The lever should not go into Low unless the lever is lifted.

4. Lift the lever toward the steering wheel and permit the lever to be placed in Neutral by the transmission detent.

5. Release the lever; it should not go into Reverse unless the lever is lifted.

6. If the linkage is adjusted correctly, the shift lever will not move past the Neutral detent and the Drive detent unless the lever is lifted so it can pass over the mechanical stop in the steering column.

7. If adjustment is necessary, place the lever in the Drive or High detent position. If the indicator pointer is out of alignment, you must rely upon the detent position to determine what gear you are in (see Steps 2 and 3).

Turbo Hydra-Matic shift linkage, 1970–72

8. Loosen the adjustment swivel or clamp at the cross-shaft and move the shift lever so that it contacts the drive stop in the column.

9. Tighten the swivel and recheck the adjustment (see Steps 2 and 6).

10. If the indicator pointer fails to line up properly with the gear symbol (P, R, N, D, L) or aligns with a wrong symbol (being in Reverse when the pointer indicates Neutral, etc.), the cause may be a bent indicator wire. Inspect it and repair.

11. If necessary, readjust the neutral safety switch to agree with the detent positions. The ignition key should move into "lock" only when the shift lever is in Park.

CAUTION: *The above adjustments must be made correctly to prevent early transmission failure caused by controls not being fully engaged with the detent. This results in a situation in which fluid pressure is reduced causing only partial engagement of the clutches. It may appear to run well but the pressure reduction may be just enough to cause clutch failure after only a few miles of operation.*

1973–81

1. The shift tube and lever assembly must be free in the mast jacket.

2. Lift the selector lever toward the steering wheel and allow the selector lever to be positioned in Drive by the detent. Do not use the selector lever pointer as a reference.

3. Release the selector lever. The lever should not be able to go into Low unless the lever is lifted.

4. Lift the selector lever toward the steering wheel and allow the lever to be positioned in Neutral by the transmission detent.

5. Release the selector lever. The lever should not be able to engage Reverse unless the lever is lifted. A properly adjusted linkage will prevent the lever from moving beyond both the Neutral and Drive detents unless the lever is lifted.

6. If adjustment is required, remove the screw and spring washer from the swivel.

7. Set the transmission lever in Neutral by moving it counterclockwise to L and then three detents clockwise to Neutral.

8. Put the transmission selector lever in Neutral as determined by the mechanical stop in the steering column.

9. Do not use the pointer to determine these positions.

10. Assemble the swivel spring and washer to the lever and tighten to 20 ft. lbs.

11. Readjust the Neutral safety switch if necessary.

12. Check the operation. With the key in

Turbo Hydra-Matic shift linkage, 1973–81

RUN, and the transmission in Reverse, be sure that the key cannot be removed and the steering wheel is not locked.

With the key in LOCK and the shift lever in PARK, be sure that the key can be removed, the steering wheel is locked, and that the transmission remains in PARK when the steering column is locked.

NOTE: *Any inaccuracies in the above adjustments may result in premature transmission failure, due to operation of the transmission with the controls not in the full detent. Partial engagement of clutches and other internal parts will result in transmission failure after only a few miles.*

1982 and Later

1. Set the trans lever "A" in the neutral position by moving it clockwise to the "Park" detent, then counterclockwise two detents to "Neutral".

1982 and later Turbo Hydra-Matic automatic transmission linkage adjustment, column shift shown

2. Set the column shift lever to the "Neutral" gate notch, by rotating it until the shift lever drops into the "Neutral" gate. Do not use the indicator pointer as a reference to position the shift lever, as this will not be accurate.

3. Attach rod "C" to the transmission shaft assembly as shown.

4. Slide the swivel and clamp onto rod "C" and align it with the column shift lever. Complete the attachment.

5. Hold the column lever against the "Neutral" stop on the "Park" position side. Tighten the nut.

DETENT CABLE ADJUSTMENT (TURBO HYDRA-MATIC 350)

1970–71

1. Remove the air cleaner.
2. Loosen the detent cable screw.
3. With the choke off and the accelerator linkage adjusted, position the carburetor lever in the wide open position.
4. Pull the detent cable rearward until the wide open throttle stop in the transmission is felt. The cable must be pulled through the detent position to reach the wide open throttle stop in the transmission.
5. Tighten the detent cable screw and check the linkage for proper operation.

Detent cable adjustment, 1970–72

1972

1. Remove the air cleaner.
2. Pry up on each side of the snap-lock with a screwdriver to release the lock.
3. Compress the locking tabs and disconnect the locking tabs from the bracket.
4. Attach the snap-lock to the accelerator control lever and install the retaining ring.
5. Pull the carburetor to the wide open throttle position against the stop on the carburetor.

Detent switch adjustment, 1970 396 V8

6. With the carburetor held in this position, pull the cable housing rearward until the wide open throttle stop in the transmission is felt.

7. Push the snap lock on the cable downward until it is flush with the cable.

8. Do not lubricate the cable. Install the air cleaner.

1973 and Later

1. With the snap-lock disengaged from the bracket, position the carburetor at the wide open throttle position. Push the snap-lock downward until the top is flush with the rest of the cable.

DETENT SWITCH ADJUSTMENT (TURBO HYDRA-MATIC 400)

1970–71

1. Adjust the detent switch as shown in the accompanying illustrations.

1972 and Later

1. Install the detent switch as shown.
2. After installing the switch, press the switch plunger as far forward as possible. This will preset the switch for adjustment. The switch will automatically adjust itself with the first wide open throttle application of the accelerator pedal.

NEUTRAL SAFETY/BACKUP LIGHT SWITCH REPLACEMENT AND ADJUSTMENT

This switch is on top of the steering column, behind the instrument panel. It prevents the starting circuit from being completed unless the shift lever is in Neutral or Park. The same switch causes the backup light to go on in Reverse.

NOTE: *The three speed manual transmission backup light switch is on the column. On the four speed, it is on the transmission, near the top cover.*

"SNAP LOCK"

B

A

"SNAP LOCK"

6

V-8

C-K MODEL

C-K MODEL
VIEW A

C-K MODEL
V-8 350 ENGINE
VIEW B

Detent cable adjustment, 1972 and later

WITH ACCELERATOR CONTROLS
PROPERLY ADJUSTED, ROTATE
LEVER TO OBTAIN WIDE OPEN
THROTTLE. FULLY DEPRESS
PLUNGER AND POSITION SWITCH
TO OBTAIN DIM. **A** SHOWN IN
TABLE BETWEEN PLUNGER AND
LEVER. TIGHTEN SWITCH ATTACHING
SCREWS.

	DIM. A
ALL EXCEPT 350 V8	.05
350 V8	.20

LEVER

6 CYLINDER ENGINE

SWITCH   PLUNGER   A

307 V-8 ENGINE

350   ENGINE

Detent switch adjustment, 1970–71 except 396 V8

TRANSMISSION
CONTROL SWITCH

PLUNGER

Detent cable adjustment, 1972 and later

.098 DIA.
GAUGE PIN

STEERING
COLUMN

Neutral start switch adjustment, 1973 and later

1970–72

1. Disconnect the wiring plug. Remove the screws and the switch.

2. Place the shift lever in Drive. Locate the lever tang against the transmission selector plate.

3. Align the slot in the contact support with the hole in the switch and insert a ³⁄₃₂ in. drill bit to hold the support in place.

4. Place the contact support drive slot over the shifter tube drive tang and tighten the screws. Remove the bit.

5. Connect the wiring plug and check that the engine will start only in Neutral and Park (foot on the brake!) and that the backup lights work only in reverse. Loosen the screws and move the switch to correct.

1973 and Later

1. Disconnect the switch wiring plug. Remove the screws and the switch.

2. Place the shift lever in Neutral.

3. Insert a ³⁄₃₂ in. drill bit, ³⁄₈ in. into the switch hole on a used switch. A new switch is held in the Neutral position by a plastic shear pin, so the bit isn't needed.

4. Insert the switch tang into the column slot and install the screws.

5. Remove the locating bit. With a new switch, shift out of Neutral to shear the plastic pin.

6. Connect the wiring plug and check that the engine will start only in Neutral and Park (foot on the brake!) and that the backup lights work only in Reverse. Loosen the screws and move the switch to correct.

TRANSMISSION REMOVAL AND INSTALLATION

NOTE: *It would be best to drain the transmission before starting.*
It may be necessary to disconnect and remove the exhaust crossover pipe on V8s, and to disconnect the catalytic converter and remove its support bracket, on models so equipped.

Two Wheel Drive

1. Disconnect the battery ground cable. Disconnect the detent cable at the carburetor.

2. Raise and support the truck on jack stands.

3. Remove the driveshaft, after matchmarking its flanges.

4. Disconnect the speedometer cable, downshift cable, vacuum modulator line, shift linkage, and fluid cooler lines at the transmission. Remove the filler tube.

5. Support the transmission and unbolt the rear mount from the crossmember. Remove the crossmember.

6. Remove the torque converter underpan, matchmark the flywheel and converter, and remove the converter bolts.

7. Support the engine and lower the transmission slightly for access to the upper transmission to engine bolts.

8. Remove the transmission to engine bolts

and pull the transmission back. Rig up a strap or keep the front of the transmission up so the converter doesn't fall out.

9. Reverse the procedure for installation. Bolt the transmission to the engine first (30 ft. lbs.), then the converter to the flywheel (35 ft. lbs.). Make sure that the converter attaching lugs are flush and that the converter can turn freely before installing the bolts. Tighten the bolts finger tight, then torque to specification, to insure proper converter alignment.

NOTE: *Lubricate the internal yoke splines at the transmission end of the driveshaft with lithium base grease. The grease should seep out through the vent hole.*

1970–72 Four Wheel Drive

1. Disconnect the battery ground cable. Disconnect the detent cable at the carburetor.
2. Raise and support the truck.
3. Remove the driveshafts, after matchmarking their flanges.
4. Remove the transfer case shift lever.
5. Disconnect the speedometer cable, downshift cable, vacuum modulator line, shift linkage, and fluid cooler lines at the transmission. Remove the filler tube.
6. Support the transmission and transfer case separately. Remove the transmission to adapter case bolts. Unbolt the transfer case from the frame bracket and remove it.
7. Proceed with Steps 5 through 9 of the two wheel drive procedure. See transfer case Removal and Installation for adapter bolt torques.

1973 and Later Four Wheel Drive

1. Disconnect the battery ground cable and remove the transmission dipstick. Detach the downshift cable at the carburetor. Remove the transfer case shift lever knob and boot.
2. Raise and support the truck on jack stands.
3. Remove the skid plate, if any. Remove the flywheel cover.
4. Matchmark the flywheel and torque converter, remove the bolts, and secure the converter so it doesn't fall out of the transmission.
5. Detach the shift linkage, speedometer cable, vacuum modulator line, downshift cable, and cooler times at the transmission. Remove the filler tube.
6. Remove the exhaust crossover pipe to manifold bolts.
7. Unbolt the transfer case adapter from the crossmember. Support the transmission and transfer case. Remove the crossmember.
8. Move the exhaust system aside. Detach the driveshafts after matchmarking their flanges. Disconnect the parking brake cable.

9. Unbolt the transfer case from the frame bracket. Support the engine. Unbolt the transmission from the engine, pull the assembly back, and remove.

10. Reverse the procedure for installation. Bolt the transmission to the engine first (30 ft. lbs.), then the converter to the flywheel (35 ft. lbs.). Make sure that the converter attaching lugs are flush and that the converter can turn freely before installing the bolts. See Transfer Case Removal and Installation for adapter bolt torques.

TRANSFER CASE

There are three cases used. The New Process 205 is used in part time systems with all transmissions through 1975, and in 1980, and with manual transmissions only 1976–79. It has a large New Process emblem on the back of the case. The full time New Process 203 is used with all transmissions in 1974 and early 1975, and only with automatics from mid-1975, to 1979. It can be identified by the H LOC and L LOC positions on the shifter. 1981 and later ½ and ¾ ton trucks use the model 208 transfer case. All 1 ton trucks use model 205.

NOTE: *Models with the New Process 203 full time four wheel drive transfer case, especially with manual transmissions, may give a front wheel "chatter" or vibration on sharp turns. This is a normal characteristic of this drivetrain combination. If it occurs shortly after shifting out of a LOC position, the transfer case is probably still locked up. This should correct itself after about a mile of driving, or can be alleviated by backing up for a short distance.*

CAUTION: *Owners of full time four wheel drive trucks (New Process 203 transfer case) often consider either removing the front driveshaft, or installing locking front hubs and operating in a LOC position, as a means of improving gas mileage. This practice will submit the transfer case to stresses beyond its design limits and will void all warranties. Use of any lubricant additive in the transfer case is also not recommended.*

REMOVAL AND INSTALLATION
All Models

NOTE: *See illustrations of 205 and 208 series transfer cases under "Transmission Removal" in this chapter.*

1. Raise and support the truck.
2. Drain the transfer case.
3. Disconnect the speedometer cable, back-up light switch, and the TCS switch.

NOTE: NO INSULATION TO BE INSTALLED UNDER RETAINER

NOTE: SHIFT PATTERN SHOULD BE IN HORIZONTAL POSITION TO DRIVER

NOTE: INSTALL BOOT PRIOR TO INSTALLATION OF NUT & KNOB

NOTE: WITH TRANS CASE IN "NEUTRAL" POSITION, ALIGN INDICATOR PLATE TO CENTER OF SHIFT LEVER

FWD

VIEW A

VIEW B

New Process model 203 transfer case shift linkage adjustment

4. If necessary, remove the skid plate and crossmember support.

5. Disconnect the front and rear driveshafts and support them out of the way.

On New Process 205 models, disconnect the shift lever rod from the shift rail link.

On New Process 203 models, disconnect the shift levers at the transfer case.

6. Remove the transfer case-to-frame mounting bolts.

VIEW B

VIEW B

1970–72 manual transmission transfer case mounting

Automatic transmission transfer case mounting, 1970–72

7. Support the transfer case and remove the bolts attaching the transfer case to transmission adaptor.

8. Move the transfer case to the rear until the input shaft clears the adaptor and lower the transfer case from the truck.

9. Installation is the reverse of removal.

SHIFT LINKAGE—ADJUSTMENT

New Process Model 203

The 203 full time four wheel drive transfer case is the only one on which linkage adjustment is possible.

1. Place the selector lever in the cab in the Neutral position.

2. Detach the adjustable rod ends from the transfer case levers.

3. Insert an $^{11}/_{64}$ in. drill bit through the alignment holes in the shifter levers. This will lock the shifter in the neutral position with both levers vertical.

4. Place the range shift lever (the outer lever) on the transfer case in the Neutral position.

5. Place the lockout shift lever (the inner lever) on the transfer case in the unlocked position. Both levers should now be vertical.

6. Adjust the rods so that the linkage fits together. The indicator plate can be moved to align with the correct symbol.

7. Remove the drill bit.

DRIVELINE

Tubular driveshafts are used on all models, incorporating needle bearing U-joints. An internally splined sleeve at the forward end compensates for variation in distance between the rear axle and the transmission.

The number of driveshafts used is determined by the length of the wheelbase. On trucks that use two driveshafts there is a center support incorporating a rubber cushioned ball bearing mounted in a bracket attached to the frame crossmember. The ball bearing is permanently sealed and lubricated. 4 WD models use a front driveshaft with a constant velocity joint.

Extended life U-joints have been incorporated on most models and can be identified by the absence of a lubrication fitting.

Front Driveshaft (4 WD Only)
REMOVAL AND INSTALLATION

Chevrolet and GMC use U-bolts or straps to secure the driveshaft to the pinion flange. Use the following procedure to remove the driveshaft.

1. Jack up your vehicle and support it with jack stands.
2. Scribe aligning marks on the driveshaft and the pinion flange to aid in reassembly.
3. Remove the U-bolts or straps at the axle end of the shaft. Compress the shaft slightly and tape the bearings into place to avoid losing them.
4. Remove the U-bolts or straps at the transfer case end of the shaft. Tape the bearings into place.
5. Remove the driveshaft.
6. Installation is the reverse of removal. Make certain that the marks made earlier line up correctly to prevent possible imbalances. Be sure that the constant velocity joint is at the transfer case end.

Rear Driveshaft (All Models)
REMOVAL AND INSTALLATION

1. Jack up your truck and support it with jack stands.
2. Scribe alignment marks on the driveshaft and flange of the rear axle, and transfer case or transmission. If the truck is equipped with a two piece driveshaft, be certain to also scribe marks at the center joint near the splined connection. When reinstalling driveshafts, it is necessary to place the shafts in the same posi-

Rear drive shaft U-bolt attachment

Rear driveshaft strap attachment

Driveshaft, U-joint and bearing support, 1971 and later

tion from which they were removed. Failure to reinstall the driveshaft properly will cause driveline vibrations and reduced component life.

3. Disconnect the rear universal joint by removing U-bolts or straps. Tape the bearings into place to avoid losing them.

4. If there are U-bolts or straps at the front end of the shaft, remove them. Tape the bearings into place. For trucks with two piece shafts, remove the bolts retaining the bearing support to the frame crossmember. Compress the shaft slightly and remove it.

5. If there are no fasteners at the front end of the transmission, there will only be a splined fitting. Slide the shaft forward slightly to disengage the axle flange, lower the rear end of the shaft, then pull it back out of the transmission. Most two wheel drive trucks are of this type. For trucks with two piece driveshafts, remove the bolts retaining the bearing support to the frame crossmember.

6. Reverse the procedure for installation. It may be tricky to get the scribed alignment marks to match up on trucks with two piece driveshafts. For those models only, the following instructions may be of some help. First, slide the grease cap and gasket onto the rear splines. Then:

1977 and later K models with 16 splines, after installing the front shaft to the transmission and bolting the support to the crossmember, arrange the front trunnion vertically and the second trunnion horizontally.

1973 C and K models, 1974 C models, 1975 and later models with 32 splines have an alignment key. The driveshaft cannot be replaced incorrectly. Simply match up the key with the keyway.

1975–76 K models with 16 splines, align the trunnions vertically. The shafts should not be rotated before installing the rear shaft to the front shaft.

1975–76 C models with 16 splines, after installing the front shaft to the transmission or transfer case, must align the trunnions vertically, then the rear shaft must be rotated four splines (90°) to the left (driver's) side before installing the rear shaft to the front shaft.

1971–72 C and K models and 1974 K models, after installing the front shaft to the transmission or transfer case and bolting the support to the crossmember, rotate all the U-joints so the trunnions are vertical, then rotate the rear shaft four splines towards the left (driver's) side of the truck before installing the rear shaft to the front shaft.

U-joint alignment, 1977 and later K models with two piece driveshafts only

7. On two wheel drive automatic transmission models, lubricate the internal yoke splines at the transmission end of the shaft with lithium base grease. The grease should seep out through the vent hole.

NOTE: *A thump in the rear driveshaft sometimes occurs when releasing the brakes after braking to a stop, especially on a downgrade. This is most common with automatic transmission. It is often caused by the driveshaft splines binding and can be cured by removing the driveshaft, inspecting the splines for rough edges, and carefully lubricating. A similar thump may be caused by the clutch plates in Positraction limited slip rear axles binding. If this isn't caused by wear, it can be cured by draining and refilling the rear axle with the special lubricant and adding Positraction additive, both of which are available from dealers.*

1973 C-10 and C-1500 long wheelbase pick-ups equipped with either the Turbo Hydra-Matic

U-joint alignment, 1971–72 C and K, 1974 K models

U-joint alignment, 1975–76 C models with 16 splines,; for 1975–76 K models follow steps 1 and 2 only

350 or 400 transmission may suffer from a driveline shudder during acceleration. This can be corrected by installing a spacer between the driveshaft center bearing support and the hanger to which it is attached. The spacer should measure 7¾ in. long and 1¼ in. wide, and be ½ in. thick. Two ½ in. diameter holes should be drilled at either end, centered 9/16 from the end in the long dimension and 5/8 in. on the short dimension. This places the centers of the holes 5/8 in. apart. Install the spacer between the center bearing support and the hanger using bolts ½ in. longer than the ones removed.

U-joint alignment keyway, 32-spline shaft

U-Joint Overhaul

There are three types of U-joints used in these trucks. The first is held together by wire snap rings in the yokes. The second type, first used in 1975, is held together with injection molded plastic retainer rings. This type cannot be reassembled with the same parts, once disassembled. However, repair kits are available. The third type (four wheel drive models only) is the large constant velocity joint which looks like a double U-joint, located at the transfer case end of the front driveshaft.

SNAP RING TYPE

1. Remove the driveshaft(s) from the truck.
2. Remove the lockrings from the yoke and remove the lubrication fitting.
3. Support the yoke in a bench vise. Never clamp the driveshaft tube.
4. Use a soft drift pin and hammer to drive against one trunnion bearing to drive the opposite bearing from the yoke.
   NOTE: *The bearing cap cannot be driven completely out.*
5. Grasp the cap and work it out.
6. Support the other side of the yoke and drive the other bearing cap from the yoke and remove as in Steps 4 and 5.
7. Remove the trunnion from the driveshaft yoke.
8. If equipped with a sliding sleeve, re-

1. TRUNNION
2. SEAL
3. BEARINGS
4. WASHER
5. CAP
6. SNAP RING

U-joint repair kit, snap-ring types

Installing trunnion into bearing yoke

U-joint bearing cup removal with a vise, snap-ring type

Installing U-joint snap-rings

move the trunnion bearings from the sleeve yoke in the same manner as above. Remove the seal retainer from the end of the sleeve and pull the seal and washer from the retainer.

To remove the bearing support:

9. Remove the dust shield, or, if equipped with a flange, remove the cotter pin and nut and pull the flange and deflector assembly from the shaft.

10. Remove the support bracket from the rubber cushion and pull the cushion away from the bearing.

11. Pull the bearing assembly from the shaft. If equipped, remove the grease retainers and slingers from the bearing.

Assemble the bearing support as follows:

12. Install the inner deflector on the driveshaft and punch the deflector on 2 opposite sides to be sure that it is tight.

13. Pack the retainers with special high melting grease.

Insert a slinger (if used) inside one retainer and press this retainer over the bearing outer race.

14. Start the bearing and slinger on the shaft journal. Support the driveshaft and press the bearing and inner slinger against the shoulder of the shaft with a suitable pipe.

STRIKE TUBE YOKE EAR IN THIS AREA

Tap the tube yoke lightly to seat the U-joint bearings against the lock rings

15. Install the second slinger on the shaft and press the second retainer on the shaft.

16. Install the dust shield over the shaft (small diameter first) and depress it into position against the outer slinger or, if equipped with a flange, install the flange and deflector. Align the centerline of the flange yoke with the centerline of

the driveshaft yoke and start the flange straight on the splines of the shaft with the end of the flange against the slinger.

17. Force the rubber cushion onto the bearing and coat the outside diameter of the cushion with clean brake fluid.

18. Force the bracket onto the cushion. Assemble the trunnion bearings:

19. Repack the bearings with grease and replace the trunnion dust seals after any operation that requires disassembly of the U-joint. But be sure that the lubricant reservoir at the end of the trunnion is full of lubricant. Fill the reservoirs with lubricant from the bottom.

20. Install the trunnion into the driveshaft yoke and press the bearings into the yoke over the trunnion hubs as far as it will go.

21. Install the lockrings.

22. Hold the trunnion in one hand and tap the yoke slightly to seat the bearings against the lockrings.

23. On the rear driveshafts, install the sleeve yoke over the trunnion hubs and install the bearings in the same manner as above.

MOLDED RETAINER TYPE

An injection molded plastic retainer is used on some 1975 and later models. A service repair kit is available for overhaul.

1. Remove the driveshaft.

2. Support the driveshaft in a horizontal position. Place the U-joint so that the lower ear of the shaft yoke is supported by a 1⅛ in. socket. Press the lower bearing cup out of the yoke

BEARING RETAINER

BEARING CUP

ROUND PLASTIC WASHER

ROLLER BEARINGS

SEAL

FLAT PLASTIC WASHER

CROSS

Injected molded retainer U-joint repair kit

ear. This will shear the plastic retaining the lower bearing cup.

NOTE: *Never clamp the driveshaft tubing in a vise.*

3. If the bearing cup is not completely removed, lift the cross, insert a spacer and press the cup completely out.

4. Rotate the driveshaft, shear the opposite plastic retainer, and press the other bearing cup out in the same manner.

5. Remove the cross from the yoke. Production U-joints cannot be reassembled. There are no bearing retainer grooves in the cups. Discard all parts that we removed and substitute those in the overhaul kit.

6. Remove the sheared plastic bearing retainer. Drive a small pin or punch through the injection holes to aid in removal.

7. If the front U-joint is serviced, remove the bearing cups from the slip yoke in the manner previously described.

8. Be sure that the seals are installed on the service bearing cups to hold the needle bearings in place for handling. Grease the bearings if they aren't pregreased.

9. Install one bearing cup partway into one side of the yoke and turn this ear to the bottom.

10. Insert the cross into the yoke so that the trunnion seats freely in the bearing cup.

11. Install the opposite bearing cup partway. Be sure that both trunnions are started straight into the bearing cups.

12. Press against opposite bearing cups, working the cross constantly to be sure that it is free in the cups. If binding occurs, check the needle rollers to be sure that one needle has not become lodged under an end of the trunnion.

13. As soon as one bearing retainer groove is exposed, stop pressing and install the bearing retainer snap-ring.

14. Continue to press until the opposite bearing retainer can be installed. If difficulty installing the snap-rings is encountered, rap the yoke with a hammer to spring the yoke ears slightly.

15. Assemble the other half of the U-joint in the same manner.

Constant Velocity (CV) Joint
OVERHAUL

1. Using a punch, mark the link yoke and the adjoining yokes before disassembly to ensure proper reassembly and driveshaft balance.

NOTE: *It is easier to remove the universal joint bearings from the flange yoke first. The first pair of flange yoke universal joint bearings to be removed is the pair in the link yoke.*

FLANGE YOKE COUPLING YOKE LUBE FITTING BALL SUPPORT TUBE YOKE

ALIGNMENT PUNCH MARKS

Constant-velocity joint showing alignment marks punched for reassembly

Constant velocity joint disassembly sequence

2. With the driveshaft in a horizontal position, solidly support the link yoke (a 1⅞ in. pipe will do).

3. Apply force to the bearing cup on the opposite side with a 1⅛ in. pipe or a socket the size of the bearing cup. Use a vise or press to apply force. Force the cup inward as far as possible.

NOTE: *In the absence of a press, a heavy vise may be used, but make sure that the universal to be removed is at a right angle to the jaws of the vise. Do not cock the bearing cups in their bores.*

4. Remove the pieces of pipe and complete the removal of the protruding bearing cup by tapping around the circumference of the exposed portion of the bearing with a small hammer.

5. Reverse the position of the pieces of pipe and apply force to the exposed journal end. This will force the other bearing cup out of its bore and allow removal of the flange.

NOTE: *There is a ball joint located between the two universals. The ball portion of this joint is on the inner end of the flange yoke. Prior to 1973, the ball was not replaceable. Beginning 1973, the ball, as well as the ball seat parts, is replaceable. Care must to taken*

not to damage the ball. The ball portion of this joint is on the driveshaft. To remove the seat, pry the seal out with a screwdriver.

6. To remove the journal from the flange, use steps two through five.

7. Remove the universal joint bearings from the driveshaft using the steps from two through five. The first pair of bearing caps that should be removed is the pair in the link yoke.

8. Examine the ball stud seat and ball stud for scores or wear. Worn seats can be replaced with a kit. A worn ball, however, requires the replacement of the entire shaft yoke and flange assembly. Clean the ball seat cavity and fill it with grease. Install the spring, washer, ball seats, and spacer, if removed.

9. Install the universal joints opposite the order in which they were disassembled.

10. Install a bearing ¼ of the way into one side of the yoke.

11. Insert the journal into the yoke so that an arm of the journal seats into the bearing.

12. Press the bearing in the remaining distance and install its snap-ring.

13. Install the opposite bearing. Do not allow the bearing rollers to jam. Continually check for free movement of the journal in the bearings as they are pressed into the yoke.

14. Install the rest of the bearings in the same manner.

CENTER YOKE
REAR TRUNNION
FRONT YOKE
REAR YOKE HALF

Driving out the bearing cup constant velocity joint

BALL SEATS
WASHER
SEAL
WASHER
BALL STUD
SPRING
BALL STUD SEAT
COUPLING YOKE

Exploded view of a constant velocity joint

NOTE: *The flange yoke should snap over center to the right or left and up or down by the pressure of the ball seat spring.*

FRONT AXLE—FOUR WHEEL DRIVE ONLY

Front Hub

Locking front hubs are standard equipment on 1975–and later four wheel drive models and optional on earlier years, with the exception of 1973–79 full time four wheel drive trucks. The purpose of locking hubs is to reduce friction and wear by disengaging the front axle shaft, differential, and driveline from the front wheels when four wheel drive is not being used.

The engagement and disengagement of the hubs is a manual operation which must be performed to each hub assembly. Unlocking should only take place when the transfer case lever is in the two wheel drive position. The hubs should be placed in the full Lock or full Free position or damage will result.

CAUTION: *Do not use four wheel drive unless the hubs are in the Lock position.*

NOTE: *Locking hubs should be run in the Lock position for at least 10 miles each month to assure proper differential lubrication.*

REMOVAL AND INSTALLATION
Including Wheel Bearings

NOTE: *This procedure requires snap ring pliers and a special hub nut wrench. It is not very easy without them.*

1. Remove the wheel and tire.

2. For 1970 and later ½ and ¾ ton trucks with lock front hubs: lock the hubs. Remove the outer retaining plate Allen head bolts and take off the plate, O-ring, and knob. Take out the large snap ring inside the hub and remove the outer clutch retaining ring and actuating cam body. This is a lot easier with snap ring pliers. Relieve pressure on the axle shaft snap ring and remove it. Take out the axle shaft sleeve and clutch ring assembly and the inner clutch ring and bushing assembly. Remove the spring and retainer plate.

3. For ¾ ton truck models 1970–76, with locking front hubs, turn the hub key to the "Free" position. Remove the Allen head bolts securing the retainer cap assembly to the wheel

Four wheel drive steering knuckle

hub. Pull off the hub cap assembly and gasket, and the exterior sleeve extension housing and its gasket.

NOTE: *You will have to modify this procedure for either of the models mentioned above if you have non-factory installed locking hubs.*

4. If you don't have locking front hubs, remove the hub cap and snap ring. Next, remove the drive gear and pressure spring. To prevent the spring from popping out, place a hand over the drive gear and use a screwdriver to pry the gear out. Remove the spring.

5. Remove the wheel bearing outer lock nut, lock ring, and wheel bearing inner adjusting nut. A special wrench is required.

6. Remove the brake disc assembly and outer wheel bearing. Remove the spring retainer plate if you don't have locking hubs. See Chapter 9 for details on brake drum or disc and caliper removal.

7. Remove the oil seal and inner bearing cone from the hub using a brass drift and hammer. Discard the oil seal. Use the drift to remove the inner and outer bearing cups.

8. Check the condition of the spindle bearing. If you have drum brakes, remove the grease retainer, gasket, and backing plate after removing the bolts. Unbolt the spindle and tap it with a soft hammer to break it loose. Remove the spindle and check the condition of the thrust

1. Retaining plate bolts	8. Outer clutch retaining ring
2. Washer	9. Actuating cam body
3. Hub ring retaining knob	10. Axle shaft snap ring
4. Actuator knob "O" ring	11. Axle shaft sleeve and ring
5. Actuator knob	12. Inner clutch ring
6. "O" ring	13. Pressure spring
7. Internal snap ring	14. Spring retainer plate

Exploded view, manual-locking free wheeling hubs

1. Machine screw
2. Cover plate
3. Cover
4. Sealing ring
5. Bearing race spring
6. Bearing inner race
7. Bearing
8. Bearing retainer clip
9. Wire retaining ring
10. Outer clutch housing
11. Seal bridge—retainer
12. Retaining ring
13. Spring support washer
14. Spring retainer
15. Return spring
16. Spring retainer

17. Clutch gear
18. Hub sleeve
19. "C" type retaining ring
20. Conical spring
21. Cam follower
22. Outer cage
23. Inner cage
24. Snap ring
25. Brake band
26. Drag sleeve and detent
27. Small spacer
28. Retaining ring
29. Lock nut
30. Drag sleeve retainer washer
31. Adjusting nut, wheel bearing

Exploded view—automatic free wheeling hubs

Details of locking hubs for K-20 and K-2500 models, 1970–77

washer, replacing it if worn. Now you can remove the oil seal and spindle roller bearing.

NOTE: *The spindle bearings must be greased each time the wheel bearings are serviced.*

9. Clean all parts in solvent, dry, and check for wear or damage.

10. Pack both wheel bearings (and the spindle bearing) using wheel bearing grease. Place a healthy glob of grease in the palm of one hand and force the edge of the bearing into it so that grease fills the bearing. Do this until the whole bearing is packed. Grease packing tools are available to make this job easier.

11. To reassemble the spindle: drive the repacked bearing into the spindle and install the grease seal onto the slinger with the lip toward the spindle. It would be best to replace the axle shaft slinger when the spindle seal is replaced. See Axle Shaft Removal and Overhaul in Chapter 7 for details.

NOTE: *An improved spindle seal (no. 376855) and axle seal (no. 376851) were introduced during the 1976 model year. These can be installed on earlier (late 1972 and up) models. See the note under Axle Shaft Removal and Installation in Chapter 7 for details on identifying late 1972 models.*

If you are using the improved seals, fill the seal end of the spindle with grease. If not, apply grease only to the lip of the seal. Install the thrust washer over the axle shaft. On late 1972 through 1982 models, the chamfered side of the thrust washer should be toward the slinger.

This special four wheel drive bearing adjusting wrench is available at four wheel drive suppliers and truck parts outlets

Driving out the bearing cups

Removing the spindle

Replacing the spindle thrust washer and spindle; the components are removed from the truck for clarity

CHAMFER
TOWARD
SEAL

Replace the spindle and torque the nuts to 45 ft. lbs. through 1976, 25 ft. lbs., 1977–78, 33 ft. lbs., 1979–80, 65 ft. lbs. 1981 and later.

WHEEL BEARING ASSEMBLY AND ADJUSTMENT

1. To reassemble the wheel bearings: drive the outer bearing cup into the hub, replace the inner bearing cup, and insert the repacked bearing.

2. Install the disc or drum and outer wheel bearing to the spindle.

3. Adjust the bearings by rotating the hub and torquing the inner adjusting nut to 50 ft. lbs., then loosening it and retorquing to 35 ft. lbs. Next, back the nut off ⅜ turn or less. Turn the nut to the nearest hole in the lockwasher. Install the outer locknut and torque to a minimum of 50 ft. lbs. through 1978, or 80 ft. lbs., 1979–80, 160–205 ft. lbs. 1981 and later ½ and ¾ ton, and 65 ft. lbs. on 1 ton vehicles. There should be 0.001–0.010 in. bearing end play. This can be measured with a dial indicator.

4. Replace the brake components.

5. Lubricate the locking hub components with high temperature grease. Lubrication must be applied to prevent component failure For ½ ton 1970–82 and 1977–84 ¾ and 1 ton models, install the spring retainer plate with the flange side facing the bearing over the spindle nuts and seat it against the bearing outer cup. Install the pressure spring with the large end against the spring retaining plate. The spring is an interference fit; when seated, its end extends past the spindle nuts by approximately ⅞ in. Place the inner clutch ring and bushing assembly into the axle shaft sleeve and clutch ring assembly and install that as an assembly onto the axle shaft. Press in on this assembly and install the axle shaft ring. If there are two axle shaft snap ring grooves (1976–79), use the inner one.

NOTE: *You can install a ⁷⁄₁₆ in. bolt in the axle shaft end and pull outward on it to aid in seating the snap ring.*

Install the actuating cam body in the cams facing outward, the outer clutch retaining ring, and the internal snap ring. Install a new O-ring on the retaining plate, and then install the actuating knob in the Lock position. Install the retaining plate. The grooves in the knob must fit into the actuator cam body. Install the seals and six cover bolts and torque them to 30 ft. lbs. Turn the knob to the Free position and check for proper operation.

6. For ¾ and 1 ton models, 1970–76, apply grease generously to the axle splines and teeth of the inner and outer clutch gears.

NOTE: *Remove the head from a 5 in. long ⅜ in. bolt and use this to align the hub assembly.*

Install the headless bolt into one of the hub housing bolt holes. Install a new exterior sleeve extension housing gasket, the housing, and a new hub retainer cap assembly gasket, and the cap assembly. Install the six Allen head bolts and their washers, and torque them to 30 ft. lbs. Turn the knob to Lock and check engagement.

7. Without locking hubs, replace the snap ring and hub cap. If there are two axle shaft snap ring grooves (1976–79), use the inner one.

Axle Shaft
REMOVAL AND INSTALLATION

NOTE: *The front spindles and universal joints were changed during the 1972 model year. You must know which one you have to order the correct parts. The early design is stamped 603351 or 603352 on the front of the left axle tube; the later design is 603333 or 603334. The only interchangeable part is the inner hub seal.*

1. Follow the steps of the Front Hub section above.

2. Pull out the axle shaft and universal joint assembly.

3. When installing the axle shaft, turn the shaft slowly to align the splines with the differential.

4. Reassemble everything and adjust the wheel bearings following the steps in the "Front Hub" section in this chapter.

AXLE SHAFT U-JOINT OVERHAUL

1. Remove the axle shaft.

2. Squeeze the ends of the trunnion bearings in a vise to relieve the load on the snap rings. Remove the snap rings.

3. Support the yoke in a vise and drive on one end of the trunnion bearing with a brass drift enough to drive the opposite bearing from the yoke.

4. Support the other side of the yoke and drive the other bearing out.

5. Remove the trunnion.

6. Clean and check all parts. You can buy

U-joint repair kits to replace all the worn parts.

7. Lubricate the bearings with wheel bearing grease.

8. Replace the trunnion and press the bearings into the yoke and over the trunnion hubs far enough to install the lock rings.

9. Hold the trunnion in one hand and tap the yoke lightly to seat the bearings against the lock rings.

10. The axle slingers can be pressed off the shaft.

NOTE: *Always replace the slingers if the spindle seals are replaced.*

11. Replace the shaft.

REAR AXLE

All models use conventional hypoid axles. Half ton models use semi-floating axles, while ¾ and 1 ton models use full floating axles. Semi-floating axles use one bearing at the end of the axle housing next to the wheel hub. These bearings do not require adjustment. Full floating axles

1. Drum	14. Shim kit, pinion brg	26. Bolt, hyp drive gear
2. Bolt, rr whl	15. Gear, ring and pinion	27. Case, diff
3. Shaft, rr axle	16. Lock	28. Shaft, diff pinion
4. Seal, rr axle shaft	17. Nut, diff brg adj	29. Screw, diff pinion shaft
5. Bearing, rr axle whl	18. Bolt, adj nut lock	30. Washer, diff png thrust
6. Nut, pinion flange	19. Cap, diff brg	31. Pinion, diff
7. Washer, pinion flange	20. Bolt, diff brg cap	32. Washer, si gear thrust
8. Flange, w/defl, pinion	21. Shim, diff brg	33. Gear, diff side
9. Seal, pinion flange	22. Bearing, differential	34. Plate, rr brk flg
10. Bearing, pinion frt	23. Clip, rr brk c/ovr pipe	35. Washer, lk (½")
11. Spacer, pinion bearing	24. Bolt, diff carrier cover	36. Bolt, hex (½"-20 x 1")
12. Carrier & tube, diff	25. Cover, diff carrier	37. Lock, axle shaft
13. Bearing, pinion gear rr		

9½ in. ring gear axle, exploded view

use two bearings, and must be adjusted (in much the same manner as front wheel bearings) if removed or replaced. Full floating axle housings carry the entire weight of the chassis and cargo, permitting the axle shafts to be removed without disturbing the differential.

Axle Shaft, Bearings, and Seal
REMOVAL AND INSTALLATION

All ½ Ton Trucks Except 1974—And Later Locking Differential

This procedure applies to all standard rear axles and to those with the optional Positraction limited slip differential.

1. Support the axle on jack stands.
2. Remove the wheels and brake drums.
3. Clean off the differential cover area, loosen the cover to drain the lubricant, and remove the cover.
4. Turn the differential until you can reach the differential pinion shaft lockscrew. Remove the lockscrew and the pinion shaft.
5. Push in on the axle end. Remove the C-lock from the inner (button) end of the shaft.
6. Remove the shaft, being careful of the oil seal.
7. You can pry the oil seal out of the housing by placing the inner end of the axle shaft behind the steel case of the seal, then prying it out carefully.
8. A puller or a slide hammer is required to remove the bearing from the housing.
9. Pack the new or reused bearing with wheel bearing grease and lubricate the cavity between the seal lips with the same grease.
10. The bearing has to be driven into the housing. Don't use a drift, you might cock the bearing in its bore, use a large socket instead. Drive only on the outer bearing race. In a sim-

The correct way to install a bearing. Note that the one illustrated is being driven down over a shaft. When installing the axle tube bearing, you would drive on the outer bearing race to prevent damaging the bearing rollers. The pipe exerts even pressure all around so that the bearing goes on straight (© Chevrolet Motor Div.)

Wheel bearing puller. This tool can usually be rented from tool rental shops

Rear wheel bearing installation tool

Removing the differential pinion shaft lock pin, all ½ ton trucks, except with locking differential (© Chevrolet Motor Div.)

ilar manner, drive the seal in flush with the end of the tube.

11. Slide the shaft into place, turning it slowly until the splines are engaged with the differential. Be careful of the oil seal.

12. Install the C-lock on the inner axle end. Pull the shaft out so that the C-lock seats in the counterbore of the differential side gear.

13. Position the differential pinion shaft through the case and the pinion gears, aligning the lockscrew hole. Install the lockscrew.

14. Install the cover with a new gasket and tighten the bolts evenly in a crisscross pattern.

15. Fill the axle with lubricant.

16. Replace the brake drums and wheels.

1974–80 Series 10 and 1500 With Locking Differential

This axle uses a thrust block on the differential pinion shaft.

1. Follow Steps 1–3 of the preceding procedure.

2. Rotate the differential case so that you can remove the lockscrew and support the pinion shaft so it can't fall into the housing. Remove the differential pinion shaft lockscrew.

3. Carefully pull the pinion shaft partway out and rotate the differential case until the shaft touches the housing at the top.

Correct C-lock positioning, 1974–80 locking differential

Push the axle shaft inward to remove the C-lock

4. Use a drift pin to position the C-lock with its open end directly inward. You can't push in the axle shaft till you do this.

5. Push the axle shaft in and remove the C-lock.

6. Follow Steps 6–11 of the preceding procedure.

7. Keep the pinion shaft partway out of the differential case while installing the C-lock on the axle shaft. Put the C-lock on the axle shaft and carefully pull out on the axle shaft until the C-lock is clear of the thrust block.

8. Follow steps 13–16 of the previous procedure.

1970–82 ¾ and 1 Ton

These models all use axles of full floating design. The procedures are the same for locking and non-locking axles. Some 1970–72 trucks use

Removing the lock screw

Positioning the differential case for best clearance for pinion shaft removal, 1974 and later locking differential.

Removing the full floating axle shaft, 1970–72; 1973 and later similar

Dana axles, but the same procedures should be used.

The best way to remove the bearings from the wheel hub is with an arbor press. Use of a press reduces the chances of damaging the bearing races, cocking the bearing in its bore, or scoring the hub walls. A local machine shop is probably equipped with the tools to remove and install bearings and seals. However, if one is not available, the hammer and drift method outlined can be used.

1. Support the axle on jacking stands.
2. Remove the wheels.
3. Remove the bolts and lock washers that attach the axle shaft flange to the hub.
4. On 1970–72 trucks, install two ½ in. by 13 in. bolts in the threaded holes provided in the axle shaft flange. By turning these bolts alternately the axle shaft may be easily started and then removed from the housing.
5. On 1973 and later trucks, rap on the flange with a soft faced hammer to loosen the shaft. Grip the rib on the end of the flange with a pair of locking pliers and twist to start shaft removal. Remove the shaft from the axle tube.
6. The hub and drum assembly must be removed to remove the bearings and oil seals. You will need a large socket to remove and later adjust the bearing adjustment nut.

7. Remove the locknut retainer, then the locknut.
8. Remove the adjusting nut from the housing tube.
9. Remove the thrust washer from the housing tube.
10. Pull the hub and drum straight off the axle housing.
11. Remove the oil seal and discard.
12. Use a hammer and a long draft pin to knock the inner bearing, cup, and oil seal from the hub assembly.
13. Remove the outer bearing snap ring with a pair of pliers. It may be necessary to tap the bearing outer race away from the retaining ring slightly by tapping on the ring to remove the ring.
14. Drive the outer bearing from the hub with a hammer and drift pin.
15. To reinstall the bearings, place the outer bearing into the hub. The larger outside diameter of the bearing should face the outer end of the hub. Drive the bearing into the hub using a washer that will cover both the inner and outer races of the bearing. Place a socket on the top of this washer, then drive the bearing into place with a series of light taps. If avail-

This tool is available for removing and adjusting the bearing locknut and adjusting nut

1. Axle Shaft
2. Shaft-to-Hub Bolt
3. Locknut
4. Locknut Retainer
5. Adjusting Nut
6. Thrust Washer
7. Hub Outer Bearing
8. Snap Ring
9. Hub Inner Bearing
10. Oil Seal
11. Wheel Bolt
12. Hub Assembly
13. Drum Assembly
14. Gasket

Cross section of the hub and drum assembly for ¾ and 1 ton models

SEAL INSTALLER
(J-21128 (8½) or J-29713 (9½))

Seal installation

able, an arbor press should be used for this job.

16. Drive the bearing past the snap ring groove, and install the snap ring. Then, turning the hub assembly over, drive the bearing back against the snap ring. Again, protect the bearing by placing a washer on top of it. You can use the thrust washer that fits between the bearing and the adjusting nut for this job.

17. Place the inner bearing into the hub. The thick edge should be toward the shoulder in the hub. Press the bearing into the hub until it seats against the shoulder, using a washer and socket as outlined earlier. Make certain that the bearing is not cocked and that it is fully seated on the shoulder.

18. Pack the wheel bearings with the grease, and lightly coat the inside diameter of the hub bearing contact surface and the outside diameter of the axle housing tube.

19. Make sure that the inner bearing, oil seal, axle housing oil deflector, and outer bearing are properly positioned. Install the hub and drum assembly on the axle housing, exercising care so as not to damage the oil seal or dislocate other internal components.

20. Install the thrust washer so that the tang on the inside diameter of the washer is in the keyway on the axle housing.

21. Install the adjusting nut. Tighten to 50 ft. lbs., at the same time rotating the hub to make sure that all the bearing surfaces are in contact. Back off the nut and retighten to 35 ft. lbs., then back off ¼ of a turn.

22. Install the tanged retainer against the inner adjusting nut. Align the adjusting nut so that the short tang of the retainer will engage the nearest slot on the adjusting nut.

23. Install the outer locknut and tighten to 65 ft. lbs. Bend the long tang of the retainer into the slot of the outer nut. This method of adjustment should provide .001 to .010 in. of end play.

24. Place a new gasket over the axle shaft and position the axle shaft in the housing so that the shaft splines enter the differential side gear. Position the gasket so that the holes are in alignment, and install the flange-to-hub attaching bolts. Torque to 90 ft. lbs. through 1975, 115 ft. lbs. 1976 and later.

NOTE: *To prevent lubricant from leaking through the flange holes, apply a nonhardening sealer to the bolt threads. Use the sealer sparingly.*

25. Replace the wheels.

Determining Axle Ratio

Axle ratios available in these trucks range from 2.56:1 to 4.57:1 with nine stops in between. However, not all ratios are available with all axles. If you are contemplating a change of axle ratios, your dealer can advise you as to what gears are available for your particular axle.

Front axle ratios installed on four wheel drive models are the same as the rear.

An axle ratio is obtained by dividing the number of teeth on the drive pinion gear into the number of teeth on the ring gear. For instance, on a 4.11 ratio, the driveshaft will turn 4.11 times for every turn of the rear wheel.

The most accurate way to determine axle ratios is to drain the differential, remove the cover, and count the number of teeth on the ring and pinion.

An easier method is to jack and support the truck so that both rear wheels are off the ground. Make a chalk mark on the rear wheel and the driveshaft. Block the front wheels and put the transmission in Neutral. Turn the rear wheel one complete revolution and count the number of turns made by the driveshaft. The number of driveshaft rotations is the axle ratio. You can get more accuracy by going more than one tire rotation and dividing the result by the number of tire rotations.

The axle ratio is also identified by the axle serial number prefix on the axles. Dana axles usually have a tag under one of the cover bolts, giving either the ratio or the number of pinion/ring gear teeth.

Suspension and Steering

FRONT SUSPENSION

All models except four wheel drive use an independent front suspension with upper and lower control arms and coil springs. Four wheel drive pick-ups are tapered leaf springs and the traditional solid front axle.

CAUTION: *Coil springs are under considerable tension. Be very careful when removing and installing them; they can exert enough force to cause serious injury.*

Coil Spring

REMOVAL AND INSTALLATION

1. Raise and support the truck under the frame rails. The control arms should hang free.

2. Disconnect the shock absorber at the lower end and move it aside. Disconnect the stabilizer bar from the lower control arm.

3. Support the cross-shaft and install a spring compressor or chain the spring to the control arm as a safety precaution.

4. Raise the jack to remove the tension from the lower control arm cross-shaft and remove the two U-bolts securing the crossshaft to the crossmember.

NOTE: *The cross-shaft and lower control arm keeps the coil spring compressed. Use care when you lower the assembly.*

5. Slowly release the jack and lower the control arm until the spring can be removed. Be sure that all compression is relieved from the spring.

6. Remove the spring.

7. Installation is the reverse of removal, with the following recommendations: Position the control arm cross-shaft on the crossmember and install the U-bolts. Be sure that the front indexing hole in the cross-shaft is aligned with the crossmember attaching saddle stud.

Have the front suspension alignment checked. Torque the U-bolts to 45 ft. lbs., 1970–75 ½

Front coil spring removal showing spring compressor. Make sure the fork in the top of the spring compressor is in position whenever the tool is used

Coil spring compressed. The lower control arm pivot bolts have been removed.

Spring compressed and ready to install

ton trucks, 110 ft. lbs. ¾ and 1 ton models; all other trucks 85 ft. lbs.

Leaf Spring

REMOVAL AND INSTALLATION

1. Raise and support the vehicle so that all tension is taken off of the front suspension.

2. Remove the shackle upper retaining bolt and the front spring eye bolt.

3. Remove the spring-to-axle U-bolt nuts. Pull of the spring, the lower plate, and the spring pads.

4. Remove the shackle-to-spring bolt, bushings, and shackle.

To replace the bushing, place the spring in a press or vise and press out the bushing. Press in the new bushing. The new bushing should protrude evenly on both sides of the spring.

5. Installation is the reverse of removal. The following torques are necessary; 1970–72 U-Bolts 120 ft. lbs. 1973 and later 150 ft. lbs., Spring shackle 50 ft. lbs., Front eye bolt 90 ft. lbs., Rear eye bolt 50 ft. lbs.

Typical front suspensions. 4X4 top, 2WD lower

Shock Absorbers
REMOVAL AND INSTALLATION

1. Raise and support the truck.
2. Remove the nuts and eye bolts securing the upper and lower shock absorber eyes.
3. Remove the shock absorber and inspect the rubber eye bushings. If these are defective, replace the shock absorber assembly.
4. Installation is the reverse of removal.

TESTING

Adjust the tire pressure before testing the shocks. If the truck is equipped with heavy-duty equipment, this can sometimes be misleading. A stiff ride normally accompanies a stiff or heavy-duty suspension. Be sure that all weight in the truck is distributed evenly.

Each shock absorber can be tested by bouncing the corner of the truck until maximum up and down movement is obtained. Let go of the truck. It should stop bouncing in 1–2 bounces. If not, the shock should be replaced.

Ball Joints—Two Wheel Drive Models
INSPECTION
Upper—1970–71

1. Raise and support the truck so that the control arms hang free.
2. Remove the wheel.
3. Support the lower control arm with a jacking stand and disconnect the upper ball stud from the steering knuckle.
4. Reinstall the nut on the ball stud and measure the torque required to rotate the stud. If the torque is not within 1–10 ft. lbs., replace the ball joint.
5. If no defects are evident, connect the steering knuckle to the upper stud and torque the nut to 70 ft. lbs. Tighten further to install the cotter pin, but don't exceed 90 ft. lbs.

Upper—1972 and Later

1. Perform Steps 1–3 of the 1970–71 inspection procedure.

Lower

1. Support the weight of the control arm at the wheel hub.

Two wheel drive front shock absorber

Lower ball joint inspection

Four wheel drive front shock absorber

Loosening the ball joint stud with the special tool (© Chevrolet Motor Div.)

2. Measure the distance between the tip of the ball joint stud and the grease fitting below the ball joint.

3. Move the support to the control arm and allow the hub and drum to hang free. Measure the distance again. If the variation between the two measurements exceeds ³⁄₃₂ in. the ball joint should be replaced.

REMOVAL AND INSTALLATION

Lower

1. Raise and support the truck with jack stands. Support the lower control arm with a floor jack.

2. Remove the tire and wheel.

3. Remove the lower stud cotter pin and loosen, but do not remove, the stud nut.

4. Loosen the ball joint with the tool illustrated or its equivalent. It may be necessary to remove the brake caliper and wire it to the frame to gain enough clearance.

5. When the stud is loose, remove the tool and ball stud nut.

Pressing out the 2WD lower ball-joint using a ball-joint tool

Installing the lower ball-joint, 2WD models

6. Install a spring compressor on the coil spring for safety.

7. Pull the brake disc and knuckle assembly up and off the ball stud and support the upper arm with a block of wood.

8. Remove the ball joint from the control arm with a ball joint fork or another suitable tool.

To install:

9. Start the new ball joint into the control arm. Position the bleed vent in the rubber boot facing inward.

10. Turn the screw until the ball joint is seated in the control arm.

11. Lower the upper arm and match the steering knuckle to the lower ball stud.

12. Install the brake caliper, if removed.

13. Install the ball stud nut and torque it to 80–100 ft. lbs. plus the additional torque necessary to align the cotter pin hole. Do not exceed 130 ft. lbs. or back the nut off to align the holes with the pin.

14. Install a new lube fitting and lubricate the new joint.

15. Install the tire and wheel.

16. Lower the truck.

Upper

1. Raise and support the truck with jack stands. Remove wheel.

2. Support the lower control arm with a floor jack.

3. Remove the cotter pin from the upper ball stud and loosen, but do not remove the stud nut.

4. Using the special tool or its equivalent, loosen the ball stud in the steering knuckle. When the stud is loose, remove the tool and the stud nut. It may be necessary to remove the brake caliper and wire it to the frame to gain clearance.

5. Drill out the rivets. Remove the ball joint assembly.

To install:

6. Install the service ball joint, using the nuts supplied or special hardened fasteners.

7. Torque the ball stud nut as follows: ½ ton trucks: 60 ft. lbs. plus the additional torque to align the cotter pin. Do not exceed 90 ft. lbs. and never back the nut off to align the pin.

¾ and 1 ton trucks: 80–100 ft. lbs. plus additional torque necessary to align the cotter pin. Do not exceed 130 ft. lbs. and never back off the nut to align the pin.

8. Install a new cotter pin.

9. Install a new lube fitting and lubricate the new joint.

10. If removed, install the brake caliper.

11. Install the wheel and lower the truck.

Four Wheel Drive Models

REPLACEMENT

All Except K30 Series

The steering knuckle pivot ball joints may need replacement when there is excessive steering play, hard steering, irregular tire wear (especially on the inner edge), or persistent tie rod loosening.

This procedure requires the removal of the steering knuckle before the ball joints can be removed. K30 models with king-pins have their own knuckle removal procedure later in this chapter.

1. Support the front axle on jack stands.
2. Remove the axle shaft as detailed earlier.
3. Remove the steering linkage. The best method is to use a tire rod end puller.
4. If you remove the steering arm from the top of the knuckle, the nuts cannot be reused.
5. Remove the cotter pin and ball joint stud nuts.
6. Remove the knuckle from the housing yoke by forcing a wedge between the lower ball

Pressing the lower ball-joint out of the knuckle

Lower ball-joint removal, 4X4s.

Removing the steering arm nuts, 4X4 models. Replace the nuts with new ones when installing

Removing the ball socket retaining nuts on 4X4s

stud and the yoke, then between the upper ball stud and the yoke.

NOTE: *If you have to loosen the upper ball stud adjusting sleeve to remove the knuckle, don't loosen it more than two threads. The soft threads in the yoke are easily damaged.*

7. Remove the lower ball joint snap-ring. Press the lower ball joint out first.
8. Press out the upper ball joint and unscrew the adjusting sleeve. A spanner wrench is required for the sleeve.
9. Press the new lower ball joint into the knuckle and install the snap-ring. The lower joint doesn't have a cotter pin hole.
10. Press the upper ball joint into the knuckle.
11. Position the knuckle to the yoke. Install new stud nuts finger tight.
12. Push up on the knuckle and tighten the lower nut to 70 ft. lbs.
13. Using a spanner wrench, install and torque the upper ball stud adjusting sleeve to 100 ft. lbs. and install the cotter pin. Don't loosen the castellated nut, but make it tighter to line up the cotter pin hole.

14. Replace the steering arm, using new nuts and torquing to 90 ft. lbs.

15. Check the knuckle turning torque with a spring scale hooked to the tie rod hole in the steering arm. With the knuckle straight ahead, measure the right angle pull to keep the knuckle turning after initial breakaway, in both directions. The pull should be 25 lbs. or less for axles assembled after Feb. 10, 1976, and 33 lbs. for earlier models.

16. Replace the axle shaft and other components. Tighten the steering linkage nuts to 45 ft. lbs.

King Pins

REPLACEMENT

K30 Series 4x4 Models

1. Remove the hub and spindle as previously outlined. Check the bronze spacer between the axle shaft joint assembly and bearing, if worn it must be replaced.

2. Remove the upper king pin cap nuts alternately, as the spring pressure will be forcing the cap up.

Removing the tapered bushing

Use a large breaker bar to remove the upper king pin. When installing the king pin, torque to 500–600 ft. lbs.

Remove the upper king pin cap nuts alternately

Removing the cap, spring and gasket

3. Remove the cap, compression spring, and gasket. Discard the gasket.

4. Remove the four cap screws from the lower king pin bearing cap. Remove the gearing cap and king pin.

5. Remove the upper king pin tapered bushing and knuckle from the yoke. Remove the felt seal and remove the knuckle.

6. Remove the upper king pin from the yoke with a large breaker bar.

7. Remove the lower king pin bearing cup, cone, grease retainer, and seal. Discard the seal. If the grease retainer is damaged, replace it.

Install in the following manner:

1. Install the new grease retainer and lower king pin bearing cap using special tool J-7817 or its equivalent.

2. Fill the grease retainer, grease the bearing and install. Install the lower seal using tool J22281 or its equivalent.

NOTE: *Do not distort the oil seal. It will*

Remove the cap, cone and seal. Discard the seal and replace with a new one during assembly. If the grease retainer is damaged, replace it

Installing the knuckle to the yoke

protrude slightly from the surface of the yoke when installed.

3. Install the upper king pin using tool J28871 or its equal. Torque to 500–600 ft. lbs.

4. Install the felt seal on the king pin.

5. Install the knuckle and tapered bushing over the king pin.

6. Install the lower bearing cap and king pin. Torque the cap screws to 90 ft. lbs.

7. Place the compression spring on the upper king pin bushing. Install the bearing cap with a new gasket. Torque the nuts to 90 ft. lbs.

Upper Control Arm

REMOVAL AND INSTALLATION

1. Raise and support the truck on jack stands.

2. Support the lower control arm with a floor jack.

3. Remove the wheel and tire.

4. Remove the cotter pin from the upper ball joint and loosen the stud nut one turn.

Upper control arm mounting, 2WD models

5. Install a spring compressor on the coil spring for safety.

6. Loosen the upper ball joint using a ball joint removal tool. Remove the nut from the ball joint and raise the upper arm to clear the steering knuckle. It may be necessary to remove the brake caliper and wire it to the frame to gain clearance.

7. Remove the nuts securing the control arm shaft studs to the crossmember bracket and remove the control arm.

8. Tape the shims and spacers together and tag for proper reassembly.

9. Installation is the reverse of removal. Before tightening the nuts to 70 ft. lbs. for ½ ton trucks, or 105 ft. lbs. for ¾ and 1 ton models. Have the front end alignment checked, and adjusted.

Lower Control Arm

REMOVAL AND INSTALLATION

1. Raise and support the truck on jack stands.

2. Remove the spring (see "Spring Removal and Installation").

3. Support the inboard end of the control arm after spring removal.

4. Remove the cotter pin from the lower ball joint and loosen the nut one turn.

5. Loosen the lower ball joint using a ball joint removal tool. When the stud is loose, remove the nut from the stud. It may be necessary to remove the brake caliper and wire it to the frame to gain clearance.

6. Remove the lower control arm.

7. Installation is the reverse of removal. See the "Spring Removal and Installation" for bolt torques.

Front End Alignment

Correct alignment of the front suspension is necessary to provide optimum tire life and for proper and safe handling of the vehicle. Caster and camber cannot be set or measured accurately without professional equipment. Toe-in

Front end geometry

LEFT HAND FRONT VIEW

Front wheel camber

can be adjusted with some degree of success without any special equipment.

CASTER

Caster is the tilt of the front steering axis either forward or backward away from the vertical. A tilt toward the rear is said to be positive and a forward tilt is negative. Caster is calculated with a special instrument but one can see the caster angle by looking straight down from the top of the upper control arm. You will see that the ball joints are not aligned if the caster angle is more or less than 0°. If the vehicle has positive caster, the lower ball joint would be ahead of the upper ball joint center line. Caster is designed into the four wheel drive front suspension. Small caster adjustments can be made on four wheel drive front axles by the use of tapered shims between the springs and the axle.

2WD front suspension shwoing caster adjustment shims

CAMBER

Camber is the slope of the front wheels from the vertical when viewed from the front of the vehicle. When the wheels tilt outward at the top, the camber is positive. When the wheels tilt inward at the top, the camber is negative. The amount of positive and negative camber is measured in degrees from the vertical and the measurement is called camber angle. Camber is designed into the front axle of all four wheel drive vehicles. Small camber adjustments can be made on four wheel drive front axles by the use of an adjusting shim between the spindle and the steering knuckle. Any major corrections require axle straightening equipment.

CASTER AND CAMBER ADJUSTMENTS

Two Wheel Drive

Caster and camber adjustments are made by removing or adding shims between the upper control arm shaft and the mounting bracket which is attached to the suspension crossmember.

Front wheel alignment on Chevrolet and GMC trucks is a complex operation. Specifications for camber and caster are given in relation to a measurement (the distance from the lower control arm to the bump stop bracket). This takes into account all sorts of individuality among trucks: heavy-duty suspensions, tires, spring rates, and even wear on the front suspension. As a result specifications are not included in this book. Camber should not vary more than ½° from side to side.

TOE-IN

Toe-in is the amount, measured in a fraction of an inch, that the wheels are closer together in front than at the rear.

Virtually all trucks are set with toe-in. Some four wheel drive trucks require toe-out to prevent excessive toe-in under power.

NOTE: *Some alignment specialists set toe-in to the lower specified limit on vehicles with radial tires. The reason is that radial tires have less drag, and therefore a lesser tendency to toe-out at speed. By the same reasoning, off-road tires would require the upper limit of toe-in.*

Toe-in must be checked after caster and camber have been adjusted, but it can be adjusted without disturbing the other two settings. You can make this adjustment without special equipment, if you make careful measurements. The adjustment is made at the tie-

"B" IS LESS THAN "A" WHEN WHEELS TOE-IN

TIE ROD ADJUSTING SLEEVES

Toe-in adjustment

Toe-in (in.)

Year	Model	Toe-In
1970	C-10, 1500, 20, 2500	⅛–¼
	K-10, 1500, 20, 2500	³⁄₃₂–³⁄₁₆
1971	All	⅛–¼
1972–73	All	³⁄₁₆
1974–80	C-10, 1500, 20, 2500	³⁄₁₆
	K-10, 1500, 20, 2500	0
1981–84	All	³⁄₁₆

NOTE: EQUAL THREAD LENGTHS MUST BE VISIBLE AT INNER AND OUTER ENDS OF ADJUSTER SLEEVE WHEN ASSEMBLED TO STEERING KNUCKLE

NOTE: LOCATE CLAMPS WITHIN TOLERANCE SHOWN

CAUTION: CLAMP MUST BE BETWEEN & CLEAR OF DIMPLES BEFORE TORQUING NUT

FWD

A

SLOT

HORIZONTAL LINE

ADJUSTER SLEEVE

45°

FWD

REARWARD ROTATION

NOTE: SLOT IN ADJUSTER SLEEVE MUST NOT BE WITHIN THIS AREA OF CLAMP JAWS

VIEW A

C-K SERIES

Tie-rod sleeve clamp installation

rod sleeves. The wheels must be straight ahead.

1. Toe-in can be determined by measuring the distance between the centers of the tire treads, front and rear. If the tread pattern of your tires makes this impossible, you can measure between the edges of the wheel rims, but make sure to move the truck forward and measure in a couple of places to avoid errors caused by bent rims or wheel runout.

2. Loosen the clamp bolts on the tie-rod sleeves.

3. Rotate the sleeves equally (in opposite directions) to obtain the correct measurement. If the sleeves are not adjusted equally, the steering wheel will be crooked.

NOTE: *If your steering wheel is already crooked, it can be straightened by turning the sleeves equally in the same direction.*

4. When the adjustment is complete, tighten the clamps.

REAR SUSPENSION

All two wheel drive trucks from 1970–72 use a coil spring with lateral control arm rear suspension. An auxiliary leaf spring is also used on ½ and ¾ ton trucks. In 1973 this was changed to a conventional leaf spring rear suspension. Four wheel drive trucks in all years use the traditional leaf springs in the rear. All models use one shock absorber at each rear wheel.

CAUTION: *Springs are under considerable tension. Be careful when removing and installing them; they can exert enough force to cause very serious injuries.*

Coil Spring
REMOVAL AND INSTALLATION

1. Jack up the vehicle and support it with jack stands. Position another jack under the control arm.

Removing the upper clamp bolt from the rear coil spring

Lower clamp bolt, rear coil spring

2. Remove the lower shock absorber bolt from its mounting on the lower control arm.

3. Remove the upper and lower clamps from the spring by releasing the lower bolt from the lower side of the control arm. The upper bolt is situated in the middle of the spring.

CAUTION: *Insert a safety chain through the spring and lower control arm to prevent the spring from flying out.*

4. Lower the jack under the control arm slowly until there is sufficient room to remove the spring.

5. Installation is the reverse of removal.

Auxiliary Spring (1970–72)
REMOVAL AND INSTALLATION

The auxiliary spring is attached to the frame and is removed as follows.

1. Remove all tension from the spring before attempting to remove it. Be certain that the spring leaf does not contact the bumper on the control arm.

2. Pull the cotter pin from the spring retaining bolt and then remove the nut. Remove the spring from the frame bracket.

3. If you are removing the contact bumper, support the axle with a jack, remove the U-bolts, and remove the bumper.

To install:

4. Place the spring bumper between the control arm and the axle housing. Make certain that the holes in the spring bracket are aligned with those in the control arm. Place the shock absorber bracket on the underside of the control arm. Place the U-bolt over the axle and through the auxiliary spring control arm and shock absorber bracket. Tighten the U-bolt retaining nuts alternately to 150 ft. lbs.

5. Position the auxiliary spring assembly in the frame bracket so that the free end of the spring is above the bumper and aligned with the spring-to-bracket bolt holes. Place the bolt and washer through the top side of the bracket

Auxiliary rear spring, 1970–72 C series

and then install the nut and washer on the bolt. The nut should be torqued to 370 ft. lbs. Install the cotter pin.

Leaf Spring

REMOVAL AND INSTALLATION

1. Raise the vehicle and support it so that there is no tension on the leaf spring assembly.

2. Loosen the spring-to-shackle retaining bolts. (Do not remove these bolts).

3. Remove the securing bolts with attach the shackle to the spring hanger.

4. Remove the nut and bolt which attach the spring to the front hanger.

5. Remove the U-bolt nuts and remove the spring plate.

6. Pull the spring from the vehicle.

7. Inspect the spring and replace any damaged components.

NOTE: *If the spring bushings are defective, use the following procedures for removal and installation. 1975 and later ¾ ton and 1 ton trucks use bushings that are staked in place. The stakes must first be straightened. When a new bushing is installed stake it in 3 equally spaced locations.*

Using a press or vise, remove the bushing and install the new one.

8. Place the spring assembly onto the axle housing.

NOTE: *The shackle assembly must be attached to the rear spring eye before the rear shackle is installed.*

9. Position the spring retaining plate and the U-bolts (loosely).

10. It will be necessary to jack the frame in some manner to align the spring and shackle with the spring hangers.

11. Install the shackle bolt and nut and re-

CK 10,20 (06)   CK 10 (03,16) & CK 20 (03)   C 20 (43) & CK 30

Leaf spring installation

position the spring if necessary in order to align the front eye. Position the front eyebolt and nut.

12. Torque the hanger ans shackle fasteners to 110 ft. lbs. 1977 and later, 90 ft. lbs. 1973–76.

NOTE: *Make sure that the bolts are free turning in their bushings prior to torquing.*

13. Lower the truck so that the weight is on the suspension components. Torque the U-bolt nuts to 140 ft. lbs.

14. Lower the truck completely and remove the jacks.

Shock Absorbers

REMOVAL AND INSTALLATION

1. Raise and support the truck.
2. Support the rear axle with a floor jack.
3. If the truck is equipped with air lift shocks, bleed the air from the lines and disconnect the line from the shock absorber.
4. Disconnect the shock absorber at the top by removing the nut and washers.
5. Remove the nut, washers and bolt from the bottom mount.
6. Remove the shock from the truck.
7. Installation is the reverse of removal. Torque the upper mount to 140 ft. lbs. through 1977, or 150 ft. lbs., 1978 and later; the lower to 115 ft. lbs.

TESTING

See "Shock Absorber Testing" under "Front Suspension."

STEERING

Steering Wheel

REMOVAL AND INSTALLATION

1. Disconnect the battery ground cable.
2. Remove the horn button and the receiving cap, belleville washer and bushing (if equipped).
3. Mark the steering wheel-to-steering shaft relationship.
4. On 1975 and later models, remove the snap ring from the steering shaft.
5. Remove the nut and washer from the steering shaft.
6. Remove the steering wheel with a puller.
CAUTION: *Don't hammer on the steering shaft.*
7. Installation is the reverse of removal. The turn signal control assembly must be in the Neutral position to prevent damaging the cancelling cam and control assembly. Tighten the

Steering wheel removal

nut to 40 ft. lbs. 1970–72, 30 ft. lbs. 1973 and later.

NOTE: *A steering wheel puller can be made by drilling two holes in a piece of steel the same distance apart as the two threaded holes in the steering wheel. Sometimes an old spring shackle will have the right dimensions. Drill another hole in the center. Place a center bolt with the head against the steering shaft and a nut against the bottom of the homemade puller bar. Thread the two outer bolts into the holes into the wheel. Unscrew the nut on the center bolt to draw the wheel off the shaft.*

Turn Signal Switch

REPLACEMENT

1970–72

1. Disconnect the battery ground cable.
2. Remove the steering wheel, preload spring, and cancelling cam.
3. Remove the shaft lever roll pin and shaft lever (if applicable).
4. Remove the turn signal lever screw and the lever.
5. Push the hazard warning knob in. This must be done to avoid damaging the switch.
6. Disconnect the switch wire from the chassis harness located under the dash.
7. Remove the mast jacket upper bracket.
8. Remove the switch wiring cover from the column.
9. Unscrew the mounting screws and remove the switch, bearing housing, switch cover, and shaft housing from the column.
10. Installation is the reverse of removal.

1973 and Later

1. Remove the steering wheel as previously outlined.

1. Cancelling cam
2. Directional lever retaining screw
3. Switch mounting screw
4. Switch
5. Upper bearing
6. Bearing support
7. Switch cover
8. Lever arm
9. Washer
10. Wiring connector

1970–72 turn signal switch

2. Loosen the three cover screws and lift the cover off the shaft. On 1976–80 models, place a drift pin in the cover slot and pry out to free the cover.

3. The round lockplate must be pushed down to remove the wire snap-ring from the shaft. A special tool is available to do this. The tool is an inverted U-shape with a hole for the shaft. The shaft nut is used to force it down. Pry the wire snap-ring out of the shaft groove. Discard the snap-ring.

4. Remove the tool and lift the lockplate off the shaft.

5. Slip the cancelling cam, upper bearing preload spring, and thrust washer off the shaft.

6. Remove the turn signal lever. Push the flasher knob in and unscrew it.

7. Pull the switch connector out of the mast jacket and tape the upper part to facilitate switch removal. On tilt wheels, place the turn signal and shifter housing in Low position and remove the harness cover.

8. Remove the three switch mounting screws. Remove the switch by pulling it straight up while guiding the wiring harness cover through the column.

9. Install the replacement switch by working the connector and cover down through the housing and under the bracket. On tilt models, the connector is worked down through the housing, under the bracket, and then the cover is installed on the harness.

10. Install the switch mounting screws and the connector on the mast jacket bracket. Install the column-to-dash trim plate.

11. Install the flasher knob and the turn signal lever.

12. With the turn signal lever in neutral and the flasher knob out, slide the thrust washer, upper bearing pre-load spring, and cancelling cam onto the shaft.

13. Position the lockplate on the shaft and

SNAP
RING

Removing the lockplate retaining ring

press it down until a new snap-ring can be inserted in the shaft groove.

14.   Install the cover and the steering wheel.

Ignition Switch

For procedures covering the 1970–72 ignition switch, see Chapter 5.

LOCK CYLINDER REMOVAL AND INSTALLATION

1973–78

1.   Remove steering wheel and turn signal switch.

NOTE: *It is not necessary to completely remove the turn signal switch. Pull the switch over the end of the shaft—no further.*

2.   Place lock cylinder in Run position.

CAUTION: *Do not remove the ignition key buzzer.*

3.   Insert a small drift pin into the turn signal housing slot. Keeping the drift pin to the right-side of the slot, break the housing flash loose and depress the spring latch at the lower end of the lock cylinder. Remove the lock cylinder.

NOTE: *Considerable force may be necessary to break this casting flash, but be careful not to damage any other parts. When or-*

Ignition lock cylinder, 1973–78; later models similar

Ignition lock cylinder removal, 1973–78

dering a new lock cylinder, specify a cylinder assembly. This will save assembling the cylinder, washer, sleeve and adapter.

4.   To install, hold the lock cylinder sleeve and rotate the knob clockwise against the stop. Insert the cylinder into the housing, aligning the key and keyway. Hold a .070 in. drill between the lock bezel and housing. Rotate the cylinder counterclockwise, maintaining a light pressure until the drive section of the cylinder mates with the sector. Push in until the snap-ring pops into the grooves. Remove drill. Check cylinder operation.

CAUTION: *The drill prevents forcing the lock cylinder inward beyond its normal position. The buzzer switch and spring latch can hold the lock cylinder in too far. Complete disassembly of the upper bearing housing is necessary to release an improperly installed lock cylinder.*

1979 and Later

1.   Remove the steering wheel.

2.   Remove the turn signal switch. It is not necessary to completely remove the switch from the column. Pull the switch rearward far enough to slip it over the end of the shaft, but do not pull the harness out of the column.

3.   Turn the lock to Run.

4.   Remove the lock retaining screw and remove the lock cylinder.

CAUTION: *If the retaining screw is dropped on removal, it may fall into the column, requiring complete disassembly of the column to retrieve the screw.*

5.   To install, rotate the key to the stop while holding onto the cylinder.

6.   Push the lock all the way in.

7.   Install the screw. Tighten the screw to 3 ft. lbs. for regular columns, 2 ft. lbs. for adjustable columns.

8.   Install the turn signal switch and the steering wheel.

1973 AND LATER IGNITION SWITCH REMOVAL AND INSTALLATION

The switch is on the steering column, behind the instrument panel.

1.   Lower the steering column, making sure that it is supported.

CAUTION: *Extreme care is necessary to prevent damage to the collapsible column.*

2.   Make sure the switch is in the Lock position. If the lock cylinder is out, pull the switch rod up to the stop, then go down one detent.

3.   Remove the two screws and the switch.

4.   Before installation, make sure the switch is in the Lock position.

5.   Install the switch using the original screws.

CAUTION: *Use of screws that are too long*

1979 and later ignition lock cylinder removal and installation

1973 and later ignition switch assembly showing switch in "Lock" position for removal

could prevent the column from collapsing on impact.

6. Replace the column.

Power Steering Pump

REMOVAL AND INSTALLATION

All Models

1. Disconnect the hoses at the pump. When the hoses are disconnected, secure the ends in a raised position to prevent leakage. Cap the ends of the hoses to prevent the entrance of dirt.

2. Cap the pump fittings.

3. Loosen the bracket-to-pump mounting nuts.

4. Remove the pump drive belt.

5. Remove the bracket-to-pump bolts and remove the pump from the truck.

6. Installation is the reverse of removal. Fill the reservoir and bleed the pump by turning the pulley counterclockwise (as viewed from the front) until bubbles stop forming. Adjust the belt tension.

BLEEDING THE HYDRAULIC SYSTEM

1. Fill the reservoir to the proper level and let the fluid remain undisturbed for at least 2 minutes.

2. Start the engine and run it for only about 2 seconds.

3. Add fluid as necessary.

4. Repeat Steps 1–3 until the fluid level remains constant.

5. Raise the front of the vehicle so that the front wheels are off the ground. Set the parking brake and block both rear wheels front and rear. Manual transmissions should be in Neutral; automatic transmissions should be in Park.

6. Start the engine and run it at approximately 1,500 rpm.

7. Turn the wheels to the right and left, lightly contacting the stops.

8. Add fluid as necessary.

9. Lower the vehicle and turn the wheels right and left on the ground.

10. Check the fluid level and refill as necessary.

11. If the fluid is extremely foamy, let the truck stand for a few minutes with the engine off and repeat the above procedure. Check the belt tension and check for a bent or loose pulley. The pulley should not wobble with the engine running.

12. Check that no hoses are contacting any parts of the truck, particularly sheet metal.

13. Check the level and refill as necessary. This step and the next are very important.

14. Check for air in the fluid. Aerated fluid appears milky. If air is present, repeat the above operations. If it is obvious that the pump will not respond to bleeding after several attempts, refer it to a qualified shop for further service.

Tie-Rod Ends

REMOVAL AND INSTALLATION

1. Loosen the tie-rod adjuster sleeve clamp nuts.

2. Remove the tie-rod end stud cotter pin and nut.

3. You can use a tie-rod removal tool to loosen the stud, or you can loosen it by tapping on the steering arm with a hammer while using a heavy hammer as a backup.

4. Remove the inner stud in the same way.

5. Unscrew the tie-rod end from the threaded sleeve. The threads may be left or right hand threads. Count the number of turns required to remove it.

6. To install, grease the threads and turn the new tie-rod end in as many turns as were needed to remove it. This will give approximately correct toe-in. Tighten the clamp bolts.

7. Tighten the stud nuts to 45 ft. lbs. and

Freeing the tie-rod end; use another hammer as a backup

install new cotter pins. You may tighten the nut to align the cotter pin, but don't loosen it.

8. Adjust the toe-in.

Brakes

BRAKE SYSTEM

All Chevrolet and GMC trucks from 1970 are equipped with a split hydraulic braking system. The system is designed with separate systems for the front and rear brakes using a dual master cylinder with separate reservoirs. If a wheel cylinder or brake line should fail in either the front or the rear system, the truck can still be stopped with reasonable control.

In 1970, trucks were equipped with drum brakes front and rear. The front brakes are duo-servo anchor pin type which are self-adjusting. The rear brakes are of the same basic type.

Beginning 1971, trucks were equipped with disc brakes at the front and drum brakes at the rear. The drum brakes are still of the duo-servo anchor pin self-adjusting type, while the front disc brakes are single-piston sliding caliper types. The front disc brakes are self-adjusting.

The parking brake is either hand or foot operated, but in any event, acts upon the rear service brakes.

Adjustment

FRONT OR REAR DRUM BRAKES

These brakes are equipped with self-adjusters and no manual adjustment is necessary, except when brake linings are replaced.

FRONT DISC BRAKES

These brakes are self-adjusting and no adjustment is possible.

HYDRAULIC SYSTEM

Master Cylinder
REMOVAL AND INSTALLATION

1. Using a clean cloth, wipe the master cylinder and its lines to remove excess dirt and

Typical master cylinder installations

then place cloths under the unit to absorb spilled fluid.

NOTE: *Clean master cylinder parts in alcohol or brake fluid. Never use mineral-based cleaning solvents such as gasoline, kerosene, carbon-tetrachloride, acetone, or paint thinner as these will destroy rubber parts.*

2. Remove the hydraulic lines from the master cylinder and plug the outlets to prevent the entrance of foreign material.

3. Disconnect the brake pushrod from the brake pedal (non-power brakes).

4. Remove the attaching bolts and remove the master cylinder from the firewall or the brake booster. Remove the master cylinder from the booster.

5. Connect the pushrod to the brake pedal with the pin and retainer.

6. Connect the brake lines and fill the master cylinder reservoirs to the proper levels.

7. Bleed the brake system.

8. If necessary, adjust the brake pedal free-play.

OVERHAUL

In most years, there are two sources for master cylinders: Delco-Moraine and Bendix. The Bendix unit can readily be identified by the secondary stop bolt on the bottom, which is not present on the Delco-Moraine unit. Mas-

BAIL

COVER

DIAPHRAGM

STOP SCREW

BODY

PRIMARY SEAL

SPRING

SEAL PROTECTOR

RETAINER

LOW PRESSURE

SECONDARY SEAL

PISTON

HIGH PRESSURE

SECONDARY SEAL

RETAINER RING

NO CHECK VALVES

SECONDARY PISTON

PRIMARY PISTON

Exploded view of a typical master cylinder

ter cylinders bearing identifying code letters should only be replaced with cylinders bearing the same code letters. Secondary pistons are also coded by rings or grooves on the shank or center section of the piston, and should only be replaced with pistons having the same code. The primary pistons also are of two types. One has a deep socket for the pushrod and the other has a very shallow socket. Be sure to replace pistons with identical parts. Failure to do this could result in a malfunction of the master cylinder.

NOTE: *This is a tedious, time-consuming job. You can save yourself the trouble if you buy a rebuilt or new master cylinder.*

1. Remove the secondary piston stop screw (if equipped) which is located at the bottom of the master cylinder front reservoir.

2. Position the master cylinder in a vise covering the jaws with cloth to prevent damage. (Do not tighten the vise too tightly.)

3. Remove the lockring from the inside of the piston bore. Once this is done, the primary piston assembly may be removed.

4. The secondary piston, piston spring, and the retainer may be removed by blowing compressed air through the stop screw hole. If compressed air is not available, the piston may be removed with a small piece of wire. Bend the wire ¼ in. from the end into a right angle. Hook this end to the edge of the secondary piston and pull it from the bore. The brass insert should not be removed unless it is being replaced.

5. Inspect the piston bore for corrosion or other obstructions. Make certain that the outer ports are clean and the fluid reservoirs are free of foreign matter. Check the by-pass and the compensating ports to see if they are clogged.

6. Remove the primary seal, seal protector, and secondary seals from the secondary piston.

Clean all parts in denatured alcohol or brake fluid. Use a soft brush to clean metal parts and compressed air to dry all parts. If corrosion is found inside the housing, either a crocus cloth or fine emery paper can be used to remove these deposits. Remember to wash all parts after this cleaning. Be sure to keep the parts clean until assembly. All rubber parts should be clean and free of fluid. Check each rubber part for cuts, nicks, or other damage. If there is any doubt as to the condition of any rubber part, it is best to replace it.

NOTE: *Since there are differences between master cylinders, it is important that the assemblies are identified correctly. There is a two-letter metal stamp located at the end of the master cylinder. The stamp indicates the displacement capabilities of the particular master cylinder. If the master cylinder is replaced, it must be replaced with a cylinder with the same markings.*

7. Install the new secondary piston assembly.

NOTE: *The seal which is nearest the flat end has its lips facing toward the flat end. On Delco units, the seal in the second groove has its lips facing toward the compensating holes of the secondary piston. On Bendix units, the seal is an O-ring*

8. Install the new primary seal and seal protector over the end of the secondary piston opposite the secondary seals. It should be positioned so that the flat side of the seal seats against the flange of the piston with the compensating holes.

NOTE: *The seal protector isn't used on 1977 and later models.*

9. Install the complete primary piston assembly included in every repair kit.

10. Coat the master cylinder bore and the primary and secondary seals with brake fluid. Position the secondary seal spring retainer into the secondary piston spring.

11. Place the retainer and spring over the end of the secondary piston so that the retainer is placed inside the lips of the primary seal.

12. Seat the secondary piston. It may be necessary to manipulate the piston to get it to seat.

13. Position the master cylinder with the open end up and coat the primary and secondary seal on the primary piston with brake fluid. Push the primary piston into the bore of the master cylinder. Hold the piston and position the lockring.

14. Still holding the piston down, install and tighten the stop screw to a torque of 25 to 40 in. lbs.

15. Install the reservoir cover and also the

cover on the master cylinder and its retaining clip.

16. Bleed the master cylinder of air. Do this by positioning the cylinder with the front slightly down, filling it with brake fluid, and working the primary piston until all the bubbles are gone.

Bleeding the Brakes

The brake system must be bled when any brake line is disconnected or there is air in the system.

NOTE: *Never bleed a wheel cylinder when a drum is removed.*

1. Clean the master cylinder of excess dirt and remove the cylinder cover and the diaphragm.

2. Fill the master cylinder to the proper level. Check the fluid level periodically during the bleeding process, and replenish it as necessary. Do not allow the master cylinder to run dry, or you will have to start over.

3. Before opening any of the bleeder screws, you may want to give each one a shot of penetrating solvent. This reduces the possibility of breakage when they are unscrewed.

4. Attach a length of vinyl hose to the bleeder screw of the brake to be bled. Insert the other end of the hose into a clear jar half full of brake fluid, so that the end of the hose is beneath the level of fluid. The correct sequence for bleeding is to work from the brake farthest from the master cylinder to the one closest; right rear, left rear, right front, left front.

Combination valves are usually mounted blow the master cylinder on the frame rail. Clip or tape the metering pin "in" while bleeding the disc brakes

Have an assistant pump, then hold in the brake pedla while you bleed each wheel

5. The combination valve (all vehicles with disc brakes) must be held open during the bleeding process. A clip, tape, or other similar tool (or an assistant) will hold the metering pin in.

6. With power brakes, depress and release the brake pedal three or four times to exhaust any residual vacuum.

7. Have an assistant push down on the brake pedal. Open the bleeder valve slightly. As the pedal reaches the end of its travel, close the bleeder screw. Repeat this process until no air bubbles are visible in the expelled fluid.

NOTE: *Make sure your assistant presses the brake pedal to the floor slowly. Pressing too fast will cause air bubbles to form in the fluid.*

8. Repeat this procedure at each of the brakes. Remember to check the master cylinder level occasionally. Use only fresh fluid to refill the master cylinder, not the stuff bled from the system.

9. When the bleeding process is complete, refill the master cylinder, install its cover and diaphragm, and discard the fluid bled from the brake system.

BLEEDER WRENCH

BLEEDER TUBE

TUBE MUST BE SUBMERGED IN BRAKE FLUID

Brake bleeding equipment

Hydro-Boost

Diesel-engined trucks are equipped with the Bendix Hydro-boost system. This power brake booster obtains hydraulic pressure from the power steering pump, rather than vacuum pressure from the intake manifold as in most gasoline engine brake booster systems. Procedures for removing, overhauling, and replacing the master cylinder are the same as previously outlined. The master cylinder uses the same DOT 3 brake fluid recommended for other systems.

HYDRO-BOOST SYSTEM CHECKS

1. A defective Hydro-Boost cannot cause any of the following conditions:
   a. Noisy brakes
   b. Fading pedal
   c. Pulling brakes

If any of these occur, check elsewhere in the brake system.

2. Check the fluid level in the master cylinder. It should be within ¼ in. of the top. If it isn't, add only DOT-3 or DOT-4 brake fluid until the correct level is reached.

3. Check the fluid level in the power steering pump. The engine should be at normal running temperature and stopped. The level should register on the pump dipstick. Add power steering fluid to bring the reservoir level up to the correct level. Low fluid level will result in both poor steering and stopping ability.

CAUTION: *The brake hydraulic system uses brake fluid only, while the power steering and Hydro-Boost systems use power steering fluid only. Don't mix the two.*

4. Check the power steering pump belt tension, and inspect all of the power steering/Hydro-Boost hoses for kinks or leaks.

5. Check and adjust the engine idle speed, as necessary.

6. Check the power steering pump fluid for bubbles. If air bubbles are present in the fluid, bleed the system:
   a. Fill the power steering pump reservoir to specifications with the engine at normal operating temperature.
   b. With the engine running, rotate the steering wheel through its normal travel 3 or 4 times, without holding the wheel against the stops.
   c. Check the fluid level again.

7. If the problem still exists, go on to the Hydro-Boost test sections and troubleshooting chart.

HYDRO-BOOST TESTS

Functional Test

1. Check the brake system for leaks or low fluid level. Correct as necessary.

2. Place the transmission in Neutral and stop the engine. Apply the brakes 4 or 5 times to empty the accumulator.

3. Keep the pedal depressed with moderate (25–40 lbs.) pressure and start the engine.

4. The brake pedal should fall slightly and then push back up against your foot. If no movement is felt, the Hydro-Boost system is not working.

Accumulator Leak Test

1. Run the engine at normal idle. Turn the steering wheel against one of the stops; hold it there for no longer than 5 seconds. Center the steering wheel and stop the engine.

2. Keep applying the brakes until a "hard" pedal is obtained. There should be a minimum

Removal and installation of Hydro-Booster

SPOOL RETURN SPRING

"O" RING

SPOOL PLUG

RETAINER
PUSH SPOOL PLUG IN AND
REMOVE RETAINER WITH
SMALL SCREWDRIVER.

27 N·m (20 FT. LBS.)

DO NOT DISCONNECT
BRAKE LINES

Removing Hydro-Boost spool valve and seal

of 1 power-assisted brake application when pedal pressure of 20–25 lbs. is applied.

3. Start the engine and allow it to idle. Rotate the steering wheel against the stop. Listen for a light "hissing" sound; this is the accumulator being charged. Center the steering wheel and stop the engine.

4. Wait one hour and apply the brakes without starting the engine. As in step 2, there should be at least 1 stop with power assist. If not, the accumulator is defective and must be replaced.

HYDRO-BOOST SYSTEM BLEEDING

The system should be bled whenever the booster is removed and installed. 1. Fill the power steering pump until the fluid level is at the base of the pump reservoir neck. Disconnect the battery lead from the distributor.

NOTE: *Remove the electrical lead to the fuel solenoid terminal on the injection pump before cranking the engine.*

2. Jack up the front of the car, turn the wheels all the way to the left, and crank the engine for a few seconds.

3. Check steering pump fluid level. If necessary, add fluid to the "Add" mark on the dipstick.

4. Lower the car, connect the battery lead, and start the engine. Check fluid level and add fluid to the "Add" mark if necessary.

With the engine running, turn the wheels from side to side to bleed air from the system. Make sure that the fluid level stays above the internal pump casting.

5. The Hydro-Boost system should now be

fully bled. If the fluid is foaming after bleeding, stop the engine, let the system set for one hour, then repeat the second part of Step 4.

The preceding procedures should be effective in removing excess air from the system, however sometimes air may still remain trapped. When this happens the booster may make a "gulping" noise when the brake is applied. Lightly pumping the brake pedal with the engine running should cause this noise to disappear. After the noise stops, check the pump fluid level and add as necessary.

HYDRO-BOOST TROUBLESHOOTING CHART

HIGH PEDAL AND STEERING EFFORT (IDLE)

1. Loose/broken power steering pump belt
2. Low power steering fluid level
3. Leaking hoses or fittings
4. Low idle speed
5. Hose restriction
6. Defective power steering pump

HIGH PEDAL EFFORT (IDLE)

1. Binding pedal/linkage
2. Fluid contamination
3. Defective Hydro-Boost unit

POOR PEDAL RETURN

1. Binding pedal linkage
2. Restricted booster return line
3. Internal return system restriction

Remove And Install Spool Valve, Power Piston/Acuumulator And Seal.

REMOVE

1. Remove parts as shown.
2. If removing spool valve plug refer to Remove and Install Spool Valve Plug In Car.

INSTALL

1. Install parts as shown.
2. If installing spool valve plug refer to Remove And Install Spool Valve Plug In Car.

RETAINER DOES NOT HAVE TO BE REMOVED. IF RETAINER CAME OUT IT DOES NOT HAVE TO BE REPLACED. IT IS USED FOR PRODUCTION PURPOSES.

BRACKET

HOUSING COVER

HOUSING SEAL

SPOOL VALVE

RETURN PORT FITTING

HOUSING

"O" RING

SPOOL VALVE SLEEVE

RETAINER

POWER PISTON/ACCUMULATOR

"O" RING

OUTPUT ROD (RETAINED BY "O" RING)

PISTON SEAL

BOLT
27 N·m (20 FT. LBS.)

POWER PISTON RETURN SPRING

WHEN INSTALLING SPRING PUSH SPRING UNTIL IT SEATS BEHIND LEDGE IN HOUSING

POWER PISTON/ACCUMULATOR SPRING

SCREWDRIVER

REMOVE POWER PISTON/ACCUMULATOR SPRING

CLEAN GROOVE BOTTOM BEFORE INSTALLING SEAL

PISTON SEAL

HOUSING

INSTALL POWER PISTON/ACCUMULATOR SEAL

BE SURE SPOOL VALVE IS ENGAGE

SPOOL VALVE

BE SURE "U" SHAPE BRACKET ON INPUT ROD IS ENGAGED WITH LOWER LEVER PINS.

INSTALL SPOOL VALVE

WHEN REPLACING POWER PISTON/ACCUMULATOR DRILL A 1/8" HOLE BEFORE DISPOSING

DRILL

1/8" BIT

DISPOSE POWER PISTON/ACCUMULATOR

Hydro Boost overhaul

PEDAL CHATTER/PULSATION

1. Power steering pump drive belt slipping
2. Low power steering fluid level
3. Defective power steering pump
4. Defective Hydro-Boost unit

BRAKES OVERSENSITIVE

1. Binding linkage
2. Defective Hydro-Boost unit

NOISE

1. Low power steering fluid level
2. Air in the power steering fluid
3. Loose power steering pump drive belt
4. Hose restrictions

OVERHAUL

GM Hydro-Boost units may be rebuilt. Kits are available through auto parts jobbers and GMC/Chevrolet truck dealers.

NOTE: *Have a drain pan ready to catch and discard leaking fluid during disassembly.*

Use the accompanying illustrations to overhaul the Hydro-Boost system. If replacing the power piston/accumulator, dispose of the old one as shown.

SPOOL VALVE PLUG AND SEAL REMOVAL AND INSTALLATION

1. Turn the engine off and pump the brake pedal 4 or 5 times to deplete the accumulator inside the boost unit.
2. Remove the master cylinder from the boost unit with the brake lines attached. Fasten the master cylinder out of the way with tape or wire.
3. Push the spool valve plug in and use a small screwdriver to carefully remove the retaining ring.
4. Remove the spool valve plug and O-ring.
5. Installation is the reverse of removal. Bleed the system upon installation, following the above bleeding instructions.

HYDRO-BOOST UNIT REMOVAL AND INSTALLATION

CAUTION: *Power steering fluid and brake fluid cannot be mixed. If brake seals contact the steering fluid or steering seals contact the brake fluid, damage will result.*

1. Turn the engine off and pump the brake pedal 4 or 5 times to deplete the accumulator inside the unit.
2. Remove the two nuts from the master cylinder, and remove the cylinder keeping the brake lines attached. Secure the master cylinder out of the way.
3. Remove the three hydraulic lines from the booster.

4. Remove the booster unit from the firewall.
5. To install, reverse the removal procedure. Bleed the Hydro-Boost system.

FRONT DISC BRAKES

All models from 1971 have front disc brakes. This single-piston caliper is a sliding type. No brake adjustment is necessary once the brake pads have been seated against the rotor.

NOTE: *1977 and later vehicles (Over 9000 GVWR) use a Bendix disc brake assembly.*

The single-piston system is a closed system with fluid pressure being exerted on two surfaces: on the piston itself and in the opposite direction against the bottom of the bore of the caliper housing. There is equal pressure since the area of the piston and the bottom of the caliper bore are equal.

When hydraulic pressure is applied to the piston, it is transmitted to the inner brake pad lining assembly which contacts the inner surface of the disc. This pulls the caliper assembly inboard as it slides on the four rubber bushings. As the caliper slides, the outer lining applies force to the outer surface of the disc and in this manner the two surfaces brake the vehicle.

Since the hydraulic pressure is equally applied to both brake pads there will be no flexing or distortion of the pad and if the unit is operating correctly, the pad wear should be equal.

Cross-section of a front disc brake caliper

This type of disc brake uses a very small running clearance between pad and rotor. As the brake linings wear, the caliper assembly moves inward and the brake fluid from the reservoir fills the area behind the piston so that brake pedal travel is not increased. Therefore, you will still have a high pedal even though the pad could be worn to the metal backing.

Because the brake pads are in close contact with the rotor, this gives the advantage of increased brake response, reduced brake pedal travel, and faster generation of hydraulic line pressure. The pad being close to the rotor disc also cleans it of foreign material.

The system is composed of the hub and disc assembly, the shield, the support, the caliper assembly, and the linings. The disc is vented with cooling fins which dissipate heat.

Brake Pads
INSPECTION

NOTE: *The Bendix system does not use a wear warning sensor.*

Support the front suspension or axle on jack stands and remove the wheels. Look in at the ends of the caliper to check the lining thickness of the outer pad. Look through the inspection hole in the top of the caliper to check the thickness of the inner pad. Minimum acceptable pad thickness is $\frac{1}{32}$ in. from the river heads on original equipment riveted linings and $\frac{1}{32}$ in. lining thickness on bonded linings.

NOTE: *These manufacturer's specifications may not agree with your state inspection law.*

All original equipment pads are the riveted type; unless you want to remove the pads to measure the actual thickness from the rivet heads, you will have to make the limit for visual inspection $\frac{1}{16}$ in. or more. The same applies if you don't know what kind of lining you have. 1974 and later original equipment pads and GM replacement pads have an integral wear sensor. This is a spring steel tab on the rear edge of the inner pad which produces a squeal by rubbing against the rotor to warn that the pads have reached their wear limit. They do not squeal when the brakes are applied.

CAUTION: *The squeal will eventually stop if the worn pads aren't replaced. Should this happen, replace the pads immediately to prevent expensive rotor (disc) damage.*

REPLACEMENT

The caliper has to be removed to replace the pads, so go on to that procedure. Skip steps 8–10, as there is no need to detach the brake line.

Disc Brake Caliper
REMOVAL AND INSTALLATION

1. Remove the cover on the master cylinder and siphon enough fluid out of the reservoirs to bring the level to $\frac{1}{3}$ full. This step prevents spilling fluid when the piston is pushed back. Discard the fluid.
2. Raise and support the vehicle. Remove the front wheels and tires.
3. Push the brake piston back into its bore using a C-clamp.
4. Remove the two Allen head bolts which hold the caliper and then lift the caliper off the disc.

CAUTION: *Do not let the caliper assembly hang by the brake hose. Tie it out of the way with wire.*

5. Remove the inboard and outboard pads. The shoe support spring will come off with the inner pad.
6. Installation is the reverse of removal with the following suggestions:
1. Use a pair of channel lock pliers to bend over the ears of the outer pad.
2. Torque the mounting bolts to 35 ft. lbs. Remember to refill the master cylinder.

NEW SHOE & LINING   READY
FOR REPLACEMENT

New and worn brake pads

Use a C-clamp to retract the caliper piston

NOTE END OF BOLT
PASSES UNDER
RETAINING EAR

Disc brake caliper removal and installation

CALIPER INBOARD SHOE
AND LINING

OUTBOARD SHOE
AND LINING

SCREW

SUPPORT
KEY

DISC

SPLASH SHIELD

Bendix front disc brake assembly

BOLTS BUSHINGS

SLEEVES

CALIPER

BUSHINGS

▨ LUBRICATE AREAS INDICATED

Caliper lubrication points at installation

SUPPORT
KEY

BRASS ROD

Removing the caliper support key

NOTE: *Check the inside of the caliper for fluid leakage; if so, the caliper should be overhauled.*
CAUTION: *Do not use compressed air to clean the inside of the caliper as this may unseat the dust boot.*
The brake lining should be replaced if there is ⅛ in. of lining or less present on the shoe.

BENDIX

1. Remove approximately ⅓ of the brake fluid from the master cylinder. Discard the used brake fluid.
2. Jack up your vehicle and support it with jack stands.
3. Push the piston back into its bore. This can be done by using a C-clamp.
4. Remove the bolt at the caliper support

key. Use a brass drift pin to remove the key and spring.
5. Tie the caliper out of the way with a piece of wire. Be careful not to damage the brake line.
6. Remove the inner shoe from the rear caliper support. Discard the inner shoe clip. Remove the outer shoe.
7. Installation is the reverse of removal. Lubricate the caliper support and support spring, with silicone. Be sure to install a new inner shoe clip. Remember to add brake fluid if necessary.

OVERHAUL

Use only denatured alcohol or brake fluid to clean caliper parts. Never use any mineral based cleaning solvents such as gasoline or kerosene as these solvents will deteriorate rubber parts.

1. Remove the caliper, clean it and place it on a clean and level work surface.
2. Remove the brake hose from the caliper

Piston removal using compressed air. Keep fingers out of the way of the piston when the air is applied.

Caliper piston boot installation

and discard the copper gasket. Check the brake hose for cracks or deterioration. Replace the hose as necessary.

3. Drain the brake fluid from the caliper.

4. Pad the interior of the caliper with cloth and then apply compressed air to the caliper inlet hose.

WARNING: *Do not place hands or fingers in front of the piston in an attempt to catch it. Use just enough air pressure to ease the piston out of the bore.*

5. Remove the piston dust boot by prying

it out with a drift pin. Use caution when performing this procedure.

6. Remove the piston seal from the caliper piston bore using a small piece of wood or plastic. DO NOT use any type of metal tool for this procedure.

7. Remove the bleeder valve from the caliper.

IMPORTANT: *Dust boot, piston seal, rubber bushings and sleeves are included in every rebuilding kit. These should be replaced at every caliper rebuild.*

Exploded view of the brake caliper

8. Clean all parts in solvent and dry them completely.

NOTE: *The use of lubricated shop air may leave an oil film on metal parts. This may damage rubber parts.*

9. Examine the mounting bolts for rust or corrosion. Replace them as necessary.

10. Examine the piston for scoring, nicks, or worn plating. If any of these conditions are present, replace the piston.

CAUTION: *Do not use any type of abrasive on the piston.*

11. Check the piston bore. Small defects can be removed with crocus cloth. (Do not use emery cloth.) If the bore cannot be cleaned in this manner, replace the caliper.

12. Lubricate the piston bore and the new piston seal with brake fluid. Place the seal in the caliper bore groove.

13. Lubricate the piston and position the new boot into the groove in the piston so that the fold faces the open end of the piston.

14. Place the piston into the caliper bore using caution not to damage the seal. Force the piston to the bottom of the bore. This will require a force of 50–100 lbs.

15. Place the dust boot in the caliper coun-

Inner brake pad installation in caliper

Bendix brake caliper assembly

Installing the brake shoe; note proper shoe support spring installation

Piston boot seating

Measure the disc run-out with a dial indicator

terbore and seat the boot. Make sure that the boot is positioned correctly and evenly. Proper seating of the boot is very important for sealing out contaminants.

16. Lubricate the new sleeves and rubber bushings. Install the bushings in the caliper ears. Install the sleeves so that the end toward the disc pad is flush with the machined surface.

NOTE: *Lubrication of the sleeves and bush-*

ings is essential to ensure the proper operation of the sliding caliper design.

17. Install the shoe support spring in the piston.

18. Install the disc pads in the caliper and remount the caliper in the hub. See pad removal and installation under "Disc Brake Caliper".

19. Reconnect the brake hose to the steel brake line. Install the retainer clip. Bleed the brakes (see "Brake Bleeding").

20. Replace the wheels, check the brake fluid level, check the brake pedal travel, and road-test the vehicle.

Four Wheel Drive

Rotor removal and installation requires disassembly of the front hub components. This is covered in Chapter 7, under "Front Axle Hub", Four Wheel Drive.

Wheel Bearings

Four wheel drive front wheel bearing service is covered under "Four Wheel Drive Front Hub" removal and installation in Chapter 7. The following wheel bearing service procedure is for two wheel drive trucks only.

Two Wheel Drive

1. Remove the wheel, tire assembly, and the brake drum or brake caliper. See Chapter 9 for details.

2. Remove the hub and disc as an assembly. Remove the caliper mounting bolts and insert a block between the brake pads as the caliper is removed. Remove the caliper and wire it out of the way.

3. Pry off the grease cap, remove the cotter pin, spindle nut, and washer, and then remove the hub. Be careful that you do not drop the wheel bearings.

4. Remove the outer roller bearing assembly from the hub. The inner bearing assembly will remain in the hub and may be removed after prying out the inner seal. Discard this seal.

5. Clean all parts in solvent and allow to air dry. Check the parts for excessive wear or damage.

6. If the bearing cups are worn or scored, they must be replaced. Using a hammer and a drift, remove the bearing cups from the hub. When installing new cups, make sure that they are not cocked, and that they are fully seated against the hub shoulder.

7. Pack both wheel bearings using high melting point wheel bearing grease. Ordinary grease will melt, and ruin the pads. High temperature grease provides an extra margin of protection. Place a healthy glob of grease in the palm of one hand and force the edge of the bearing into it so that the grease fills the bearing. Do this until the whole bearing is packed. Grease packing tools are available to make this job a lot less messy. There are also tools which make it possible to grease the inner bearing without removing it or the disc from the spindle.

8. Place the inner bearing in the hub and install a new inner seal, making sure that the seal flange faces the bearing cup.

9. Carefully install the wheel hub over the spindle.

10. Using your hands, firmly press the outer bearing into the hub. Install the spindle washer and nut.

11. To adjust the bearings on 1970–71 models, tighten the adjusting nut to 15 ft. lb. while rotating the hub. Back the nut off one flat (⅙ turn) and insert a new cotter pin. If the nut and spindle hole do not align, back the nut off slightly. There should be 0.001–0.008 in. end play in the bearing. This can be measured with a dial indicator, if you wish. Install the dust cap, wheel, and tire.

12. To adjust the bearings on 1972 through 1984 models, spin the wheel hub by hand and tighten the nut until it is just snug (12 ft. lbs.). Back off the nut until it is loose, then tighten it finger tight. Loosen the nut until either hole in the spindle lines up with a slot in the nut, and insert a new cotter pin. There should be 0.001–

Exploded view of 2WD knuckle and hub assembly showing inner and outer wheel bearings

0.008 in. end play in the bearing through 1973, and 0.001–0.005 in. 1974 and later. This can be measured with a dial indicator, if you wish. Replace the dust cap, wheel, and tire.

DRUM BRAKES

Brake Drums

REMOVAL AND INSTALLATION

Drums on all models can be removed by raising the vehicle, removing the wheel lugs and the tire, and pulling the drum from the brake assembly. If the brake drums have been scored from worn linings, the brake adjuster must be backed off so that the brake shoes will retract from the drum. Some drums are retained by two screws to the hub, and can be removed after removing the screws.

The adjuster can be backed off by inserting a brake adjusting tool through the access hole provided. In some cases the access hole is provided in the brake drum. A metal cover plate is over the hole. This may be removed by using a hammer and chisel.

NOTE: *Make sure all metal particles are removed from the brake drum before reassembly.*

To install, reverse the removal procedure.

CAUTION: *Do not blow the brake dust out of the drums with compressed air or lung power. The brake linings contain asbestos, a known cancer causing agent. Wipe the drums and linings with a clean, grease-free rag, and dispose of the rag immediately.*

INSPECTION

Lining

Remove the drum and inspect the lining thickness on both brake shoes. A front brake lining

Measure the drum inside diameter with an inside micrometer

INSERT SMALL SCREWDRIVER OR AWL THROUGH BACKING PLATE SLOT AND HOLD ADJUSTER LEVER AWAY FROM SPROCKET BEFORE BACKING OFF BRAKE SHOE ADJUSTMENT

Cross-sectional view of drum brake adjustment using brake adjusting spoon

should be replaced if it is less than ⅛ in. thick at the lowest point on the brake shoe. The limit for rear brake linings is ¹⁄₁₆. However, these lining thickness measurements may disagree with your state inspection laws.

NOTE: *Brake shoes should always be replaced in axle sets.*

Drum

When a drum is removed, it should be inspected for cracks, scores, or other imperfections. These must be corrected before the drum is replaced.

CAUTION: *If the drum is found to be cracked, replace it. Do not attempt to service a cracked drum.*

Minor drum score marks can be removed with fine emery cloth. Heavy score marks must be removed by "turning the drum." This procedure removes metal from the entire inner surface of the drum in order to level the surface. Automotive machine shops and some parts stores are equipped to perform this operation.

If the drum is not scored, it should be polished with fine emery cloth before replacement. If the drum is resurfaced, it should not be enlarged past 0.060 in. of the original diameter.

NOTE: *All brake drums have a maximum diameter number cast into their outer surface. This number is a maximum wear diameter and not a refinish diameter. Do not refinish a brake drum that will not meet specifications after refinishing.*

It is advisable, while the drums are off, to check them for out-of-round. An inside micrometer is necessary for an exact measurement; therefore unless this tool is available, the drums should be taken to a machine shop to be checked. Any drum which is more than 0.006 in. out-of-round will result in an inaccurate brake

WHEEL CYLINDER LINKS
SECONDARY SHOE & LINING
SHOE GUIDE
PARKING BRAKE STRUT
STRUT SPRING
ADJUSTER LEVER
ACTUATING LINK
WHEEL CYLINDER SCREWS
BACKING PLATE
HOLD DOWN PINS
PARKING BRAKE LEVER
WHEEL CYLINDER
PRIMARY SHOE AND LINING
HOLD DOWN SPRING
ADJUSTING SCREW SPRING
ADJUSTING SCREW
LEVER RETURN SPRINGS
HOLD DOWN SPRING & CUP
BRAKE SHOE RETURN SPRING

Exploded view of a typical drum brake

adjustment and should be refinished or replaced.

NOTE: *If the micrometer is available, make all measurements at right angles to each other and at the open and closed edges of the drum machined surface.*

Check the drum with a micrometer in the following manner:

1. Position the drum on a level surface.

2. Insert the micrometer with its adapter bars if necessary.

3. Obtain a reading on the micrometer at the point of maximum contact. Record this.

4. Rotate the micrometer 45° and take a similar reading. The two readings must not vary more than 0.006 in.

Brake Shoes

REMOVAL AND INSTALLATION

1. Jack up and support your vehicle with jack stands.

2. Remove the check nuts from the end of the parking brake equalizer bracket and remove all tension on the brake cable (rear brakes only).

3. Remove the brake drums.

CAUTION: *The brake pedal must not be depressed while the drums are removed.*

4. Using a brake tool, remove the shoe springs from their holder.

5. Remove the self-adjuster actuator spring.

6. Remove the spring from the secondary shoe by pulling it from the anchor pin.

7. Remove the hold-down pins. They can be removed with a pair of pliers. Reach around the rear of the backing plate and hold the back of the pin. Turn the top of the pin retainer with the pliers. This will align the elongated tang with the slot in the retainer. Be careful, as the pin is spring-loaded and may fly off when released. Use the same procedure for the other pin assembly.

8. Remove the adjuster actuating lever assembly by removing the hold-down pin which is attached to the secondary brake shoe.

NOTE: *Since the actuator, pivot, and override spring are considered an assembly it is not recommended that they be disassembled.*

9. Remove the shoes from the backing plate. Make sure that you have a secure grip on the assembly as the bottom spring will still exert pressure on the shoes. Slowly let the tops of the shoes come together and the tension will decrease and the adjuster and spring may be removed.

NOTE: *If the linings are to be reused, mark them for identification.*

Self-adjusting brake, assembled

Labels: PRIMARY SHOE, WIRE LINK, OVERRIDE LEVER, OVERRIDE SPRING, ACTUATING LEVER, RETURN SPRING, PAWL, STAR WHEEL

Checking the actuator

10. Remove the parking brake lever from the secondary shoe (rear brakes). Using a pair of pliers, pull back on the spring which surrounds the cable. At the same time, remove the cable from the notch in the shoe bracket. Make sure that the spring does not snap back or injury may result.

11. Use a cloth to remove dirt from the brake drum. Check the drums for scoring and cracks. Have the drums checked for out-of-round and service the drums as necessary.

12. Check the wheel cylinders by carefully pulling the lower edges of the wheel cylinder boots away from the cylinders. Excessive leakage requires rebuilding or replacement of the wheel cylinder.

NOTE: *A small amount of fluid will be present to act as a lubricant for the wheel cylinder pistons.*

Unhooking the pull-back springs

Removing the hold-down springs

Lubricate the brake backing plate pads

13. Installation is the reverse of removal. Adjust the brakes as necessary.

CAUTION: *It is important to keep your hands free of dirt and grease when handling the brake shoes. Foreign matter will be absorbed into the linings and result in unpredictable braking.*

Brake Backing Plate
REMOVAL AND INSTALLATION

1. Remove the brakes as previously outlined.

2. Remove the axles.

3. Remove the attaching bolts and pull off the backing plate.

4. To install, reverse the removal procedure.

Wheel Cylinders
REMOVAL AND INSTALLATION

1. Jack up your truck and support it with jack stands.

2. Remove the wheel and tire.

3. Back off the brake adjustment and remove the drum.

4. Disconnect and plug the brake line.

5. Remove the brake shoe pull-back springs.

Later wheel cylindes are held in place by a retainer (arrow)

BLEEDER SCREW

WHEEL CYL BODY

SPRING ASSEMBLY

SEAL

PISTON

BOOT

Wheel cylinder, exploded view

BLEEDER

BODY

EXPANDERS

BOOT

BOOT

PISTON   CUPS

PISTON

Sectional view of an assembled wheel cylinder

6. Remove the screws securing the wheel cylinder to the backing plate. Later models have their wheel cylinders retained by a round retainer. To release the locking tabs, insert two awls (see illustration) into the access slots to bend the tabs back. Install the new retainer over the wheel cylinder abutment using a 1⅛ in., 12-point socket and socket extension.

7. Disengage the wheel cylinder pushrods from the brake shoes and remove the wheel cylinder.

8. Installation is the reverse of removal. Bleed the brake system.

Overhaul

As is the case with master cylinders, overhaul kits for wheel cylinders are readily available. When rebuilding and installing wheel cylinders, avoid getting any contaminants into the system. Always install clean, new high-quality brake fluid. If dirty or improper fluid has been used, it will be necessary to drain the entire system, flush the system with proper brake fluid,

Bend back the tabs on the retainer using two awls simultaneously

Install the new retainer over the wheel cylinder using a 1⅛ in., 12-point socket and extension

replace all rubber components, refill, and bleed the system.

1. Remove the rubber boots from the cylinder ends with pliers. Discard the boots.

2. Remove and discard the pistons and cups.

3. Wash the cylinder and metal parts in denatured alcohol or clean brake fluid.

CAUTION: *Never use a mineral-based solvent such as gasoline, kerosene, or paint thinner for cleaning purposes. These solvents will swell rubber components and quickly deteriorate them.*

4. Allow the parts to air dry or use compressed air. Do not use rags for cleaning since lint will remain in the cylinder bore.

5. Inspect the piston and replace it if it shows scratches.

6. Lubricate the cylinder bore and counterbore with clean brake fluid.

7. Install the rubber cups (flat side out) and then the pistons (flat side in).

8. Insert new boots into the counterbores by hand. Do not lubricate the boots.

Wheel Bearings

Four wheel drive front wheel bearings are covered in Chapter 7. Two wheel drive front wheel bearings are covered earlier in this chapter.

PARKING BRAKE

Adjustment

The rear brakes serve a dual purpose. They are used as service brakes and as parking brakes. To obtain proper adjustment of the parking

Typical parking brake system, 1971 shown. Adjustments are made at the equalizer nut

brake, the service brakes must first be properly adjusted as outlined earlier.

1. Apply the parking brake 1 notch from the fully released position, 4 notches for 1976 and later.

2. Raise and support the vehicle.

3. Loosen the jam nut at the equalizer.

4. Tighten or loosen the adjusting nut until a light drag is felt when the rear wheels are rotated forward.

5. Tighten the check nut.

6. Release the parking brake and rotate the rear wheels. No drag should be felt. If even a light drag is felt, readjust the parking brake.

7. Lower the vehicle.

NOTE: *If a new parking brake cable is being installed, prestretch it by applying the parking brake hard about three times before making adjustments.*

COMBINATION VALVE

This valve is used on all models with disc brakes. The valve itself is a combination of: 1) the metering valve, which will not allow the front disc brakes to engage until the rear brakes contact the drum, 2) the failure warning switch, which notifies the driver if one of the systems has a leak, and 3) the proportioner which limits rear brake pressure and delays rear wheel skid.

Combination valve

Centering the Switch

Whenever work on the brake system is done it is possible that the brake warning light will come on and refuse to go off when the work is finished. In this event, the switch must be centered.

1. Raise and support the truck.

2. Attach a bleeder hose to the rear brake bleed screw and immerse the other end of the hose in a jar of clean brake fluid.

3. Be sure that the master cylinder is full.

4. When bleeding the brakes, the pin in the end of the metering portion of the combination valve must be held in the open position (with the tool described in the brake bleeding sec-

tion installed under the pin mounting bolt). Be sure to tighten the bolt after removing the tool.

5. Turn the ignition key ON. Open the bleed screw while an assistant applies heavy pressure on the brake pedal. The warning lamp should light. Close the bleed screw before the helper releases the pedal.

To reset the switch, apply heavy pressure to the pedal. This will apply hydraulic pressure to the switch which will recenter it.

6. Repeat Step 5 for the front bleed screw.

7. Turn the ignition OFF and lower the truck.

NOTE: *If the warning lamp does not light during Step 5, the switch is defective and must be replaced.*

Troubleshooting

This section is designed to aid in the quick, accurate diagnosis of automotive problems. While automotive repairs can be made by many people, accurate troubleshooting is a rare skill for the amateur and professional alike.

In its simplest state, troubleshooting is an exercise in logic. It is essential to realize that an automobile is really composed of a series of systems. Some of these systems are interrelated; others are not. Automobiles operate within a framework of logical rules and physical laws, and the key to troubleshooting is a good understanding of all the automotive systems.

This section breaks the car or truck down into its component systems, allowing the problem to be isolated. The charts and diagnostic road maps list the most common problems and the most probable causes of trouble. Obviously it would be impossible to list every possible problem that could happen along with every possible cause, but it will locate MOST problems and eliminate a lot of unnecessary guesswork. The systematic format will locate problems within a given system, but, because many automotive systems are interrelated, the solution to your particular problem may be found in a number of systems on the car or truck.

USING THE TROUBLESHOOTING CHARTS

This book contains all of the specific information that the average do-it-yourself mechanic needs to repair and maintain his or her car or truck. The troubleshooting charts are designed to be used in conjunction with the specific procedures and information in the text. For instance, troubleshooting a point-type ignition system is fairly standard for all models, but you may be directed to the text to find procedures for troubleshooting an individual type of electronic ignition. You will also have to refer to the specification charts throughout the book for specifications applicable to your car or truck.

TOOLS AND EQUIPMENT

The tools illustrated in Chapter 1 (plus two more diagnostic pieces) will be adequate to troubleshoot most problems. The two other tools needed are a voltmeter and an ohmmeter. These can be purchased separately or in combination, known as a VOM meter.

In the event that other tools are required, they will be noted in the procedures.

Tach-dwell hooked-up to distributor

Troubleshooting Engine Problems

See Chapters 2, 3, 4 for more information and service procedures.

Index to Systems

System	To Test	Group
Battery	Engine need not be running	1
Starting system	Engine need not be running	2
Primary electrical system	Engine need not be running	3
Secondary electrical system	Engine need not be running	4
Fuel system	Engine need not be running	5
Engine compression	Engine need not be running	6
Engine vacuum	Engine must be running	7
Secondary electrical system	Engine must be running	8
Valve train	Engine must be running	9
Exhaust system	Engine must be running	10
Cooling system	Engine must be running	11
Engine lubrication	Engine must be running	12

Index to Problems

Problem: Symptom	Begin at Specific Diagnosis, Number ____
Engine Won't Start:	
Starter doesn't turn	1.1, 2.1
Starter turns, engine doesn't	2.1
Starter turns engine very slowly	1.1, 2.4
Starter turns engine normally	3.1, 4.1
Starter turns engine very quickly	6.1
Engine fires intermittently	4.1
Engine fires consistently	5.1, 6.1
Engine Runs Poorly:	
Hard starting	3.1, 4.1, 5.1, 8.1
Rough idle	4.1, 5.1, 8.1
Stalling	3.1, 4.1, 5.1, 8.1
Engine dies at high speeds	4.1, 5.1
Hesitation (on acceleration from standing stop)	5.1, 8.1
Poor pickup	4.1, 5.1, 8.1
Lack of power	3.1, 4.1, 5.1, 8.1
Backfire through the carburetor	4.1, 8.1, 9.1
Backfire through the exhaust	4.1, 8.1, 9.1
Blue exhaust gases	6.1, 7.1
Black exhaust gases	5.1
Running on (after the ignition is shut off)	3.1, 8.1
Susceptible to moisture	4.1
Engine misfires under load	4.1, 7.1, 8.4, 9.1
Engine misfires at speed	4.1, 8.4
Engine misfires at idle	3.1, 4.1, 5.1, 7.1, 8.4

Sample Section

Test and Procedure	Results and Indications	Proceed to
4.1—Check for spark: Hold each spark plug wire approximately ¼" from ground with gloves or a heavy, dry rag. Crank the engine and observe the spark.	→ If no spark is evident:	→4.2
	→ If spark is good in some cases:	→4.3
	→ If spark is good in all cases:	→4.6

Specific Diagnosis

This section is arranged so that following each test, instructions are given to proceed to another, until a problem is diagnosed.

Section 1—Battery

Test and Procedure	Results and Indications	Proceed to
1.1—Inspect the battery visually for case condition (corrosion, cracks) and water level.	If case is cracked, replace battery:	**1.4**
	If the case is intact, remove corrosion with a solution of baking soda and water (**CAUTION:** *do not get the solution into the battery*), and fill with water:	**1.2**

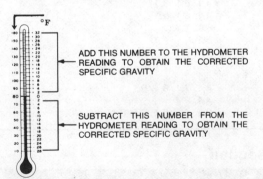

DIRT ON TOP OF BATTERY
CORROSION
PLUGGED VENT
LOOSE CABLE OR POSTS
CRACKS
LOW WATER LEVEL

Inspect the battery case

1.2—Check the battery cable connections: Insert a screwdriver between the battery post and the cable clamp. Turn the headlights on high beam, and observe them as the screwdriver is gently twisted to ensure good metal to metal contact.	If the lights brighten, remove and clean the clamp and post; coat the post with petroleum jelly, install and tighten the clamp:	**1.4**
	If no improvement is noted:	**1.3**

TESTING BATTERY CABLE CONNECTIONS USING A SCREWDRIVER

1.3—Test the state of charge of the battery using an individual cell tester or hydrometer.	If indicated, charge the battery. **NOTE:** *If no obvious reason exists for the low state of charge (i.e., battery age, prolonged storage), proceed to:*	**1.4**

°F

ADD THIS NUMBER TO THE HYDROMETER READING TO OBTAIN THE CORRECTED SPECIFIC GRAVITY

SUBTRACT THIS NUMBER FROM THE HYDROMETER READING TO OBTAIN THE CORRECTED SPECIFIC GRAVITY

Specific Gravity (@ 80° F.)

Minimum	Battery Charge
1.260	100% Charged
1.230	75% Charged
1.200	50% Charged
1.170	25% Charged
1.140	Very Little Power Left
1.110	Completely Discharged

The effects of temperature on battery specific gravity (left) and amount of battery charge in relation to specific gravity (right)

1.4—Visually inspect battery cables for cracking, bad connection to ground, or bad connection to starter.	If necessary, tighten connections or replace the cables:	**2.1**

Section 2—Starting System
See Chapter 3 for service procedures

Test and Procedure	Results and Indications	Proceed to
Note: Tests in Group 2 are performed with coil high tension lead disconnected to prevent accidental starting.		
2.1—Test the starter motor and solenoid: Connect a jumper from the battery post of the solenoid (or relay) to the starter post of the solenoid (or relay).	If starter turns the engine normally:	**2.2**
	If the starter buzzes, or turns the engine very slowly:	**2.4**
	If no response, replace the solenoid (or relay).	**3.1**
	If the starter turns, but the engine doesn't, ensure that the flywheel ring gear is intact. If the gear is undamaged, replace the starter drive.	**3.1**
2.2—Determine whether ignition override switches are functioning properly (clutch start switch, neutral safety switch), by connecting a jumper across the switch(es), and turning the ignition switch to "start".	If starter operates, adjust or replace switch:	**3.1**
	If the starter doesn't operate:	**2.3**
2.3—Check the ignition switch "start" position: Connect a 12V test lamp or voltmeter between the starter post of the solenoid (or relay) and ground. Turn the ignition switch to the "start" position, and jiggle the key.	If the lamp doesn't light or the meter needle doesn't move when the switch is turned, check the ignition switch for loose connections, cracked insulation, or broken wires. Repair or replace as necessary:	**3.1**
	If the lamp flickers or needle moves when the key is jiggled, replace the ignition switch.	**3.3**

Checking the ignition switch "start" position

STARTER RELAY
(IF EQUIPPED)

2.4—Remove and bench test the starter, according to specifications in the engine electrical section.	If the starter does not meet specifications, repair or replace as needed:	**3.1**
	If the starter is operating properly:	**2.5**
2.5—Determine whether the engine can turn freely: Remove the spark plugs, and check for water in the cylinders. Check for water on the dipstick, or oil in the radiator. Attempt to turn the engine using an 18″ flex drive and socket on the crankshaft pulley nut or bolt.	If the engine will turn freely only with the spark plugs out, and hydrostatic lock (water in the cylinders) is ruled out, check valve timing:	**9.2**
	If engine will not turn freely, and it is known that the clutch and transmission are free, the engine must be disassembled for further evaluation:	**Chapter 3**

Section 3—Primary Electrical System

Test and Procedure	Results and Indications	Proceed to
3.1—Check the ignition switch "on" position: Connect a jumper wire between the distributor side of the coil and ground, and a 12V test lamp between the switch side of the coil and ground. Remove the high tension lead from the coil. Turn the ignition switch on and jiggle the key.	If the lamp lights:	**3.2**
	If the lamp flickers when the key is jiggled, replace the ignition switch:	**3.3**
	If the lamp doesn't light, check for loose or open connections. If none are found, remove the ignition switch and check for continuity. If the switch is faulty, replace it:	**3.3**

Checking the ignition switch "on" position

3.2—Check the ballast resistor or resistance wire for an open circuit, using an ohmmeter. See Chapter 3 for specific tests.	Replace the resistor or resistance wire if the resistance is zero. **NOTE:** *Some ignition systems have no ballast resistor.*	**3.3**

RESISTOR BLOCK

CALIBRATED RESISTANCE LEAD

Two types of resistors

3.3—On point-type ignition systems, visually inspect the breaker points for burning, pitting or excessive wear. Gray coloring of the point contact surfaces is normal. Rotate the crankshaft until the contact heel rests on a high point of the distributor cam and adjust the point gap to specifications. On electronic ignition models, remove the distributor cap and visually inspect the armature. Ensure that the armature pin is in place, and that the armature is on tight and rotates when the engine is cranked. Make sure there are no cracks, chips or rounded edges on the armature.	If the breaker points are intact, clean the contact surfaces with fine emery cloth, and adjust the point gap to specifications. If the points are worn, replace them. On electronic systems, replace any parts which appear defective. If condition persists:	**3.4**

Test and Procedure	Results and Indications	Proceed to
3.4—On point-type ignition systems, connect a dwell-meter between the distributor primary lead and ground. Crank the engine and observe the point dwell angle. On electronic ignition systems, conduct a stator (magnetic pickup assembly) test. See Chapter 3.	On point-type systems, adjust the dwell angle if necessary. **NOTE:** *Increasing the point gap decreases the dwell angle and vice-versa.*	**3.6**
	If the dwell meter shows little or no reading;	**3.5**
	On electronic ignition systems, if the stator is bad, replace the stator. If the stator is good, proceed to the other tests in Chapter 3.	

CLOSE OPEN

NORMAL DWELL

WIDE GAP

SMALL DWELL

INSUFFICIENT DWELL

NARROW GAP

LARGE DWELL

EXCESSIVE DWELL

Dwell is a function of point gap

3.5—On the point-type ignition systems, check the condenser for short: connect an ohmeter across the condenser body and the pigtail lead.	If any reading other than infinite is noted, replace the condenser	**3.6**

OHMMETER

Checking the condenser for short

3.6—Test the coil primary resistance: On point-type ignition systems, connect an ohmmeter across the coil primary terminals, and read the resistance on the low scale. Note whether an external ballast resistor or resistance wire is used. On electronic ignition systems, test the coil primary resistance as in Chapter 3.	Point-type ignition coils utilizing ballast resistors or resistance wires should have approximately 1.0 ohms resistance. Coils with internal resistors should have approximately 4.0 ohms resistance. If values far from the above are noted, replace the coil.	**4.1**

Check the coil primary resistance

Section 4—Secondary Electrical System

See Chapters 2–3 for service procedures

Test and Procedure	Results and Indications	Proceed to
4.1—Check for spark: Hold each spark plug wire approximately ¼″ from ground with gloves or a heavy, dry rag. Crank the engine, and observe the spark.	If no spark is evident:	**4.2**
	If spark is good in some cylinders:	**4.3**
	If spark is good in all cylinders:	**4.6**

Check for spark at the plugs

4.2—Check for spark at the coil high tension lead: Remove the coil high tension lead from the distributor and position it approximately ¼″ from ground. Crank the engine and observe spark. **CAUTION: *This test should not be performed on engines equipped with electronic ignition.***	If the spark is good and consistent:	**4.3**
	If the spark is good but intermittent, test the primary electrical system starting at 3.3:	**3.3**
	If the spark is weak or non-existent, replace the coil high tension lead, clean and tighten all connections and retest. If no improvement is noted:	**4.4**
4.3—Visually inspect the distributor cap and rotor for burned or corroded contacts, cracks, carbon tracks, or moisture. Also check the fit of the rotor on the distributor shaft (where applicable).	If moisture is present, dry thoroughly, and retest per 4.1:	**4.1**
	If burned or excessively corroded contacts, cracks, or carbon tracks are noted, replace the defective part(s) and retest per 4.1:	**4.1**
	If the rotor and cap appear intact, or are only slightly corroded, clean the contacts thoroughly (including the cap towers and spark plug wire ends) and retest per 4.1:	
	If the spark is good in all cases:	**4.6**
	If the spark is poor in all cases:	**4.5**

CORRODED OR LOOSE WIRE

EXCESSIVE WEAR OF BUTTON

HIGH RESISTANCE CARBON

ROTOR TIP BURNED AWAY

Inspect the distributor cap and rotor

Test and Procedure	Results and Indications	Proceed to
4.4—Check the coil secondary resistance: On point-type systems connect an ohmmeter across the distributor side of the coil and the coil tower. Read the resistance on the high scale of the ohmmeter. On electronic ignition systems, see Chapter 3 for specific tests.	The resistance of a satisfactory coil should be between 4,000 and 10,000 ohms. If resistance is considerably higher (i.e., 40,000 ohms) replace the coil and retest per 4.1. **NOTE: This does not apply to high performance coils.**	

Testing the coil secondary resistance

4.5—Visually inspect the spark plug wires for cracking or brittleness. Ensure that no two wires are positioned so as to cause induction firing (adjacent and parallel). Remove each wire, one by one, and check resistance with an ohmmeter.	Replace any cracked or brittle wires. If any of the wires are defective, replace the entire set. Replace any wires with excessive resistance (over 8000 Ω per foot for suppression wire), and separate any wires that might cause induction firing.	4.6

Misfiring can be the result of spark plug leads to adjacent, consecutively firing cylinders running parallel and too close together

On point-type ignition systems, check the spark plug wires as shown. On electronic ignitions, do not remove the wire from the distributor cap terminal; instead, test through the cap

Spark plug wires can be checked visually by bending them in a loop over your finger. This will reveal any cracks, burned or broken insulation. Any wire with cracked insulation should be replaced

4.6—Remove the spark plugs, noting the cylinders from which they were removed, and evaluate according to the color photos in the middle of this book.	See following.	**See following.**

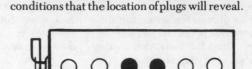

Test and Procedure	Results and Indications	Proceed to
4.7—Examine the location of all the plugs.	The following diagrams illustrate some of the conditions that the location of plugs will reveal.	4.8

Two adjacent plugs are fouled in a 6-cylinder engine, 4-cylinder engine or either bank of a V-8. This is probably due to a blown head gasket between the two cylinders

The two center plugs in a 6-cylinder engine are fouled. Raw fuel may be "boiled" out of the carburetor into the intake manifold after the engine is shut-off. Stop-start driving can also foul the center plugs, due to overly rich mixture. Proper float level, a new float needle and seat or use of an insulating spacer may help this problem

An unbalanced carburetor is indicated. Following the fuel flow on this particular design shows that the cylinders fed by the right-hand barrel are fouled from overly rich mixture, while the cylinders fed by the left-hand barrel are normal

If the four rear plugs are overheated, a cooling system problem is suggested. A thorough cleaning of the cooling system may restore coolant circulation and cure the problem

Finding one plug overheated may indicate an intake manifold leak near the affected cylinder. If the overheated plug is the second of two adjacent, consecutively firing plugs, it could be the result of ignition cross-firing. Separating the leads to these two plugs will eliminate cross-fire

Occasionally, the two rear plugs in large, lightly used V-8's will become oil fouled. High oil consumption and smoky exhaust may also be noticed. It is probably due to plugged oil drain holes in the rear of the cylinder head, causing oil to be sucked in around the valve stems. This usually occurs in the rear cylinders first, because the engine slants that way

Test and Procedure	Results and Indications	Proceed to
4.8—Determine the static ignition timing. Using the crankshaft pulley timing marks as a guide, locate top dead center on the compression stroke of the number one cylinder.	The rotor should be pointing toward the No. 1 tower in the distributor cap, and, on electronic ignitions, the armature spoke for that cylinder should be lined up with the stator.	4.8
4.9—Check coil polarity: Connect a voltmeter negative lead to the coil high tension lead, and the positive lead to ground (**NOTE:** *Reverse the hook-up for positive ground systems*). Crank the engine momentarily.	If the voltmeter reads up-scale, the polarity is correct:	5.1
	If the voltmeter reads down-scale, reverse the coil polarity (switch the primary leads):	5.1

Checking coil polarity

Section 5—Fuel System
See Chapter 4 for service procedures

Test and Procedure	Results and Indications	Proceed to
5.1—Determine that the air filter is functioning efficiently: Hold paper elements up to a strong light, and attempt to see light through the filter.	Clean permanent air filters in solvent (or manufacturer's recommendation), and allow to dry. Replace paper elements through which light cannot be seen:	5.2
5.2—Determine whether a flooding condition exists: Flooding is identified by a strong gasoline odor, and excessive gasoline present in the throttle bore(s) of the carburetor.	If flooding is not evident:	5.3
	If flooding is evident, permit the gasoline to dry for a few moments and restart. If flooding doesn't recur:	5.7
	If flooding is persistent:	5.5

If the engine floods repeatedly, check the choke butterfly flap

5.3—Check that fuel is reaching the carburetor: Detach the fuel line at the carburetor inlet. Hold the end of the line in a cup (not styrofoam), and crank the engine.	If fuel flows smoothly:	5.7
	If fuel doesn't flow (**NOTE:** *Make sure that there is fuel in the tank*), or flows erratically:	5.4

Check the fuel pump by disconnecting the output line (fuel pump-to-carburetor) at the carburetor and operating the starter briefly

Test and Procedure	Results and Indications	Proceed to
5.4—Test the fuel pump: Disconnect all fuel lines from the fuel pump. Hold a finger over the input fitting, crank the engine (with electric pump, turn the ignition or pump on); and feel for suction.	If suction is evident, blow out the fuel line to the tank with low pressure compressed air until bubbling is heard from the fuel filler neck. Also blow out the carburetor fuel line (both ends disconnected):	5.7
	If no suction is evident, replace or repair the fuel pump: NOTE: *Repeated oil fouling of the spark plugs, or a no-start condition, could be the result of a ruptured vacuum booster pump diaphragm, through which oil or gasoline is being drawn into the intake manifold (where applicable).*	5.7
5.5—Occasionally, small specks of dirt will clog the small jets and orifices in the carburetor. With the engine cold, hold a flat piece of wood or similar material over the carburetor, where possible, and crank the engine.	If the engine starts, but runs roughly the engine is probably not run enough. If the engine won't start:	5.9
5.6—Check the needle and seat: Tap the carburetor in the area of the needle and seat.	If flooding stops, a gasoline additive (e.g., Gumout) will often cure the problem:	5.7
	If flooding continues, check the fuel pump for excessive pressure at the carburetor (according to specifications). If the pressure is normal, the needle and seat must be removed and checked, and/or the float level adjusted:	5.7
5.7—Test the accelerator pump by looking into the throttle bores while operating the throttle. **Check for gas at the carburetor by looking down the carburetor throat while someone moves the accelerator**	If the accelerator pump appears to be operating normally:	5.8
	If the accelerator pump is not operating, the pump must be reconditioned. Where possible, service the pump with the carburetor(s) installed on the engine. If necessary, remove the carburetor. Prior to removal:	5.8
5.8—Determine whether the carburetor main fuel system is functioning: Spray a commercial starting fluid into the carburetor while attempting to start the engine.	If the engine starts, runs for a few seconds, and dies:	5.9
	If the engine doesn't start:	6.1

CHILTON'S
AUTO BODY REPAIR TIPS

EASY
STEP-BY-STEP
TIPS FROM PROS

**Tools and Materials • Step-by-Step Illustrated Procedures
How To Repair Dents, Scratches and Rust Holes
Spray Painting and Refinishing Tips**

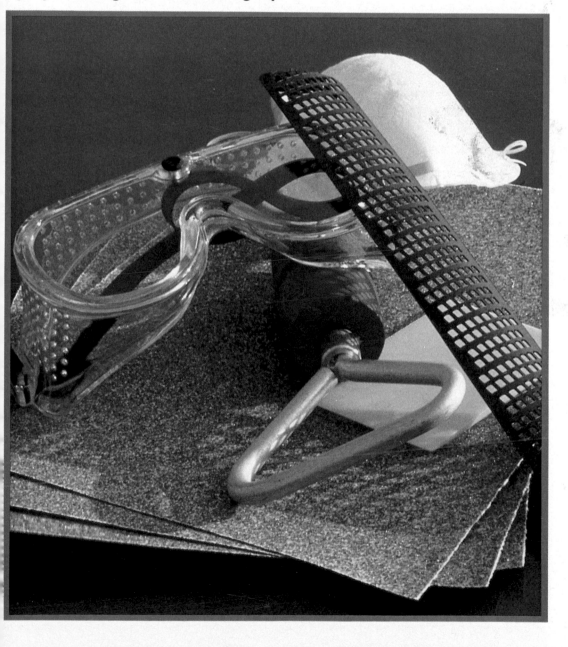

With a little practice, basic body repair procedures can be mastered by any do-it-yourself mechanic. The step-by-step repairs shown here can be applied to almost any type of auto body repair.

TOOLS & MATERIALS

You may already have basic tools, such as hammers and electric drills. Other tools unique to body repair — body hammers, grinding attachments, sanding blocks, dent puller, half-round plastic file and plastic spreaders — are relatively inexpensive and can be obtained wherever auto parts or auto body repair parts are sold. Portable air compressors and paint spray guns can be purchased or rented.

Auto Body Repair Kits

The best and most often used products are available to the do-it-yourselfer in kit form, from major manufacturers of auto body repair products. The same manufacturers also merchandise the individual products for use by pros.

Kits are available to make a wide variety of repairs, including holes, dents and scratches and fiberglass, and offer the advantage of buying the materials you'll need for the job. There is little waste or chance of materials going bad from not being used. Many kits may also contain basic body-working tools such as body files, sanding blocks and spreaders. Check the contents of the kit before buying your tools.

BODY REPAIR TIPS

Safety

Many of the products associated with auto body repair and refinishing contain toxic chemicals. Read all labels before opening containers and store them in a safe place and manner.

• Wear eye protection (safety goggles) when using power tools or when performing any operation that involves the removal of any type of material.

• Wear lung protection (disposable mask or respirator) when grinding, sanding or painting.

Sanding

1 Sand off paint before using a dent puller. When using a non-adhesive sanding disc, cover the back of the disc with an overlapping layer or two of masking tape and trim the edges. The disc will last considerably longer.

2 Use the circular motion of the sanding disc to grind *into* the edge of the repair. Grinding or sanding away from the jagged edge will only tear the sandpaper.

3 Use the palm of your hand flat on the panel to detect high and low spots. Do not use your fingertips. Slide your hand slowly back and forth.

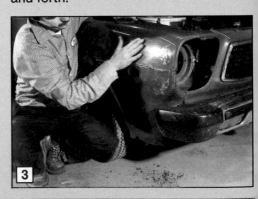

WORKING WITH BODY FILLER

Mixing The Filler

Cleanliness and proper mixing and application are extremely important. Use a clean piece of plastic or glass or a disposable artist's palette to mix body filler.

1 Allow plenty of time and follow directions. No useful purpose will be served by adding more hardener to make it cure (set-up) faster. Less hardener means more curing time, but the mixture dries harder; more hardener means less curing time but a softer mixture.

2 Both the hardener and the filler should be thoroughly kneaded or stirred before mixing. Hardener should be a solid paste and dispense like thin toothpaste. Body filler should be smooth, and free of lumps or thick spots.

Getting the proper amount of hardener in the filler is the trickiest part of preparing the filler. Use the same amount of hardener in cold or warm weather. For contour filler (thick coats), a bead of hardener twice the diameter of the filler is about right. There's about a 5% margin on either side, but, if in doubt use less hardener.

3 Mix the body filler and hardener by wiping across the mixing surface, picking the mixture up and wiping it again. Colder weather requires longer mixing times. Do not mix in a circular motion; this will trap air bubbles which will become holes in the cured filler.

Applying The Filler

1 For best results, filler should not be applied over 1/4″ thick.

Apply the filler in several coats. Build it up to above the level of the repair surface so that it can be sanded or grated down.

The first coat of filler must be pressed on with a firm wiping motion.

Apply the filler in one direction only. Working the filler back and forth will either pull it off the metal or trap air bubbles.

REPAIRING DENTS

Before you start, take a few minutes to study the damaged area. Try to visualize the shape of the panel before it was damaged. If the damage is on the left fender, look at the right fender and use it as a guide. If there is access to the panel from behind, you can reshape it with a body hammer. If not, you'll have to use a dent puller. Go slowly and work the metal a little at a time. Get the panel as straight as possible before applying filler.

1 This dent is typical of one that can be pulled out or hammered out from behind. Remove the headlight cover, headlight assembly and turn signal housing.

2 Drill a series of holes ½ the size of the end of the dent puller along the stress line. Make some trial pulls and assess the results. If necessary, drill more holes and try again. Do not hurry.

3 If possible, use a body hammer and block to shape the metal back to its original contours. Get the metal back as close to its original shape as possible. Don't depend on body filler to fill dents.

4 Using an 80-grit grinding disc on an electric drill, grind the paint from the surrounding area down to bare metal. Use a new grinding pad to prevent heat buildup that will warp metal.

5 The area should look like this when you're finished grinding. Knock the drill holes in and tape over small openings to keep plastic filler out.

6 Mix the body filler (see Body Repair Tips). Spread the body filler evenly over the entire area (see Body Repair Tips). Be sure to cover the area completely.

7 Let the body filler dry until the surface can just be scratched with your fingernail. Knock the high spots from the body filler with a body file ("Cheesegrater"). Check frequently with the palm of your hand for high and low spots.

8 Check to be sure that trim pieces that will be installed later will fit exactly. Sand the area with 40-grit paper.

9 If you wind up with low spots, you may have to apply another layer of filler.

10 Knock the high spots off with 40-grit paper. When you are satisfied with the contours of the repair, apply a thin coat of filler to cover pin holes and scratches.

11 Block sand the area with 40-grit paper to a smooth finish. Pay particular attention to body lines and ridges that must be well-defined.

12 Sand the area with 400 paper and then finish with a scuff pad. The finished repair is ready for priming and painting (see Painting Tips).

Materials and photos courtesy of Ritt Jones Auto Body, Prospect Park, PA.

REPAIRING RUST HOLES

There are many ways to repair rust holes. The fiberglass cloth kit shown here is one of the most cost efficient for the owner because it provides a strong repair that resists cracking and moisture and is relatively easy to use. It can be used on large and small holes (with or without backing) and can be applied over contoured areas. Remember, however, that short of replacing an entire panel, no repair is a guarantee that the rust will not return.

1 Remove any trim that will be in the way. Clean away all loose debris. Cut away all the rusted metal. But be sure to leave enough metal to retain the contour or body shape.

2 Grind away all traces of rust with a 24-grit grinding disc. Be sure to grind back 3-4 inches from the edge of the hole down to bare metal and be sure all traces of paint, primer and rust are removed.

3 Block sand the area with 80 or 100 grit sandpaper to get a clear, shiny surface and feathered paint edge. Tap the edges of the hole inward with a ball peen hammer.

4 If you are going to use release film, cut a piece about 2-3″ larger than the area you have sanded. Place the film over the repair and mark the sanded area on the film. Avoid any unnecessary wrinkling of the film.

5 Cut 2 pieces of fiberglass matte to match the shape of the repair. One piece should be about 1″ smaller than the sanded area and the second piece should be 1″ smaller than the first. Mix enough filler and hardener to saturate the fiberglass material (see Body Repair Tips).

6 Lay the release sheet on a flat surface and spread an even layer of filler, large enough to cover the repair. Lay the smaller piece of fiberglass cloth in the center of the sheet and spread another layer of filler over the fiberglass cloth. Repeat the operation for the larger piece of cloth.

7 Place the repair material over the repair area, with the release film facing outward. Use a spreader and work from the center outward to smooth the material, following the body contours. Be sure to remove all air bubbles.

8 Wait until the repair has dried tack-free and peel off the release sheet. The ideal working temperature is 60°-90° F. Cooler or warmer temperatures or high humidity may require additional curing time. Wait longer, if in doubt.

9 Sand and feather-edge the entire area. The initial sanding can be done with a sanding disc on an electric drill if care is used. Finish the sanding with a block sander. Low spots can be filled with body filler; this may require several applications.

10 When the filler can just be scratched with a fingernail, knock the high spots down with a body file and smooth the entire area with 80-grit. Feather the filled areas into the surrounding areas.

11 When the area is sanded smooth, mix some topcoat and hardener and apply it directly with a spreader. This will give a smooth finish and prevent the glass matte from showing through the paint.

12 Block sand the topcoat smooth with finishing sandpaper (200 grit), and 400 grit. The repair is ready for masking, priming and painting (see Painting Tips).

Materials and photos courtesy Marson Corporation, Chelsea, Massachusetts

PAINTING TIPS

Preparation

1 SANDING — Use a 400 or 600 grit wet or dry sandpaper. Wet-sand the area with a 1/4 sheet of sandpaper soaked in clean water. Keep the paper wet while sanding. Sand the area until the repaired area tapers into the original finish.

2 CLEANING — Wash the area to be painted thoroughly with water and a clean rag. Rinse it thoroughly and wipe the surface dry until you're sure it's completely free of dirt, dust, fingerprints, wax, detergent or other foreign matter.

3 MASKING — Protect any areas you don't want to overspray by covering them with masking tape and newspaper. Be careful not get fingerprints on the area to be painted.

4 PRIMING — All exposed metal should be primed before painting. Primer protects the metal and provides an excellent surface for paint adhesion. When the primer is dry, wet-sand the area again with 600 grit wet-sandpaper. Clean the area again after sanding.

Painting Techniques

P aint applied from either a spray gun or a spray can (for small areas) will provide good results. Experiment on an old piece of metal to get the right combination before you begin painting.

SPRAYING VISCOSITY (SPRAY GUN ONLY) — Paint should be thinned to spraying viscosity according to the directions on the can. Use only the recommended thinner or reducer and the same amount of reduction regardless of temperature.

AIR PRESSURE (SPRAY GUN ONLY) — This is extremely important. Be sure you are using the proper recommended pressure.

TEMPERATURE — The surface to be painted should be approximately the same temperature as the surrounding air. Applying warm paint to a cold surface, or vice versa, will completely upset the paint characteristics.

THICKNESS — Spray with smooth strokes. In general, the thicker the coat of paint, the longer the drying time. Apply several thin coats about 30 seconds apart. The paint should remain wet long enough to flow out and no longer; heavier coats will only produce sags or wrinkles. Spray a light (fog) coat, followed by heavier color coats.

DISTANCE — The ideal spraying distance is 8"-12" from the gun or can to the surface. Shorter distances will produce ripples, while greater distances will result in orange peel, dry film and poor color match and loss of material due to overspray.

OVERLAPPING — The gun or can should be kept at right angles to the surface at all times. Work to a wet edge at an even speed, using a 50% overlap and direct the center of the spray at the lower or nearest edge of the previous stroke.

RUBBING OUT (BLENDING) FRESH PAINT — Let the paint dry thoroughly. Runs or imperfections can be sanded out, primed and repainted.

Don't be in too big a hurry to remove the masking. This only produces paint ridges. When the finish has dried for at least a week, apply a small amount of fine grade rubbing compound with a clean, wet cloth. Use lots of water and blend the new paint with the surrounding area.

WRONG	CORRECT	WRONG
Thin coat. Stroke too fast, not enough overlap, gun too far away.	Medium coat. Proper distance, good stroke, proper overlap.	Heavy coat. Stroke too slow, too much overlap, gun too close.

Test and Procedure	Results and Indications	Proceed to
5.9—Uncommon fuel system malfunctions: See below:	If the problem is solved:	6.1
	If the problem remains, remove and recondition the carburetor.	

Condition	Indication	Test	Prevailing Weather Conditions	Remedy
Vapor lock	Engine will not restart shortly after running.	Cool the components of the fuel system until the engine starts. Vapor lock can be cured faster by draping a wet cloth over a mechanical fuel pump.	Hot to very hot	Ensure that the exhaust manifold heat control valve is operating. Check with the vehicle manufacturer for the recommended solution to vapor lock on the model in question.
Carburetor icing	Engine will not idle, stalls at low speeds.	Visually inspect the throttle plate area of the throttle bores for frost.	High humidity, 32–40° F.	Ensure that the exhaust manifold heat control valve is operating, and that the intake manifold heat riser is not blocked.
Water in the fuel	Engine sputters and stalls; may not start.	Pump a small amount of fuel into a glass jar. Allow to stand, and inspect for droplets or a layer of water.	High humidity, extreme temperature changes.	For droplets, use one or two cans of commercial gas line anti-freeze. For a layer of water, the tank must be drained, and the fuel lines blown out with compressed air.

Section 6—Engine Compression
See Chapter 3 for service procedures

6.1—Test engine compression: Remove all spark plugs. Block the throttle wide open. Insert a compression gauge into a spark plug port, crank the engine to obtain the maximum reading, and record.	If compression is within limits on all cylinders:	7.1
	If gauge reading is extremely low on all cylinders:	6.2
	If gauge reading is low on one or two cylinders: (If gauge readings are identical and low on two or more adjacent cylinders, the head gasket must be replaced.)	6.2

Checking compression

6.2—Test engine compression (wet): Squirt approximately 30 cc. of engine oil into each cylinder, and retest per 6.1.	If the readings improve, worn or cracked rings or broken pistons are indicated:	See Chapter 3
	If the readings do not improve, burned or excessively carboned valves or a jumped timing chain are indicated:	7.1
	NOTE: *A jumped timing chain is often indicated by difficult cranking.*	

Section 7—Engine Vacuum
See Chapter 3 for service procedures

Test and Procedure	Results and Indications	Proceed to
7.1—Attach a vacuum gauge to the intake manifold beyond the throttle plate. Start the engine, and observe the action of the needle over the range of engine speeds.	See below.	**See below**

INDICATION: normal engine in good condition

Proceed to: 8.1

Normal engine
Gauge reading: steady, from 17–22 in./Hg.

INDICATION: sticking valves or ignition miss

Proceed to: 9.1, 8.3

Sticking valves
Gauge reading: intermittent fluctuation at idle

INDICATION: late ignition or valve timing, low compression, stuck throttle valve, leaking carburetor or manifold gasket

Proceed to: 6.1

Incorrect valve timing
Gauge reading: low (10–15 in./Hg) but steady

INDICATION: improper carburetor adjustment or minor intake leak.

Proceed to: 7.2

Carburetor requires adjustment
Gauge reading: drifting needle

INDICATION: ignition miss, blown cylinder head gasket, leaking valve or weak valve spring

Proceed to: 8.3, 6.1

Blown head gasket
Gauge reading: needle fluctuates as engine speed increases

INDICATION: burnt valve or faulty valve clearance. Needle will fall when defective valve operates

Proceed to: 9.1

Burnt or leaking valves
Gauge reading: steady needle, but drops regularly

INDICATION: choked muffler, excessive back pressure in system

Proceed to: 10.1

Clogged exhaust system
Gauge reading: gradual drop in reading at idle

INDICATION: worn valve guides

Proceed to: 9.1

Worn valve guides
Gauge reading: needle vibrates excessively at idle, but steadies as engine speed increases

White pointer = steady gauge hand   Black pointer = fluctuating gauge hand

Test and Procedure	Results and Indications	Proceed to
7.2—Attach a vacuum gauge per 7.1, and test for an intake manifold leak. Squirt a small amount of oil around the intake manifold gaskets, carburetor gaskets, plugs and fittings. Observe the action of the vacuum gauge.	If the reading improves, replace the indicated gasket, or seal the indicated fitting or plug: If the reading remains low:	**8.1** **7.3**
7.3—Test all vacuum hoses and accessories for leaks as described in 7.2. Also check the carburetor body (dashpots, automatic choke mechanism, throttle shafts) for leaks in the same manner.	If the reading improves, service or replace the offending part(s): If the reading remains low:	**8.1** **6.1**

Section 8—Secondary Electrical System
See Chapter 2 for service procedures

Test and Procedure	Results and Indications	Proceed to
8.1—Remove the distributor cap and check to make sure that the rotor turns when the engine is cranked. Visually inspect the distributor components.	Clean, tighten or replace any components which appear defective.	**8.2**
8.2—Connect a timing light (per manufacturer's recommendation) and check the dynamic ignition timing. Disconnect and plug the vacuum hose(s) to the distributor if specified, start the engine, and observe the timing marks at the specified engine speed.	If the timing is not correct, adjust to specifications by rotating the distributor in the engine: (Advance timing by rotating distributor opposite normal direction of rotor rotation, retard timing by rotating distributor in same direction as rotor rotation.)	**8.3**
8.3—Check the operation of the distributor advance mechanism(s): To test the mechanical advance, disconnect the vacuum lines from the distributor advance unit and observe the timing marks with a timing light as the engine speed is increased from idle. If the mark moves smoothly, without hesitation, it may be assumed that the mechanical advance is functioning properly. To test vacuum advance and/or retard systems, alternately crimp and release the vacuum line, and observe the timing mark for movement. If movement is noted, the system is operating.	If the systems are functioning: If the systems are not functioning, remove the distributor, and test on a distributor tester:	**8.4** **8.4**
8.4—Locate an ignition miss: With the engine running, remove each spark plug wire, one at a time, until one is found that doesn't cause the engine to roughen and slow down.	When the missing cylinder is identified:	**4.1**

Section 9—Valve Train
See Chapter 3 for service procedures

Test and Procedure	Results and Indications	Proceed to
9.1—Evaluate the valve train: Remove the valve cover, and ensure that the valves are adjusted to specifications. A mechanic's stethoscope may be used to aid in the diagnosis of the valve train. By pushing the probe on or near push rods or rockers, valve noise often can be isolated. A timing light also may be used to diagnose valve problems. Connect the light according to manufacturer's recommendations, and start the engine. Vary the firing moment of the light by increasing the engine speed (and therefore the ignition advance), and moving the trigger from cylinder to cylinder. Observe the movement of each valve.	Sticking valves or erratic valve train motion can be observed with the timing light. The cylinder head must be disassembled for repairs.	**See Chapter 3**
9.2—Check the valve timing: Locate top dead center of the No. 1 piston, and install a degree wheel or tape on the crankshaft pulley or damper with zero corresponding to an index mark on the engine. Rotate the crankshaft in its direction of rotation, and observe the opening of the No. 1 cylinder intake valve. The opening should correspond with the correct mark on the degree wheel according to specifications.	If the timing is not correct, the timing cover must be removed for further investigation.	**See Chapter 3**

Section 10—Exhaust System

Test and Procedure	Results and Indications	Proceed to
10.1—Determine whether the exhaust manifold heat control valve is operating: Operate the valve by hand to determine whether it is free to move. If the valve is free, run the engine to operating temperature and observe the action of the valve, to ensure that it is opening.	If the valve sticks, spray it with a suitable solvent, open and close the valve to free it, and retest. If the valve functions properly: If the valve does not free, or does not operate, replace the valve:	**10.2** **10.2**
10.2—Ensure that there are no exhaust restrictions: Visually inspect the exhaust system for kinks, dents, or crushing. Also note that gases are flowing freely from the tailpipe at all engine speeds, indicating no restriction in the muffler or resonator.	Replace any damaged portion of the system:	**11.1**

Section 11—Cooling System
See Chapter 3 for service procedures

Test and Procedure	Results and Indications	Proceed to
11.1—Visually inspect the fan belt for glazing, cracks, and fraying, and replace if necessary. Tighten the belt so that the longest span has approximately ½″ play at its mid-point under thumb pressure (see Chapter 1).	Replace or tighten the fan belt as necessary:	**11.2**

Checking belt tension

Test and Procedure	Results and Indications	Proceed to
11.2—Check the fluid level of the cooling system.	If full or slightly low, fill as necessary:	**11.5**
	If extremely low:	**11.3**
11.3—Visually inspect the external portions of the cooling system (radiator, radiator hoses, thermostat elbow, water pump seals, heater hoses, etc.) for leaks. If none are found, pressurize the cooling system to 14–15 psi.	If cooling system holds the pressure:	**11.5**
	If cooling system loses pressure rapidly, reinspect external parts of the system for leaks under pressure. If none are found, check dipstick for coolant in crankcase. If no coolant is present, but pressure loss continues:	**11.4**
	If coolant is evident in crankcase, remove cylinder head(s), and check gasket(s). If gaskets are intact, block and cylinder head(s) should be checked for cracks or holes. If the gasket(s) is blown, replace, and purge the crankcase of coolant:	**12.6**
	NOTE: *Occasionally, due to atmospheric and driving conditions, condensation of water can occur in the crankcase. This causes the oil to appear milky white. To remedy, run the engine until hot, and change the oil and oil filter.*	
11.4—Check for combustion leaks into the cooling system: Pressurize the cooling system as above. Start the engine, and observe the pressure gauge. If the needle fluctuates, remove each spark plug wire, one at a time, noting which cylinder(s) reduce or eliminate the fluctuation.	Cylinders which reduce or eliminate the fluctuation, when the spark plug wire is removed, are leaking into the cooling system. Replace the head gasket on the affected cylinder bank(s).	

Pressurizing the cooling system

Test and Procedure	Results and Indications	Proceed to
11.5—Check the radiator pressure cap: Attach a radiator pressure tester to the radiator cap (wet the seal prior to installation). Quickly pump up the pressure, noting the point at which the cap releases.	If the cap releases within ± 1 psi of the specified rating, it is operating properly:	**11.6**
	If the cap releases at more than ± 1 psi of the specified rating, it should be replaced:	**11.6**

Checking radiator pressure cap

Test and Procedure	Results and Indications	Proceed to
11.6—Test the thermostat: Start the engine cold, remove the radiator cap, and insert a thermometer into the radiator. Allow the engine to idle. After a short while, there will be a sudden, rapid increase in coolant temperature. The temperature at which this sharp rise stops is the thermostat opening temperature.	If the thermostat opens at or about the specified temperature:	**11.7**
	If the temperature doesn't increase: (If the temperature increases slowly and gradually, replace the thermostat.)	**11.7**
11.7—Check the water pump: Remove the thermostat elbow and the thermostat, disconnect the coil high tension lead (to prevent starting), and crank the engine momentarily.	If coolant flows, replace the thermostat and retest per 11.6:	**11.6**
	If coolant doesn't flow, reverse flush the cooling system to alleviate any blockage that might exist. If system is not blocked, and coolant will not flow, replace the water pump.	

Section 12—Lubrication
See Chapter 3 for service procedures

Test and Procedure	Results and Indications	Proceed to
12.1—Check the oil pressure gauge or warning light: If the gauge shows low pressure, or the light is on for no obvious reason, remove the oil pressure sender. Install an accurate oil pressure gauge and run the engine momentarily.	If oil pressure builds normally, run engine for a few moments to determine that it is functioning normally, and replace the sender.	—
	If the pressure remains low:	**12.2**
	If the pressure surges:	**12.3**
	If the oil pressure is zero:	**12.3**
12.2—Visually inspect the oil: If the oil is watery or very thin, milky, or foamy, replace the oil and oil filter.	If the oil is normal:	**12.3**
	If after replacing oil the pressure remains low:	**12.3**
	If after replacing oil the pressure becomes normal:	—

Test and Procedure	Results and Indications	Proceed to
12.3—Inspect the oil pressure relief valve and spring, to ensure that it is not sticking or stuck. Remove and thoroughly clean the valve, spring, and the valve body.	If the oil pressure improves: If no improvement is noted:	— **12.4**
12.4—Check to ensure that the oil pump is not cavitating (sucking air instead of oil): See that the crankcase is neither over nor underfull, and that the pickup in the sump is in the proper position and free from sludge.	Fill or drain the crankcase to the proper capacity, and clean the pickup screen in solvent if necessary. If no improvement is noted:	**12.5**
12.5—Inspect the oil pump drive and the oil pump:	If the pump drive or the oil pump appear to be defective, service as necessary and retest per 12.1: If the pump drive and pump appear to be operating normally, the engine should be disassembled to determine where blockage exists:	**12.1** **See Chapter 3**
12.6—Purge the engine of ethylene glycol coolant: Completely drain the crankcase and the oil filter. Obtain a commercial butyl cellosolve base solvent, designated for this purpose, and follow the instructions precisely. Following this, install a new oil filter and refill the crankcase with the proper weight oil. The next oil and filter change should follow shortly thereafter (1000 miles).		

TROUBLESHOOTING EMISSION CONTROL SYSTEMS

See Chapter 4 for procedures applicable to individual emission control systems used on specific combinations of engine/transmission/model.

TROUBLESHOOTING THE CARBURETOR
See Chapter 4 for service procedures

Carburetor problems cannot be effectively isolated unless all other engine systems (particularly ignition and emission) are functioning properly and the engine is properly tuned.

Condition	Possible Cause
Engine cranks, but does not start	1. Improper starting procedure 2. No fuel in tank 3. Clogged fuel line or filter 4. Defective fuel pump 5. Choke valve not closing properly 6. Engine flooded 7. Choke valve not unloading 8. Throttle linkage not making full travel 9. Stuck needle or float 10. Leaking float needle or seat 11. Improper float adjustment
Engine stalls	1. Improperly adjusted idle speed or mixture **Engine hot** 2. Improperly adjusted dashpot 3. Defective or improperly adjusted solenoid 4. Incorrect fuel level in fuel bowl 5. Fuel pump pressure too high 6. Leaking float needle seat 7. Secondary throttle valve stuck open 8. Air or fuel leaks 9. Idle air bleeds plugged or missing 10. Idle passages plugged **Engine Cold** 11. Incorrectly adjusted choke 12. Improperly adjusted fast idle speed 13. Air leaks 14. Plugged idle or idle air passages 15. Stuck choke valve or binding linkage 16. Stuck secondary throttle valves 17. Engine flooding—high fuel level 18. Leaking or misaligned float
Engine hesitates on acceleration	1. Clogged fuel filter 2. Leaking fuel pump diaphragm 3. Low fuel pump pressure 4. Secondary throttle valves stuck, bent or misadjusted 5. Sticking or binding air valve 6. Defective accelerator pump 7. Vacuum leaks 8. Clogged air filter 9. Incorrect choke adjustment (engine cold)
Engine feels sluggish or flat on acceleration	1. Improperly adjusted idle speed or mixture 2. Clogged fuel filter 3. Defective accelerator pump 4. Dirty, plugged or incorrect main metering jets 5. Bent or sticking main metering rods 6. Sticking throttle valves 7. Stuck heat riser 8. Binding or stuck air valve 9. Dirty, plugged or incorrect secondary jets 10. Bent or sticking secondary metering rods. 11. Throttle body or manifold heat passages plugged 12. Improperly adjusted choke or choke vacuum break.
Carburetor floods	1. Defective fuel pump. Pressure too high. 2. Stuck choke valve 3. Dirty, worn or damaged float or needle valve/seat 4. Incorrect float/fuel level 5. Leaking float bowl

Condition	Possible Cause
Engine idles roughly and stalls	1. Incorrect idle speed 2. Clogged fuel filter 3. Dirt in fuel system or carburetor 4. Loose carburetor screws or attaching bolts 5. Broken carburetor gaskets 6. Air leaks 7. Dirty carburetor 8. Worn idle mixture needles 9. Throttle valves stuck open 10. Incorrectly adjusted float or fuel level 11. Clogged air filter
Engine runs unevenly or surges	1. Defective fuel pump 2. Dirty or clogged fuel filter 3. Plugged, loose or incorrect main metering jets or rods 4. Air leaks 5. Bent or sticking main metering rods 6. Stuck power piston 7. Incorrect float adjustment 8. Incorrect idle speed or mixture 9. Dirty or plugged idle system passages 10. Hard, brittle or broken gaskets 11. Loose attaching or mounting screws 12. Stuck or misaligned secondary throttle valves
Poor fuel economy	1. Poor driving habits 2. Stuck choke valve 3. Binding choke linkage 4. Stuck heat riser 5. Incorrect idle mixture 6. Defective accelerator pump 7. Air leaks 8. Plugged, loose or incorrect main metering jets 9. Improperly adjusted float or fuel level 10. Bent, misaligned or fuel-clogged float 11. Leaking float needle seat 12. Fuel leak 13. Accelerator pump discharge ball not seating properly 14. Incorrect main jets
Engine lacks high speed performance or power	1. Incorrect throttle linkage adjustment 2. Stuck or binding power piston 3. Defective accelerator pump 4. Air leaks 5. Incorrect float setting or fuel level 6. Dirty, plugged, worn or incorrect main metering jets or rods 7. Binding or sticking air valve 8. Brittle or cracked gaskets 9. Bent, incorrect or improperly adjusted secondary metering rods 10. Clogged fuel filter 11. Clogged air filter 12. Defective fuel pump

TROUBLESHOOTING FUEL INJECTION PROBLEMS

Each fuel injection system has its own unique components and test procedures, for which it is impossible to generalize. Refer to Chapter 4 of this Repair & Tune-Up Guide for specific test and repair procedures, if the vehicle is equipped with fuel injection.

TROUBLESHOOTING ELECTRICAL PROBLEMS

See Chapter 5 for service procedures

For any electrical system to operate, it must make a complete circuit. This simply means that the power flow from the battery must make a complete circle. When an electrical component is operating, power flows from the battery to the component, passes through the component causing it to perform its function (lighting a light bulb), and then returns to the battery through the ground of the circuit. This ground is usually (but not always) the metal part of the car or truck on which the electrical component is mounted.

Perhaps the easiest way to visualize this is to think of connecting a light bulb with two wires attached to it to the battery. If one of the two wires attached to the light bulb were attached to the negative post of the battery and the other were attached to the positive post of the battery, you would have a complete circuit. Current from the battery would flow to the light bulb, causing it to light, and return to the negative post of the battery.

The normal automotive circuit differs from this simple example in two ways. First, instead of having a return wire from the bulb to the battery, the light bulb returns the current to the battery through the chassis of the vehicle. Since the negative battery cable is attached to the chassis and the chassis is made of electrically conductive metal, the chassis of the vehicle can serve as a ground wire to complete the circuit. Secondly, most automotive circuits contain switches to turn components on and off as required.

Every complete circuit from a power source must include a component which is using the power from the power source. If you were to disconnect the light bulb from the wires and touch the two wires together (don't do this) the power supply wire to the component would be grounded before the normal ground connection for the circuit.

Because grounding a wire from a power source makes a complete circuit—less the required component to use the power—this phenomenon is called a short circuit. Common causes are: broken insulation (exposing the metal wire to a metal part of the car or truck), or a shorted switch.

Some electrical components which require a large amount of current to operate also have a relay in their circuit. Since these circuits carry a large amount of current, the thickness of the wire in the circuit (gauge size) is also greater. If this large wire were connected from the component to the control switch on the instrument panel, and then back to the component, a voltage drop would occur in the circuit. To prevent this potential drop in voltage, an electromagnetic switch (relay) is used. The large wires in the circuit are connected from the battery to one side of the relay, and from the opposite side of the relay to the component. The relay is normally open, preventing current from passing through the circuit. An additional, smaller, wire is connected from the relay to the control switch for the circuit. When the control switch is turned on, it grounds the smaller wire from the relay and completes the circuit. This closes the relay and allows current to flow from the battery to the component. The horn, headlight, and starter circuits are three which use relays.

It is possible for larger surges of current to pass through the electrical system of your car or truck. If this surge of current were to reach an electrical component, it could burn it out. To prevent this, fuses, circuit breakers or fusible links are connected into the current supply wires of most of the major electrical systems. When an electrical current of excessive power passes through the component's fuse, the fuse blows out and breaks the circuit, saving the component from destruction.

Typical automotive fuse

A circuit breaker is basically a self-repairing fuse. The circuit breaker opens the circuit the same way a fuse does. However, when either the short is removed from the circuit or the surge subsides, the circuit breaker resets itself and does not have to be replaced as a fuse does.

A fuse link is a wire that acts as a fuse. It is normally connected between the starter relay and the main wiring harness. This connection is usually under the hood. The fuse link (if installed) protects all the

Most fusible links show a charred, melted insulation when they burn out

The test light will show the presence of current when touched to a hot wire and grounded at the other end

chassis electrical components, and is the probable cause of trouble when none of the electrical components function, unless the battery is disconnected or dead.

Electrical problems generally fall into one of three areas:

1. The component that is not functioning is not receiving current.

2. The component itself is not functioning.

3. The component is not properly grounded.

The electrical system can be checked with a test light and a jumper wire. A test light is a device that looks like a pointed screwdriver with a wire attached to it and has a light bulb in its handle. A jumper wire is a piece of insulated wire with an alligator clip attached to each end.

If a component is not working, you must follow a systematic plan to determine which of the three causes is the villain.

1. Turn on the switch that controls the inoperable component.

2. Disconnect the power supply wire from the component.

3. Attach the ground wire on the test light to a good metal ground.

4. Touch the probe end of the test light to the end of the power supply wire that was disconnected from the component. If the component is receiving current, the test light will go on.

NOTE: *Some components work only when the ignition switch is turned on.*

If the test light does not go on, then the problem is in the circuit between the battery and the component. This includes all the switches, fuses, and relays in the system. Follow the wire that runs back to the battery. The problem is an open circuit between the

battery and the component. If the fuse is blown and, when replaced, immediately blows again, there is a short circuit in the system which must be located and repaired. If there is a switch in the system, bypass it with a jumper wire. This is done by connecting one end of the jumper wire to the power supply wire into the switch and the other end of the jumper wire to the wire coming out of the switch. If the test light lights with the jumper wire installed, the switch or whatever was bypassed is defective.

NOTE: *Never substitute the jumper wire for the component, since it is required to use the power from the power source.*

5. If the bulb in the test light goes on, then the current is getting to the component that is not working. This eliminates the first of the three possible causes. Connect the power supply wire and connect a jumper wire from the component to a good metal ground. Do this with the switch which controls the component turned on, and also the ignition switch turned on if it is required for the component to work. If the component works with the jumper wire installed, then it has a bad ground. This is usually caused by the metal area on which the component mounts to the chassis being coated with some type of foreign matter.

6. If neither test located the source of the trouble, then the component itself is defective. Remember that for any electrical system to work, all connections must be clean and tight.

Troubleshooting Basic Turn Signal and Flasher Problems
See Chapter 5 for service procedures

Most problems in the turn signals or flasher system can be reduced to defective flashers or bulbs, which are easily replaced. Occasionally, the turn signal switch will prove defective.
F = Front   R = Rear   ● = Lights off   ○ = Lights on

Condition		Possible Cause
Turn signals light, but do not flash		Defective flasher
No turn signals light on either side		Blown fuse. Replace if defective. Defective flasher. Check by substitution. Open circuit, short circuit or poor ground.
Both turn signals on one side don't work		Bad bulbs. Bad ground in both (or either) housings.
One turn signal light on one side doesn't work		Defective bulb. Corrosion in socket. Clean contacts. Poor ground at socket.
Turn signal flashes too fast or too slowly		Check any bulb on the side flashing too fast. A heavy-duty bulb is probably installed in place of a regular bulb. Check the bulb flashing too slowly. A standard bulb was probably installed in place of a heavy-duty bulb. Loose connections or corrosion at the bulb socket.
Indicator lights don't work in either direction		Check if the turn signals are working. Check the dash indicator lights. Check the flasher by substitution.
One indicator light doesn't light		On systems with one dash indicator: See if the lights work on the same side. Often the filaments have been reversed in systems combining stoplights with taillights and turn signals. Check the flasher by substitution. On systems with two indicators: Check the bulbs on the same side. Check the indicator light bulb. Check the flasher by substitution.

Troubleshooting Lighting Problems
See Chapter 5 for service procedures

Condition	Possible Cause
One or more lights don't work, but others do	1. Defective bulb(s) 2. Blown fuse(s) 3. Dirty fuse clips or light sockets 4. Poor ground circuit
Lights burn out quickly	1. Incorrect voltage regulator setting or defective regulator 2. Poor battery/alternator connections
Lights go dim	1. Low/discharged battery 2. Alternator not charging 3. Corroded sockets or connections 4. Low voltage output
Lights flicker	1. Loose connection 2. Poor ground. (Run ground wire from light housing to frame) 3. Circuit breaker operating (short circuit)
Lights "flare"—Some flare is normal on acceleration—If excessive, see "Lights Burn Out Quickly"	High voltage setting
Lights glare—approaching drivers are blinded	1. Lights adjusted too high 2. Rear springs or shocks sagging 3. Rear tires soft

Troubleshooting Dash Gauge Problems
Most problems can be traced to a defective sending unit or faulty wiring. Occasionally, the gauge itself is at fault. See Chapter 5 for service procedures.

Condition	Possible Cause
COOLANT TEMPERATURE GAUGE	
Gauge reads erratically or not at all	1. Loose or dirty connections 2. Defective sending unit. 3. Defective gauge. To test a bi-metal gauge, remove the wire from the sending unit. Ground the wire for an instant. If the gauge registers, replace the sending unit. To test a magnetic gauge, disconnect the wire at the sending unit. With ignition ON gauge should register COLD. Ground the wire; gauge should register HOT.
AMMETER GAUGE—TURN HEADLIGHTS ON (DO NOT START ENGINE). NOTE REACTION	
Ammeter shows charge Ammeter shows discharge Ammeter does not move	1. Connections reversed on gauge 2. Ammeter is OK 3. Loose connections or faulty wiring 4. Defective gauge

Condition	Possible Cause

OIL PRESSURE GAUGE

Gauge does not register or is inaccurate	1. On mechanical gauge, Bourdon tube may be bent or kinked. 2. Low oil pressure. Remove sending unit. Idle the engine briefly. If no oil flows from sending unit hole, problem is in engine. 3. Defective gauge. Remove the wire from the sending unit and ground it for an instant with the ignition ON. A good gauge will go to the top of the scale. 4. Defective wiring. Check the wiring to the gauge. If it's OK and the gauge doesn't register when grounded, replace the gauge. 5. Defective sending unit.

ALL GAUGES

All gauges do not operate	1. Blown fuse 2. Defective instrument regulator
All gauges read low or erratically All gauges pegged	3. Defective or dirty instrument voltage regulator 4. Loss of ground between instrument voltage regulator and frame 5. Defective instrument regulator

WARNING LIGHTS

Light(s) do not come on when ignition is ON, but engine is not started	1. Defective bulb 2. Defective wire 3. Defective sending unit. Disconnect the wire from the sending unit and ground it. Replace the sending unit if the light comes on with the ignition ON.
Light comes on with engine running	4. Problem in individual system 5. Defective sending unit

Troubleshooting Clutch Problems

It is false economy to replace individual clutch components. The pressure plate, clutch plate and throwout bearing should be replaced as a set, and the flywheel face inspected, whenever the clutch is overhauled. See Chapter 6 for service procedures.

Condition	Possible Cause
Clutch chatter	1. Grease on driven plate (disc) facing 2. Binding clutch linkage or cable 3. Loose, damaged facings on driven plate (disc) 4. Engine mounts loose 5. Incorrect height adjustment of pressure plate release levers 6. Clutch housing or housing to transmission adapter misalignment 7. Loose driven plate hub
Clutch grabbing	1. Oil, grease on driven plate (disc) facing 2. Broken pressure plate 3. Warped or binding driven plate. Driven plate binding on clutch shaft
Clutch slips	1. Lack of lubrication in clutch linkage or cable (linkage or cable binds, causes incomplete engagement) 2. Incorrect pedal, or linkage adjustment 3. Broken pressure plate springs 4. Weak pressure plate springs 5. Grease on driven plate facings (disc)

Troubleshooting Clutch Problems (cont.)

Condition	Possible Cause
Incomplete clutch release	1. Incorrect pedal or linkage adjustment or linkage or cable binding 2. Incorrect height adjustment on pressure plate release levers 3. Loose, broken facings on driven plate (disc) 4. Bent, dished, warped driven plate caused by overheating
Grinding, whirring grating noise when pedal is depressed	1. Worn or defective throwout bearing 2. Starter drive teeth contacting flywheel ring gear teeth. Look for milled or polished teeth on ring gear.
Squeal, howl, trumpeting noise when pedal is being released (occurs during first inch to inch and one-half of pedal travel)	Pilot bushing worn or lack of lubricant. If bushing appears OK, polish bushing with emery cloth, soak lube wick in oil, lube bushing with oil, apply film of chassis grease to clutch shaft pilot hub, reassemble. NOTE: Bushing wear may be due to misalignment of clutch housing or housing to transmission adapter
Vibration or clutch pedal pulsation with clutch disengaged (pedal fully depressed)	1. Worn or defective engine transmission mounts 2. Flywheel run out. (Flywheel run out at face not to exceed 0.005") 3. Damaged or defective clutch components

Troubleshooting Manual Transmission Problems
See Chapter 6 for service procedures

Condition	Possible Cause
Transmission jumps out of gear	1. Misalignment of transmission case or clutch housing. 2. Worn pilot bearing in crankshaft. 3. Bent transmission shaft. 4. Worn high speed sliding gear. 5. Worn teeth or end-play in clutch shaft. 6. Insufficient spring tension on shifter rail plunger. 7. Bent or loose shifter fork. 8. Gears not engaging completely. 9. Loose or worn bearings on clutch shaft or mainshaft. 10. Worn gear teeth. 11. Worn or damaged detent balls.
Transmission sticks in gear	1. Clutch not releasing fully. 2. Burred or battered teeth on clutch shaft, or sliding sleeve. 3. Burred or battered transmission mainshaft. 4. Frozen synchronizing clutch. 5. Stuck shifter rail plunger. 6. Gearshift lever twisting and binding shifter rail. 7. Battered teeth on high speed sliding gear or on sleeve. 8. Improper lubrication, or lack of lubrication. 9. Corroded transmission parts. 10. Defective mainshaft pilot bearing. 11. Locked gear bearings will give same effect as stuck in gear.
Transmission gears will not synchronize	1. Binding pilot bearing on mainshaft, will synchronize in high gear only. 2. Clutch not releasing fully. 3. Detent spring weak or broken. 4. Weak or broken springs under balls in sliding gear sleeve. 5. Binding bearing on clutch shaft, or binding countershaft. 6. Binding pilot bearing in crankshaft. 7. Badly worn gear teeth. 8. Improper lubrication. 9. Constant mesh gear not turning freely on transmission mainshaft. Will synchronize in that gear only.

Condition	Possible Cause
Gears spinning when shifting into gear from neutral	1. Clutch not releasing fully. 2. In some cases an extremely light lubricant in transmission will cause gears to continue to spin for a short time after clutch is released. 3. Binding pilot bearing in crankshaft.
Transmission noisy in all gears	1. Insufficient lubricant, or improper lubricant. 2. Worn countergear bearings. 3. Worn or damaged main drive gear or countergear. 4. Damaged main drive gear or mainshaft bearings. 5. Worn or damaged countergear anti-lash plate.
Transmission noisy in neutral only	1. Damaged main drive gear bearing. 2. Damaged or loose mainshaft pilot bearing. 3. Worn or damaged countergear anti-lash plate. 4. Worn countergear bearings.
Transmission noisy in one gear only	1. Damaged or worn constant mesh gears. 2. Worn or damaged countergear bearings. 3. Damaged or worn synchronizer.
Transmission noisy in reverse only	1. Worn or damaged reverse idler gear or idler bushing. 2. Worn or damaged mainshaft reverse gear. 3. Worn or damaged reverse countergear. 4. Damaged shift mechanism.

TROUBLESHOOTING AUTOMATIC TRANSMISSION PROBLEMS

Keeping alert to changes in the operating characteristics of the transmission (changing shift points, noises, etc.) can prevent small problems from becoming large ones. If the problem cannot be traced to loose bolts, fluid level, misadjusted linkage, clogged filters or similar problems, you should probably seek professional service.

Transmission Fluid Indications

The appearance and odor of the transmission fluid can give valuable clues to the overall condition of the transmission. Always note the appearance of the fluid when you check the fluid level or change the fluid. Rub a small amount of fluid between your fingers to feel for grit and smell the fluid on the dipstick.

If the fluid appears:	It indicates:
Clear and red colored	Normal operation
Discolored (extremely dark red or brownish) or smells burned	Band or clutch pack failure, usually caused by an overheated transmission. Hauling very heavy loads with insufficient power or failure to change the fluid often result in overheating. Do not confuse this appearance with newer fluids that have a darker red color and a strong odor (though not a burned odor).
Foamy or aerated (light in color and full of bubbles)	1. The level is too high (gear train is churning oil) 2. An internal air leak (air is mixing with the fluid). Have the transmission checked professionally.
Solid residue in the fluid	Defective bands, clutch pack or bearings. Bits of band material or metal abrasives are clinging to the dipstick. Have the transmission checked professionally.
Varnish coating on the dipstick	The transmission fluid is overheating

TROUBLESHOOTING DRIVE AXLE PROBLEMS

First, determine when the noise is most noticeable.

Drive Noise: Produced under vehicle acceleration.

Coast Noise: Produced while coasting with a closed throttle.

Float Noise: Occurs while maintaining constant speed (just enough to keep speed constant) on a level road.

External Noise Elimination

It is advisable to make a thorough road test to determine whether the noise originates in the rear axle or whether it originates from the tires, engine, transmission, wheel bearings or road surface. Noise originating from other places cannot be corrected by servicing the rear axle.

ROAD NOISE

Brick or rough surfaced concrete roads produce noises that seem to come from the rear axle. Road noise is usually identical in Drive or Coast and driving on a different type of road will tell whether the road is the problem.

TIRE NOISE

Tire noise can be mistaken as rear axle noise, even though the tires on the front are at fault. Snow tread and mud tread tires or tires worn unevenly will frequently cause vibrations which seem to originate elsewhere; *temporarily, and for test purposes only,* inflate the tires to 40–50 lbs. This will significantly alter the noise produced by the tires, but will not alter noise from the rear axle. Noises from the rear axle will normally cease at speeds below 30 mph on coast, while tire noise will continue at lower tone as speed is decreased. The rear axle noise will usually change from drive conditions to coast conditions, while tire noise will not. Do not forget to lower the tire pressure to normal after the test is complete.

ENGINE/TRANSMISSION NOISE

Determine at what speed the noise is most pronounced, then stop in a quiet place. With the transmission in Neutral, run the engine through speeds corresponding to road speeds where the noise was noticed. Noises produced with the vehicle standing still are coming from the engine or transmission.

FRONT WHEEL BEARINGS

Front wheel bearing noises, sometimes confused with rear axle noises, will not change when comparing drive and coast conditions. While holding the speed steady, lightly apply the footbrake. This will often cause wheel bearing noise to lessen, as some of the weight is taken off the bearing. Front wheel bearings are easily checked by jacking up the wheels and spinning the wheels. Shaking the wheels will also determine if the wheel bearings are excessively loose.

REAR AXLE NOISES

Eliminating other possible sources can narrow the cause to the rear axle, which normally produces noise from worn gears or bearings. Gear noises tend to peak in a narrow speed range, while bearing noises will usually vary in pitch with engine speeds.

Noise Diagnosis

The Noise Is:	Most Probably Produced By:
1. Identical under Drive or Coast	Road surface, tires or front wheel bearings
2. Different depending on road surface	Road surface or tires
3. Lower as speed is lowered	Tires
4. Similar when standing or moving	Engine or transmission
5. A vibration	Unbalanced tires, rear wheel bearing, unbalanced driveshaft or worn U-joint
6. A knock or click about every two tire revolutions	Rear wheel bearing
7. Most pronounced on turns	Damaged differential gears
8. A steady low-pitched whirring or scraping, starting at low speeds	Damaged or worn pinion bearing
9. A chattering vibration on turns	Wrong differential lubricant or worn clutch plates (limited slip rear axle)
10. Noticed only in Drive, Coast or Float conditions	Worn ring gear and/or pinion gear

Troubleshooting Steering & Suspension Problems

Condition	Possible Cause
Hard steering (wheel is hard to turn)	1. Improper tire pressure 2. Loose or glazed pump drive belt 3. Low or incorrect fluid 4. Loose, bent or poorly lubricated front end parts 5. Improper front end alignment (excessive caster) 6. Bind in steering column or linkage 7. Kinked hydraulic hose 8. Air in hydraulic system 9. Low pump output or leaks in system 10. Obstruction in lines 11. Pump valves sticking or out of adjustment 12. Incorrect wheel alignment
Loose steering (too much play in steering wheel)	1. Loose wheel bearings 2. Faulty shocks 3. Worn linkage or suspension components 4. Loose steering gear mounting or linkage points 5. Steering mechanism worn or improperly adjusted 6. Valve spool improperly adjusted 7. Worn ball joints, tie-rod ends, etc.
Veers or wanders (pulls to one side with hands off steering wheel)	1. Improper tire pressure 2. Improper front end alignment 3. Dragging or improperly adjusted brakes 4. Bent frame 5. Improper rear end alignment 6. Faulty shocks or springs 7. Loose or bent front end components 8. Play in Pitman arm 9. Steering gear mountings loose 10. Loose wheel bearings 11. Binding Pitman arm 12. Spool valve sticking or improperly adjusted 13. Worn ball joints
Wheel oscillation or vibration transmitted through steering wheel	1. Low or uneven tire pressure 2. Loose wheel bearings 3. Improper front end alignment 4. Bent spindle 5. Worn, bent or broken front end components 6. Tires out of round or out of balance 7. Excessive lateral runout in disc brake rotor 8. Loose or bent shock absorber or strut
Noises (see also "Troubleshooting Drive Axle Problems")	1. Loose belts 2. Low fluid, air in system 3. Foreign matter in system 4. Improper lubrication 5. Interference or chafing in linkage 6. Steering gear mountings loose 7. Incorrect adjustment or wear in gear box 8. Faulty valves or wear in pump 9. Kinked hydraulic lines 10. Worn wheel bearings
Poor return of steering	1. Over-inflated tires 2. Improperly aligned front end (excessive caster) 3. Binding in steering column 4. No lubrication in front end 5. Steering gear adjusted too tight
Uneven tire wear (see "How To Read Tire Wear")	1. Incorrect tire pressure 2. Improperly aligned front end 3. Tires out-of-balance 4. Bent or worn suspension parts

HOW TO READ TIRE WEAR

The way your tires wear is a good indicator of other parts of the suspension. Abnormal wear patterns are often caused by the need for simple tire maintenance, or for front end alignment.

Excessive wear at the center of the tread indicates that the air pressure in the tire is consistently too high. The tire is riding on the center of the tread and wearing it prematurely. Occasionally, this wear pattern can result from outrageously wide tires on narrow rims. The cure for this is to replace either the tires or the wheels.

This type of wear usually results from consistent under-inflation. When a tire is under-inflated, there is too much contact with the road by the outer treads, which wear prematurely. When this type of wear occurs, and the tire pressure is known to be consistently correct, a bent or worn steering component or the need for wheel alignment could be indicated.

Feathering is a condition when the edge of each tread rib develops a slightly rounded edge on one side and a sharp edge on the other. By running your hand over the tire, you can usually feel the sharper edges before you'll be able to see them. The most common causes of feathering are incorrect toe-in setting or deteriorated bushings in the front suspension.

When an inner or outer rib wears faster than the rest of the tire, the need for wheel alignment is indicated. There is excessive camber in the front suspension, causing the wheel to lean too much putting excessive load on one side of the tire. Misalignment could also be due to sagging springs, worn ball joints, or worn control arm bushings. Be sure the vehicle is loaded the way it's normally driven when you have the wheels aligned.

Cups or scalloped dips appearing around the edge of the tread almost always indicate worn (sometimes bent) suspension parts. Adjustment of wheel alignment alone will seldom cure the problem. Any worn component that connects the wheel to the suspension can cause this type of wear. Occasionally, wheels that are out of balance will wear like this, but wheel imbalance usually shows up as bald spots between the outside edges and center of the tread.

Second-rib wear is usually found only in radial tires, and appears where the steel belts end in relation to the tread. It can be kept to a minimum by paying careful attention to tire pressure and frequently rotating the tires. This is often considered normal wear but excessive amounts indicate that the tires are too wide for the wheels.

Over-inflation

Under-inflation

Feathering

One side wear

Cupping

Second-rib wear

Troubleshooting Disc Brake Problems

Condition	Possible Cause
Noise—groan—brake noise emanating when slowly releasing brakes (creep-groan)	Not detrimental to function of disc brakes—no corrective action required. (This noise may be eliminated by slightly increasing or decreasing brake pedal efforts.)
Rattle—brake noise or rattle emanating at low speeds on rough roads, (front wheels only).	1. Shoe anti-rattle spring missing or not properly positioned. 2. Excessive clearance between shoe and caliper. 3. Soft or broken caliper seals. 4. Deformed or misaligned disc. 5. Loose caliper.
Scraping	1. Mounting bolts too long. 2. Loose wheel bearings. 3. Bent, loose, or misaligned splash shield.
Front brakes heat up during driving and fail to release	1. Operator riding brake pedal. 2. Stop light switch improperly adjusted. 3. Sticking pedal linkage. 4. Frozen or seized piston. 5. Residual pressure valve in master cylinder. 6. Power brake malfunction. 7. Proportioning valve malfunction.
Leaky brake caliper	1. Damaged or worn caliper piston seal. 2. Scores or corrosion on surface of cylinder bore.
Grabbing or uneven brake action— Brakes pull to one side	1. Causes listed under "Brakes Pull". 2. Power brake malfunction. 3. Low fluid level in master cylinder. 4. Air in hydraulic system. 5. Brake fluid, oil or grease on linings. 6. Unmatched linings. 7. Distorted brake pads. 8. Frozen or seized pistons. 9. Incorrect tire pressure. 10. Front end out of alignment. 11. Broken rear spring. 12. Brake caliper pistons sticking. 13. Restricted hose or line. 14. Caliper not in proper alignment to braking disc. 15. Stuck or malfunctioning metering valve. 16. Soft or broken caliper seals. 17. Loose caliper.
Brake pedal can be depressed without braking effect	1. Air in hydraulic system or improper bleeding procedure. 2. Leak past primary cup in master cylinder. 3. Leak in system. 4. Rear brakes out of adjustment. 5. Bleeder screw open.
Excessive pedal travel	1. Air, leak, or insufficient fluid in system or caliper. 2. Warped or excessively tapered shoe and lining assembly. 3. Excessive disc runout. 4. Rear brake adjustment required. 5. Loose wheel bearing adjustment. 6. Damaged caliper piston seal. 7. Improper brake fluid (boil). 8. Power brake malfunction. 9. Weak or soft hoses.

Troubleshooting Disc Brake Problems (cont.)

Condition	Possible Cause
Brake roughness or chatter (pedal pumping)	1. Excessive thickness variation of braking disc. 2. Excessive lateral runout of braking disc. 3. Rear brake drums out-of-round. 4. Excessive front bearing clearance.
Excessive pedal effort	1. Brake fluid, oil or grease on linings. 2. Incorrect lining. 3. Frozen or seized pistons. 4. Power brake malfunction. 5. Kinked or collapsed hose or line. 6. Stuck metering valve. 7. Scored caliper or master cylinder bore. 8. Seized caliper pistons.
Brake pedal fades (pedal travel increases with foot on brake)	1. Rough master cylinder or caliper bore. 2. Loose or broken hydraulic lines/connections. 3. Air in hydraulic system. 4. Fluid level low. 5. Weak or soft hoses. 6. Inferior quality brake shoes or fluid. 7. Worn master cylinder piston cups or seals.

Troubleshooting Drum Brakes

Condition	Possible Cause
Pedal goes to floor	1. Fluid low in reservoir. 2. Air in hydraulic system. 3. Improperly adjusted brake. 4. Leaking wheel cylinders. 5. Loose or broken brake lines. 6. Leaking or worn master cylinder. 7. Excessively worn brake lining.
Spongy brake pedal	1. Air in hydraulic system. 2. Improper brake fluid (low boiling point). 3. Excessively worn or cracked brake drums. 4. Broken pedal pivot bushing.
Brakes pulling	1. Contaminated lining. 2. Front end out of alignment. 3. Incorrect brake adjustment. 4. Unmatched brake lining. 5. Brake drums out of round. 6. Brake shoes distorted. 7. Restricted brake hose or line. 8. Broken rear spring. 9. Worn brake linings. 10. Uneven lining wear. 11. Glazed brake lining. 12. Excessive brake lining dust. 13. Heat spotted brake drums. 14. Weak brake return springs. 15. Faulty automatic adjusters. 16. Low or incorrect tire pressure.

Condition	Possible Cause
Squealing brakes	1. Glazed brake lining. 2. Saturated brake lining. 3. Weak or broken brake shoe retaining spring. 4. Broken or weak brake shoe return spring. 5. Incorrect brake lining. 6. Distorted brake shoes. 7. Bent support plate. 8. Dust in brakes or scored brake drums. 9. Linings worn below limit. 10. Uneven brake lining wear. 11. Heat spotted brake drums.
Chirping brakes	1. Out of round drum or eccentric axle flange pilot.
Dragging brakes	1. Incorrect wheel or parking brake adjustment. 2. Parking brakes engaged or improperly adjusted. 3. Weak or broken brake shoe return spring. 4. Brake pedal binding. 5. Master cylinder cup sticking. 6. Obstructed master cylinder relief port. 7. Saturated brake lining. 8. Bent or out of round brake drum. 9. Contaminated or improper brake fluid. 10. Sticking wheel cylinder pistons. 11. Driver riding brake pedal. 12. Defective proportioning valve. 13. Insufficient brake shoe lubricant.
Hard pedal	1. Brake booster inoperative. 2. Incorrect brake lining. 3. Restricted brake line or hose. 4. Frozen brake pedal linkage. 5. Stuck wheel cylinder. 6. Binding pedal linkage. 7. Faulty proportioning valve.
Wheel locks	1. Contaminated brake lining. 2. Loose or torn brake lining. 3. Wheel cylinder cups sticking. 4. Incorrect wheel bearing adjustment. 5. Faulty proportioning valve.
Brakes fade (high speed)	1. Incorrect lining. 2. Overheated brake drums. 3. Incorrect brake fluid (low boiling temperature). 4. Saturated brake lining. 5. Leak in hydraulic system. 6. Faulty automatic adjusters.
Pedal pulsates	1. Bent or out of round brake drum.
Brake chatter and shoe knock	1. Out of round brake drum. 2. Loose support plate. 3. Bent support plate. 4. Distorted brake shoes. 5. Machine grooves in contact face of brake drum (Shoe Knock). 6. Contaminated brake lining. 7. Missing or loose components. 8. Incorrect lining material. 9. Out-of-round brake drums. 10. Heat spotted or scored brake drums. 11. Out-of-balance wheels.

Troubleshooting Drum Brakes (cont.)

Condition	Possible Cause
Brakes do not self adjust	1. Adjuster screw frozen in thread. 2. Adjuster screw corroded at thrust washer. 3. Adjuster lever does not engage star wheel. 4. Adjuster installed on wrong wheel.
Brake light glows	1. Leak in the hydraulic system. 2. Air in the system. 3. Improperly adjusted master cylinder pushrod. 4. Uneven lining wear. 5. Failure to center combination valve or proportioning valve.

Mechanic's Data

General Conversion Table

Multiply By	To Convert	To	
	LENGTH		
2.54	Inches	Centimeters	.3937
25.4	Inches	Millimeters	.03937
30.48	Feet	Centimeters	.0328
.304	Feet	Meters	3.28
.914	Yards	Meters	1.094
1.609	Miles	Kilometers	.621
	VOLUME		
.473	Pints	Liters	2.11
.946	Quarts	Liters	1.06
3.785	Gallons	Liters	.264
.016	Cubic inches	Liters	61.02
16.39	Cubic inches	Cubic cms.	.061
28.3	Cubic feet	Liters	.0353
	MASS (Weight)		
28.35	Ounces	Grams	.035
.4536	Pounds	Kilograms	2.20
—	To obtain	From	Multiply by

Multiply By	To Convert	To	
	AREA		
.645	Square inches	Square cms.	.155
.836	Square yds.	Square meters	1.196
	FORCE		
4.448	Pounds	Newtons	.225
.138	Ft./lbs.	Kilogram/meters	7.23
1.36	Ft./lbs.	Newton-meters	.737
.112	In./lbs.	Newton-meters	8.844
	PRESSURE		
.068	Psi	Atmospheres	14.7
6.89	Psi	Kilopascals	.145
	OTHER		
1.104	Horsepower (DIN)	Horsepower (SAE)	.9861
.746	Horsepower (SAE)	Kilowatts (KW)	1.34
1.60	Mph	Km/h	.625
.425	Mpg	Km/1	2.35
—	To obtain	From	Multiply by

Tap Drill Sizes

National Coarse or U.S.S.

Screw & Tap Size	Threads Per Inch	Use Drill Number
No. 5	40	.39
No. 6	32	.36
No. 8	32	.29
No. 10	24	.25
No. 12	24	.17
1/4	20	8
5/16	18	F
3/8	16	5/16
7/16	14	U
1/2	13	27/64
9/16	12	31/64
5/8	11	17/32
3/4	10	21/32
7/8	9	49/64

National Coarse or U.S.S.

Screw & Tap Size	Threads Per Inch	Use Drill Number
1	8	7/8
1 1/8	7	63/64
1 1/4	7	1 7/64
1 1/2	6	1 11/32

National Fine or S.A.E.

Screw & Tap Size	Threads Per Inch	Use Drill Number
No. 5	44	.37
No. 6	40	.33
No. 8	36	.29
No. 10	32	.21

National Fine or S.A.E.

Screw & Tap Size	Threads Per Inch	Use Drill Number
No. 12	28	.15
1/4	28	3
6/16	24	1
3/8	24	Q
7/16	20	W
1/2	20	29/64
9/16	18	33/64
5/8	18	37/64
3/4	16	11/16
7/8	14	13/16
1 1/8	12	1 3/64
1 1/4	12	1 11/64
1 1/2	12	1 27/64

Drill Sizes In Decimal Equivalents

Inch	Decimal	Wire	mm	Inch	Decimal	Wire	mm	Inch	Decimal	Wire & Letter	mm	Inch	Decimal	Letter	mm	Inch	Decimal	mm
1/64	.0156		.39		.0730	49			.1614		4.1		.2717		6.9		.4331	11.0
	.0157		.4		.0748		1.9		.1654		4.2		.2720	I		7/16	.4375	11.11
	.0160	78			.0760	48			.1660	19			.2756		7.0		.4528	11.5
	.0165		.42		.0768		1.95		.1673		4.25		.2770	J		29/64	.4531	11.51
	.0173		.44	5/64	.0781		1.98		.1693		4.3		.2795		7.1	15/32	.4688	11.90
	.0177		.45		.0785	47			.1695	18			.2810	K			.4724	12.0
	.0180	77			.0787		2.0	11/64	.1719		4.36	9/32	.2812		7.14	31/64	.4844	12.30
	.0181		.46		.0807		2.05		.1730	17			.2835		7.2		.4921	12.5
	.0189		.48		.0810	46			.1732		4.4		.2854		7.25	1/2	.5000	12.70
	.0197		.5		.0820	45			.1770	16			.2874		7.3		.5118	13.0
	.0200	76			.0827		2.1		.1772		4.5		.2900	L		33/64	.5156	13.09
	.0210	75			.0846		2.15		.1800	15			.2913		7.4	17/32	.5312	13.49
	.0217		.55		.0860	44			.1811		4.6		.2950	M			.5315	13.5
	.0225	74			.0866		2.2		.1820	14			.2953		7.5	35/64	.5469	13.89
	.0236		.6		.0886		2.25		.1850	13		19/64	.2969		7.54		.5512	14.0
	.0240	73			.0890	43			.1850		4.7		.2992		7.6	9/16	.5625	14.28
	.0250	72			.0906		2.3		.1870		4.75		.3020	N			.5709	14.5
	.0256		.65		.0925		2.35	3/16	.1875		4.76		.3031		7.7	37/64	.5781	14.68
	.0260	71			.0935	42			.1890		4.8		.3051		7.75		.5906	15.0
	.0276		.7	3/32	.0938		2.38		.1890	12			.3071		7.8	19/32	.5938	15.08
	.0280	70			.0945		2.4		.1910	11			.3110		7.9	39/64	.6094	15.47
	.0292	69			.0960	41			.1929		4.9	5/16	.3125		7.93		.6102	15.5
	.0295		.75		.0965		2.45		.1935	10			.3150		8.0	5/8	.6250	15.87
	.0310	68			.0980	40			.1960	9			.3160	O			.6299	16.0
1/32	.0312		.79		.0981		2.5		.1969		5.0		.3189		8.1	41/64	.6406	16.27
	.0315		.8		.0995	39			.1990	8			.3228		8.2		.6496	16.5
	.0320	67			.1015	38			.2008		5.1		.3230	P		21/32	.6562	16.66
	.0330	66			.1024		2.6		.2010	7			.3248		8.25		.6693	17.0
	.0335		.85		.1040	37		13/64	.2031		5.16		.3268		8.3	43/64	.6719	17.06
	.0350	65			.1063		2.7		.2040	6		21/64	.3281		8.33	11/16	.6875	17.46
	.0354		.9		.1065	36			.2047		5.2		.3307		8.4		.6890	17.5
	.0360	64			.1083		2.75		.2055	5			.3320	Q		45/64	.7031	17.85
	.0370	63		7/64	.1094		2.77		.2067		5.25		.3346		8.5		.7087	18.0
	.0374		.95		.1100	35			.2087		5.3		.3386		8.6	23/32	.7188	18.25
	.0380	62			.1102		2.8		.2090	4			.3390	R			.7283	18.5
	.0390	61			.1110	34			.2126		5.4		.3425		8.7	47/64	.7344	18.65
	.0394		1.0		.1130	33			.2130	3		11/32	.3438		8.73		.7480	19.0
	.0400	60			.1142		2.9	7/32	.2188		5.5		.3445		8.75	3/4	.7500	19.05
	.0410	59			.1160	32			.2205		5.6		.3465		8.8	49/64	.7656	19.44
	.0413		1.05		.1181		3.0						.3480	S			.7677	19.5
	.0420	58			.1200	31			.2210	2			.3504		8.9	25/32	.7812	19.84
	.0430	57			.1220		3.1		.2244		5.7		.3543		9.0		.7874	20.0
	.0433		1.1	1/8	.1250		3.17		.2264		5.75		.3580	T		51/64	.7969	20.24
	.0453		1.15		.1260		3.2		.2280	1			.3583		9.1		.8071	20.5
	.0465	56			.1280		3.25		.2283		5.8	23/64	.3594		9.12	13/16	.8125	20.63
3/64	.0469		1.19		.1285	30			.2323		5.9		.3622		9.2		.8268	21.0
	.0472		1.2		.1299		3.3		.2340	A			.3642		9.25	53/64	.8281	21.03
	.0492		1.25		.1339		3.4	15/64	.2344		5.95		.3661		9.3	27/32	.8438	21.43
	.0512		1.3		.1360	29			.2362		6.0		.3680	U			.8465	21.5
	.0520	55			.1378		3.5		.2380	B			.3701		9.4	55/64	.8594	21.82
	.0531		1.35		.1405	28			.2402		6.1		.3740		9.5		.8661	22.0
	.0550	54		9/64	.1406		3.57		.2420	C		3/8	.3750		9.52	7/8	.8750	22.22
	.0551		1.4		.1417		3.6		.2441		6.2		.3770	V			.8858	22.5
	.0571		1.45		.1440	27			.2460	D			.3780		9.6	57/64	.8906	22.62
	.0591		1.5		.1457		3.7		.2461		6.25		.3819		9.7		.9055	23.0
	.0595	53			.1470	26			.2480		6.3		.3839		9.75	29/32	.9062	23.01
	.0610		1.55		.1476		3.75	1/4	.2500	E	6.35		.3858		9.8	59/64	.9219	23.41
1/16	.0625		1.59		.1495	25			.2520		6.		.3860	W			.9252	23.5
	.0630		1.6		.1496		3.8		.2559		6.5		.3898		9.9	15/16	.9375	23.81
	.0635	52			.1520	24			.2570	F		25/64	.3906		9.92		.9449	24.0
	.0650		1.65		.1535		3.9		.2598		6.6		.3937		10.0	61/64	.9531	24.2
	.0669		1.7		.1540	23			.2610	G			.3970	X			.9646	24.5
	.0670	51		5/32	.1562		3.96		.2638		6.7		.4040	Y		31/32	.9688	24.6
	.0689		1.75		.1570	22		17/64	.2656		6.74	13/32	.4062		10.31		.9843	25.0
	.0700	50			.1575		4.0		.2657		6.75		.4130	Z		63/64	.9844	25.0
	.0709		1.8		.1590	21			.2660	H			.4134		10.5	1	1.0000	25.4
	.0728		1.85		.1610	20			.2677		6.8	27/64	.4219		10.71			

Index

Chilton's Repair & Tune-Up Guides

The complete line covers domestic cars, imports, trucks, vans, RV's and 4-wheel drive vehicles.

CODE	TITLE	CODE	TITLE
#7199	AMC 75–82; all models	#7171	Ford Vans 61–82
#7165	Alliance 1983	#7165	Fuego 82–83
#7323	Aries 81–82	#6935	GM Sub-compact 71–81 inc. Vega, Monza, Astre, Sunbird, Starfire & Skyhawk
#7344	Arrow 78–83		
#7193	Aspen/Volaré 76–80	#7311	Granada 78–83
#5902	Audi 70–73	#7204	Honda 73–82
#7028	Audi 4000/5000 77–81	#5912	International Scout 67–73
#6337	Audi Fox 73–75	#7136	Jeep CJ 1945–81
#5807	Barracuda 65–72	#6739	Jeep Wagoneer, Commando, Cherokee 66–79
#7203	Blazer 69–82	#7203	Jimmy 69–82
#5576	BMW 59–70	#7059	J-2000 1982
#7315	BMW 70–82	#7165	Le Car 76–83
#7308	Buick 75–83 all full sized models	#7323	Le Baron 1982
#7307	Buick Century/Regal 75–83	#7055	Lynx 81–82 inc. EXP & LN-7
#7045	Camaro 67–81	#6634	Maverick/Comet 70–77
#7317	Camaro 82–83	#7198	Mazda 71–82
#6695	Capri 70–77	#7031	Mazda RX-7 79–81
#7195	Capri 79–82	#6065	Mercedes-Benz 59–70
#7059	Cavalier 1982	#5907	Mercedes-Benz 68–73
#7309	Celebrity 82–83	#6809	Mercedes-Benz 74–79
#7309	Century 82–83	#7318	Mercury 68–83 all full sized models
#5807	Challenger 65–72	#7194	Mercury Mid-Size 71–82 inc. Continental, Cougar, XR-7 & Montego
#7343	Challenger (Import) 71–83		
#7344	Champ 78–83	#7173	MG 61–80
#6316	Charger/Coronet 71–75	#7311	Monarch 75–80
#7162	Chevette 76–82 inc. diesel	#7405	Mustang 65–73
#7313	Chevrolet 68–83 all full sized models	#6812	Mustang II 74–78
#7167	Chevrolet/GMC Pick-Ups 70–82	#7195	Mustang 79–82
#7169	Chevrolet/GMC Vans 67–82	#6841	Nova 69–79
#7310	Chevrolet S-10/GMC S-15 Pick-Ups 82–83	#7308	Oldsmobile 75–83 all full sized models
#7051	Chevy Luv 72–81 inc. 4wd	#7335	Omega 80–83
#7056	Chevy Mid-Size 64–81 inc. El Camino, Chevelle, Laguna, Malibu & Monte Carlo	#7191	Omni/Horizon 78–82
		#6575	Opel 71–75
#6841	Chevy II 62–79	#5982	Peugeot 70–74
#7309	Ciera 82–83	#7335	Phoenix 80–83
#7059	Cimarron 1982	#7027	Pinto/Bobcat 71–80
#7335	Citation 80–83	#8552	Plymouth 68–76 full sized models
#7343	Colt 71–83	#7168	Plymouth Vans 67–82
#7194	Continental 1982	#7308	Pontiac 75–83 all full sized models
#6691	Corvair 60–69 inc. Turbo	#7309	Pontiac 6000 82–83
#6576	Corvette 53–62	#5822	Porsche 69–73
#7192	Corvette 63–82	#7048	Porsche 924 & 928 77–81 inc. Turbo
#7405	Cougar 65–73	#7323	Reliant 81–82
#7190	Cutlass 70–82	#7165	Renault 75–83
#6324	Dart/Demon 68–76	#7383	S-10 Blazer 82–83
#5790	Datsun 61–72	#7383	S-15 Jimmy 82–83
#7196	Datsun F10, 310, Nissan Stanza 77–82	#5988	Saab 69–75
#7170	Datsun 200SX, 510, 610, 710, 810 73–82	#7344	Sapporo 78–83
#7197	Datsun 1200, 210/Nissan Sentra 73–82	#5821	Satellite/Roadrunner, Belvedere, GTX 68–73
#7172	Datsun Z & ZX 70–82	#7059	Skyhawk 1982
#7050	Datsun Pick-Ups 70–81 inc. 4wd	#7335	Skylark 80–83
#6554	Dodge 68–77 all full sized models	#7208	Subaru 70–82
#7323	Dodge 400 1982	#5905	Tempest/GTO/LeMans 68–73
#6486	Dodge Charger 67–70	#5795	Toyota 66–70
#7168	Dodge Vans 67–82	#7314	Toyota Celica & Supra 71–83
#7032	Dodge D-50/Plymouth Arrow Pick-Ups 77–81	#7316	Toyota Corolla, Carina, Tercel, Starlet 70–83
#7055	Escort 81–82 inc. EXP & LN-7	#7044	Toyota Corona, Cressida, Crown, Mark II 70–81
#6320	Fairlane/Torino 62–75	#7035	Toyota Pick-Ups 70–81
#7312	Fairmont 78–83	#5910	Triumph 69–73
#7042	Fiat 69–81	#7162	T-1000 1982
#6846	Fiesta 78–80	#6326	Valiant/Duster 68–76
#7046	Firebird 67–81	#5796	Volkswagen 49–71
#7345	Firebird 82–83	#6837	Volkswagen 70–81
#7059	Firenza 1982	#7339	Volkswagen Front Wheel Drive 74–83 inc. Dasher, GTI, Jetta, Quantum, Pick-Up, Rabbit, Scirocco
#7318	Ford 68–83 all full sized models		
#7140	Ford Bronco 66–81		
#7341	Ford Courier 72–82	#6529	Volvo 56–69
#7194	Ford Mid-Size 71–82 inc. Torino, Gran Torino, Ranchero, Elite, LTD II & Thunderbird	#7040	Volvo 70–80
		#7312	Zephyr 78–83
#7166	Ford Pick-Ups 65–82 inc. 4wd		

Chilton's Repair & Tune-Up Guides are available at your local retailer or by mailing a check or money order for **$11.95** plus **$1.00** to cover postage and handling to:

Chilton Book Company
Dept. DM
Radnor, PA 19089

NOTE: When ordering be sure to include your name & address, book code & title.